The A–Z Guide to
Modern Literary and
Cultural Theorists

The A–Z Guide to Modern Literary and Cultural Theorists

Edited by
Stuart Sim

 PRENTICE HALL
HARVESTER WHEATSHEAF

LONDON • NEW YORK • TORONTO • SYDNEY • TOKYO • SINGAPORE •
MADRID • MEXICO CITY • MUNICH

First published 1995 by
Prentice Hall/Harvester Wheatsheaf
Campus 400, Maylands Avenue
Hemel Hempstead
Hertfordshire, HP2 7EZ
A division of
Simon & Schuster International Group

Typeset in 9pt Palatino
by Photoprint, Torquay, S. Devon

Printed and bound in Great Britain by
Biddles Ltd, Guildford and King's Lynn

Library of Congress Cataloging-in-Publication Data

The A-Z guide to modern literary & cultural theorists /
    edited by Stuart Sim.
        p. cm.
    Includes bibliographical references and index.
    ISBN 0–13–355553–4
    1. Critics-Dictionaries. 2. Authors-Dictionaries.
    3. Litterateurs Dictionaries. 4. Criticism-Dictionaries.
    I. Sim, Stuart.
    PN74.A2 1995
    301-dc20   94–46372
                                                              CIP

British Library Cataloguing in Publication Data

A catalogue record for this book is available from the British
Library

ISBN 0–13–355553–4

---

1 2 3 4 5   99 98 97 96 95

To Dr Helene Brandon

Contents

Contents

Acknowledgements

My original editor at Harvester, Jackie Jones, played a very significant role in the design of this project, and I would like to thank her for her help and encouragement right up to the final stages.

I would also like to express my gratitude to the School of Arts, Design and Communications at the University of Sunderland for providing me with sabbatical time towards the completion of this project.

Introduction

The fields of literary and cultural theory continue to expand and change in restless fashion: new names come into prominence, debates shift direction, concerns subtly alter, such that it is increasingly difficult for both students and teachers to keep track of developments. This book sets out to map these fields as they appear in the mid 1990s by providing a series of concise essays (100 in all) on leading theorists, an A–Z series that encompasses not just established figures but also, crucially, up-and-coming figures whose influence will undoubtedly increase over the next few years. Thus one can find in these pages essays on Paul Gilroy, Meaghan Morris and John Fiske as well as on Roland Barthes, Raymond Williams and Jacques Derrida. Every effort has been made to cover the spectrum of modern literary and cultural theory so that all the main areas of current concern are represented, with feminist, black, and Third World theorists, for example, constituting a highly significant bloc in the volume's 100 entries.

Where theorists are best known for their work in collaboration with others – Wimsatt/Beardsley, Deleuze/Guattari, and Gilbert/Gubar, for example – they are treated in a joint entry.

It might be wondered why such nineteenth-century figures as Marx and Nietzsche feature in our list of significant moderns. We have taken the conscious decision to reach as far back as these two on the grounds that their ideas inform so many current theoretical debates that they can hardly be omitted in any serious survey. Indeed, they line up with Saussure and Freud as arguably the four great sources for modern literary and cultural theory: a quartet whose ideas continue to reverberate throughout the work of even the most recent theorists (as the entries will show), and who therefore stake an equal claim on our attention. Taken collectively, the essays in this volume constitute a tribute to the richness and diversity of literary and cultural theory today, and an indispensable aid in coming to grips with their complexity and many levels of interconnection.

How to use the guide

Each entry is designed to give the essential information about the theorist in question, and is formatted as follows:

1. theorist's name and dates;
2. discussion of academic and cultural background;
3. exposition of main ideas;
4. consideration of cultural impact;
5. main published works;
6. further reading (up to six selected texts);
7. glossary of technical terms (if required).

A line marks the division between each section of individual entries. When cross-references are made to other entries, theorists' names will be picked out in bold type. The heart of each entry is Section 3, which aims to provide a quick and easy-to-follow rundown of the theorist's ideas, not neglecting to draw attention to any weak or problematical aspects of these. Section 2 will vary in length from theorist to theorist – some people lead more interesting lives than others, and some people's lives have more relevance to an understanding of their work than is the case with others (Simone de Beauvoir being a prime example) – as will Section 4. Section 5 will list all the main works by which the theorist is known in their most accessible editions (that is, in translation where the original work is not in English); while Section 6 will suggest further reading on the theorist up to six titles maximum. Technical terms are in general defined in the course of each entry, but where this has been felt to hold up the progress of the argument they can be found in the glossary at the conclusion of said entry.

The collective goal of the volume's several contributors has been to provide concise and – as far as possible – jargon-free introductions to all the chosen theorists, and to direct readers to more specialist work should they choose to delve more deeply into the literature in future.

Stuart Sim.

List of Contributors

David Amigoni
University of Sunderland

Frank Beardow
University of Sunderland

Pieter Bekker
Leeds Metropolitan University

Kay Boardman
University of Central Lancashire

Fred Botting
Lancaster University

Donna Brody
Essex University

Peter Dempsey
University of Sunderland

Antony Easthope
Manchester Metropolitan University

Sarah Gamble
University of Sunderland

Elspeth Graham
Liverpool John Moores University

Maggie Humm
University of East London

Kathleen Kerr
University of Sunderland

Barry Lewis
University of Stavanger

Anthony McGowan
Open University

Kate McGowan
Manchester Metropolitan University

George McKay
University of Central Lancashire

Paul Marris
University of Sunderland

David Owen
University of Central Lancashire

Noel Parker
University of Surrey

Mike Peters
Leeds Metropolitan University

Carl Plasa
University of Wales College of Cardiff

Joanna Price
Liverpool John Moores University

Brian Rosebury
University of Central Lancashire

Michael Rossington
University of Newcastle upon Tyne

Stuart Sim
University of Sunderland

Tamsin Spargo
Liverpool John Moores University

John Storey
University of Sunderland

John Strachan
University of Sunderland

Richard Terry
University of Sunderland

List of Contributors

Sue Thornham
University of Sunderland

Joss West–Burnham
Manchester Metropolitan University

Caroline Ukoumunne
Manchester Metropolitan University

Patrick Williams
Nottingham Trent University

David Amigoni, Frank Beardow, Peter Dempsey, Sarah Gamble, Kathleen Kerr, Paul Marris, Stuart Sim, John Storey, John Strachan and Sue Thornham are all members of the Raman Selden Centre for the Study of Cultural and Textual Theory, in the School of Arts, Design and Communications at the University of Sunderland.

A

Achebe, Chinua (1930–)

Achebe is one of the most prominent of African writers, political theorists and political activists. He was born in Ogidi village in Eastern Nigeria, and educated at Government College, Umuahia and University College, Ibadan, which was affiliated to the University of London. Achebe has been employed as a lecturer at numerous universities, both in Nigeria and abroad. During the Nigerian Civil War he acted as a spokesman on behalf of Biafra, and in this capacity he made a number of visits to America, Europe and various African states. At present he is the Dean of Humanities in Annandale-on-Hudson, New York.

Achebe's works include five novels, three critical works and a sizeable collection of short stories, poems and essays. *Things Fall Apart*, his most acclaimed novel, has sold over three million copies to date. His enduring appeal is probably his ability to fuse the political concerns of the newly emergent African nations with a commitment to forging and creating a new African aesthetic within the framework of the modern novel in English.

The intercultural exchanges Achebe experienced while he was growing up, and the precarious position of democracy in the modern African states, are issues which are rigorously explored in his work. The question of power has also been integral to all his novels; he raises many questions as to the use and abuse of power in both the public and private spheres. He also appears to have an abiding interest in the transitory period between the demise of traditional society and the advent of colonialism. Consequently, his novels are characterized by the exploration of religious, political and cultural conflicts. Like many post-colonial writers, Achebe is also concerned with the role of the writer in the modern African state, the function of the English language in African literatures, and the problems to which that writing in a borrowed lingua franca gives rise. He asks whether it is ever possible for African writers who use foreign languages to engage in political or literary dissent, which can institute challenges to the metropolitan institutions which simultaneously include and exclude them.

The question of the use of the English language by African writers is also explored in his critical writings, *Morning Yet on Creation Day* (1975) and *Hopes and Impediments* (1988). Both these texts are seminal in a reconstruction of many of the issues which have been hotly debated in the field of African literature. In his essay 'The novelist as teacher', first published in 1965, Achebe states that as an African writer, his primary purpose was to enable his society to regain belief in itself, and put away the years of 'denigration and self abasement'. The years of colonial rule had so denigrated the African peoples that their histories as con-structed within the discourse of colonialism had become 'one long night of savagery from which the first Europeans, acting on God's behalf, delivered them'.

It is clear from Achebe's early work that he is concerned with the reconstruction of an African identity, which is a crucial step in the process of the creation of a national identity and the building of a nation-state. The role of the writer in a post-colonial state is made extremely complex by the fact that the modern writer cannot commune with his people in the same way as a traditional artist. The writer in a modern African state is, in Achebe's view, essentially an individualist, produced by particular historical circumstances Consequently, he has stated:

> In the very different wide open, multicultural and highly volatile condition known as modern Nigeria, for example, can a writer ever begin to know who his community is, let alone devise strategies for relating to it? If I write my novels in a country in which most citizens are illiterate, who then is my community? If I write in English in a country in which English may still be called a foreign language, or in any case is spoken only by a minority, what use is my writing?

Achebe has always problematized his use of the English language, yet his final justification for writing in English has been a somewhat fatalistic acceptance of the 'unassailable logic' of its convenience. His major concerns are, thus; the role of the artist in a society which is riven with a diversity of conflicts, the notion of rewriting an Afrocentric history, and the creation of linguistic tools which would be best suited to this enterprise.

These ideas are important for an understanding of *Things Fall Apart*, one of the first great post-colonial novels. In this text Achebe rewrites African history, offering a new version of African identity from the position of a colonial subject. He critiques the images of Africa which were delineated by philosophers such as Kant and Hegel, and specifically attacks the constructions of Africa which were posited in Conrad's *Heart of Darkness* and Cary's *Mr Johnson*. Whereas the characters in both these colonial novels are, fundamentally, savages who exist in the twilight zone between barbarity and civilization, Achebe's characters are multidimensional constructs, who are endowed with humanity.

Achebe also unsettles the dialectics that characterize Europe's relationship with Africa. To some extent he seems to have worked within the paradigms of the Negritude movement – where Africa and Africans are understood in terms of a supposed female disposition towards emotion and sensuality, and Europe is often explained in terms of the patriarchal qualities of logic and reason. Achebe challenges the binary construct on which these assumptions are based in the form of Okonkwo, the protagonist – and, to a certain extent, the tragic hero – of *Things Fall Apart*. Okonkwo symbolizes the warring factions of the male and female principles, which are the axis on which Achebe's mythical re-creation of the Ibo culture revolves. Okonkwo – and, by implication, the Ibo culture which produces him – is unable to reconcile these opposing elements, and this leads finally to the self-destruction of both.

The textual form of the novel reiterates the political ideas inherent throughout Achebe's work. He attempts to construct a new English which is at once familiar and alienating, the novel making a conscious effort to re-create the speech patterns of the Ibo community. Achebe also utilizes Ibo words, and this serves as a constant reminder to the reader that the novel is produced in a significantly different cultural context. This is underlined by the interweaving of Ibo proverbs, idioms and imagery with the narrative. Consequently, in common with Achebe's later novels, *Things Fall Apart* forces the reader constantly to question the ways and means by which language constructs particular types of realities.

The radical changes and political turmoil which have gone hand in hand with decolonization is also charted in Achebe's writing. *A Man of the People* is a satirical attack on the failure of leadership in African countries, which superbly captures the disillusionment of the petty-bourgeois class with the 'spoils' of decolonization. The text is an important landmark in that it pre-empted the dissolution of Nigeria's First Republic, which gave way to military rule. *Anthills of the Savannah*, Achebe's latest novel, also explores similar issues; it is a text which encapsulates his commitment to the political role of the writer as storyteller and critic in the post-colonial state.

It is difficult to assess the cultural impact of Achebe's work, since the work of African writers has not become fully established in the canon of English literature. The fact that he writes in English has also meant that his work has been reclaimed, when it is taught, under a liberal humanist, universalist banner. The problems inherent in this are obvious – the texts simply cannot be explored within their historical, cultural and political contexts. Nevertheless, he has made an invaluable contribution to the field of post-colonial studies, and echoes of his ideas are to be found in numerous African literary texts.

Main works

Things Fall Apart, London: Heinemann, 1958.

A Man of the People, London: Heinemann, 1966.

Morning Yet on Creation Day: Essays, London: Heinemann, 1975.

Anthills of the Savannah, London: Heinemann, 1987.

The African Trilogy, London: Picador, 1988a.

Hopes and Impediments: Selected Essays, London: Heinemann, 1988b.

Further reading

Balogun, F.O., *Tradition and Eternity in the African Short Story*, New York: Greenwood, 1991

Ehling, H.G. (ed.). *Critical Approaches to Anthills of the Savannah*, Amsterdam and Atlanta, GA: Rodopi, 1991.

Gikandi, S., *Reading Achebe*, Currey London: A6 1991.

Innes, C.L., *Chinua Achebe*, Cambridge: Cambridge University Press, 1990.

Innes, C.L. and Bernth, Lindfors *Critical Perspectives on Chinua Achebe*, Washington DC: Three Continents Press 1978.

Killam, G.D., *The Novels of Chinua Achebe*, London: Heinemann, 1977.

Adorno, Theodor Wiesengrund (1903–69)

Theodor W. Adorno, one of the most influential thinkers associated with the Frankfurt Institute of Social Research, was also among the most difficult to comprehend. Indeed, as Fredric **Jameson** notes, his work everywhere asserts that the value of modernity – its art and its thought – lies in its denial of habitual response, in its reawakening of 'numb thinking and deadened perception to a raw, wholly unfamiliar real world' (Jameson, 1971). Adorno was born into the Jewish bourgeoisie at a time when it was still a stable force in Europe, and his early education was privileged: he studied piano with Bernard Schles and, at the age of just 12, classical German philosophy with the philosopher, culture critic and film theorist Seigfried Kracauer. In fact, this combination of musical and philosophical training came to inform his thinking over the course of his lifetime. After graduating from the Kaiser Wilhelm Gymnasium in Frankfurt in 1921, Adorno entered the Wolfgang Goethe University, where he studied philosophy, sociology, psychology and music, emerging three years later with a doctorate, which he wrote, under the direction of Hans Cornelius, on Edmund Husserl. Among the most important people influencing his thinking, besides Siegfried Kracauer, were Max Horkheimer and Walter **Benjamin**. Of these three he came to collaborate most intimately with Horkheimer, specifically in the studies undertaken as part of the Frankfurt School of Critical Theory.

Adorno's professional fate was closely linked to that of the Institute of Social Research, later the Frankfurt School of Critical Theory. Established in 1923 in Frankfurt, Germany, as an independent body associated with the University of Frankfurt, it began as an orthodox Marxist organization (closely associated with the **Marx**–Engels Institute in Moscow) committed to an inductive method of research. But under the directorship of Horkheimer it developed an interdisciplinary orientation; thus the singularly materialist approach to research came to include an analysis of the relationship between the political/economic motion of society, the psychic development of the individual and cultural changes. Adorno's work as a philosopher and musicologist had an enormous influence on the economists, sociologists, psychologists, philosophers and political scientists working at the Institute. When the school was forced to leave Germany for New York in 1933, he was already one of its most prominent members.

Horkheimer believed that traditional philosophical concerns had become redundant; that the revival of the discipline would require addressing different questions better served by the social sciences. Adorno, on the other hand, thought that the forms of different philosophies were closely connected to objective structures in society, and that the revival of philosophy would require an *immanent critique*; to this end he devoted much of his time to analyzing the concept of truth. However, despite this fundamental difference, in 1947 they published a work, conceived jointly during the reign of Nazism, called *Dialectic of the Enlightenment*. This is a volume of 'united fragments' which attempts to address the question of increased barbarism in the aftermath of the Enlightenment. In this book Adorno and Horkheimer argue that reason is the hegemonic force that objectifies and hence reifies nature in its effort to totalize in the interests of the subject: what begins as a resistance to the seductions of myth becomes rationalization, and hence itself a new myth. The mastery of nature implicit in this dialectical movement extends to human beings, who become objects available for exploitation. Fascism stands at the centre of this dialectical progression, first using reason to dislodge oppressive myth for the purpose of liberating nature, and then using liberated nature as a totalizing concept which rationalizes the objectifying, reifying process.

Of all the Western Marxists, Adorno, in both the style and the content of his work, found it difficult to affirm the utopian hope of human redemption and an emancipated future. The horror of Auschwitz haunted his writing of the 1940s and 1950s: 'To write poetry after Auschwitz,' he said, 'is barbaric' (1981). To have survived the Holocaust was a mark of the cold subjectivity that could prescribe the Final Solution in the first place. He was highly critical of what he called *identity thinking*, or the kind of thinking that assumes the identity of subjects and objects, the existence of the Absolute Idea (Hegel), and refuses the idiosyncratic nature of particulars by too easily subsuming them under the general. Although identity thinking functions pragmatically by providing the means by which particulars are brought under universals, and concepts are referred to objects, the capitalist mode of production prevents concepts linking with the *ideal* existence of objects. Hence identity thinking is a false or *reified* thinking. For Adorno, the purpose of a critical theory is to provide the means for unmasking the distorted social reality that emerges when conceptual thought is taken as corresponding unproblematically with an objective world.

One extremely influential book on the development of Adorno's thought was Walter Benjamin's *Origin of German Tragic Drama*, which drew correspondences between art and philosophy by proposing that the truth-content of both was to be found in the complete immersion in the tiniest details of subject matter, which in the case of philosophy is language. Thus both these thinkers reject the assumption that everything about the object is covered by its concept, that every object is easily classified as part of a whole. To counteract this way of thinking, Adorno proposes *non-identity thinking* or *negative dialectics*, which examines the relations between the object and its concept in order to discover discrepancies and reveal hidden potentialities. Viewing the object from different angles allows the inner history to emerge in its 'truth' as part of a *constellation* of concepts which are themselves in motion. *Negative Dialectics* closes with: 'the micrological view cracks the shells of what, measured by the subsuming cover concept, is helplessly isolated and explodes its identity, the delusion that it is but a specimen' (1973).

Adorno is unique in that he is the only Western Marxist who focused extensively on music (the majority of his writing was in the area of musicology, and most of this work remains untranslated) in his cultural criticism, and then used his knowledge of musical composition in his theoretical speculations. In 1925 Adorno began studying with Alban Berg in Vienna, where he learned an appreciation for Schoenberg, in particular his early 'expressive' work. He was especially drawn to the atonality of Schoenberg's 'new music', which attempted to represent objective truth through the logic of musical development. Adorno's interest in this music was in the way it refused the façade of universalism built upon the strengthening of cold subjectivism: progressive music, like progressive art, determinately negated the illusion of the whole. Schoenberg's music represented the objective relations of a reality born out of crisis and deteriorated in decadence. Moreover, this did not invalidate the synthesizing force of music, its power to prefigure a future totality. For Adorno:

> The whole, as a positive entity, cannot be antithetically extracted from an estranged and splintered reality by means of the will and power of the individual; if it is not to denigrate into deception and ideology, it must assume the form of negation. (1981)

Schoenberg's non-referential representation of tone might be considered the musical equivalent of Benjamin's paratactic style: just as Benjamin's style precluded simple understanding, so Schoenberg's atonality complicated the language of the emotions. This understanding of the importance of form to the meaning of the work's content is implicit in Adorno's own writing. His preferred use of the essay and the aphorism not only allowed for the kind of interventions into totalizing systems characteristic of his thought, but also enacted the idiosyncratic nature of the particular.

Adorno's aesthetics, like his other philosophical speculations, drew him to works which resist the easy subsumption of particulars under generals and the attending illusion of totality. This resistance to totality informs two other major themes in his essays on modern culture: first, the way the culture industry, in an age of monopoly capitalism, promotes a totalizing perspective in order to adapt the individual to the real conditions of daily life; second, the reason why 'serious' modern art must, if it is to realize its truly subversive potential, render correctly the antinomial and contradictory character of the relation between the particular and the general. It is not only modern art, however, that must realize its subversive potential. All thought – and this includes enlightened thought itself – if it is to claim such a name, must exercise critical self-reflection and be antithetical. From his earliest work onwards, Adorno insisted on the importance of displacing the impulse to a mindless acceptance of the familiar.

Adorno's influence on the development and direction of research in the Frankfurt School was considerable in its heyday of the 1930s and 1940s, and in the 1950s and 1960s his very name came to signify the Institute itself. Nevertheless, his refusal to translate negative philosophy into activist politics during the student unrest of the 1960s made him an object of much revilement. When he died in 1969 he was still at the height of his intellectual powers, though ostracized by the student pundits.

Main works

Negative Dialectics, trans. E.B. Ashton, London: Routledge & Kegan Paul, 1973a.

The Jargon of Authenticity, trans. Knut Tarnowski and Fredric Will, London: Routledge & Kegan Paul, 1973b.

Minima Moralia: Reflections from a damaged life, trans. E.F.N. Jephcott, London: Verso, 1974.

Dialectic of Enlightenment (with Max Horkheimer), trans. John Cumming, London: Verso, 1979.

Prisms, trans. Samuel and Shierry Weber, Cambridge, MA: MIT Press, 1981a.

In Search of Wagner, trans. Rodney Livingston, London: Verso, 1981b.

Against Epistemology: A metacritique, trans. Willis Domingo, Oxford: Basil Blackwell, 1982.

Aesthetic Theory, ed. Gretel Adorno and Rolf Tiedemann, trans. C. Lenhardt, London, Boston, Melbourne and Henley: Routledge & Kegan Paul, 1984.

Notes to Literature vol.1, trans. Shierry Weber Nicholsen, New York: Columbia University Press, 1991.

Notes to Literature vol.2, trans. Shierry Weber Nicholsen, New York: Columbia University Press, 1992.

The Culture Industry, ed. J.M. Bernstein, London: Routledge, 1991.

Further reading

Buck-Morss, Susan, *The Origin of Negative Dialectics: Theodor W. Adorno, Walter Benjamin and the Frankfurt Institute*, New York and London: Routledge, 1977.

Jameson, Frederic, *Marxism and Form: Twentieth-century dialectical theories of literature*, Princeton, NJ: Princeton University Press, 1971.

Jameson, Frederic, *Late Marxism: Adorno, or the persistence of the dialectic*, London: Verso, 1990.

Jay, Martin, *Adorno*, London: Fontana, 1984a.

Jay, Martin, *Marxism and Totality: The adventures of a concept from Lukács to Habermas*, Cambridge and Oxford: Polity Press, 1984b.

Rose, Gillian, *The Melancholy Science: An introduction to the thought of Theodor Adorno*, London and Basingstoke: Macmillan, 1978.

Althusser, Louis (1918–90)

Louis Althusser was born in Algiers and educated at schools in Algiers and Marseilles, and at the Ecole Normale Supérieure, where he subsequently taught philosophy. In 1948 he became a member of the French Communist Party. In 1980 Althusser murdered his wife. Declared mentally ill, he was placed in St Anne's Psychiatric Hospital in Paris. He was released in 1983. The last seven years of his life were marked by periods of mental illness.

It is almost impossible to overestimate the influence that the ideas of Louis Althusser had on literary and cultural theory in the 1970s. In a series of profoundly influential works, Althusser presented a rereading of Marx which provoked both enthusiastic support and acrimonious disagreement, but rarely indifference.

Althusser's most significant contribution to cultural and literary theory is his retheorization of the Marxist concept of ideology. Althusser's reformulation begins with a rejection of both the mechanistic interpretation of the base/superstructure model of society and the Hegelian view of society as a social totality. He insists instead on seeing society as a social formation consisting of three practices: the economic, the political and the ideological. In this model, the relationship between base and superstructure is not expressive (i.e. the superstructure being an expression or passive reflection of the base); rather, the superstructure is seen as necessary to the existence and reproduction of the base. The model allows for the 'relative autonomy' of the superstructure, and for a much more central place for the concept of ideology. Determination remains, but it is 'determination in the last instance'. This works through what Althusser calls the 'structure in dominance'; that is, although the economic practice is always determinant, this does not mean that in a particular historical conjuncture it will necessarily be dominant. Feudalism, for example, produced a social formation in which the political was the dominant practice. Determination remains, however, because the practice which is dominant will always depend on the specific form of economic production. According

9

to Althusser, the economic contradictions of a social formation never take a pure form: 'the lonely hour of the last instance never comes'. Determination remains, but (borrowing from **Freud**'s dream theory) as 'overdetermination': the structured articulation of a number of contradictions and determinations. The economic is determinant in the last instance – not because the other practices of the social formation are its expressive epiphenomena, but because it determines which practice is dominant.

Althusser's theorizations of ideology are a direct consequence of his model of the social formation. He produced three concepts of ideology, two of which have proved particularly fruitful for the student of cultural and literary theory. The first formulation is the claim that it is through ideology that men and women live their relation to the real conditions of existence. In this formulation, ideology is a practice: 'By practice in general I shall mean any process of transformation of a determinate product, a transformation effected by a determinate human labour, using determinate means (of "production")' (*For Marx*). Althusser argues that just as the economic practice, the historically specific mode of production, transforms certain raw materials into products by determinate means of production, involving determinate relations of production, so political practice, in the same way, transforms social relations and, in the same way, ideological practice is the transformation of a subject's lived relations to the social formation. In this formulation, ideology exists to dispel the perception of contradictions in lived experience. It manages this by offering false, but seemingly true, resolutions to real problems. This is not a 'conscious' process; ideology 'is profoundly unconscious' in its mode of operation. Ideology 'presupposes both a real relation and an "imaginary", "lived" relation' between men and women and the social conditions of existence (*For Marx*). The relationship is both real and imaginary in the sense that ideology is the way we live our relationship to the real conditions of existence at the level of representations (myths, concepts, ideas, images, etc.): there are real conditions and there are the ways we represent these conditions to ourselves and to others. This applies to both dominant and subordinate groups and classes; ideologies do not just convince oppressed groups and classes that all is well (more or less) with the world, they also reassure dominant groups and classes that what others might call exploitation and oppression is in fact something quite different: the operations and processes of universal necessity. Only a 'scientific' discourse (Althusser's Marxism, for example) can read through ideology to the real conditions of existence.

Because ideology for Althusser is a closed system, it can set itself, as it were, only such problems as it can answer; that is, to remain within its boundaries (a mythic realm without contradictions) it must stay silent on questions which threaten to take it outside these boundaries.

This formulation leads Althusser to the concept of the 'problematic'. He first uses the concept to explain the 'epistemological break' he claims occurs in Marx's work in 1845. Marx's problematic, according to Althusser – 'the objective internal reference . . . the system of questions commanding the answers given' (*Reading Capital*) – determines not only the questions and answers he is able to bring into play, but also the absence of problems and concepts in his work. A problematic is the theoretical (and ideological) structure which both frames and produces the repertoire of crisscrossing and competing discourses out of which a text or practice is materially organized. The problematic of a text relates to its moment of historical existence as much by what it excludes as by what it includes. That is to say, it encourages a text to answer questions posed by itself, but at the same time, it generates the production of 'deformed' answers to the questions it attempts to exclude. Thus a problematic is structured as much by what is absent (what is not said/what is not done) as by what is present (what is said/what is done). The task of an Althusserian critical practice is to deconstruct the problematic: to perform what Althusser (again borrowing from Freud) calls a 'symptomatic reading'.

Althusser characterizes Marx's method of reading Adam Smith as 'symptomatic' in that

> it divulges the undivulged event in the text it reads, and in the same movement relates it to a *different text*, present as a necessary absence in the first. Like his first reading, Marx's second reading presupposes the existence of *two texts*, and the measurement of the first against the second. But what distinguishes this new reading from the old is the fact that in the new one the second text is articulated with the lapses in the first text. (*ibid.*)

By a symptomatic reading of Smith, Marx is able to measure 'the problematic contained in the paradox of *an answer which does not correspond to any question posed*' (*ibid.*). Therefore, to read a text symptomatically is to perform a double reading: reading first the manifest text, and then, through the lapses, distortions, silences and absences (the 'symptoms' of a problem struggling to be posed) in the manifest text, to produce and read the latent text. For example, a symptomatic reading of the film *Taxi Driver* would articulate a problematic in which answers are posed to questions it can hardly name: 'How does the Vietnam veteran return home to America after the imperialist horrors of Vietnam?' At the core of the film's problematic are questions relating to real historical problems, albeit deformed and translated into a fantasy quest and a bloody resolution. A symptomatic reading of *Taxi Driver*, *reading the 'symptoms' for evidence of an underlying dis-ease*, would construct from the film's contradictions, its evasions, its silences, its inexplicable violence, its fairytale ending, the central and structuring absence: *Vietnam*.

Undoubtedly the most sustained attempt to apply this method of reading to cultural texts is Pierre **Macherey**'s *A Theory of Literary*

Production. In his essay on Jules Verne, Macherey demonstrates the way in which Verne gives fictional form to the ideology of French imperialism, and how, if it is read symptomatically, Verne's fiction can be made to stage the contradictions between the myth and the reality of late-nineteenth-century French imperialism. In 'A letter on art', Althusser argues that although 'genuine' and 'authentic' literature and art can never provide us with a 'scientific' denunciation of, say, imperialism, it can, when read symptomatically (a reading 'which dislodges the work internally'), 'make us see', 'make us perceive', 'make us feel' the contradictions of the ideological discourses from which the cultural text is constituted: 'from which it is born, in which it bathes, from which it detaches itself . . . and to which it alludes' (*Lenin and Philosophy*). In this way the cultural text can be made to show us – though not necessarily in the way intended – the ideological and historical conditions of its existence.

In Althusser's second formulation, ideology is retheorized as a lived, material practice – rituals, customs, patterns of behaviour, ways of thinking taking practical form – reproduced through the practices and productions of the Ideological State Apparatuses (ISAs): education, organized religion, the family, organized politics, the media, the cultural industries, and so on. In this formulation, 'all ideology has the function (which defines it) of "constructing" concrete individuals as subjects'. Ideological subjects are generated by acts of 'hailing' or 'interpellation' (*ibid.*). Althusser uses the analogy of a police officer hailing an individual: 'Hey, you there!' When the individual hailed turns in response, she has been interpellated, has become a subject of the police officer's discourse. In this way, ideology is the creation of subjects who are subjected to the material practices of ideology. It was this second formulation of ideology which had a particularly powerful effect on cultural and literary theory.

Throughout the 1970s Althusser's influence on cultural theory, especially in the field of film studies, was profound. Studies were produced to demonstrate the ways in which cultural texts interpellate their readers as subjects of, and subjected to, specific ideological discourses and subject positions. In studies of advertising, for example, it was argued that consumers are interpellated to make meaning, and to purchase and consume. When I am told, for example, that 'people like you' are turning to this or that product, I am interpellated as a member of a group, but more importantly as an individual 'you' of that group. I am addressed as an individual who can recognize myself in the imaginary space opened up by the pronoun 'you'. Thus I am invited to become the imaginary 'you' spoken to in the advertisement. But for Althusser, my response to the advertisement's invitation is an act of ideological 'misrecognition'. First, it is an act of misrecognition in the sense that in order for the advertisement to work, it must attract many others who also (mis)recognize themselves in the 'you' of its discourse. Second, it is a misrecognition in another sense: the 'you' I (mis)recognize in the advertisement is in fact a 'you' created by the advertisement. Advertising thus flatters us into thinking that we are the special 'you' of its discourse; in so doing we become subjects of, and subjected to, its material practices: acts of consumption.

From the perspective of cultural and literary theory, the main problem with Althusser's formulations of the concept of ideology is that ideology is presented as something which appears to function too well. It proposes an ideology that can be relied on to ensure that men and women are always successfully reproduced with all the necessary ideological habits and patterns of thought as required by the capitalist mode of production; there is no sense of ideological failure, let alone any notion of conflict, struggle or resistance. Do advertisements, for example, always successfully interpellate us as consuming subjects? It was against the background of such doubts and questions that students of cultural and literary theory began to turn their backs on the work of Louis Althusser.

Main works

For Marx, trans. Ben Brewster, London: Verso, 1969.

Reading Capital, trans. Ben Brewster (with Etienne Balibar), London: Verso, 1970.

Lenin and Philosophy and Other Essays, trans. Ben Brewster, London: Verso, 1971.

Politics and History, trans. Ben Brewster, London: Verso, 1972.

Essays in Self-Criticism, trans. G. Lock, London: Verso, 1976.

Essays in Ideology, trans. Ben Brewster, London: Verso, 1983.

Further reading

Benton, Ted, *The Rise and Fall of Structural Marxism: Althusser and his influence*, London: Macmillan, 1984.

Clarke, Simon *et al.*, *One-Dimensional Marxism*, London: Allison and Busby, 1980.

Callinicos, Alex, *Althusser's Marxism*, London: Pluto Press, 1976.

Hall, Stuart, 'Signification, representation, ideology: Althusser and the post-structuralist debates', *Critical Studies in Mass Communication*, 2, 2 (1985).

Hall, Stuart, Ben Lumley and Gregor McLennan (eds), *On Ideology*, London: Hutchinson, 1978.

Thompson, E.P., *The Poverty of Theory*, London: Merlin, 1978.

Anzaldúa, Gloria (1942–)

Gloria Anzaldúa is a Chicana writer, theorist and cultural critic currently writing and teaching in the United States of America. She has, to date, produced five major works, all of which combine the creative writing process with explorations of theory, language and history in a palpably political context.

Born on a ranch settlement in Southern Texas, Anzaldúa worked for many years alongside her family as a field labourer. In the 1960s her success at school won her the distinction of becoming the first person from her region ever to attend university. She gained a BA degree from the Pan American University, and an MA in English and Education from the University of Texas at Austin. Since 1976 she has lectured at a number of universities across the United States, and in 1988 was appointed as Distinguished Visiting Professor in Women's Studies at the University of California, Santa Cruz.

Gloria Anzaldúa describes herself as a border woman, a subject produced between two cultures: 'the Mexican (with a heavy Indian influence) and the Anglo (as a member of a colonized people in our own territory)'. Her writing comes from a similar borderland space. It has its roots in the politics of the Chicano nationalist movement of the 1970s, and in the discourses of feminism and of gay liberation. At the same time, however, it does not exist entirely within either one or the other of those territories. Its existence is 'los intersticios', the places where those roots intersect, overlap, clash and produce anew.

It is also, textually, an enactment of the borderland existence it seeks to elucidate. Mixing genres and linguistic codes (it switches from English to North Mexican dialect, to Tex–Mex with a sprinkling of Nahuatl), Anzaldúa's writing experiments with what she calls a 'language of the borderlands'. This, it would seem, is a language within which identity itself is neither stable nor fixed, but slides from one linguistic construction to the next in a perpetual process of redefinition.

As a writer, Anzaldúa is steeped in the knowledges of an ancient Indian past, and of the mystical knowledge of what she calls the 'Coatlicue state' – dreams which rupture our everyday world. She also draws upon the terms and the paradigms of psychoanalysis, particularly its conceptualization of the unconscious in the work of Lacan and French feminist theory. In a sense, her work represents the blending and clashing of a series of knowledges in an attempt to produce a notion of the multicultural subject upon which a politics of change can be secured. The notion of the subject which underpins this attempt is very firmly that of the subject-in-process.

While part of the project of this work, particularly in the early days of *This Bridge Called My Back*, is to bring a marginalized existence into representation, the process of representation itself is always problematic in Anzaldúa's terms. It is not so much a putting into discourse of a subject already in existence as an interrogation of the very category of the subject itself.

The work of Chicano nationalists, and in particular the Chicano student movement, was very firmly a move towards establishing a solid Chicano identity. It was an important gesture in the face of denigration and erasure at the hands of a hostile white culture. But in its resistance to existing cultural stereotypes, it produced its own regimes and regulations. In particular, its emphasis upon the return to Aztlán (the legendary homeland of the Aztecs) demanded the recovery of a common past in order to produce a common culture and a oneness within the 'Chicano nation'. Since Aztlán does not exist in the present, it was thought to be located within the deepest spiritual layers of every Chicano consciousness. What ensued from this was a politics of resistance based upon the production of an essential Chicano subject.

The notion of a pre-Columbian past and the mystical presence of Aztlán are evident at times in Anzaldúa's analyses of her culture and identity. But her writing moves away from its static and one-dimensional roots. It questions (often guiltily) the erasure of differences amongst Chicanos and of the multiplicity of cultural identities they, as a people, embody. 'Political correctness', she writes, separates off issues of 'color, class and gender' as though they were distinct and unrelated categories of identification. This in turn produces boundaries which are rarely traversed politically and which, in a masquerade of difference, create their own internal notions of sameness and unity – so much so, she insists, that 'I have been terrified to write this essay because I will have to own up to the fact that I do not exclude whites from the people I love', or 'that I must be hard on people of color' (*Bridge*).

However difficult that task may be politically, it is necessary in Anzaldúa's terms if progress is to be made. The concept of a singular or unified identity is merely an illusion. It also produces a notion of solidarity which is won only at the expense of exclusion. In the essay

'La Prieta' in *This Bridge Called My Back* she asks: 'who are my people?' The Chicano movement demands her allegiance to 'La Raza', her Black and Asian friends to the 'Third World' and feminists to her gender, to women. But there are also her allegiances to 'the gay movement, to the socialist revolution, to the New Age, to magic and the occult'. Finally she asks:

> What am I? *A third world lesbian feminist with Marxist and mystic leanings.* They would chop me up into little fragments and tag each piece with a label.

The self of which Anzaldúa writes is not wholly defined by the discourses of political allegiance amongst which she is split. The subject she writes exists in the borderlands, the margins of available discourses, and it is this borderland existence which drives what she calls 'one's shifting and multiple identity'. If the US–Mexican border 'es una herida abierta [is an open wound] where the Third World grates against the first and bleeds', the subject of that borderland space is itself the site of a grating. It is the site of an intersection of discourses, a site of struggle and contradiction which keeps it continually in process, shifting, changing, always in excess of its own definitions.

Identity in these terms is never an already accomplished fact, but a process of production which is never complete. It is a transient process, within which rupture and discontinuity are its real material conditions.

Anzaldúa's work has been vastly important within a Chicana context. For women, particularly lesbians, who have been ostracized as sell-outs to the Chicano race, or marginalized as exotic 'other' to the white feminist movement, her writings are more than significant. For the feminist movement, with its prioritization of gender as a category of oppression and unity among women, Anzaldúa's analyses of race and sexuality have been challenging and often disturbing. For the gay liberation movement, which assumes a common identity based upon sexual practice, her analyses of race and gender have been equally challenging.

With its fragmented style and its rupturing of the linear rationalist discourse of common sense, Anzaldúa's work carries within it the potential for rethinking the ways in which cultural communities conceptualize themselves and the subjects they produce. Whether the present intellectual and political climate is one in which that challenge can be fully met, however, is something that remains to be seen.

Main works

This Bridge Called My Back: Writings by radical women of color, with Cherríe Moraga, Massachusetts: Persephone Press, 1981.

Borderlands/La Frontera: The New Mestiza, San Francisco: Spinsters/Aunt Lute, 1987.

Making Face, Making Soul/Haciendo Caras: Creative and critical perspectives by women of color, San Francisco: Aunt Lute Foundation, 1990.

Friends from the Other Side: Amigos del otro lado, San Francisco: Children's Book Press, 1993a.

La Prieta, San Francisco: Aunt Lute, 1993a.

Further reading

Alarcón, Norma, 'Chicana feminism: in the tracks of "the" native woman', *Cultural Studies*, 4, 3 (1990): 248–56.

Mohanty, Chandra, *Third World Women and the Politics of Feminism*, Bloomington: Indiana University Press, 1991.

Quintana, Alvina, 'Politics, representation and the emergence of a Chicana aesthetic', *Cultural Studies*, 4, 3 (1990): 257–63.

Glossary

Chicana: The term Chicano is taken from the oral working-class culture of the Mexican peoples who live and work in the United States. It is an attempt to name an existence which is neither Mexican nor American, and represents a move away from the constitution of a people as hyphenated Americans (the alternative designation being Mexican-Americans). **Chicana** is the feminine equivalent of that term.

B

Bachelard, Gaston (1884–1962)

A self-taught mathematician and philosopher, Bachelard held chairs in the philosophy of science at Dijon and, from 1940 to 1955, at the Sorbonne. He had a major influence on the French scientific epistemology of his day, bequeathing to **Althusser**, for example, the concept of an 'epistemological break', whereby a discipline escapes intuitive biases through the rationality of its self-consistent rules for interpretation and explanation. Beginning in the late 1930s, however, he published a series of books discussing the dynamics of the image and setting it on an equal, albeit distinct, footing alongside the rationalized creativity of scientific thought. Bachelard accorded a special status to the poetic image *vis-à-vis* the psyche and the deeper realities of human experience. His literary studies fused surrealism, Jungian psychoanalysis, and a phenomenological view of the constructive activity of the human psyche, and developed a distinctive way of exploring images in written and unwritten sources. In the belief that 'Man's being is an unfixed being' (*The Poetics of Space*), they also proclaimed a radical alternative to the fixed human subject of idealism, of rationalism, and even of sychoanalysis itself.

Bachelard departed from the Bergsonian approach dominant in the early decades of the century. Bergson, the vitalist, had sought intuitions of the continuous 'creative impulse' which underlies all change and all experience of the world; Bachelard, the philosopher of science, pursued a phenomenological reflection built on concepts from theoretical physics: relativity and quantum mechanics. He claimed that time and order are created in consciousness out of the rhythm and juxtaposition of the discrete instants of time.

But the poetic image permits a rejection of time and order as they are given in such processes. It escapes from what Bachelard calls (in *La Dialectique de la durée*) objective, 'horizontal time'; that is, 'the time of others, the time of life, the world's time'. Where poetry can achieve lyrical reverie, images may flow quite outside of any given temporal order – and thus overstep causality itself. To gain access to this other, 'vertical time', Bachelard announces a 'Copernican revolution' in which the reader's imagination commits itself to the movements of its own imaginings.

Bachelard was avowedly ignorant of modern linguistics and its tenets. His thinking was hostile to metaphors, which he regarded as formalized shackles on insight, especially where (as in pre-scientific thinking) they sustain unconscious obstacles to true understanding. He was uninterested in repeated patterns, which are the stuff of much literary analysis. Instead, Bachelardian reading focused on images, which, because they exist in vertical time, elude anticipation and causal necessity. 'The poetic image', he tells us (in *The Poetics of Space*), 'is not subject to an inner thrust. It is not an echo of the past. . . . [It] has an entity and a dynamism of its own.' In order to reflect that dynamism, his readings use all the polysemic potential of language, unfixing the reader and renewing the creative activity of the imagination. He aims to revive the image as 'the very well-spring of the imagination's life', which, when fully developed, can experience 'that absolute of reverie that is *poetic reverie*' (*La Flamme d'une chandelle*). He associated that liberated imagination with the inspiration of surrealism, describing its target (in *La Psychanalyse du feu*) as 'the dadaist region where dreams . . . test out experience and reverie transforms forms already transformed . . .'.

Rather than an analysis of a given text, then, the activity of reading is primarily a liberating, transforming experience for the reader. According to Bachelard, the reader should 'strain forward, driven by the improbable need to be another being' (*La Poétique de la rêverie*). His expositions on poetry progress through inventive sideways steps which traverse the multiple meanings of a group of primal images. Sometimes they make only passing reference to specific texts.

The image is also followed to deeper levels of response towards the materiality of the world in itself. As can be readily seen from the titles of his books, Bachelard himself drew on Jung's account of alchemical archetypes (earth, fire, water and air) to map out these deeper responses (though he was opposed to any formulaic application of interpretative devices from psychoanalysis). Water images, for example, may be pursued through the pull of self-substantive narcissism and of the death-wish, to a gentle malleability in matter itself, to forms of cosmic anger and aggression, or to experiences of the infinitude of the universe. Bachelard also embraced a Jungian preference for the all-enveloping 'anima', as opposed to the exclusive, analytical 'animus'. In *La Poétique de la rêverie*, for example, he finds that the image of the flame permits us to 'fuse with the world', and rediscover 'the essence of being . . . rooted in our ancient being'.

Bachelard was awarded the French *Grand Prix National des Lettres* in 1961. Bachelardian reading was taken up in France and the United States in the 1960s, and continues today, though there are few avowed practitioners. Disciples often work, as did Bachelard, on fields of images rather than on individual cases. Though its dislike of pattern and its taste for reverie limit its analytical use on specific texts, Bachelardian reading does provide a reference point for anti-authoritarian, psychoanalytic readings divorced from the **Freud**ian tradition. And it can be a powerful tool where a writer's voice expresses his or her deep-seated response to families of symbols – one thinks of Arnold's intimations of death, or Shelley's responses to water. By exploring poetry neither as the expression of an idealized, singular author nor as the effect of any kind of structure (as in the model derived from **Lévi-Strauss**), it offers a genuine alternative to both the fetishization of the authorial consciousness and structuralism's suppression of all creativity.

Main works

L'Intuition de l'instant, Paris: Stock, 1932.

Le Nouvel esprit scientifique, Paris: Alcan, 1934.

La Dialectique de la durée, Paris: Boivin, 1936.

La Formation de l'esprit scientifique, Paris: Vran, 1938.

L'Eau et les rêves, Paris: Jofé Corti, 1942.

La Terre et les rêveries du repos, Paris: Jofé Corti, 1948.

La Flamme d'une chandelle, Paris: Presses Universitaires de France, 1961.

The Poetics of Space, trans. Maria Jolas, Boston: Beacon Press, 1964a.

The Psychoanalysis of Fire, trans. Alan C.M. Ross, Boston: Beacon Press, 1964b.

The Poetics of Reverie, trans. D. Russell, New York: Orion Press, 1969.

A selection of excerpts in translation appeared in *On Poetic Imagination and Reverie: Selections from the work of Gaston Bachelard*, trans. Colette Gaudin, Indianapolis: Bobbs-Merrill, 1971.

Further reading

McAllester, Mary, *Gaston Bachelard, Subversive Humanist*, Madison: University of Wisconsin Press, 1991.

McAllester Mary, (ed.), *The Philosophy and Poetics of Gaston Bachelard*, Washington DC: University Press of America, 1989.

Revue de la Littérature comparée, 58 (1984).

University of Ottawa Quarterly, 57, 1 (1987).

Smith, Roch C., *Gaston Bachelard*, Boston: Twayne, 1982.

Tiles, Mary, *Bachelard: Science and objectivity*, Cambridge: Cambridge University Press, 1984.

Bakhtin, Mikhail Mikhailovich (1895–1975)

From 1914 Bakhtin studied Greek and Latin at St Petersburg University. Between 1918 and 1924 he was based in Nevel and Vitebsk, and was at the centre of an intellectual formation which has subsequently been designated 'the Bakhtin circle'; this circle included V.N. **Voloshinov**, who wrote a Marxist treatise on the philosophy of language for which Bakhtin, late in life, claimed authorship. Between 1924 and 1945 Bakhtin elaborated his intellectual system amid the life-threatening conditions of the political paranoia of Stalinism, purges, invasion and war. He was variously unemployed, exiled and imprisoned – though as a prisoner he was permitted to work as a teacher. In 1945 he was given the Chair of Russian and World Literature at the new University of Saransk, and in 1947 his controversial dissertation – on Rabelais – was accepted but awarded the lower degree of Candidate rather than Doctor. During the 1960s, when he was permitted to move to the Moscow area, Bakhtin's writings from the 1920s and 1930s started to appear, and to gain recognition in the Soviet Union.

Bakhtin was centrally concerned with the importance of context: utterances (verbal or written) were addressed to particular audiences, and contexts shaped the meaning of those utterances in particular locations at particular times. The context of Soviet intellectual and political orthodoxy crucially shaped the meaning of his writings – whether he was arguing against **Lukács's** party line on the novel ('Discourse in the novel') or against Stalinist authoritarianism (*Rabelais and His World*). However, because of the unstable conditions in which they were formed, Bakhtin's writings are marked by a number of difficulties. First, there are the difficulties relating to the texts ascribed to Voloshinov but later claimed by Bakhtin. Second, there are the two versions of Bakhtin's book on Dostoevsky (1929, 1963: the former produced in dangerous conditions, the latter in relatively liberal conditions). Third, there is Bakhtin's style itself; the writings on the novel comprising the text known in English as *The Dialogic Imagination* are repetitive and often appear to be without structure. So while an understanding of context shapes a response to Bakhtin's writings, a context does not pin them down to *one* meaning.

Plurality of meaning was explored in Bakhtin's writings through the important concept of dialogue, in which the words of language were active participants. For Bakhtin, words are uttered in particular locations, but they are addressed and evaluatively accented to meet a context of reception. They thus come to any speaker or writer marked by both their previous and anticipated uses. Words are marked with plural meanings because they never belong wholly to one speaker or to one context; they are marked by the traces of dialogic activity.

Bakhtin's view of language was thus historical, for history inscribed the signs of human language with the complex effects of social and cultural interaction. Bakhtin distinguished between early monoglot languages which had not witnessed interaction between culturally diverse groups, and heteroglot languages which were marked by the language practices of diverse, often competing groups. Homeric Greek was, for him, a monoglot culture: late medieval/early Renaissance Europe was a heteroglot culture, and in his study of Rabelais, Bakhtin looked at sixteenth-century France as a site of competing languages and social groups.

For language was also inscribed with historically accumulated forms of prestige and authority which were both asserted and resisted: the language of the Church and its clerics was the language of high culture, whereas the language of the marketplace or public square and the people was the language of low culture. This process of assertion and resistance was registered in the field of artistic discourse. According to Bakhtin, the prestigious poetic genres in European cultures, such as the epic, were produced in line with authoritarian, centripetal exclusivity. However, writers such as Rabelais actively sought to represent the clash and competition between high and low forms of language: in Bakhtin's view, Rabelais was a writer of novels.

The idea of the novel is an immensely powerful one in Bakhtin's writing. His understanding of the novel was not confined to representational prose narratives of length: rather, the novel was a kind of discourse which acted as a site of convergence for the heteroglossic elements of a given culture and society. This understanding of the novel is presented in two important essays: 'From the prehistory of novelistic Discourse' and 'Discourse in the novel'. In these essays, novelistic discourse is characterized by its mingling of 'language images', or 'the image of another's language'. For Bakhtin, this is discourse which *represents* a particular style of language characteristic of a person in a particular social group. In saying that this style is represented as an image of another's language, Bakhtin implies that there is some social and ideological distance between the authorial position of the discourse in which the image is cast, and the position represented. The authorial position can thus evaluatively accent the language image in an ironic or a parodic light. Novelistic discourse has the capacity to ironize and parody authoritative forms of language which, historically, have come to be dominant. The clashing voices of novelistic discourse are a source of carnival, which is an important concept in Bakhtin's writings.

The emancipatory potential of carnival is examined in *Rabelais and His World*. This might seem less concerned with written texts than Bakhtin's other writings, and more of a social and cultural history. Bakhtin argues that carnival was an anarchic festival during which freedom was unleashed: social hierarchies were inverted and authority was transgressed. Carnival finds its emblem in the grotesque, pleasure – seeking human body: fat and fleshy, eating, drinking, fornicating and defecating to excess. For Bakhtin the carnivalized body connects humanity to the materiality of the earth and the cycle of reproduction. But while he stresses the materiality of both body and world, Bakhtin's insistence on the primacy of the word for human understanding means that the body is inscribed in traditions of semiosis, so that the body is connected to novelistic practices of discourse – enter Rabelais and *Gargantua and Pantagruel*. In fact the idea of carnival in history is present in the writings on novelists and the history and prehistory of the novel: in the later version of *Problems of Dostoevsky's Poetics* Bakhtin argues that Dostoevsky weaves the laughter of carnival into his novels through genres of discourse which had their origins in carnival and the popular language of the marketplace.

Ken Hirschkop has pointed to failures of rigorous political and historical thinking in Bakhtin's formulations: can political interests really be coterminous with a linguistic style, and to what extent did Bakhtin simply impose a monolithically negative image of modernity on a complex history of medieval and early Renaissance culture? The rigour of Bakhtin's concepts might also be questioned in the light of their apparently limitless availability to appropriation – something that becomes evident as his cultural impact is examined.

Bakhtin's writings have had an impact on **Marx**ist aesthetic debates within the British cultural studies tradition. Bakhtin enables Marxists to take a 'linguistic turn' without abandoning materialism and class – Tony Bennett's *Formalism and Marxism* (1979) being exemplary here. This formation has drawn upon *Rabelais and His World*, and the emphasis is on carnival as an act of populist subversion. Julia **Kristeva**'s seminal post-structuralist reading of Bakhtin's theory of the novel in

Desire in Language (1980) opened up deconstructive possibilities; in an English context a post-structuralist/deconstructionist Bakhtin has been politically endorsed by Graham Pechey, and critiqued by the late Allon White – both are important commentators on Bakhtin's work. Bakhtin's writings have also been appropriated by humanist scholars such as Katerina Clark and Michael Holquist, who seek to return Bakhtin to what they see as his 'roots' in the Russian Orthodox Church, neo-Kantianism and German aesthetic theory. But we are returned here to the problem of context and multiple meanings in Bakhtin's writings: if Bakhtin can be appropriated simultaneously by two distinctive and, in crucial respects, incompatible theoretical traditions – the French and the German – then as Robert Young has argued, just about anyone can, and probably will, appropriate Bakhtin for more or less anything. However, some of the latest and most valuable work to appear on Bakhtin confronts this problem: Michael Gardiner seeks critically to reappraise the grounds on which Bakhtin can be related to French structuralism and post-structuralism, and the German tradition of hermeneutics and critique.

Main works

The Dialogic Imagination, trans. Caryl Emerson and Michael Holquist, Austin, Texas University Press, 1981; contains 'Epic and novel', 'From the prehistory of novelistic discourse' and 'Discourse in the novel'.

Problems of Dostoevsky's Poetics (1963), trans. Caryl Emerson, Minneapolis: Minnesota University Press, 1984.

Rabelais and His World (1965), trans. Hélène Iswolsky, Bloomington: Indiana University Press, 1984.

Speech Genres and Other Late Essays, trans. Vern W. McGee, Austin: Texas University Press, 1986.

Further reading

Clark, Katerina and Michael Holquist, *Mikhail Bakhtin*, Cambridge, MA: Harvard University Press, 1984.

Gardiner, Michael, *The Dialogics of Critique: M.M. Bakhtin and the theory of ideology*, London: Routledge, 1992.

Hirschkop, Ken and David Shepherd (eds), *Bakhtin and Cultural Theory*, Manchester: Manchester University Press, 1989: contains essays by Hirschkop and Pechey.

Kristeva, Julia, *Desire in Language*, trans. Thomas Gora *et al.*, Oxford: Blackwell, 1980.

White, Allon, 'Bakhtin, sociolinguistics and deconstruction', in *The Theory of Reading*, ed. Frank Gloversmith, Brighton: Harvester, 1984.

Young, Robert, 'Back to Bakhtin', *Cultural Critique* 2 (1985).

Barthes, Roland (1915–80)

Roland Barthes allied himself, albeit temporarily, with most of the intellectual fashions that dominated French cultural life from the end of the Second World War to the 1980s. He was influenced by **Marx**ism and existentialism in the forties; by structuralism in the fifties, semiology in the sixties and post-structuralism in the seventies. His structuralism placed him close to **Lévi-Strauss**, **Lacan** and **Foucault**, whilst the critical work of **Derrida** and **Kristeva** clearly helped to shift his work towards a post-structuralist position. Barthes was never a politically committed intellectual in the **Sartre**/Foucault mould; he preferred to assault dominant interests and ruling elites through his constantly demystifying intellectual engagement. Between 1947 and 1976 he held a number of positions on the margins of French academic life, after which he was made a professor of the Collège de France, a position he held until his death in 1980.

It is tempting, but dangerous, to view Barthes's work as falling into a number of 'phases'. In the first – beginning with *Writing Degree Zero* and ending with *Mythologies*, and including most of his writing on the theatre – Barthes was under the influence of Sartre, **Marx** and **Brecht**. *Writing Degree Zero* is in some ways a response to Sartre's *What is Literature?* He challenges Sartre's view that literature must, in order to engage with society and history, be unambiguous and transparent. Literature, Barthes argues, should question its own practices in order to realize its revolutionary potential. Barthes introduces three terms around which his argument develops. A writer's *language* is the inherited set of rules that an individual can neither choose nor change. *Style* on the other hand, is the set of reflexes and habits, conditioned by a writer's personal history and biology. Neither style nor language can be the ground of commitment; for that Barthes introduces the concept of *écriture*, the mode of writing, which is the field of politics. Thus Céline and Camus, while they share the same *language* have, by virtue of who they are, different *styles* and, virtue of their political relations, very different *écritures*.

The most important work in Barthes's early period is the series of reflections on contemporary French culture, originally written for the magazine *Les Lettres nouvelles* between 1954 and 1956 and published, along with a long theoretical essay, in 1957 as *Mythologies*. In these pieces, Barthes demonstrates how racism, sexism and colonialism lurk behind the apparently natural and innocent. He shows how certain images or ideas – which constitute a first layer of meaning, consisting of a signified and a signifier united in a sign – are transformed into 'myth'. The original sign has its concept emptied out, and it becomes a signifier for a second, mythical level of meaning. A photograph of a black soldier on the cover of *Paris Match* functions as a sign of that particular individual, who exists at a particular time in a particular place. He has a history. Myth destroys that history, and the image becomes instead the form that carries the concept of French imperialism, the myth of different nations and races living together in harmony under the same flag.

The function of myth in bourgeois culture is to obscure the manufactured nature of that very culture, to make the contingent and historical appear natural and eternal. In this it resembles strongly some of Marx's arguments in his *Critique of Hegel's View of the State*. What distinguishes Barthes's analysis is first his concentration on the apparently trivial – the striptease, wrestling, advertisements for soap powders – and second, his employment of a linguistic model.

From the publication of *Mythologies* onwards, Barthes was identifiably part of the structuralist movement. He himself has defined structuralism as the use of the methods of structuralist linguistics to analyze other language systems. Barthes's initial contact with structuralist linguistics came from Louis Hjelmslev, and it was from Hjelmslev that he acquired his commitment to a *scientific* approach to the analysis of language systems. This impulse towards science – what Barthes has called his 'euphoric dream of scientificity' – is manifested in his contributions to **Saussure's** anticipated science of signs. *The Elements of Semiology* codifies his practice, elucidating the series of opposed terms by which the semiologist analyzes the meaning-generating power of language: diachronic/synchronic; language/speech; signifier/signified; connotation/denotation. It commits the seniologist to analyzing non-linguistic phenomena using the structuralist model, by first clearly specifying the field to be studied, a language system existing at a particular moment in time (therefore synchronic rather than diachronic) and then selecting only those elements which contribute towards meaning through their differential relations. Central to the structuralist project is the concept of the death of the author, famously announced by Barthes in an essay in 1967. The point was not that authors had ceased to write, or were no longer important, but that authorial intention could no longer be appealed to as the final arbiter of the meaning of a text.

The Fashion System is Barthes's most rigorous attempt to apply the principles of scientific semiology to a facet of culture, in this case the world of fashion as depicted in the magazines *Elle* and *Jardin des Modes*. He first selects his field – not, as one might expect, the photographs of particular garments ('image clothing') but, rather, the captions describing them ('written clothing'), which serve to direct and order our perceptions. From these, Barthes constructs a 'grammar' of fashion, and demonstrates the different levels at which meanings are generated. We are told what is fashionable, what elements can be combined and which exclude each other. The project is allied to *Mythologies* in that the captions naturalize what is arbitrary: we are informed by a caption that 'dresses are becoming longer', as if that was in some way inevitable.

The Fashion System has been criticized on its own terms as an example of a structural analysis, but a more fundamental challenge to structuralism itself was beginning to make itself felt in French intellectual circles by the time it was published in 1967. Derrida's essay 'Force and signification', in *Writing and Difference* (1967), attacked the metaphysical, teleological concepts underpinning notions of structure applied to the literary text. The post-structuralism of Derrida and Julia Kristeva carried Saussure's insight into the arbitrariness of the sign to its extreme, destroying any attempt to discover ultimate meaning in the infinite play of signifiers. The scientific structuralism of *The Fashion System* was itself out of fashion by the time it appeared.

The first important work of what might be termed Barthes's post-structuralist phase is *The Empire of Signs*. It takes the form of a series of detailed descriptions of various aspects of Japanese culture – food, the puppet theatre, haiku, calligraphy – from which he creates a confessedly utopian account of a culture in which everything signifies, but meanings are never final. No metaphysical notion of a soul lurks behind the Japanese eye; in the same way, the most beautifully wrapped Japanese parcel contains nothing of significance. We are not presented with what claims to be a true picture of the 'real' Japan; Barthes is creating a myth in which all meaning is differential and nothing has an essence or a history.

S/Z is perhaps Barthes's most fertile and challenging text. In it he takes *Sarrasine*, a short story by Balzac, and shatters it into a series of fragments. These are then allocated to one of five codes that enable the text to signify. The intention is to demonstrate that texts, even those which aspire to 'realism', are woven from other texts. Balzac's originality vanishes as 'observations' are traced to the cultural commonplaces they express. Yet the text itself proves surprisingly fertile, shimmering with unexpected meanings. Barthes contrasts the classic *lisible*, or readable, in which the reader is a passive consumer, to the *scriptible* or 'writable' text, in which the reader becomes an active producer, collaborating in the creation of meaning. Unexpectedly, the effect of *S/Z* is to undermine that distinction – the classic work *Sarrasine* proves to be eminently *scriptible* with a reader as creative as Barthes.

After *S/Z* Barthes became preoccupied with the actual physical experience of reading, with the sensuous body rather than the signifying system. He viewed this as an attempt to emphasize the material basis of language, and as a challenge to the critical orthodoxy his own practice had helped to develop. Nevertheless, it too often appears as a return to the same myth of the 'natural' he had done so much to exorcize in the 1950s and 1960s. From this phase, *The Pleasure of the Text* has been one of Barthes's most influential – if perplexing – works. In a series of alphabetically arranged sections he develops what has been called an 'erotics of reading'. The contrast between the *writerly* and *readerly* encountered in *S/Z* is translated into the two types of sensation experienced by a reader: *Plaisir* and *jouissance*. The text of pleasure offers the traditional joys of the classic novel: intelligence, irony, delicacy, euphoria, mastery and security. *Jouissance*, or ecstasy, is the shock of the unexpected, where the reader's comfort is destroyed, where language is fissured. The suggestion is made that a reconciliation should be possible, that the classic can be rent by *jouissance*, and the avant-garde made readable: we encounter the erotic at the 'seam' between culture and anarchy.

Roland Barthes by Roland Barthes is an ironic and highly selective autobiography in which Barthes gently mocks his earlier enthusiasms, without critically engaging with those other selves. It is an often amusing and self-deflating account of his compulsive need to try out new ideas – to confront *doxa*, accepted opinion, with paradox. His impoverished, bourgeois upbringing, his long struggle with TB and his homosexuality are touched on without revealing what could ever be regarded as the 'real' Roland Barthes – indeed, Barthes claims that he exists only as the product of his own texts.

A Lover's Discourse was a bestseller in France, and it is sometimes thought of as the novel that Barthes had often spoken of writing. It depicts the confused, fragmentary language of sentimental love, gleaned from Romantic fiction, philosophy and psychoanalysis. The lover finds himself 'in the brazier of meaning' in which every gesture, every accidental caress, is charged with significance. It is an extraordinary and melancholy work. Love – or rather, its discourse – never progresses, but circulates endlessly.

Barthes's final text, *Camera Lucida*, is both a theoretical work – a phenomenology of photography – and a personal exploration of his relationship with his mother. He privileges photography as giving an unmediated picture of the world, and particularly of the past, in opposition to language, in which meanings are encoded. This gives photography the power to move, and to shock us into our knowledge of love and death. In this sense *Camera Lucida* is diametrically opposed to *Empire of Signs*, in which the emptiness of signs is celebrated.

Barthes was among the most influential cultural critics of the postwar period. He was a generator of new discourses, which he would then attack when they became widely accepted. This range of theoretical approaches can be baffling – he picks up Marxism, structuralism and post-structuralism, examines them from various angles, leaves them alone and then comes back to them – but his fertility is a consequence of his critical restlessness.

Main works

On Racine, trans. Richard Howard, New York: Hill & Wang, 1964.

Writing Degree Zero, trans. Annette Lavers and Colin Smith, London: Jonathan Cape, 1967a.

Elements of Semiology, trans. Annette Lavers and Colin Smith, London: Jonathan Cape, 1967a.

Mythologies, trans. Annette Lavers, London: Jonathan Cape, 1972a.

Critical Essays, trans. Richard Howard, Evanston, IL: Northwestern University Press, 1972b.

S/Z, trans. Richard Miller, London: Jonathan Cape, 1975.

The Pleasure of the Text, trans. Richard Miller, London: Jonathan Cape, 1976.

A Lover's Discourse: Fragments, trans. Richard Howard, London: Jonathan Cape, 1979.

A Barthes Reader, ed. Susan Sontag, London: Jonathan Cape, 1982a.

Camera Lucida: Reflections on Photography, trans. Richard Howard, London: Jonathan Cape, 1982b.

Empire of Signs, trans. Richard Howard, London: Jonathan Cape, 1983.

The Fashion System, trans. Matthew Ward and Richard Howard, London: Jonathan Cape, 1985.

The Rustle of Language, trans. Richard Howard, Oxford: Blackwell, 1986.

Further reading

Culler, Jonathan, *Structuralist Poetics: Structuralism, linguistics and the study of literature*, London: Routledge & Kegan Paul, 1975.

Culler, Jonathan, *Barthes*, London: Fontana, 1990.

Lavers, Annette, *Roland Barthes: Structuralism and after*, London: Methuen, 1982.

Moriarty, Michael, *Roland Barthes*, Cambridge: Polity, 1991.

Sturrock, John (ed.), *Structuralism and Since: From Lévi–Strauss to Derrida*, Oxford: 1979.

Wiseman, Mary Bittner, *The Ecstasies of Roland Barthes*, London: Routledge & Kegan Paul, 1989.

Baudrillard, Jean (1929–)

Baudrillard taught sociology at the University of Nanterre for over twenty years (1966–87). In recent years he has come to international prominence as a writer of 'coffee-table' format books on postmodern life, such as *America* and *Cool Memories*. Among his range of influences is the Situationist movement (Guy **Debord** *et al.*) whose aesthetic theories were much in vogue during Baudrillard's early career, as well as the work of his sociology teacher Henri Lefebvre, noted for his call for a **Marx**ist-orientated 'critique of everyday life'; but it would also be true to say that Baudrillard drew freely on a whole range of intellectual discourses that emerged during the 1960s in France, and is a fairly eclectic thinker overall.

Baudrillard's intellectual trajectory marks a dramatic shift from a 1960s left-revolutionary radicalism (he was a translator of the plays of both Peter Weiss and Bertolt **Brecht** in this period) to a resolutely post-Marxist postmodernism apparently unconcerned with practical politics. In his early sociological studies, such as *Le Système des objets*, *La Société de consommation*, and *For a Critique of the Political Economy of the Sign*, Baudrillard investigates various aspects of the new mass consumer society (a subject of considerable interest to French cultural theorists of the time, **Barthes** being another notable commentator on the phenomenon) from a Marxist perspective, showing a particular concern with the semiology of consumerism and the social attitudes and behaviour that accompanied this. He can be considered part of a general movement in radical Marxist circles in the postwar era to emphasize the role of culture in the formation of capitalist ideology (economic factors had generally been accorded precedence in Marxist thinking up to that point); hence his desire to elaborate a 'political economy of the sign'. The impact of the cultural sphere on everyday life – areas such as sexuality, fashion, the media, and technology coming under scrutiny, for example – becomes the main focus of Baudrillard's inquiry into the new consumer society, and he tends to view consumerism as a force that dominates and controls the lives of individuals.

From the mid 1970s onwards, however, Baudrillard proceeds to veer sharply away from his earlier political radicalism and Marxist orientation to become a hostile critic of the French Communist Party and what he considers to be its outdated policies – policies which have not fully absorbed the sociological implications of the technological revolution that has overtaken us in the later twentieth century. He becomes increasingly concerned with the impact of cybernetics on society (a phenomenon he refers to as 'cyberblitz'), and eventually concludes that it leads to the creation of a new social order that transcends the principles of classical Marxist theory (class conflict, etc.), the postmodern society where simulation and simulacra rule. Simulacra are reproductions of objects or events, and they are pictured as being arranged in various historical orders: an order of fixed signs in the feudal era which will allow simulation only in the form of counterfeiting; an order of infinitely reproducible objects in the industrial era, with its methods of mass production (there is an echo of Walter **Benjamin's** ideas here); and then the third order of postmodern society, in which cybernetics-generated simulation models have taken over, and now dictate the nature of reality and pattern of human existence. In this latter society the individual self is reduced to the condition of being a mere 'switching centre for all the networks of influence' that technology is able to generate.

In his postmodernist guise Baudrillard is a highly provocative thinker, whether he is proclaiming the end of history as we know it and the joys of American life at its most ruthless and inhuman in *America*, or outraging the feminist movement by his conception of femininity in *Séduction*. Describing himself as an avowed enemy of meaning and interpretation in the traditional sense of the terms, he speaks of the need to dissolve or even exterminate them, and there is a distinctly apocalyptic tone to much of his work (one of his essays is, appropriately enough, entitled 'The year 2000 will not take place') that fits in with the **Nietzsche**an strain so prominent in French theoretical discourse from post-structuralism onwards (the same influence can be seen at work in thinkers such as **Foucault, Derrida** and **Lyotard**). Whereas some theorists of the postmodern, such as the highly influential architectural theorist Charles **Jencks**, have called for a self-conscious dialogue with the discourses of the past, Baudrillard seems to want a complete break with them, and his later work is an unashamed celebration of technological revolution in all its apparently disorientating and dislocating forms. In this later work Baudrillard presents us with a strange, dreamlike realm, where reality has become confused with its own simulation in the condition he refers to as 'hyperrealism' (there are definite echoes of 'the medium is the message' notion here, and in many respects later Baudrillard amounts to a kind of 'hyper-**McLuhan**ism').

America finds Baudrillard at his most iconoclastic, and the text as a whole reveals a fascination with the paradoxes and excesses of late-twentieth-century American life. The brutal and alienating architecture, the collapsing inner cities, the huge disparity between rich and poor, the omnipresent threat of violence, the rampant consumerism, the self-centred ideology – Baudrillard can wax lyrical about all these things, while throwing out often outrageous asides about Disneyland and television being America's true reality (more *real* than reality, that is, *hyperreal*) and the demolition of skyscrapers constituting a marvellous new art form (the Situationist vision of the city as spectacle no doubt plays a part in such assessments). Outrageous though such observations are, there is more than a grain of truth in some of them: television *does* exercise a disproportionate amount of authority in the Western world, and one that is steadily on the increase. What becomes more contentious is Baudrillard's uncritical acceptance of such cultural trends. He seems to be seeking in America something like the obliteration of his still residually value-conscious European self (the concept of value itself being a relic of a lost cultural past in this reading), and he makes a determined effort to adopt the role of spectator rather than judge of American culture. America is in effect a model of our hyperreal future, where reality and simulation have become all but indistinguishable. The desert becomes for Baudrillard an image of the self stripped down to its basics – 'desertification', as he calls it – and this is taken to be the condition to which we should all ultimately aspire as postmodern individuals: 'No desire: the desert'. There is a Zen Buddhist-like quality to much of this attitudinizing, and overall *America* represents a giant step towards the creation of a post-aesthetic sensibility – a process continued in *Cool Memories*, where Baudrillard preaches the virtues of chance encounters and the complete suspension of value judgement – 'there is a charm and a particular freedom about letting just anything come along', as he puts it, conjuring up the spectre of an aimless and passive individual existence in the midst of massively disorientating, technology-driven cultural change. The apparent apoliticism of his later work has outraged many on the left who regard it as little better than an abject surrender to the ideology of late capitalism, especially coming as it does from an ex-sixties Marxist radical and one-time bitter critic of the consumer society and its mores.

One of the ways by which we can undermine the power and authority of systems is through the process of 'seduction', in Baudrillard's view a specifically feminine trait which neither confronts nor directly challenges authority but instead beguiles it into submission. It then becomes a case of individual guile against an authoritarian (that is, masculine) system, with the system being reduced to a position of disadvantage by femininity, envisaged as a principle of uncertainty and unpredictability. The system can mount no effective defence against such behaviour, Baudrillard argues. Not surprisingly, feminist theorists have been quick to attack the author's emotively sexist terminology which, they feel, merely serves to reinforce culturally unacceptable gender stereotypes, where women are encouraged to cajole or work behind the scenes rather than stand up for their rights against an exploitative patriarchy. Defining femininity as 'ironic' in character and masculinity as 'eccentric, paradoxical, paranoid and tiresome' fails to offer much protection against such charges, and once again it seems as if Baudrillard's desire to be provocative at all costs serves to obscure his very real insights into the nature of authority and its weak points. His argument about the inherent weakness of patriarchal ideology and the systems that maintain it has many affinities with Lyotard's critique of 'grand narrative'; but to its ultimate detriment, it signally lacks the intellectual rigour and moral seriousness associated with the latter.

Baudrillard is one of the gurus of postmodernism ('a sharp-shooting lone ranger of the post-Marxist left', as he has been dubbed), and his later work in particular has been a source of considerable controversy, which he gives every impression of studiously cultivating with his outrageous asides and iconoclastic attitudes. A media personality of some note in recent years, he created something of a stir with his views on the Gulf War as a quintessentially postmodern event which seemed to exist only as a simulation for television, rousing Christopher **Norris**, among others, to a bitter reply against such apparent intellectual dilettantism. Baudrillard's influence has even extended as far as inspiring an art movement in New York (the Simulationists) during the 1980s – although, ironically enough, he was not particularly enthusiastic about any of its productions.

Despite his perceived weaknesses as a theorist – he is neither a particularly systematic nor rigorous thinker in the main, as even his supporters quite readily admit ('patience and immersion in the particular' not being amongst his virtues, as Douglas Kellner has quite rightly observed) – Baudrillard is nevertheless an important source of perceptive insights into the postmodern condition, with its radically altered relationship between the individual and technology. He may well overstate the power of simulation and simulacra in determining our perception of the world, but there is no denying that these entities are playing an increasingly important role in the construction of social reality as we approach the millennium.

Main works

Le Systeme des objets, Paris: Denoel-Gonthier, 1968.

La Societe de consommation, Paris: Gallimard, 1970.

The Mirror of Production, trans. Mark Poster, St Louis, MO: Telos, 1975.

L'Echange symbolique et la mort, Paris: Gallimard, 1976.

For a Critique of a Political Economy of the Sign, trans. Charles Levin, St Louis, MO: Telos, 1981.

Les Stratégies fatales, Paris: Grasset, 1983a.

Simulations, trans. Paul Foss, Paul Patton and Philip Beitchman, New York: Semiotext(e), 1983b.

In the Shadow of the Silent Majorities, trans. Paul Foss, Paul Patton and John Johnston, New York: Semiotext(e), 1983c.

Forget Foucault, trans. Nicole Dufresne, New York: Semiotext(e), 1987.

America, trans. Chris Turner, London and New York: Verso, 1988a.

The Ecstasy of Communication, trans. B. and C. Schutze, New York: Semiotext(e), 1988b.

Cool Memories, trans. Chris Turner, London and New York: Verso, 1990a.

Séduction, trans. Brian Singer, London and Basingstoke: Macmillan, 1990b.

La Guerre du Golfe n'a pas eu lieu, Paris: Editions Galilée, 1991.

Further reading

Best, Steven and Douglas Kellner, *Postmodern Theory: Critical interrogations* New York: Guilford Press, 1991.

Featherstone, Mike, *Consumer Culture and Postmodernism*, London: Sage, 1991.

Frankovits, Alan (ed.), *Seduced and Abandoned: The Baudrillard scene*, Glebe, NSW: Stonemoss, 1984.

Kellner, Douglas, *Jean Baudrillard: From Marxism to postmodernism and beyond*, Cambridge and Oxford: Polity and Blackwell, 1989).

Norris, Christopher, *Uncritical Theory: Postmodernism, intellectuals and the Gulf War*, London: Lawrence and Wishart, 1992.

Pefanis, Julian, *Heterology and the Postmodern: Bataille, Baudrillard, and Lyotard*, Durham, NC and London: Duke University Press, 1991.

Beauvoir, Simone de (1908–86)

Simone de Beauvoir has a complex and much-disputed reputation. She is internationally recognized as one of the most distinguished and famous French intellectuals of the twentieth century, and as probably the most significant figure in second-wave feminism. Her analysis of what it is to be a woman, *The Second Sex* (published in English 1953; first published as *Le Deuxième Sexe* in 1949) is a founding text of postwar Western feminism. But her work has often been disparaged by both non-feminist and feminist critics and commentators. Some French post-structural feminists in particular, from the 1970s onwards, have been determined to distance themselves politically from her. Her reputation, in both its negative and positive formulations, whether as a philosopher, as a novelist or as a feminist, is tied as much to her life story as to her fictional and philosophical writings. In part, this is a result of her own literary activity: the volume of her published letters, newspaper interviews and autobiographical writings is enormous. Nor is it possible to separate clearly autobiography, fiction and philosophical theory in her work. All her writings are intertextually related. This is further complicated by issues concerning her lived relationship with her lover and lifelong companion Jean-Paul **Sartre**, their individual and shared political activism and the intertextual relationship between their works. Beauvoir's intellectual, emotional, sexual and political life and her writing are inseparable.

Beauvoir was born in 1908 into a middle-class Parisian family. She was educated at Catholic schools and at the Sorbonne, where she gained her Certificate of Letters in 1927. While enrolled at the Sorbonne and studying there and at the Ecole Normale Supérieure for the postgraduate *agrégation* in philosophy, she met Sartre, and in 1929, at the age of 21, she became the youngest candidate ever to pass the *agrégation*. Sartre, in his second attempt at the examination, came first in the ranking of the candidates; Beauvoir came second. Until 1943 Beauvoir worked as a teacher in *lycées* in Marseilles, Rouen and finally Paris. During the Nazi Occupation of Paris, Beauvoir, like others, temporarily left the city, but maintained the stance of political 'commitment'. After the end of World War II she took a prominent anti-imperialist position on French policy in Algeria, and opposed McCarthyism and later the involvement of the United States in Vietnam. Beauvoir's commitment to socialism as the sole possible solution to all forms of oppression was modified only in 1970, when she publicly declared herself as a feminist. From this point onwards, as a Marxist feminist, she became active in the French Women's Liberation Movement, campaigned for women's abortion rights, and announced her militant, radical feminism in 1972. She edited the feminist journal *Questions Féministes*, launched in 1977. In her much-publicized sexual and emotional life – which also provided, in various forms, material for her novels and her philosophical writing as well as her direct autobiography – Beauvoir avoided the constraints of a conventional woman's life of the period. Sartre defined his and Beauvoir's relationship as 'necessary', but as allowing other 'contingent' relationships. Throughout her life, Beauvoir had a series of other significant liaisons with both men and women (although she always defined herself as heterosexual), including Nathalie Sorokine in 1939–40; the American writer Nelson Algren from 1947 to 1951; and Claude Lanzmann, with whom she lived from 1952 to 1958. Her first novel, *She Came to Stay*, was published in 1943, and she produced numerous novels, essays and autobiographical writings throughout the rest of her life. In 1954 her novel *The Mandarins* won the Prix Goncourt. Since her death in 1986, her work has begun to be radically reappraised.

In the third volume of her autobiography, *Force of Circumstance* (first published as *La Force des Choses* in 1963), Beauvoir records that the stimulation to write her most profoundly influential and passionately debated book, *The Second Sex*, came from a conversation with Sartre, during which she recognized the difference between being born as a woman and as a man. In *The Second Sex* she addresses the question 'What is woman?' She recognizes that it is men who have defined woman's being, and that they have done so in relation to the assumed norm of the male. She argues that it has been assumed historically that 'humanity is male' and that 'man defines woman not in herself but as relative to him; she is not regarded as an autonomous being'. She goes on famously to declare:

> For [man, woman] is sex – absolute sex, no less. She is defined and differentiated with reference to man and not he with reference to her; she is the incidental, the inessential as opposed to the essential. He is the Subject, he is the Absolute – she is the Other.

Just as famously, Beauvoir further states in *The Second Sex*: 'One is not born, but rather becomes, a woman', as a result of the social and cultural processes through which adult being is formed. Her argument here, as throughout *The Second Sex*, is premised on her existentialist belief. Existentialism, in general, maintains that humans are free to act by choice. Necessary awareness of other people complicates this, producing the impulse, particularly in sexual encounters and relationships, to possess and control others. Beauvoir's work introduces awareness of the systematic difference in effect of this for men and women, and comprises a feminist revision and development of existentialism. Her long analysis of how women come to internalize and live out feminine attributes – including passivity, dependence on men and acceptance of their inferior status – is divided into sections covering investigation of: historical accounts of social division of women's and men's roles from prehistory; literary and mythic representations of woman; woman's development as she grows up; and contemporary women's roles, social situation and negotiations of their social and sexual being. The particularly strong impact of her survey and analysis of misogynistic myth on early-second-wave feminist writers is exemplified by its influence on Kate **Millett**'s classic text *Sexual Politics* (1970).

In much of her fiction Beauvoir deals with questions and material deriving from her own life, and with existentialist themes. Her first novel, *She Came to Stay* (first published in French as *L'Invitée* in 1943), examines the aetiology and implications of sexual jealousy and licence through a narrative detailing the competition and intense jealousy between two women for one man. *The Blood of Others* (in French *Le Sang des Autres*, 1948) similarly investigates issues of personal freedom, choice and the individual's responsibility towards others, through the fictionalized account of a group of members of the French Resistance during the Nazi Occupation. *The Mandarins* (*Les Mandarins*, 1954) her most celebrated novel, depicts an affair between its female central character and a male American writer, their sexual choices and commitments in the context of postwar French socialist political thought and activity. Issues dealt with fictionally in her novels are re-presented in the four volumes of her autobiography proper: *Memoirs of a Dutiful Daughter* (*Mémoires d'une jeune fille rangée*, 1958) describes her upbringing, education, first romantic and sexual encounters and meeting with Sartre, and the early development of her philosophical position; *The Prime of Life* (*La Force de l'Age*, 1960) details her relationship with Sartre; *Force of Circumstance* (*La Force des Choses*, 1963) covers the period of her greatest involvement in socialist politics and her relationships with Algren and Lanzmann; and *All Said and Done* (*Tout compte fait*, 1972). Apart from these formal autobiographical volumes, she also published accounts of her mother's and Sartre's deaths (*A Very Easy Death* [in French *Une Mort très douce*, 1964]; and *Adieux: A Farewell to Sartre* [in French *La Cérémonie des Adieux*, 1981]). These descriptions of and meditations on the deaths of crucially significant figures in her life develop her long preoccupation with issues of death.

On its first publication and later translation *The Second Sex* had a phenomenal impact. To a generation of Western (largely white, middle-class) women who felt isolated and trapped in the purely domestic roles designated to them by the prevailing ideology of the 1950s and early 1960s, *The Second Sex* provided a confirmation that their feelings were not idiosyncratic or pathological, and that women had potential to lead another form of life. Beauvoir received thousands of letters testifying to ways in which *The Second Sex* had changed individual women's lives. It became a key text for discussion in women's consciousness-raising groups in the early 1970s. Yet it was also much criticized. Although Beauvoir's declared solution to the problem of women's oppression was socialist revolution, left-wing critics challenged her separation of women's oppression as an issue from that of other forms of oppression. Most controversial, however, has been Beauvoir's perceived complicity in masculine power structures. Many feminists have pointed to her idealization of masculinity in *The Second Sex* (and elsewhere), suggesting that despite her exposure of habits of thought that assume masculinity as the norm, she herself is enmeshed in these, uncritically presenting men as unrestricted by the social, cultural and bodily, and as being not alienated but free: in other words, as unreconstructed existentialist heroes. Psychoanalytically informed post-structuralist feminism frequently dismisses her as a phallic woman whose humanist beliefs have little to offer.

Amongst influential French feminists of the 1980s, only Monique **Wittig** has acknowledged the important influence of Beauvoir. In feminist evaluation of her work, her own autobiographical representation of her life with Sartre is often brought into play, as much as it is in non-feminist criticism. Her promotion of Sartre as the foremost existentialist philosopher of the twentieth century, at her own expense, has begun to be critically discussed. Kate and Edward Fullbrooke, for instance, work from evidence that in the 1970s Beauvoir deliberately falsified the chronology of her writings, implying that she had hardly begun *She Came to Stay* before Sartre wrote *Being and Nothingness*, thus obscuring issues about her influence on Sartre's development of his theories. Fullbrooke and Fullbrooke argue from this for an inversion of the reputations of Sartre and Beauvoir, as do some other feminist revisionists, claiming her as the greater philosopher. To others, such evidence of Beauvoir's protection and unquestioning admiration of Sartre merely confirms her personal and intellectual collusion in patriarchal relations. Although critical battles over Beauvoir's importance as a novelist, philosopher and feminist – on these and more purely textual fronts – seem set to continue for some time, recent analyses such as Toril Moi's *Simone de Beauvoir: The making of an intellectual woman* have provided the basis for a less polarized and more sophisticated assessment of this major – if controversial – twentieth-century intellectual figure.

Main works

Reference is to editions in English in the chronological order of original French editions. The date of these is given in square brackets [ ].

The Ethics of Ambiguity, trans. Bernard Frechtman, New York: Citadel Press, 1976 [1946].

A Very Easy Death, trans. Patrick O'Brian, Harmondsworth: Penguin, 1983 [1964].

She Came to Stay, trans. Yvonne Moyse and Roger Senhouse, London: Fontana, 1984 [1943].

The Second Sex, trans. H.M. Pashley, Harmondsworth: Penguin, 1984 [1949].

The Blood of Others, trans. Yvonne Moyse and Roger Senhouse, Harmondsworth: Penguin, 1986 [1945].

The Mandarins, trans. Leonard M. Friedman, London: Fontana, 1986 [1954].

Old Age, trans. Patrick O'Brian, Harmondsworth: Penguin, 1986 [1970].

Adieux: A farewell to Sartre, trans. Patrick O'Brian, Harmondsworth: Penguin, 1986 [1981].

Memoirs of a Dutiful Daughter, trans. James Kirkup, Harmondsworth: Penguin, 1987 [1958].

Force of Circumstance, trans. Richard Howard, Harmondsworth: Penguin, 1987 [1963].

All Said and Done, trans. Patrick O'Brian, Harmondsworth: Penguin, 1987 [1972].

The Prime of Life, trans. Peter Green, Harmondsworth: Penguin, 1988 [1960].

Letters to Sartre, ed. and trans. Quintin Hoare, New York: Arcade, 1991 [1990].

Further reading

Evans, Mary, *Simone de Beauvoir: A feminist mandarin*, London: Tavistock, 1985.

Fallaize, Elizabeth, *The Novels of Simone de Beauvoir*, London: Routledge, 1988.

Fullbrooke, Kate and Edward Fullbrooke, *Simone de Beauvoir and Jean-Paul Sartre: The remaking of a twentieth-century legend*, Hemel Hempstead: Harvester Wheatsheaf, 1993.

Keefe, Terry, *Simone de Beauvoir: A study of her writings*, London: Harrap, 1983.

Moi, Toril, *The Making of an Intellectual Woman*, Oxford and Cambridge, MA: Blackwell, 1994.

Okley, Judith, *Simone de Beauvoir*, London: Virago, 1986.

Belsey, Catherine (1940–)

Catherine Belsey took her first degree at Oxford University and a doctorate at Warwick University. She has taught at Cardiff University since 1975, founding the Centre for Critical Theory there in 1989.

Catherine Belsey's project takes off from British post-structuralism, especially as this was inaugurated by the film journal *Screen*. In the 1970s, with writers including Colin **MacCabe** and Stephen Heath, *Screen* set itself the aim of theorizing cinema through 'the encounter of Marxism and psychoanalysis on the terrain of semiotics'.[1] Belsey's first major text, *Critical Practice*, reworks and rethinks that aim for literature. Arguing from **Saussure** that language is founded in 'a system of differences with no positive terms' *Critical Practice* begins by breaking with the naturalist fallacy, the belief that literature may be understood either as a reflection of reality, true or false, or as the expression of personal experience. Since language is primary and all meanings are constructed, literature must be read as a textual event or operation which provides a position for its reader.

Leaning on **Althusser**'s account of how 'ideology suppresses the role of language in the construction of the subject' as well as the work of **Brecht**, Belsey contrasts the 'expressive realist' with the 'interrogative' text. Effacing its own textuality, predicated on some version of truth (either in reality or personal experience), the expressive realist text 'interpellates the reader as a transcendent and non-contradictory subject', whereas the interrogative text 'disrupts the unity of the reader' by demonstrating its own textuality, so discouraging identification with a fixed position (that of the supposed 'author', for example). After exemplifying the realist text with a reading of Dickens's *Bleak House* and the interrogative text from *Julius Caesar*, *Critical Practice* points out that since, in fact, every text originates in the signifier, every text is open to plurality and a rereading, which may transform the realist text into something much more radical. Belsey cites with approval the view of Roland **Barthes** that a progressive literary politics makes 'the reader no longer a consumer, but a producer of the text'.

Critical Practice hovers a little in transition between being an Althusserian and a more radically post-structuralist work. Althusser's theory of ideology retains a notion of the real as opposite to the imaginary of ideology; it also encourages a somewhat pre-post-structuralist view of the text as having inherent *effects* on the implied reader prior to and apart from its production in a reading. In Belsey's next work, *The Subject of Tragedy*, the influence of Althusser is subsumed into that of **Foucault** and **Derrida**.

In the mid-1980s a series of books made Shakespeare and Renaissance drama the chosen battleground for radical new theory in Britain. Somewhat on the model of Foucault's *Discipline and Punish*, Belsey's *Subject of Tragedy* begins by contrasting the feudal and bourgeois subjects – or rather, the subjects of 'discursive' and 'empirical' knowledge. While the discursive subject seeks to be at one with its object – God, Logos, truth, being – 'absorbed in total presence' in a relation for which knowledge is not instrumental but constitutive, the new (bourgeois) empirical subject emerges in

> a difference between the knowing subject and the objects of its knowledge, and this difference becomes definitive for the subject. The subject is now defined as that which knows, in contradistinction to that which is known . . .

This subject effectively takes the place of God, and becomes author and guarantee of its own (subjective) truth. *The Subject of Tragedy* argues that the empirical subject endeavoured, in the seventeenth century, to validate its own authority as bearer of knowledge by relying on an institutional establishment of knowledges in the social order – only to find its sovereignty undercut by contradictions within the social order itself. Absolutism, supposed to guarantee the sovereign subject, in fact came rapidly to deny it, and so also did the attempt to impose sovereignty in the domain of gender and of sexuality.

At first the absolutist version of marriage sought to instate women as the subordinate term in the oppositions father/mother, husband/wife, parent/child, but these proved contradictory (children, for example, were meant to honour both father and mother equally), and as empirical subjects women could not hold both positions. But the later development of the affective family and liberal marriage as free choice between two empirical subjects came up against the contradiction so tersely exposed by Mary Astell in *Some Reflections upon Marriage* (1700): 'If *all men are born free*, how is it that all women are born slaves?'.

Supplanting Althusser with Foucault wins a number of benefits for *The Subject of Tragedy*. By bracketing the real, a Foucauldian account of subjectivity permits analysis to cross without difficulty any frontier between textual practice and social practice, while moving with similar facility between discussion of the historical formation and accounts of relations of gender, not always easy to theorize adequately in terms of 'social roles'. It is also able to revitalize the familiar **Marxist** notion of contradiction by thinking it in terms of power and its inescapable underside, resistance. Furthermore, *The Subject of Tragedy* realizes and confirms something more, already potential in *Critical Practice*. Discarding the opposition between high and popular culture, *The Subject of Tragedy* ranges in comfort between *Hamlet* and *Arden of Faversham*, between soliloquy, theatre design and family portrait-painting.

Belsey always writes with clarity and refreshing wit. From the French post-structuralist writers she has put together an original synthesis which is at once directed specifically at textuality (as her fine book on Milton details), comprehends issues of sexuality and gender along with the conventionally historical, and always indicates a progressive politics. That coalescent formation, committedly postmodern, might be brutally summarized as follows.

If, as Derrida proposes, difference is older than Being, then any version of sameness, unity, presence, is just that – a version. Identity, even the identity of the real, is an effect which effaces difference, that privilege being held in place by power, in fact defining the operation of power. It is always open, therefore, for a radical politics to insist on difference, thus interrogating and relativizing power, whether it appears as the supposed truth a text refers to, the 'real nature' of woman, or good old-fashioned political sovereignty. Able to fuse modes of analysis from **Lacan**, Foucault and Derrida, Belsey's synthesis is predicated, arguably, on the centre or truth it aims to undo. Some queries might follow from this slightly unnerving work of integration. Does power (ideology) take only the form of naturalization, the rendering of difference as identity? What happens to the real as understood, for example, by modern physics? Foucault's notion of the subject is a consequence of (social) power: can this be sustained when a major theorization, in **Freud**'s psychoanalysis, points to a radically other process in the subject, that of the unconscious?

As one of the first books published in the new literary theory, *Critical Practice* has become the one most conventional critics love to hate, invariably without having read or understood it carefully enough. *The Subject of Tragedy* intervenes alongside **Dollimore** and **Sinfield**'s *Political Shakespeare*, Drakakis's *Alternative Shakespeares*, and **Eagleton**'s *Shakespeare*, but extends its theoretical claims well beyond its chosen syllabus area. Belsey was one of the first to step aside from the opposition between the canon and its popular cultural other. Crossing the line between *Antony and Cleopatra* and Mills & Boon, her new work on *Desire: Love stories in Western culture* aims to show the impossibility of the sexual relation as well as its privatizing allure. It is certain to carry her project forward into a wide-ranging substantiation.

Main works

Critical Practice, London: Methuen, 1980.

The Subject of Tragedy: Identity and difference in Renaissance drama, London: Methuen, 1985.

John Milton: Language, gender, power, Oxford: Blackwell, 1988.

The Feminist Reader: Essays in gender and the politics of literary criticism, London: Macmillan, 1989.

Desire: Love stories in Western culture, Oxford: Blackwell, 1994.

Further reading

Easthope, Anthony, *British Post-Structuralism*, London: Routledge, 1988.

Heath, Stephen, *Questions of Cinema*, London: Macmillan, 1982.

Parrinder, Patrick, *The Failure of Theory*, Brighton: Harvester, 1987.

Smallwood, Philip, *Modern Critics in Practice*, Hemel Hempstead: Harvester Wheatsheaf, 1990.

MacCabe, Colin, *Tracking the Signifier*, Manchester: Manchester University Press, 1985.

Barker, Francis *et al.* (eds), *Literature, Politics and Theory*, London: Routledge, 1986.

Notes

1. Stephen Heath, '*Jaws*, ideology and film theory' originally published in *Times Higher Education Supplement* in 1976, reprinted in Tony Bennett *et al.* (eds), *Popular Television and Film*, London: BFI, 1981, pp. 200–205, (p. 201).

2. Jacques Derrida, *Margins of Philosophy*, Brighton: Harvester, 1982, p. 67.

Benjamin, Walter (1892–1940)

'In the doomed, poignant figure of a Benjamin', says Terry **Eagleton**, 'we find reflected back to us something of our contradictory desire for some undreamt-of emancipation and persistent delight in the contingent' (Eagleton, 1982). Indeed, it is that troubled coupling of nomadism and monadism in Walter Benjamin's thinking which has made him one of the most interesting and influential cultural theorists of the twentieth century. Born of the German–Jewish middle class at a historical moment when the European Jewish intellectuals were being tempted by both Zionism and Communism, his fascination for the 'messianic and the materialist' produced an idiosyncratic style which captures perfectly the trajectory of a number of modern philosophical and aesthetic preoccupations. Benjamin was educated in Switzerland during the First World War. His academic career began with an interest in German Baroque drama: after writing a doctoral dissertation on the German Romantic movement and art criticism, and an analysis of Goethe's *Elective Affinities*, he went on to prepare for his *Habilitation* in Germany with a study called *The Origin of German Tragic Drama*. Although this work would make his reputation posthumously, it was declared 'incomprehensible' at the time of its completion – owing not only to the radicality of its argument, which effectively redefined the aim of philosophy, but also to its fragmentary, aphoristic style of presentation. Despite the fact that this work failed to win Benjamin his *Habilitation*, and hence the academic career he had coveted, it was his most comprehensive theoretical statement, and became immensely important to the Frankfurt School critical theorists, in particular Theodor **Adorno**. At the time, however, this failure forced him into an itinerate lifestyle sustained only by his work as a critic and the commissions he received from a variety of sources.

The year 1924 secured his turn to **Marx**ism, for it was then that he read and admired George **Lukács**'s *History and Class Consciousness*, became friendly with Ernst Bloch, and fell in love with Asja Lacis, a Latvian Communist theatre director and friend of Bertolt **Brecht**. 1924 was also the year after Benjamin had met Adorno, who had read his *Origin* with interest. This association brought with it much-needed commissions from the Frankfurt Institute for Social Research, a supplement to Benjamin's income that allowed him to continue writing in Paris when the political climate in Germany became uncomfortable. Benjamin's peripatetic career, however, ended tragically in 1940, when he took his own life following an unsuccessful attempt to cross over to Spain to escape the Nazis.

Benjamin's work, which attempts to merge the philosophical, aesthetic and political realms, is a continual exploration of the interrelationship between history and modernity, and of the possibility of producing a modernist theory of history which includes both the concept of forgetting and that of memory. This translates into an attempt to rethink modern human subjectivity as simultaneously constructed from fragments of often discontinuous moments, but subjective moments nevertheless capable of political agency. In his critical rethinking of history, Benjamin is increasingly sceptical of traditional narrative, and of the notions of a progressive, linear development that it assumes, preferring instead the defamiliarizing technique of fragment and montage. His idiosyncratic 'critical aesthetic' is indexed by a preference for epic theatre, as theorized and practised by Bertold Brecht. Brecht, of course, while accepting Aristotle's definition of tragedy as the medium for presenting the possible, moved away from the classic notion of the end of tragedy as catharsis. Indeed, Brecht's 'undramatic' theatre sought both to present the problems of history and to problematize 'present history'. Accordingly, his theatre characterized itself by representing to a thinking audience moments for reflection, not entertainment. Interruptions, interventions, fragments, the actor's gesturing to the actuality of the play as a play, ultimately undermine a realist conception of the illusion of reality, replacing it with the reality of illusion. Within the representational space of Brecht's epic theatre, then, Aristotle's concern for the possible returns as a contemplation on the possibility for change.

In *The Origin of German Tragic Drama*, Benjamin attempts to combine an understanding of the tractarian method, defined as '(re)presentation as detour', and a paratactical montage form, a style that uses interruption in order to renounce the discursive flow of arguments which follow a single logic, direction or 'intention'. In the 'Epistemo-Critical Prologue' with which this book begins, Benjamin condemns nineteenth-century philosophy for its totalizing pretensions. What he objects to is the way in which the philosophy of this time, working on the assumption that science had a universal grammar the truth of which applied to all systems of knowledge, forced unity between the objective dimension and the subjective. The effect of this was to produce a false reconciliation between heterogeneous systems of knowledge, weaving 'a spider's web between separate kinds of knowledge in an attempt to ensnare the truth' (Benjamin, 1977). A proper philosophical style, for Benjamin, pursued many different questions simultaneously in a movement that remained conscious of itself as it preserved the integrity of concrete objects: when this movement is momentarily arrested, the constellation of concepts that emerges can be considered objectively as an 'event'. The discovery of these constellations is an interpretative activity, but one that is controlled by the real existence of ideas:

> truth is an intentionless state of being, made up of ideas. The proper approach to it is therefore not one of intention and knowledge, but rather a total immersion and absorption in it. Truth is the death of intention. (Benjamin, 1977)

There is the assumption here that human subjectivity has the power to search for, recognize and draw to itself the 'authentic' structure of the idea. This authentic structure is revealed through the juxtaposing of the 'remotest extremes and the apparent excesses of the process of development', and exists as the sum of all possible meaningful combinations. Human redemption is therefore achieved through the revelation of this 'origin', through the 'science of origin' which is philosophical history.

The 'Epistemo–Critical Critique' emerges out of Benjamin's analysis of German tragic drama of the 'decadent' Baroque period, a period that he viewed as closely associated with his own in the way that the striving for aesthetic wholeness combined uncomfortably with the lack of community ethos. Allegorical as opposed to symbolic modes of representation were used to convey this disparity, and Benjamin defended this Baroque style over the aesthetics of the symbol, which he saw as derived from the Romantic period as an attempt to recuperate a waning religious tradition. This hope for a correspondence between the world and the mind is carried over into modernism. But for Benjamin, only through allegory can the constructed, fragmentary nature of images of a perceived past wholeness be adequately conveyed: the sadness of the sorrow play is a lamentation for the loss of wholeness, and redemption is in the form of the recognition of the illusion. In this defamiliarized context, truth is not a concept of totalization but a fragmentary finitude consisting of constantly shifting relationships between heterogeneous material images.

Although the *Origin* prefigures most of Benjamin's later thought, it was literary-philosophical rather than political in orientation. The next 'materialist' phase of his intellectual development was to examine more fully the political possibilities of the epistemological problems his previous thinking had revealed. It is probable that his interest in 'a radical Communism' was facilitated by the intellectual and financial insecurity that followed the failure of his *Habilitation*.

In the late 1920s and 1930s Benjamin published a number of theoretical works in *Zeitschrift für Sozialforschung*, the journal of the Institute for Social Research, including an analysis of the movement of bourgeois intellectuals like himself from the position of avant-garde to organized political involvement; but the work that occupied him most fully was the famous *Arcades Project*. This work was thirteen years in the making, and much of it remained unpublished in his lifetime. Benjamin's interest was in reconstructing the Paris of the nineteenth century, in 'arresting' its primal history through an investigation of certain tropes which were configured and limited by the changing contours of the city; these tropes – 'the *flâneur*', 'the arcades', 'panoramas', 'fashion', 'gambling', 'prostitution', 'boredom' – were thought to represent the urban experience of modernity.

One important article connected with this work and published in the journal was 'The work of art in the age of mechanical reproduction'. In this essay Benjamin discusses the unique situation of art in an age of reproducibility; mechanical reproducibility destroys *both* the 'aura' of a work of art which is linked to its authenticity, its unique historical existence, *and*, effectively, the ritual and cult aspects of art, allowing for a cathartic release of energy through the destruction of tradition. Thus the question of how the products of mechanical reproduction get mobilized within a culture becomes a primary consideration; for Benjamin, political orientation matters very much in the handling of reproduction:

> Some of the players whom we meet in Russian films are not actors in our sense but people who portray themselves – and primarily in their own work process. In Western Europe the capitalist exploitation of the film denies consideration to modern man's legitimate claim to being reproduced. Under these circumstances the film industry is trying hard to spur the interest of the masses through illusion-promoting spectacles and dubious speculations. (Benjamin, 1978)

The *Arcades Project* also included two articles on Baudelaire: the first, 'The Paris of the Second Empire in Baudelaire' (published in *Aesthetics and Politics*) was the source of controversy between Adorno and Benjamin; the revision of this first article, called 'On some motifs in Baudelaire', was printed at the time. Although Adorno praises certain aspects of Benjamin's materialist orientation, his concern is for the undialectical nature of his analysis: the primary objection is to the way in which Benjamin reads consciousness as having a cohesion that exceeds its existence as a 'constellation of reality'; this leads him to consider dialectical images as immanent in consciousness, rather than produced by the commodity fetish. Benjamin himself acknowledges an antagonism in his work, but one that he considers productive if it is worked through in the construction of the work. Thus, in the fragmentary 'Theses on the philosophy of history' he asserts that 'every image of the past that is not recognized by the present as one of its own concerns threatens to disappear irretrievably', and also observes that our capacity to recognize these proleptic or anticipatory images is itself historically conditioned, that it is the changing horizon of the present which allows hitherto concealed and mute works from the past to speak and convey a contour, if only momentarily.

Gershom Sholem and Theodor Adorno agreed that Bertolt Brecht's aesthetics, with which Benjamin strongly identified, undermined the dialectical potential of his thinking. In his essay 'The author as producer', for example, Benjamin argues, against Lukács and with Brecht, that political tendency and literary quality necessarily coincide in a truly revolutionary aesthetics: techniques of production melt down and allow for the interfertilization of literary forms in a reconfiguration which always remains committed to proletariatization. The function of art, however, changes with the changing of historical conditions. The importance of Brecht's theatre, for Benjamin, is in the way he 'succeeded in altering the functional relationship between stage and audience, text and production, producer and actor. Epic theatre must not develop actions but represent conditions.' Brecht's use of interruption emulates the technique of montage familiar in film, radio, photography and press, but it also disrupts narrative illusion, and hence foregrounds the historical conditions of modernity.

Benjamin was virtually unknown in his lifetime except by his closest associates like Gershom Sholem, Theodor Adorno, Ernst Bloch, Bertolt Brecht and Hugo von Hofmannsthal, all of whom established themselves as important contributors to the intellectual debates of the 1930s and 1940s. Not until the 1960s did Benjamin's own work resurface in Europe and America as newly translated and in many cases newly published texts. Since that time his reputation as a cultural theorist on the edge of the Marxist tradition, a 'Marxist Rabbi' (Eagleton, 1981) with a facility for 'thinking poetically' (Hannah Arendt, Introduction, *Illuminations*, 1968), has increased, even despite Theodor Adorno's pronouncement that 'the essence of [Benjamin's] thought' is 'as philosophical thought'. However, Benjamin's thinking is not dialogic with the problems of philosophy; rather, as Benjamin says of Brecht's Galy Gay in *A Man's a Man*, it constitutes the wisdom of a man 'who lets the contradictions of existence enter into the only place where they can, in the last analysis, be resolved: the life of a man'.

Main works

Illuminations, ed, Hannah Arendt, trans. Harry Zohn, New York: Harcourt, Brace & World, 1968.

Charles Baudelaire: A lyric poet in the era of high capitalism, trans. Harry Zohn, London: New Left Books, 1973a.

Understanding Brecht, trans. Anna Bostock, London: New Left Books, 1973b.

The Origin of German Tragic Drama, trans. John Osbourne, London: New Left Books, 1977.

Reflections: Essays, aphorisms, autobiographical writings, ed. Peter Demetz, trans. Edmund Jephcott, New York and London: Harcourt, Brace & World, 1978.

One-Way Street and Other Writings, trans. Edmund Jephcott and Kingsley Shorter, London: New Left Books, 1979.

Moscow Diary, pref. Gershom Sholem, trans. Richard Sieburth, ed. Gary Smith, Cambridge, MA: Harvard University Press, 1986.

The Correspondence of Walter Benjamin and Gershom Scholem 1932–1940, trans. Gary Smith and Andre Lefevere, introduction by Anson Rabinbach, New York: Schocken Books, 1989.

Further reading

Taylor, Ronald, ed., *Aesthetics and Politics: Debates between Ernst Bloch, Georg Lukács, Bertolt Brecht, Walter Benjamin and Theodor Adorno*, London: Verso, 1977.

Buck–Morss, Susan, *The Origin of Negative Dialectics*, New York: Free Press, 1977.

Eagleton, Terry, *Walter Benjamin: Or towards a revolutionary criticism*, London: Verso, 1981.

Geyer–Ryan, Helga, *Fables of Desire*, Cambridge: Polity Press, 1994.

Smith, Gary, *Benjamin: Philosophy, aesthetics, history*, Chicago and London: University of Chicago Press, 1983.

Wolin, Richard, *Walter Benjamin: An aesthetic of redemption*, New York, 1982.

Bhabha, Homi K. (1949–)

Homi Bhabha was educated at the Universities of Bombay and Oxford, and has spent most of his academic career teaching at the University of Sussex, where he is now a professor. He has also been a visiting professor at the Universities of Princeton and Pennsylvania in the United States. In the 1980s Bhabha's work appeared mainly in journals, collections of essays and published conference proceedings in Britain and the United States. Most of his essays, some in revised form, have now been collected in his book *The Location of Culture* (1994), the introduction and conclusion to which lend a singularity of purpose to his diverse contributions in the fields of post-colonial theory and postmodernism.

Bhabha's main contribution to contemporary theory has been to suggest an alternative to untheorized or undertheorized analyses of post-colonial literature and culture in which the colonial condition is essentialized. For Bhabha, 'the postcolonial perspective attempts to revise those nationalist or "nativist" pedagogies that set up the relation of Third World and First World in a binary structure of opposition'. In *The Location of Culture*, he asserts (through readings of Toni Morrison's *Beloved* and Salman Rushdie's *Satanic Verses*, amongst other texts) that the post-colonial condition is emblematic of the heterogeneity of contemporary culture, not simply a marginal aspect of it. What characterizes the contemporary cultural moment we inhabit is a recognition that notions of unitary identity are no longer viable. Bhabha's work suggests a sophisticated move beyond the polarity of a cultural politics in which questions of gender and class, as well as race, are considered exclusively in terms of binary opposition. His own model for political change is that of the 'hybrid moment': 'the transformational value of change lies in the rearticulation, or translation, of elements that are *neither the One* (unitary working class) *nor the Other* (the politics of gender) *but something else besides*, which contests the terms and territories of both'. It should be emphasized that this notion of hybridity, of *'something else besides'*, is far removed from a quasi-Hegelian notion of synthesis or transcendence. Bhabha's ideas concerning cultural politics are in fact formulated within the terminology of post-structuralist and psychoanalytic theory, and in spirit, at least, appear to draw on **Bakhtin**ian notions of polyphony and the carnivalesque. If his project of critique has involved interrogating and destabilizing fixed ideas of identity, the title of his book, *The Location of Culture*, invites an examination of how he wishes to resituate the question of identity in the sphere of contemporary culture. What he offers is a celebration of the liminal identity associated with the post-colonial condition. Bhabha's desired vision is of a world in which intellectuals and critics inhabit a borderline existence, what he calls 'being in the "beyond"', 'an intervening space' in which it is possible 'to be part of a revisionary time, a return to the present to redescribe our cultural contemporaneity'.

Some idea of how Bhabha's theoretical work begins to take its characteristic shape can be gleaned from a relatively early essay (not reprinted in *The Location of Culture*), 'Representation and the colonial text: a critical exploration of some forms of mimeticism' (1983). Here Bhabha argues the need for a new critical language with which to explore and understand the colonial text (the particular example he focuses upon at the end of his essay is V.S. Naipaul's novel *A House for Mr Biswas*). The most readily available critical methods for analyzing the novel, identified by Bhabha as **Leavis**ite Universalism, Nationalist criticism and **Althusser**ian ideological analysis, are all predicated upon somewhat naive notions of the representational quality of literary texts. Each of these three critical positions fails to problematize the faith in mimesis preponderant in Western aesthetics, emphasizing instead the idea that literature mediates historical reality or ideology in either a transparent or a displaced fashion. Bhabha takes to task those critics who advocate the application of Leavisite universalist critical principles to Third World literary texts for ignoring the fact that, as **Achebe** has pointed out, 'universality' is itself a Western concept. Bhabha sees 'anti-colonialist, anti-racist "Nationalist" criticism' as mirroring the defects of universalist criticism because it is haunted by 'a preference for realist signification'. 'Nationalist' literary criticism, based on conventional notions of the stability of character, image analysis and so on, is impoverished, since it deals only with the identification of stereotypes of the colonial world in texts, be they negative or positive. Bhabha is clearly most interested in the kinds of ideological analysis practised in the work of **Marx**ists such as Althusser, **Macherey** and **Eagleton**, because here at least 'reality' is seen not as given but as *produced* by literary texts, and ideology is regarded in terms of repression and displacement, gaps and absences, rather than as explicitly mediated. But Bhabha's critique of contemporary Marxist literary theory is that it remains bound to various shibboleths such as 'ideology', 'reality' and 'history' which derive from Western preoccupations with teleology, tradition and the fixity of meaning. The solution Bhabha offers at the end cf his essay lies in an appeal to **Freud**'s notion of the destabilizing realm of fantasy. The psychoanalytic insight that the whole project of narrative intention and control in realist fiction can be seen to be decentred or subverted 'from within' is, argues Bhabha, especially appropriate to readings of post-colonial texts. In his reading of Naipaul's novel, colonial fantasy 'registers a crisis in the assumption of the narrative priority of the "first person" and the *natural* ascendancy of the First World'. Bhabha's resort to Freud is thus a convenient and economical way of exposing both the defects of mimetic literary theories, and their collusion with the hegemony of Western pre-occupations with realism and historicism.

Bhabha has offered the general argument that 'the encounters and negotiations of differential meanings and values within "colonial" textuality, its governmental discourses and cultural practices, have anticipated, *avant la lettre*, many of the problematics of signification and judgement that have become current in contemporary theory'. In other words, instead of applying the apparatus of modern literary theory to colonial texts, Bhabha sees himself as discovering within the texts themselves the very issues which condition such theory. This can be demonstrated in relation to the repeated motif of Bhabha's work, the aforementioned concept of *hybridity*, most extensively treated in one of a series of essays which examine various documents associated with British rule in India in the nineteenth century, 'Signs taken for wonders: questions of ambivalence and authority under a tree outside Delhi, May 1817' (1985). As with the earlier essay, 'Representation and the colonial text', Bhabha is concerned here with the question of how to interpret issues of representation in documents of the colonial era. He is interested not in a black-and-white characterization of colonial rule in which texts are read according to whether they evince 'the noisy command of colonialist authority' on the one hand, or 'the silent repression of native traditions' on the other; but, rather, in the texts' '*production* of hybridization'. Hybridity, in this context, is defined as the sign of the ambivalent and shifting forces of colonial power which cannot be registered at a purely mimetic level within colonial discourse but exceed it, resisting containment and closure. Thus subversion and intervention can be witnessed in the interstices of discourses of authority which deal with colonial subjects (government memoranda, written accounts of missionary practices). Such texts produce hybridity because the colonial construction of 'the other' is always necessarily incomplete, and colonial writings about the colonized are always marked by a perpetual undecidability.

Further manifestations of hybridity are elaborated in two further essays by Bhabha, 'Of mimicry and man: the ambivalence of colonial discourse' and 'Sly civility'. Borrowing from **Lacan**'s metaphor of mimicry as camouflage, Bhabha finds in the writings of the late-eighteenth-century missionary Charles Grant and Macaulay's famous 'Minute' of 1835 attempts to foster a nativist *imitation* of colonial values which, instead of resulting in compliance and the consolidation of colonial control, opens up the opportunity for resistance and disobedience on the part of the colonized. The phrase 'sly civility' comes from an account by an early-nineteenth-century British missionary who is disconcerted by the ostensibly polite though nevertheless resistant way that many natives react to attempts to renounce their own beliefs and convert to Christianity. 'Sly civility' registers the kind of ambivalent, undecidable, uneasy quality which Bhabha identifies as returning to haunt and threaten the appearance of control and order in colonial discourse.

Much of Bhabha's critical and theoretical methodology is clearly inflected with psychoanalytical thinking, and this is perhaps what most distinguishes his work from other critics in the field of post-colonial theory. The ambivalent and threatening quality of hybridity and the notion of fantasy, suggest an association of the colonized with an excess which is at least in part a function of the paranoia and repression within the colonizer. Bhabha is keen, however, to avoid the pitfalls of reductive binarism, as is evident in *The Location of Culture* in his critique of **Said** and his interest in **Fanon's** early work on image and fantasy in the colonized consciousness (particularly in *Black Skin, White Masks*) which clearly gestures towards Freud. Bhabha's warning that **Derrida's** invocation of the Nambikwara Indians and **Lyotard's** of the Cashinahua pagan's 'are part of a strategy of containment where the Other text is forever the exegetical horizon of difference, never the active agent of articulation', indicts a tendency in the institutions of contemporary critical theory 'to reproduce a relation of domination', and shows his welcome vigilance in the field of contemporary cultural studies.

Unlike those Eurocentric models of post-colonial theory in which the colonized Other has been further negated or marginalized (often albeit unwittingly) by academic theory, Bhabha (like Fanon before him) has taught cultural critics how to read the signs of resistance on the part of the colonized in colonial discourse. Rather than seeking to affirm the hegemonic status of the colonizing consciousness, he has shown how its encounters with the colonized destabilize questions of cultural identity in radical ways. His more recent work has begun to explore the compatibility of this fluid definition of the post-colonial condition, in which the rigid boundaries between colonizer and colonized are dissolved, with contemporary postmodernist debate.

Main works

'Representation and the colonial text: a critical exploration of some forms of Mimeticism', in Frank Gloversmith, ed., *The Theory of Reading*, Brighton: Harvester, 1984, pp.93–122.

(ed.), *Nation and Narration*, London: Routledge, 1990.

The Location of Culture, London: Routledge, 1994.

Further reading

Ashcroft, Bill, Gareth Griffiths and Helen Tiffin, *The Empire Writes Back: Theory and practice in Post-colonial literatures*, London: Routledge, 1989.

Leask, Nigel, *British Romantic Writers and the East: Anxieties of empire*, Cambridge: Cambridge University Press, 1992.

Parry, Benita, 'Problems in current theories of colonial discourse', *Oxford Literary Review*, 9, 1–2 (1987): 27–58.

Young, Robert, *White Mythologies: Writing, history and the West*, London: Routledge, 1990.

Bloom, Harold (1930–)

Harold Bloom was born and raised in New York into a working-class, orthodox Jewish family in which he was trained to be a Talmudist. He graduated from Cornell University in 1951, and was awarded his PhD from Yale University in 1955. He began teaching at Yale in 1955 and has remained associated with that institution ever since, becoming Sterling Professor of Humanities there in 1983. He has held visiting professorships at a variety of institutions, mainly in the United States and has been the recipient of numerous prizes, awards and fellowships. Bloom has been a prolific and prodigious writer of criticism, his output reflecting three principal areas of interest: the English Romantic poets and their heirs such as Stevens and Ashbery in the modern American tradition; the writings of **Freud**, in particular his theory of the family romance; and Kabbalism, a tradition of mystical interpretation of the Hebrew Bible. His most famous contribution to modern literary theory, the tetralogy beginning with *The Anxiety of Influence* [*AI*] (1973), marks an attempt to draw these three preoccupations together into a coherent theory of poetic influence, and thereby to revise conventional accounts of literary history. Over the past ten years or so, Bloom has increasingly concentrated on writings about Hebrew traditions of interpretation and scholarship, and has distanced himself from mainstream literary theory to the extent that he now clearly regards its institutional forms with some contempt. Since 1985 he has been the general editor of several hundred volumes of criticism published by Chelsea House.

As John Hollander suggests, it is its antithetical quality which marks out Bloom's contribution to literary theory and criticism. His first book, *Shelley's Mythmaking* [*SM*] (1959), a revised version of his PhD, demonstrates his affiliations with those 'Romantic Revivalist' critics, notably **Frye** and **Hartman**, who dissented from the strictures of Eliot, **Leavis** and the New Critics which had dominated assessments of the Romantic poets over the previous two decades. In launching his systematic defence of Shelley, Bloom provocatively champions the Romantic poet whose critical fortunes were probably then at their lowest ebb thanks to the animadversions of Eliot, Leavis and Tate on his purported deficiencies with regard to morality and poetic craftsmanship. Bloom's readings of individual texts are fresh and attentive to detail, but in terms of the critical terminology which he develops later on, *SM* is an act of monumental misprision. Shelley's poetry is read through the lens of Martin Buber (1878–1965), the Jewish theologian and author of *I and Thou* (1922), as a kind of existential programme in which the poet's mythopoeia always follows the same pattern of aspiration, struggle and inevitable defeat. Bloom's attack on the British tendency to read the Romantic poets through the genteel proprieties of Matthew Arnold's Hellenism, and his awareness of the hostility of Blake, Shelley, and Keats to many forms of Christianity, was – as Christopher **Norris** has shown – part of a staking-out of a dissenting literary tradition (including Spenser, Milton, Blake, Shelley, Yeats and Lawrence) which was to be contrasted with the conservative Catholic line established by Eliot. But – explicitly in *SM*, and implicitly elsewhere – the Romantic poets are at the same time recuperated into an alternative religious tradition, that of the heresies of Jewish gnosticism, in which Bloom himself has been immersed since his adolescence. *SM* and the other two books of his Romantic triad, *The Visionary Company* (1961) and *Blake's Apocalypse* (1963), show Bloom to take what he sees as the high Romantic argument of unorthodox poets such as Blake and Shelley on its own terms. Thus it is not simply that he forcefully articulates what he sees as their belief in the autonomy of the imagination, but that he too embraces that ideal as the founding principle of his own work. In this first phase of his criticism, Bloom thus emerges as a kind of paradigmatic Romantic himself.

From the late 1960s onwards Bloom's interpretation of the Romantics becomes mediated increasingly through the writings of **Freud**. He began immersing himself in Freud at the age of 35 during what he describes as a mid-life crisis, and his most clear articulation of how Freud influences his reading of the Romantics can be found in his essay 'The internalization of quest romance' (1968), reprinted in *The Ringers in the Tower* (1971). In this essay it is evident that Bloom finds in Freud a more general matrix within which to lay down his theory of conflict between Promethean aspiration and the obstacles to its fulfilment in the self, already articulated in his earlier readings of the Romantic poets. Like Abrams, and certain other American Romanticists writing at this time, Bloom takes as read the idea that the pre-eminent crisis in Romantic poetry is expressive of *internal* struggles of a spiritual and psychological kind rather than of engagements with historical, cultural or ideological issues external to the self. Bloom's assertion that 'Freud's embryonic theory of romance contains within it the potential for an adequate account of Romanticism' demonstrates that he had already laid the foundations for a theory of poetry based upon competing psychic drives (the essay is probably contemporaneous with the draft of most of *AI*, which was written in the summer of 1967). In the more polished language of *AI*, Bloom makes the Freudian influence even more explicit with the remark: 'Romanticism, for all its glories, may have been a vast visionary tragedy, the self-baffled enterprise not of Prometheus but of blinded Oedipus who did not know that the Sphinx was his Muse.'

Bloom's theory of poetic influence is reflected upon and reformulated for many years after the publication of *AI* (1973), but while each of the other works of the tetralogy – *A Map of Misreading* [*MM*] (1975), *Kabbalah and Criticism* (1975) and *Poetry and Repression*, [*PR*] (1976) – enriches his argument, *AI* remains the most elegant exposition of his central thesis in which **Nietzsche**, 'the prophet of the antithetical', and

Freud, who 'recognized sublimation as the highest human achievement', are the most notable influences on Bloom himself. *AI* claims to offer 'a theory of poetry by way of a description of poetic influence', and one of its stated aims is to 'de-idealize our accepted accounts of how one poet helps to form another'. Bloom's notion of influence has nothing to do with the conventional scholarly identification of the transmission of ideas and images from earlier to later poets. He is concerned, rather, with a psychodramatic account of the origins of all creative acts, the way 'strong poets make poetic history by misreading one another, so as to clear imaginative space for themselves'. The battle – or *agon*, as Bloom later terms it – that a later poet (whom he calls the *ephebe*) fights against an earlier (the precursor) for creative space takes several forms which are described in terms of six 'revisionary ratios': *clinamen* ('misreading or misprision'); *tessera* ('completion and antithesis'); *kenosis* ('a movement towards discontinuity with the precursor'); *daemonization* ('a movement towards a personalised Counter-Sublime'); *askesis* ('a movement of self-purgation'); *apophrades* ('the return of the dead . . . in which it seems . . . as though the later poet himself had written the precursor's characteristic work'). In considering these ratios, it should be remembered that Bloom repeatedly asserts his notion of influence in terms of the agonistic relationship between poems rather than poets, arguing that the meaning of a poem can 'only be a poem, but *another poem – a poem not itself* (*AI*). This claim and others – 'there are no texts but only relationships between texts'; 'Every poem we know begins as an encounter between poems' (*MM*); 'Any poem is an inter-poem, and any reading of a poem is an inter-reading' (*PR*) – show, as Graham Allen argues, that Bloom's concept of influence bears a resemblance to contemporary theories of intertextuality in the work of **Barthes** and others. His apparent concurrence with **de Man** that 'criticism is a metaphor for the act of reading' (*MM*), his idea of the proximity of the languages of criticism and poetry, and his engagement with **Derrida**'s readings of Freud in *MM*, perhaps explains why Bloom ended up editing and contributing to the formative collection, *Deconstruction and Criticism* (1979), even though his own contribution, 'The breaking of form', a reprise of the ideas of his tetralogy, is resolutely distanced from the preoccupations of the other contributors.

In terms of Romantic studies and literary theory, the high point of Bloom's influence occurred in the decade or so after *AI* was published. His interest in conceptions of authority and sublimation contributed to important debates on the Romantic sublime (in the work of Thomas Weiskel, for example), and his version of intertextuality looked just close enough to certain features of post-structuralism and deconstruction for him to be identified – misleadingly, as it turned out – with his

Yale colleagues, Hartman and de Man. But Bloom's theory of influence has been relentlessly attacked over the past ten years or so, on several fronts. The most sustained onslaught in recent years has come from historicist critics of the Romantic period who reject his indifference to the cultural and political forces which contributed to the making of many major Romantic texts. Marilyn Butler's *Romantics, Rebels, and Reactionaries* and **McGann**'s *Romantic Ideology* can be seen to have been successful in challenging the solipsistic and ahistorical terms in which Bloom and Abrams have characterized Romanticism, since Bloom's work currently looks out of place in a climate in which New Historicist and cultural materialist accounts of Romanticism are in the ascendant. In a wider sense, the language of Bloom's critical writing from the later volumes of his tetralogy onwards sounds increasingly esoteric and eccentric. His repeated invocations of authority, competition, and struggle as immanent features of the psyche which condition poetry (and criticism) as much as any other aspect of existence, his exclusive conception of those who qualify as strong poets, his resistance to the idea that feminist and black writers may be incorporated into the canon, make him appear increasingly out of tune with current critical preoccupations. Once again, Bloom finds himself in the embattled position which has characterized his whole career.

Main works

Shelley's Mythmaking, New Haven: Yale University Press, 1959.

The Visionary Company: A reading of English Romantic poetry, London: Faber, 1962.

Blake's Apocalypse: A study in poetic argument, London: Victor Gollancz, 1963.

Yeats, Oxford: Oxford University Press, 1970.

The Ringers in the Tower: Studies in Romantic tradition, Chicago: University of Chicago Press, 1971.

The Anxiety of Influence: A Theory of Poetry, Oxford: Oxford University Press, 1973.

A Map of Misreading, Oxford: Oxford University Press, 1975a.

Kabbalah and Criticism, New York: Seabury Press, 1975b.

Poetry and Repression: Revisionism from Blake to Stevens, New Haven: Yale University Press, 1976a.

Figures of Capable Imagination, New York: Seabury Press, 1976b.

Wallace Stevens: The Poems of Our Climate, Ithaca, NY: Cornell University Press, 1977.

(ed.), *Deconstruction and Criticism*, London: Routledge, 1979.

Agon: Towards a theory of revisionism, Oxford: Oxford University Press, 1982a.

The Breaking of the Vessels, Chicago: University of Chicago Press, 1982b.

(ed. John Hollander), *Poetics of Influence: New and selected criticism*, New Haven: Henry Schwab, 1988.

Ruin the Sacred Truths: Poetry and belief from the Bible to the present, Cambridge, Mass.: Harvard University Press, 1989.

The Book of J, trans. David Rosenberg, interpreted Harold Bloom, London: Faber, 1991.

Further reading

Allen, Graham, *Harold Bloom: A poetics of conflict*, Hemel Hempstead: Harvester Wheatsheaf, 1994.

de Bolla, Peter, *Harold Bloom: Towards historical rhetorics*, London: Routledge, 1988.

de Man, Paul, Review of Harold Bloom's *Anxiety of Influence*, in *Blindness and Insight: Essays in the Rhetoric of Contemporary Criticism*, 2nd edn, London: Methuen, 1983, pp.267–76.

Fite, David, *Harold Bloom: The rhetoric of Romantic vision*, Amherst: University of Massachusetts Press, 1985.

Lentricchia, Frank, *After the New Criticism*, London: The Athlone Press, 1980, pp.318–46.

Norris, Christopher, *Deconstruction: Theory and practice*, London: Methuen, 1982, pp.116–125.

Bourdieu, Pierre (1930–)

Pierre Bourdieu was born in Bearn, in France, and educated at the Ecole Normale Supérieure in Paris. He currently holds the Chair of Sociology at the Collège de France, and is Director of Studies at the Ecole des Hautes Etudes en Sciences Sociales and Director of the Centre de Sociologie Européenne.

Pierre Bourdieu argues that definitions of culture and the culture of living are a significant aspect of the struggle between dominant and subordinate classes in society. Arbitrary ways of living are transmuted into *the* legitimate way of life, casting all other ways of living into arbitrariness. He writes of 'the power of the dominant to impose, by their very existence, a definition of excellence which is nothing other than their own way of existing' (*Distinction*). Bourdieu maintains that cultural distinctions are used to support class distinctions. Taste is a deeply ideological category: it functions as a marker of 'class' (using the term in the double sense to mean both socioeconomic category and a particular level of quality). For Bourdieu, the consumption of culture is 'predisposed, consciously and deliberately or not, to fulfil a social function of legitimating social differences' (*ibid*.). Culture is used by the dominant class to ensure its social reproduction. Bourdieu's purpose is not to prove the self-evident – that different classes have different lifestyles, different tastes in culture – but to interrogate the processes by which the making of cultural distinctions secures and legitimates forms of power and domination rooted in economic inequalities. He is interested not so much in the actual differences as in how these differences are used by the dominant class to ensure their domination. He wants to establish a connection between taste and class, between aesthetic judgement and the privileges of economic power.

Cultural capital is the currency through which domination is purchased. When it is exchanged and invested, it yields both 'a profit in distinction, proportionate to the rarity of the means required to appropriate [cultural texts and practices], and a profit in legitimacy, the profit par excellence, which consists in the fact of feeling justified in being (what one is), being what it is right to be' (*ibid*.). Cultural capital should not be understood as a synonym for cultural competence (understood as the acquisition of particular skills and knowledges). Cultural capital is the currency of social distinction, its accumulation allows appropriation of legitimate culture and the legitimate manner of appropriating it. Being an unequally distributed currency, cultural capital, like economic capital, is a means to domination: it secures profits of distinction. A classless society in which the means to appropriate culture (both materially and symbolically) was equally distributed throughout the population would have no place for cultural capital.

Cultural capital is produced in the main by the education system. It is also the product of informal forms of education. But the education system's role is crucial. For Bourdieu, the education system's function is to secure and legitimate privileges which exist prior to its operations. Rather than education, understood as the transmission of information, the education system functions to reproduce pre-existing social inequalities. The education system legitimates the cultural preferences of the dominant class in society, while at the same time devaluing the cultural preferences of the dominated classes, thus defining and reproducing a hierarchy in cultural goods. Because education privileges the culture of the dominant groups and classes in society, those from outside these groups and classes experience it at an immediate disadvantage – as a second culture. In this way, education tends to function to reproduce, rather than reduce, social inequalities. By making appear natural what is in fact cultural, the education system reproduces social hierarchies as academic hierarchies. What is based on cultural capital inherited as a result of membership of a particular class is reproduced as a hierarchy supposedly based on merit proved in the field of education.

Although cultural capital is the result of education (formal and informal), this is constantly disavowed by the 'ideology of natural taste', which converts differences of cultural taste into differences of nature. It 'naturalizes' cultural acquisition, denying its relation to education (both formal and informal): 'to know without having learnt'. Bourdieu borrows a phrase from **Nietzsche**, 'the dogma of the immaculate perception', to describe this process. The ideology functions 'to legitimatize a social privilege by pretending that it is a gift of nature' (*The Field of Cultural Production*). The dominant class's commitment to culture is an attempt to establish a mode of legitimation equivalent to the aristocracy's 'blood' or 'right of birth'. The effect of the ideology is to make culture appear as nature – as cultivated nature. To sustain this myth (culture as a gift of nature) it is necessary to deny the connection between culture and education. A significant consequence of this is symbolically to shift the source of distinction from the economic field to the field of culture, making power and privilege appear to be the result of cultural differences guaranteed by nature rather than by economic power and historical contingency. The effect of such cultural distinction is to produce and reproduce social distinction, social separation and social hierarchy. It becomes a means of establishing difference between dominated and dominant classes in society (and dominant and dominated fractions within classes). The production and reproduction of cultural space thus produces and reproduces social space. Distinction finds expression through what Bourdieu calls 'fields'.

A field is a relatively autonomous space, a site for the reproduction of the authority of the groups and classes with power. According to Bourdieu, a social formation is always made up of particular fields: economic, educational, cultural, and so on. Each field is a homologous but relatively autonomous structured space in which agents invest (consciously or unconsciously) their symbolic capital in the hope of a profitable return. Each field is marked by a struggle for the maximization of symbolic capital – prestige, recognition, and so on. Fields exist to embody strategies of domination and exclusion, to maintain the status, the distinction, of those with power. They are terrains on which to mobilize the different forms of capital – cultural, educational, social, and so forth – and to engage in strategies of reconversion (from one form of capital to another) where necessary in order to secure and sustain status and distinction.

Such a mode of analysis rejects the Kantian claim of disinterestedness. For Bourdieu, all attributions of cultural value are also affirmations of the legitimacy to make such claims. Judgement is always also an insistence on the right to judge. Given this perspective, 'canon' construction, for example, is for Bourdieu an act of symbolic violence, in that whatever else it is, it is always about the assertion of authority and the reproduction of power. A work of culture is always produced twice: in its moment of production and in its moment(s) of consumption. Moreover, the discourses which accumulate around the work are 'not mere accompaniment, intended to assist its perception and appreciation, but a stage in the production of the work, of its meaning and value' (*The Field of Cultural Production*). According to this mode of analysis, a work of art can be really appreciated only when it is situated within the social relations which structure its field of production and consumption: the material production of the work and the symbolic production of the work (i.e. the production of its status as an object to be valued). This must entail an examination of the author/artist, her audience, and cultural mediators (academics, critics, publishers, etc.)

Bourdieu's analysis can often appear fatalistic, marked by a functionalist mode of thought in which the processes it analyzes are seen as inevitable operations of a perfectly managed system. There is also, at times, a tendency to separate dominant and subordinate classes, and to ascribe to them totally separate cultures and cultural experiences. This sometimes combines with an implicit assumption that 'high culture' is more than just legitimate culture, it *is* culture; its absence *is* a form of deprivation. Bourdieu has also been criticized for reducing culture to the single function of expressing and legitimating domination. Such a formulation leaves little room for contradiction or articulation across a contested terrain of hegemony; it leaves little room for cultural struggle to be understood as anything other than the attempt to impose one complete and autonomous culture on another complete and autonomous culture.

Bourdieu's influence on the sociology of education has been very marked. His influence on cultural and literary theory has been less so, due to the delayed translation into English of his books and articles on culture. However, it is certain that the increasing availability in translation of Bourdieu's work on cultural and literary theory will establish him here (as it has in France) as a major figure in cultural studies.

Main works

Reproduction in Education and Society (with Jean-Claude Passeron), trans. R. Nice, London: Sage, 1977a.

Outline of a Theory of Practice, trans. R. Nice, Cambridge: Cambridge University Press, 1977b.

Distinction: A social critique of the judgement of taste, trans. R. Nice, London: Routledge, 1984.

Photography: A middle-brow art (with Luc Boltanski, Robert Castel, Jean-Claude Chamboredon and Dominique Schnapper), trans. S. Whiteside, Cambridge: Polity, 1990a.

The Love of Art: European museums and their public (with A. Darbel and D. Schnapper), trans. C. Beattie and N. Merriman, Cambridge: Polity, 1990b.

The Field of Cultural Production: Essays on art and literature, Cambridge: Polity, 1993.

Further reading

Harker, Richard, Chelen Mahar and Chris Wilkes, *An Introduction to the Works of Pierre Bourdieu*, New York: St Martin's, 1990.

Calhoun, Craig, Edward LiPuma and Moishe Postone (eds), *Bourdieu: Critical perspectives*, Cambridge: Polity, 1993.

Frow, John, 'Accounting for tastes: some problems in Bourdieu's sociology of culture', *Cultural Studies*, 1, 1 (1987).

Garnham, Nicholas and Raymond Williams, 'Pierre Bourdieu and the sociology of culture: an introduction', *Media, Culture and Society*, 2 (1980).

Jenkins, Richard, *Pierre Bourdieu*, London: Routledge, 1992.

Robbins, Derek, *The Work of Pierre Bourdieu*, Milton Keynes: Open University Press, 1991.

Brecht, Bertolt (1898–1956)

Born in Augsburg, Germany, Bertolt Brecht was a playwright, novelist and poet. He was a lifelong socialist, but never a member of the German Communist Party. Following the rise of the Nazis he went into exile – mostly in Denmark and the USA – and settled in East Germany in 1948. In 1949 he established the Berliner Ensemble there.

Bertolt Brecht is first and foremost a playwright. His contribution to cultural and literary theory is a development of his attempt to improve his own theatrical practice. For Brecht, as a **Marxist**, theatre should never simply interpret or represent the world as it is, but must work to change it. He saw theatre as a weapon in the class struggle. To be effective, it must combine 'instruction' with 'entertainment'. To achieve this mix required an attack on what he calls 'the general drug traffic' of bourgeois theatre (the theatre of naturalism). The problem with naturalism is that it delights the senses without engaging with the intellect. The result is an audience lulled into a sense of peace with the world; an audience with a dulled desire for change. Given this analysis, it was clear that naturalism would not do as a weapon in the class struggle; it was clearly not a theatre to change the world. But to transform naturalism did not mean the introduction of politics on to the stage. For Brecht, all theatre is political: 'Good or bad, a play always includes an image of the world. . . . There is no play and no theatrical performance which does not in some way or other affect the dispositions and conceptions of the audience. Art is never without consequences' (*Brecht on Theatre*). To claim that bourgeois theatre is apolitical is dangerous nonsense. Claims to be above politics should always be understood as support for the established order, the order of the ruling class. Therefore, Brecht's attack is made not so much against the explicit politics of bourgeois theatre as against its implicit politics. His critique is aimed at the politics produced by its theatrical practices, the politics of its 'form' rather than its 'content'.

Bourgeois theatre is organized around the theatrical practice of 'illusionism'. According to Brecht, illusionism encourages an audience to leave its intellect with their coats in the cloakroom. Illusionism, because it conceals the constructedness of social reality, both reflects and encourages the view that the world is fixed and unchangeable. It is escapist entertainment for those trapped within such assumptions. Against such theatre, Brecht proposes 'epic theatre'. The key feature of this new theatre is its anti-illusionism. Brecht's principal means of achieving this is by a series of theatrical devices known as the 'alienation effect' (also translated as 'estrangement', 'defamiliarization', 'distanciation'). His aim is to make the familiar strange. 'To alienate an incident or character means simply to remove from the incident or character all that is taken for granted, all that is well known and generally accepted and to generate surprise and curiosity about them' (*ibid.*). The alienation effect attacks the tendency of the familiar, the taken-for-granted, the obvious, to protect itself from criticism (and from change) by its very unobtrusiveness. When something is (or seems) obvious, it has moved safely beyond the analytical grasp of critical understanding.

The alienation effect is an umbrella term for a set of anti-illusionist devices. Its aim is to produce 'complex seeing': a mode of viewing which operates, as it were, above the flow of the stream rather than within it; a way of seeing which situates itself at a certain critical distance from the object of appropriation. For example, Brecht advocates a theatre of 'narrative rather than plot'. Instead of a theatre in which one thing *leads* to another, epic theatre works with an episodic structure ('montage'), in which one thing *follows* another. Distance is thus created between audience and performance. 'Literization', informing the audience what will happen – using written messages, projections, narrative voice, and so on – is used to make the audience concentrate on *how* it will happen. Brecht also breaks up the flow of a performance by the use of film. Besides breaking the illusion of the organic whole, this can also add information and encourage the audience to make connections between what is happening on stage and screen. Songs can also be used in much the same way: to provide commentary, break up the organic flow (musicians are always visible). Music, on the other hand, is often used as something against which the actors can play. Whereas generally speaking (and perhaps more so in Brecht's day) in cinema music is used to fix or support meaning (setting a mood, etc.), Brecht attempted to use it 'dialectically'. The actor(s) would display happiness (thesis), while the music would connote sadness (antithesis); and it would be up to the audience actively to determine the meaning (synthesis) of the scene.

Epic theatre demands epic acting – what is sometimes referred to as 'gestic acting'. This is a complex and disputed method, but basically what Brecht demands is a style of acting in which the actor does not *become* a character but *shows* a character's behaviour, and so on. Acting is understood as a form of demonstration rather than expression. Naturalism requires its actors to pretend to be a character (method acting is the extreme form of this demand), to express her inner feelings, to maximize psychological realism. Epic theatre wants an actor to show how a character behaves within a certain social relationship, to produce a form of 'social realism' (according to Brecht: 'Realism is not a mere question of form. . . . Anyone who is not a victim of formalistic prejudices knows that the truth can be suppressed in many ways and must be expressed in many ways' [*Aesthetics and Politics*]). To achieve this effect (what Brecht calls acting in quotation marks) he coached actors in a series of techniques; for example, insisting that they speak stage directions and preface remarks with 'she said' or 'he said'. All these devices aim to maintain a critical distance and prevent an audience identifying too closely with the events and characters on stage: getting lost in the narrative flow.

Brecht hoped to create a new audience, one that would no longer leave the theatre saying: 'Yes, I have felt like that too – Just like me – It's only natural – It'll never change – The sufferings of this man appal me, because they are inescapable – That's great art; it all seems the most obvious thing in the world – I weep when they weep, I laugh when they laugh'. Instead he hoped for an audience who would leave saying:

'I'd never had thought it – That's not the way – That's extraordinary, hardly believable – It's got to stop – The sufferings of this man appal me, because they are unnecessary – That's great art: nothing obvious in it – I laugh when they weep, I weep when they laugh' (*Brecht on Theatre*). Epic theatre, Brecht hoped, would turn an audience into actors who would complete his plays – not on stage, but out on the streets and cities of history. *The Good Person of Szechwan* ends with the injunction: 'There's only one solution that we know:/That you should now consider as you go/What sort of measures would you recommend/To help good people to a happy end.' Bourgeois theatre portrays interpersonal conflicts, created and resolved by the actors on stage; epic theatre seeks to create social conflicts on stage, and to insist that they can be resolved only outside the theatre. Bourgeois theatre practices catharsis to release pent-up emotional tension; epic theatre uses the alienation effect to produce political tension which can be released only in the world outside the theatre. Bourgeois theatre invites its audience to turn from the troubles of the world for relief in the troubles of the stage; epic theatre incites its audience to turn from the troubles of the stage to confront the troubles of the world.

For Brecht, theory was of value only to the extent that it aided practice. His favourite maxim was 'the proof of the pudding is in the eating'. His theories must ultimately be judged by the practice. Whether Brecht ever in fact produced a play which fully illustrated his theatrical theories is a point open to dispute. What is beyond dispute is his influence – first his influence on theatrical theory and practice throughout the world, and second – and perhaps more central to the concerns of cultural and literary theory – his influence, especially in the 1960s and 1970s, on a mode of film analysis associated with the journal *Screen*. This journal used Brecht's theories – first in its search for a revolutionary cinema, and second in its attempt to construct a method of film analysis based on Brecht's dramaturgical theory and practice. From the second of these endeavours emerged Colin **MacCabe**'s theory of the 'classic realist text' (see entries on **Belsey** and MacCabe).

Main works

Brecht on Theatre: The development of an aesthetic, trans. J. Willett, London: Methuen, 1964.

The Messingkauf Dialogues, trans. J. Willett, London: Methuen, 1965.

Collected Plays, trans. J. Willett, R. Manheim *et al.*, London: Methuen, 1970– .

Poems 1913–1956, trans. J. Willett, R. Manheim *et al.*, London: Methuen, 1976.

Further reading

Anderson, Perry, *et al.* (eds), *Aesthetics and Politics*, London: Verso, 1980.

Benjamin, Walter, *Understanding Brecht*, London: New Left Books, 1973.

Fuegi, John, *Bertolt Brecht: Chaos, according to plan*, Cambridge: Cambridge University Press, 1987.

Suvin, Darko, *To Brecht and Beyond: Soundings in modern dramaturgy*, Brighton: Harvester, 1984.

Willet, John, *The Theatre of Bertolt Brecht*, London: Methuen, 1959.

Wright, Elizabeth, *Postmodern Brecht: A re-presentation*, London: Routledge, 1989.

C

Chodorow, Nancy Julia (1944–)

Born in New York in 1944, Nancy Chodorow was a sociologist who had recently trained as a psychoanalyst when she published *The Reproduction of Mothering: Psychoanalysis and the sociology of gender* in 1978. This book had a strong impact on feminist thought in the United States, marking a shift towards acceptance of psychoanalytic theory as a feminist tool. Many earlier American feminists had rejected psychoanalytic thought, with its **Freud**ian origins, as being deeply implicated in and contributing to the patriarchal oppression of women. Chodorow's work offers a model that derives from Anglo-American traditions of thought, and is perceived by those working in this tradition, both in the United States and Britain, as providing a more accessible and sympathetic model of the interrelationship of the psychic and sociocultural constructions of gendered identity than post-structural theories.

Chodorow sees 'the reproduction of mothering as a central and constituting element in the social organization of gender'. Beginning with a statement of the apparently obvious fact that in modern Western society, as in most other societies, it is women who mother, she seeks to analyze why it is that women do not only bear children, but are predominantly responsible for infant and child care and socialization. She considers the social organization of labour that designates mothering as fundamentally women's work, and investigates the psychic structures that enable women to fulfil a mothering role, to desire to mother and to experience mothering, or the urge to mother, as the core of feminine identity.

She explores and criticizes a series of prevailing contemporary anthropological, medical and sociological accounts which 'naturalize' women's nurturing role and psychic capacity to mother. Psychoanalysis, she suggests, offers a more plausible, systemic theory of how the social organization of gender – especially within the prime social institution, the family – is transmitted structurally to the forming personalities of children, producing them as gendered members of society with gendered psychic characteristics. After surveying the theories of a variety of psychoanalytic schools, she declares the influence of object-relations theory on her own work. She argues that this school of psychoanalytic thought – originating in the work of the British psychoanalysts W.R.D. Fairbairn, Harry Guntrip and D.W. Winnicott, who in turn developed the work of Melanie Klein – avoids the pitfalls of both biological and cultural determinism. Object-relations theorists focus on the pre-oedipal relationship between the mother, the primary care-taker, and the infant in the first year of life, suggesting that the early task of the infant, involving the first phase of movement towards individuation and a sense of self (a task which is worked upon throughout life), is to distinguish itself from its surrounding environment. In order to establish a sense of 'me', the infant needs to separate 'me' from 'not-me'. This primary process of self-formation is enacted through a series of formative relations with 'objects' (whole people, body parts, aspects of the environment) or internalized representations of these. Chief among these objects is the maternal object, who represents the surrounding, caring and containing environment to the infant, so it is the actual relationship between the infant and its mother as negotiated through its phantasizing of her as a maternal object which is crucial to early phases of psychic organization. For a self to develop, the infant must internalize its objects so that it gradually becomes its own care-taker, and gains independence. This also involves the infant in recognizing its eventual separateness from its external objects, while retaining the ability to remain in touch with others. In this manner, the infant's early object relations form the basis of its self-identity, and of its later relationships with the world and others.

In her rereading of these theories, Chodorow emphasizes her initial point that it is actual women who predominantly take on the role of mothering. The mother, as maternal object, is already psychically and socially constructed as bearing feminine traits, and her femininity inevitably informs her relationship with the infant, producing a difference in the relationships established in the mother/male infant dyad and the mother/female infant dyad. Boys' and girls' formations of identity follow differing trajectories. The girl child, in order to separate herself from the mother, has to recognize herself *as* separate, but the strength of her identification with the mother is so great as to premise her identity on the sense: 'I am separate and different, "me", but I am the same.' The boy child's emergent identity, on the other hand, is constituted on the basis 'I am separate and different, "me", and I am not like the mother.' The effect of this asymmetry is that girl children's personalities are founded on a greater sense of similarity with the maternal object, and thus with others, than boy children's. Consequently, girls have more flexible ego boundaries. They tend to look for points of likeness between themselves and others; they are less detached from their objects; in short, they develop those characteristics conventionally considered feminine: the capacities for empathy and intuition; the abilities to see others' points of view, to recognize shared feelings with others, and to nurture. They may find it difficult to 'say "no" ' to others; they seek contact rather than distance. Their personalities are relational. Boys, according to this schema, develop characteristics traditionally deemed masculine. They have more rigid ego boundaries, tending to perceive difference or separateness from 'me' before similarity. They are more able to see distinctions between self and others. Since, especially, they distance themselves from the maternal, which to them threatens regression from autonomy and individuation, they may come to denigrate the feminine. Male power, as well as feminine restriction to nurturing roles and social powerlessness, are thereby reproduced through the dynamics of parenting. Chodorow, then, locates the establishment of gendered identity within the early phases of the mother/child dyad, rather than being crucially configured during the later oedipal crisis, as in classical Freudian theory, where the role of the father, and emphasis on the phallus and castration, are fundamental. Chodorow's development of this alternative paradigm leads her to argue for shared parenting as a way of breaking out of the cycle of reproduction of rigid gender roles.

Chodorow's theory has proved stimulating to feminist literary critics who have, through application of her ideas, been able to trace the effects of feminine personality structures and the importance of the mother/daughter relationship in women's writing. And attention has been directed to analysis of submerged themes of women's writing, where, particularly in the novel, preoccupation with relationships between female characters is seen to underlie more explicit plot concerns, such as heterosexual romance. Feminist critics have deployed Chodorow's ideas in theorizing notions of a feminine tradition distinct from the male literary tradition, and of a feminine reading practice based on empathy. More complex attempts to establish theories of feminine language have also set Chodorowian concepts against Lacanian theories of the masculine Symbolic. Chodorow is seen to provide a more positive model of feminine language than those deriving from Lacanian notions of lack, since in her terms feminine language can be perceived as originating in the richness of the repressed symbiotic union of mother and female infant and is characterized by fluidity, the move towards fusion and relatedness.

However, Chodorow's theory of the reproduction of mothering has been criticized from several angles. Her assumption of the homogeneity of women's identities has been challenged: she assumes heterosexuality and displays no awareness of class, racial, ethnic and other differences. In the late 1980s and 1990s the assumption of the category 'woman' (or 'man') has increasingly been questioned. Queer theory, in particular, has complicated any easy assumption of binary oppositions based on sex, gender or sexuality. More generally, post-structural theorists regard her notion of identity as being too unitary and lacking the precision and complexity of post-Lacanian concepts of the subject. Further, logical flaws in her argument have been identified – for instance, by Rachel Bowlby. Since Chodorow argues that gendered identity is an effect of the dynamics of gendered parenting, it might be assumed that changes in child-rearing practices would erase gender difference. Yet Chodorow contradictorily assumes the necessity of a sense of gendered self to the individual, and claims that this would persist if gendered roles changed. It is not clear what would constitute gendered identity in this case, nor how it would be constructed. Nevertheless, in spite of these important criticisms of her theory, and the movement of 1990s feminism away from preoccupation with mothering, Chodorow has provided a stimulating and enriching model for analysis of women's writing, and has had influence in the social sciences and among feminist psychotherapists.

Main works

The Reproduction of Mothering: Psychoanalysis and the sociology of gender, Berkeley: University of California Press, 1978.

Feminism and Psychoanalytic Theory, New Haven, CT: Yale University Press, 1989.

Further reading

Abel, Elizabeth, *Virginia Woolf and the Fictions of Psychoanalysis*, Chicago: University of Chicago Press, 1989.

Abel, Elizabeth, Marianne Hirsch and Elizabeth Langland (eds), *The Voyage In: Fictions of female development*, Hanover and London: University Press of New England, 1983.

Bowlby, Rachel, *Still Crazy After All These Years: Women, writing and psychoanalysis*, London and New York: Routledge, 1992.

Hirsch, Marianne, *The Mother/Daughter Plot: Narrative, psychoanalysis, feminism*, Bloomington: Indiana University Press, 1989.

Homans, Margaret, *Bearing the Word: Language and female experience in nineteenth-century women's writing*, New Haven, CT and London: Yale University Press, 1986.

Radway, Janice A., *Reading the Romance: Women, patriarchy and popular literature*, Chapel Hill and London: University of North Carolina Press, 1984.

Chomsky, Avram Noam (1928–)

Noam Chomsky was born in Philadelphia, Pennsylvania, the son of the famous Jewish Hebrew scholar William Chomsky. Nevertheless, his academic career began reluctantly: his early aversion to competitive education led him to consider leaving the University of Pennsylvania after his first year. The decision to return to take up the study of philosophy, mathematics and linguistics was possibly influenced as much by the linguist Professor Zellig Harris, with whom he shared many political views, as his own father. In 1951 he obtained a Master's degree at the University of Pennsylvania with a work called 'Morphophonemics of Modern Hebrew', and after four years of research at Harvard University as a Junior Fellow of the Society of Fellows he obtained a PhD, in 1955, with a dissertation called 'Transformational Analysis'. In the 1960s Chomsky became associated with the New Left, speaking out vehemently against not only the war in Vietnam, but American imperialistic intervention in the Third World. His arguments were founded on the belief that common moral considerations had been effectively circumvented by a scientific rhetoric contrived to deceive the public about the real nature of 'American activities'. He has been teaching at the Massachusetts Institute of Technology since 1955; in 1966 he obtained the Ferrari P. Ward Chair of Modern Languages and Linguistics, which he held until 1977, when he became Institute Professor.

Chomsky's works fall into two categories: those dealing with various aspects of theoretical linguistics relating to the development of transformational grammar; and those political writings committed to recovering the truth beneath a surface structure of rhetorical decoys serving – in particular – to legitimize American foreign policy. The link between these two interests is to be found in his affiliation with the rationalist tradition which begins with Plato and is carried forward by Kant. Accordingly, he begins with the assumption that human language is fundamentally different from animal communication, and that the human mind is biologically structured to acquire and use language in a way that the animal mind is not. His claim is that human infants tacitly know the set of rules and principles for the use of their language, because they are innately endowed with the knowledge of universal grammar. Human beings do not simply learn a language as a result of a social conditioning which requires a communicative facility; rather, they are cognitively predisposed to the acquisition of language. Ferdinand de **Saussure**'s important insight that language systems are both relational and arbitrary is accommodated by making a distinction between language and grammar. For Chomsky:

> language is a much more abstract notion than the notion of grammar. The reason is that grammars have to have a real existence, that is, there is something in your brain that corresponds to the grammar. That's got to be true. But there is nothing in the real world corresponding to language. In fact it could very well turn out that there is no intelligible notion of language (Chomsky, 1982a)

It is this positing of a grammar bound to the mental faculties, over and above a grammar that emerges as an effect of environmental stimuli, which provides the ground for human agency and action; and it is precisely this orientation towards language that informs Chomsky's political judgements.

From Chomsky's point of view, linguistic research has demonstrated a shift from what he calls *externalized language linguistics* to *internalized language linguistics*: from a method that collects language samples and produces a descriptive grammar corresponding to the patterns of regularity found in their properties (as with the structuralist tradition) to a method directed towards describing the system of language as it is 'represented in the mind/brain of a particular individual' (Chomsky, 1988); or a grammar that describes linguistic knowledge rather than the products of that knowledge. This historical evolution provides the background and justification for a distinction between language *competence* and language *performance*, between knowledge of language and use of language, between 'the cognitive state that encompasses all those aspects of form and meaning and their relation' (Chomsky, 1982b) and the raw data – letters, recipes, diaries, literary works, conversations, notes to the milkman – which emerge as a result of its use in different situations. Linguistic competence accounts for creativity in language – that is, the ability of speakers to generate and understand an infinite number of sentences from a finite number of rules and principles; linguistic performance, on the other hand, accounts for the use of language in actual speech situations. Clearly, this opposition becomes questionable in considering how a speaker comes to know the appropriate use of language if competence is not somehow linked to performance. Chomsky introduces the term *pragmatic competence* to describe the relationship between knowledge and practice: it 'places language in the institutional setting of its use,

relating intentions and purposes to the linguistic means at hand'
(Chomsky, 1982b).

Chomsky has been an active and prolific thinker since the early 1950s;
as such he has received accolades from many universities and
organizations both in the United States and abroad, acknowledging his
work in the area of linguistics and cognitive psychology – not to
mention his commitment to international politics, in particular as a
critic of American intervention in the Third World. The measure of
Chomsky's influence in the field of generative grammar over the last
four decades is reflected in the fact that he is now recognized as one of
the century's most important linguists: his original, radical and
systematic study of language has fundamentally changed the way in
which language is studied in academic institutions all over the world.
The impact of his thinking, moreover, has extended well beyond
academic linguistics, reaching into psychology and also cognitive
science, a discipline that cites his work as the ground for its foundation.
Equally important is his influence on philosophy. In fact, in many ways
the relevance of the linguistics he pioneered is more fully understood in
a philosophical setting, for Chomsky, like W.V. Quine, finds no sharp
distinction between the natural sciences and philosophy. Thus, if
transformational grammar is anything, it is a grammar of the
proposition, and the many forms that the proposition can take in a
surface structure.

Noam Chomsky's influence on the study of language has been
profound, but his work in the area of language and politics demonstrates an unparalleled commitment to democracy. It is sometimes easy
to forget that his theory of the polity of grammar was, at a time when
the need was greatest, balanced equally with a continual exposition of
the grammar of politics.

Main works

Syntactic Structures, The Hague: Mouton, 1957.

Current Issues in Linguistic Theory, The Hague: Mouton, 1964.

Aspects of the Theory of Syntax, Cambridge, MA and London: MIT Press,
1965.

Cartesian Linguistics, New York and London: Harper & Row, 1966a.

Topics in the Theory of Generative Grammar, The Hague: Mouton, 1966b.

The Sound Pattern of English (with M. Haille), New York and London:
Harper & Row, 1968a.

Language and Mind, New York and London: Harcourt Brace, 1968b.

American Power and the New Mandarins, New York: Pantheon; London: Chatto & Windus; Harmondsworth: Penguin, 1969.

At War with Asia: Essays on Indochina, New York: Random House, 1970.

Problems of Knowledge and Freedom, New York: Basic Books; London; Barrie & Jenkins, Fontana, 1971.

Language and Mind, enlarged edn, New York and London: Harcourt Brace Jovanovich, 1972a.

Studies on Semantics in Generative Grammar, The Hague: Mouton, 1972b.

The Backroom Boys, New York: Pantheon, 1973a.

For Reasons of State, New York: Pantheon, 1973b.

Peace in the Middle East?, New York: Vintage; London: Fontana, 1974.

The Logical Structure of Linguistic Theory, New York and London: Plenum, 1975.

Reflections on Language, New York: Pantheon; London; Temple Smith, Fontana, 1976.

Essays on Form and Interpretation, Amsterdam and New York: Elsevier/ North Holland, 1977.

'Human Rights' and American Foreign Policy, Nottingham: Spokesman Books, 1978.

Language and Responsibility: Based on conversations with Mitsou Ronat, New York: Pantheon, 1979.

The Generative Enterprise: A discussion with Riny Huybregts and Henk van Riemsdiik, Dordrecht: Foris, 1982a.

Some Concepts and Consequences of the Theory of Government and Binding, Cambridge, MA: MIT Press, 1982b.

Towards a New Cold War: Essays on the current crisis and how we got there, New York: Pantheon, 1982c.

The Fateful Triangle: The United States, Israel and the Palestinians, Boston, MA: South End Press; London: Pluto Press, 1983.

Modular Approaches to the Study of Mind, San Diego: California State University Press, 1984a.

Réponses inédites à mes détracteurs parisiens, Paris: Spartacus, 1984b.

Turning the Tide: US intervention in Central America and the struggle for peace, London: Pluto Press, 1985.

Barriers (*Linguistic Inquiry Monograph* 13), Cambridge, MA: MIT Press, 1986a.

Knowledge of Language: Its nature origin and use, New York and London: Praeger, 1986b.

The Chomsky Reader, ed. James Peck, New York: Pantheon, 1987a; London; Serpent's Tail, 1988.

Generative Grammar: Its basis, development and prospects, Kyoto, Japan: Kyoto University, 1987.

Language in a Philosophical Setting (*Sophia Linguistica* 22), Tokyo: Sophia University, 1987c.

On Power and Ideology, Boston, MA: South End Press, 1987d.

The Culture of Terrorism, Boston MA: South End Press; London: Pluto Press, 1988a.

Language and Politics, Montreal: Black Rose Books, 1988b.

Language and Problems of Knowledge, Cambridge, MA: MIT Press, 1988.

Deterring Democracy, London: Verso, 1991.

(with Edward S. Herman)
After the Cataclysm: Postwar IndoChina and the reconstruction of American imperial ideology, Boston, MA: South End Press, 1979a.

The Washington Connection and Third World Fascism, Boston, MA: South End Press, 1979b.

Manufacturing Consent: The political economy of the mass media, New York: Pantheon, 1988.

Further reading

Botha, Rudolf P., *Challenging Chomsky: The generative garden game*. Oxford: Blackwell, 1989.

Bracken, H., *Mind and Language: Essays on Descartes and Chomsky*, Dordrecht: Foris, 1984.

Salkie, Raphael, *The Chomsky Update: Linguistics and politics*, London: Unwin Hyman, 1990.

Modgil, S. and C., Modgil, (eds), *Noam Chomsky: Consensus and controversy*, Barcombe, Sussex: Farmer Press, 1987.

Cixous, Hélène (1937–)

Hélène Cixous was born in Algeria in 1937. She is Professor of Literature at the University of Paris VIII (Vincennes), which she co-founded in 1968, and director of the Centre d'Etudes Féminines, a research centre she founded in 1976. Cixous is a prolific writer whose texts include fictions and plays as well as books, essays and articles. She is known in France primarily as the author of experimental or avant-garde fictional works, but her reputation in England and the United States is mainly as an extremely influential and controversial feminist theorist.

Hélène Cixous is a writer whose work defies conventional categorization. Her focus on the connections between sexuality and textuality has been enabling, challenging and often confusing for feminists working within Anglo-American traditions. Although she has been actively involved in feminist politics, she has refused the label 'feminism'; and while she is considered to be one of the foremost theorists of her generation, her work is often explicitly anti-theoretical. Her writing interrogates, and attempts to undermine, the logocentrism and phallocentrism of Western philosophical discourse, deploying and interrogating the theoretical models of post-structuralist thinkers such as **Derrida** and **Lacan**. It also seeks to explore and reformulate the relationship between women and writing in ways which can be connected with the work of radical or utopian feminists.

Cixous's work is often associated with that of other French feminists, notably Luce **Irigaray** and Catherine Clément.

In 'Sorties', her main contribution to *The Newly Born Woman* (*La Jeune Née* in the original French), which she co-wrote with Clément, Cixous exposes and deconstructs the hierarchically ordered binary oppositions within Western thought which have demanded and enacted the violent repression and suppression of both women and the feminine. Binary oppositions such as Activity/Passivity, Culture/Nature, Head/Emotions are seen to correspond in patriarchal thought to an underlying opposition of man/woman, and to establish a hierarchy in which the 'feminine' is negative or inferior. Cixous denounces this patriarchal logic, which allows women no positive position, and her work, as the title of 'Sorties' suggests, can be seen as a series of attempts to depart from or escape an oppressive structure of writing and thought.

The way in which Cixous writes is as much a part of her project as what she writes, and it is the relationship between women and writing which is the central preoccupation of her work. Cixous's writing style is poetic, metaphorical and allusive, creating a dense network of images and ideas which resist reduction to a clear theoretical programme. Her texts are punctuated by slips, puns and verbal echoes which are often lost in translation. Myth plays a prominent part in much of her writing, with figures such as Medusa, Medea, the Amazons and Cleopatra serving as paradigms of female experience; and the texts are full of intertextual references and allusions to the work of other writers, including Genet, Bataille, Hoffman, Kleist and Clarice Lispector. Some of these are male writers who, in Cixous's words, 'let their femininity traverse them', and all are seen to have subverted the dominant order in their writing.

Cixous argues that there is a way of writing which refuses the stasis and closure of oppositional structures, and celebrates difference which she has called *l'écriture féminine*, or feminine writing. This has been the subject of much debate, as critics have disagreed about whether or not it implies an essentialist belief in an implicit – or biological – rather than cultural – and therefore contingent and changeable – difference between men and women. Cixous has refused to give an absolute definition, and there are contradictory strands in her writing on the subject. *L'écriture féminine*, as described in one strand of Cixous's work, bears considerable resemblance to Derrida's formulation of writing as *différance*, standing for a mode of writing which subverts the dominant linguistic order and exploits the free play of the signifier. Cixous has argued that the designation of *l'écriture féminine* is not to be reserved for writing *by women*; it is a description of a type of writing rather than a reference to the empirical sex of the author. So Jean Genet's work can be celebrated as an example of *l'écriture féminine*, as can Clarice Lispector's. Cixous does, however, suggest that in current sociohistorical conditions it is more likely that women will produce this type of writing, and there are aspects of her work which seem to rely on a metaphysical formulation of the relationship between women and writing.

In her article 'Castration or decapitation?' Cixous delineates separate 'masculine' and 'feminine' libidinal economies. Masculinity is structured as a Realm of the Proper (signalling both proper and property), characterized by self-identity, an insistence on regulated exchange, on classification, categorization, hierarchization. Femininity is structured as a Realm of the Gift, characterized by generosity that expects no return, an openness to the other. These economies are presented in anti-essentialist terms, but here, as elsewhere in her writing, the term 'feminine' often slides into 'female' or 'woman'. Similarly, her concept of a 'new bisexuality', a multiple and heterogeneous sexuality which she believes to be inherent in all human beings but which women are currently more open to than men, hovers on the line between deconstruction and essentialism.

The aspects of Cixous's work which seem most apparently close to essentialism concern the relation between woman, the mother, and voice. In 'The laugh of the Medusa' Cixous exhorts women to write with 'white ink', a reference to mother's milk, which connects woman to a pre-oedipal stage and space. Elemental and bodily images of the maternal combine to evoke a space which closely resembles Lacan's Imaginary, a space which offers the subject both freedom from the restrictions of the Symbolic order and the security of unity with the mother. This space is seen as available to both men and women, but women have privileged access to it, since they have more defences against the mother and against their libidinal drives than men. It is in this space that woman discovers a voice which is both her own and that of the mother, a voice which resonates in women's writing. Here Cixous is developing a profoundly metaphysical explanation in which woman becomes present in her writing through transcribing her voice. It is at this point that her work seems furthest removed from the deconstructive or post-structuralist tradition, and nearest to an idealist or essentialist tradition.

The impact of Cixous's work on feminist studies reflects the complexity and diversity of her writing. Her stress on the relationships between writing, subjectivity, sexuality and sexual difference has constituted a stimulating and often provocative departure from existing models. Reactions to her work have – predictably – been varied. Her image of the feminine as marked by imagination, generosity and openness has been read by some feminist critics as being dangerously close to the stereotypes offered within patriarchal discourse, but her work has also been read as exploiting the sliding of the signifier in order to subvert patriarchal language structures which oppress and silence women. Cixous has explicitly acknowledged the contradictions in her work, claiming that she chooses to 'be carried off by the poetic word' rather than observing the constraints of philosophical discourse. Even here, however, the implied opposition of philosophical and poetic modes, and the apparent privileging of the latter, has given rise to some criticism.

Cixous's work has been read as a powerful utopian vision of female creativity imagined beyond the repressive norms of the dominant order. As a vision it has been criticized for failing to address the practical or actual problems and experiences of many women, and for stressing the journey to self-expression of the individual subject rather than exploring issues of collectivity or wider communities. Both criticisms have been connected with a perceived absence in Cixous's theoretical work of any sustained analysis of historical and cultural conditions. It should be noted, however, that in her recent writing for the theatre, which forms an increasing part of her work, she does engage explicitly with issues of cultural and historical difference, and of political struggle in specific contexts; and that she has chosen to explore collective ways of working with the Théâtre du Soleil.

Main works

The Exile of James Joyce, trans. S. Purcell, London: Calder, 1976.

La Venue à l'écriture, Paris: Union générale d'editions, 1977.

Portrait of Dora, trans. A. Burrows, in *Benmussa Directs: Portrait of Dora and the singular life of Albert Nobbs*, London, 1979.

Vivre l'orange/ To Live the Orange, trans. Ann Liddle and Sarah Cornell, Paris: Des femmes, 1979.

Illa, Paris: Des femmes, 1980.

'The laugh of the Medusa', trans. K. and P. Cohen, in Elaine Marks and Isabelle de Courtivron (eds), *New French Feminisms*, Brighton: Harvester Wheatsheaf, 1980.

'Castration or decapitation?', trans. A. Kuhn, *Signs* 7, 1 (1981): 36–55.

[With Catherine Clément], *The Newly Born Woman*, trans. by B. Wing, Manchester: Manchester University Press, 1986.

Inside, trans. C. Barko, New York: Schocken, 1986.

Writing Differences, Sellers, Susan (ed.), London: Free Press, 1988.

Reading with Clarice Lispector, trans. V. Andermatt Conley, Minneapolis: University of Minnesota Press, 1989.

Readings: The Poetics of Blanchot, Kleist, Kafka, Lispector and Tsvetayeva, trans. Verena Andermatt Conley, Minneapolis: University of Minnesota Press, 1991.

Further reading

Conley, Verena Andermatt, *Hélène Cixous: Writing the feminine*, Lincoln: University of Nebraska Press, 1984.

Gallop, Jane, *The Daughter's Seduction*, Ithaca, NY; Cornell University Press, 1984.

Moi, Toril A. 'Hélène Cixous: an imaginary utopia,' in *Sexual/Textual Politics: Feminist literary theory*, London: Metheun, 1985.

Sankovitch, Tilda A. 'Hélène Cixous: the pervasive myth', in *French Women Writers and the Book: Myths of access and desire*, Syracuse, NY: Syracuse University Press, 1988.

Sihach, Morag, *The politics of writing*, London: Routledge, 1992.

Wilcox, Helen *et al.* (eds), *The Body and the Text: Hélène Cixous, reading and teaching*, Hemel Hempstead: Harvester Wheatsheaf, 1990.

Glossary

Phallocentrism: A system in which the phallus stands as principal signifier, and which consequently privileges masculine sexuality and subordinates the feminine.

Culler, Jonathan (1944–)

Jonathan Culler is one of the most important ciphers through which semiotics, structuralism and post-structuralism entered into the main-stream of Anglo-American criticism. He has worked exclusively within the academic world as critic and teacher, holding posts at Cambridge and Oxford. He is currently Professor of English and Comparative Literature at Cornell University.

Culler is best known for two major works on structuralism and deconstruction. *Structuralist Poetics* was one of the first comprehensive surveys in English of the impact of structuralism on literary theory. It functions both as a general introduction to the broad range of structuralist thinking on literature and as a critique of some of the ways in which the linguistic model has been applied to the interpretation of texts.

For Culler, the relevance of modern linguistics to literary studies rests on two assumptions. First, cultural events and objects are never simply 'there'. They are inevitably bound up with meaning, and therefore function as signs. Secondly, the value of those signs is not a product of nature, or in some way inherent in them, but is a consequence of the structure of which they are a part. Meaning is determined by the place that an object or event occupies in the structure, and is a product of the arbitrary sets of distinctions and rules applicable to the structured activity under analysis. The apparent arbitrariness of linguistic signs provides the best example of how such systems function.

Culler makes an important distinction between attempts to derive the rules governing a language from a detailed description of a corpus of data that is perceived as relevant, and 'transformational grammars' which lay the ground rules by which the system makes sense – or, indeed, can be perceived as a structure at all. The former method, Culler argues, is a blind alley along which too many structuralists – among them **Barthes, Jakobson** and **Greimas** – have ventured.

The latter relies on what Noam **Chomsky** terms 'linguistic competence', which is the language user's innate knowledge of language structure, much of which may be implicit – many people who are perfectly capable of expressing themselves clearly are unable to define accurately the grammatical devices they are employing. By analogy, Culler posits a 'literary competence'. For Culler there is no such thing as a natural, unmediated response to a text. We have to learn the 'correct' way to read a poem or piece of prose, acquire a set of pre-existing conventions. The function of literature lessons in schools and universities is to pass on this literary competence. An understanding of the poetics of the lyric involves grasping the notions of distance, unity and significance without which a reader confronted by a poem for the first time would be baffled.

In the same way, the conventions of narrative structure, symbolic significance and character must be understood if we are to read a novel correctly. The reader approaches a novel expecting to find a realistic world, with recognizable elements. The avant-garde literary text may flout these conventions, but its meaning is equally dependent on the structure it attempts to go beyond. It is defined by that very transgression.

Culler allows a limited freedom to interpretation, but returns to the notions of competence and structure when confronted with the work of **Derrida** and **Kristeva**. He still craves a discernible meaning based on the relative stability of structure.

On Deconstruction marks a subtle shift from the position of *Structuralist Poetics*. Derridean deconstruction is accepted with fewer reservations, and the text advocates as well as describes deconstruction. The work begins with an investigation into what is involved in reading. Literary works are defined in terms of the actions they perform on the understanding of the reader. Culler is well aware that 'the reader' is itself far from being a simple concept. Nevertheless, studying the effects of literature on the reader has – at least since Aristotle – been part of what it means to interpret literature. What has changed for the modern critic is the nature of literature itself; in the modern work, the reader has to participate in constructing the text.

Reading, Culler asserts, can never be divided simply between reader's and author's contributions. The text is at the same time complete and a cavity to be filled by the reader. As **Sartre** puts it in *What is Literature?*, 'Thus for the reader everything is done and everything is already done'. One crucial question, for Culler, in the turn towards the reader is that of what it means to read as a woman. He is particularly receptive to feminist critics' attempts to change the experience of reading by questioning the literary, political and social assumptions on which reading has been based.

One of Culler's main aims is to show the links between the philosophical origins of deconstruction and its literary applications. He takes us through Derrida's deconstructionist readings of Plato, **Saussure**, Rousseau and J.L. Austin, illustrating the crucial concepts of presence, logocentrism, *différance*, and the logic of supplementarity. Meaning emerges as a product of the infinite, unchecked play of signifiers permitting no final resolution between rival interpretations. Deconstructing a discourse involves demonstrating how that discourse undermines the very concepts on which it is based. The contradictions exposed are never reconciled or transcended by deconstruction but, rather, reinscribed at a different level. Culler nevertheless maintains that deconstruction is not irrational; Derrida uses all the resources of the Western metaphysical tradition he deconstructs. It is not that 'anything goes' in deconstructionist readings; but rather that no reading can be final. He importantly distinguishes deconstruction from **Rorty**an pragmatism, in which truth is a matter of consensus and nothing is thinkable outside the particular tradition in which the thinker finds herself. Deconstruction is interested in exactly those things suppressed by consensus, and questions the categories which constitute a tradition.

Culler identifies four ways in which deconstruction affects literary criticism. First, it brings the very notion of literature into question by, for example, examining the split between literature and philosophy. Secondly, it provides a source of themes for critics to probe in texts through such concepts as origin, marginality, presence and absence. Thirdly, it supplies examples of reading strategies in its search for points where one text or genre is grafted on to another, or where the text seems to contradict itself. Finally, it provides a powerful tool for uncovering the nature and goals of critical inquiry, seen most clearly in deconstruction's undermining of the scientific goals of structuralism, or its critique of totalizing forms of **Marx**ist and psychoanalytic criticism. He concludes by illustrating how these concepts have been employed by a number of critics, most notably Paul **de Man**.

Culler's other main works have commanded less interest. *The Pursuit of Signs* is a survey of literary semiotics focusing particularly on the relations between semiotics and deconstruction, the role of interpretation in literary criticism and the concept of intertextuality. As ever, Culler works by testing the writings of other theorists: Michael Riffaterre and Stanley **Fish**, in particular, come in for a close and critical reading.

Culler is often at his best as an explicator and interpreter. His short studies of Barthes and Saussure are excellent examples of how to introduce the work of a difficult theorist, steering deftly between oversimplification and unduly baffling complexity. With Saussure he succeeds in outlining the main arguments of the *Course in General Linguistics* and describing its consequences for critical theory. *Roland Barthes* combines a discussion of the enormously varied range of Barthes's thought with a serious critique of both his 'high' structuralism and his late concern with the body.

Culler has been accused of avoiding the political in his criticism, an accusation he attempts to rebut in *Framing the Sign*, the only one of his books to engage with wider social issues – although his focus remains on the academic. He clearly has deep reservations about the sort of criticism practised by Terry **Eagleton**, in which the critic commits himself to a particular political programme.

Culler is not a major, original thinker but, rather, an expert interpreter, translating the complexities of continental critical discourse into a language accessible to those brought up within an entirely different tradition. His major contributions are towards the growth of reader-response criticism and in the resiting of criticism and the role of the critic as central to the study of literature.

Main works

Flaubert: The Uses of Uncertainty, London: Paul Elek, 1974.

Structuralist Poetics: Structuralism, linguistics and the study of literature, London: Routledge & Kegan Paul, 1975.

Ferdinand de Saussure, London: Fontana, 1976.

The Pursuit of Signs: Semiotics, literature, deconstruction, London: Routledge & Kegan Paul, 1981.

Roland Barthes, London: Fontana, 1983.

On Deconstruction: Theory and Criticism after Structuralism, London: Routledge & Kegan Paul, 1983.

Framing the Sign: Criticism and its institutions, Oxford: Blackwell, 1988.

Further reading

Lentricchia, Frank, *After the New Criticism*, London: Athlone Press, 1991.

Norris, C., *Deconstruction: Theory and practice*, London: Methuen, 1982.

D

Daly, Mary (1928–)

Mary Daly is an American radical feminist philosopher/theologist. Holder of three doctorates, including doctorates in both theology and philosophy from the University of Fribourg, she has been employed since 1966 in the theology department of Jesuit-run Boston College, Massachusetts, where she teaches Feminist Ethics. Boston College's repeated refusal to grant Daly the status of full professor, and its withholding of financial increments, despite her growing international reputation, are recorded in *Outercourse* (1993), Daly's philosophical autobiography, as are the resulting protests from feminists, academics and students. She remains at Boston College, however, as she explains, choosing to stand her ground 'on the Boundaries of patriarchal institutions'.

Daly's early work as a radical Catholic theologian attacks the Church as a powerful enemy of women's liberation. The Church is so powerful, she argues, because to the stereotype of the 'eternal feminine' it is able to give the 'stamp of divine approval', leading women to internalize this imposed role and so actually become the inferior beings so described. Against this stereotype Daly opposes her ideal of the 'developing, authentic person, who will be unique, self-critical, self-creating, active, and searching'. Although in her later work Daly was to reject both the concept of God and the androgynous 'person' of the above description, both the attack on patriarchal religion and the ideal of transcendent being were to remain central in her work. Indeed, she chooses the metaphor of the 'spiral voyage' to describe the development of her thought, arguing that this spiral movement continues 'to re-member/re-call/re-claim' the themes of earlier work.

In *Beyond God the Father* (1973), Daly's first major work, she develops these themes. The concept of God, the divine patriarch, serves to link 'the unsteady reality of social constructs' with 'ultimate reality' through the legitimating power of myth. The myth of patriarchal religion has not only legitimated men's oppression of women but also, through the myth of feminine evil, imposed on women the burden of guilt. Through the process of 'reversal', men's evil becomes women's, and women's creativity is reassigned to men. Traditional Christian morality then hypocritically idealizes some of the qualities (humility, self-sacrifice, service) which it imposes on the oppressed, while it serves to mask the real motivations and values operative in patriarchal society. These centre upon 'powerover', the power to use the Other as object, replacing the relation of 'I–Thou' with that of 'I–It'. In the sphere of knowledge, this means the substitution of 'technical knowledge' or instrumental reason for intuitive knowledge or 'ontological reason'. Women, then, have had the power of *naming* stolen from them, and with it their unitary identity with an authentic self. A truly radical women's movement must be above all a *spiritual* revolution, replacing the concept of God as patriarch with that of 'God as Verb', that *movement* towards wholeness which involves both 'becoming who we are' and self-transcendence. For this, a new language will be necessary, a language which will both allow women to name their own development or 'process' and also seek to reclaim pre-Christian knowledge of a female transcendent, the 'Great Mother' or 'Great Goddess'.

In *Gyn/Ecology* (1978), Daly's most influential book, these twin movements of 'exorcism' (the unmasking of the myths and strategies of patriarchy) and 'Ecstasy' (women's journey beyond patriarchy into new be-ing, knowing and naming) are repeated. Daly now argues that it is patriarchy which is 'the prevailing religion of the entire planet, and its essential message is necrophilia'. Christianity now becomes just one manifestation of this global religion, its myths one example of mythic power stolen from women and used with intent to 'destroy the divine spark in women'. If myth provides patriarchy's legitimation, however, it is through 'sado-ritual' that its destructive power is enacted. In practices separated widely in both time and space, from Indian *suttee* and Chinese footbinding to European witchburnings and American gynaecology, Daly finds enacted the same pattern of ritualized atrocities aginst women. The pattern is completed by the meta-ritual of patriarchal scholarship, in which these atrocities are 'explained' and legitimated, and their true meanings are erased. Armed with the knowledge gained from such an 'exorcism', women, Daly argues, may begin on the journey towards 'Ecstasy'. This involves not only new be-ing (a fusion of 'being' and 'becoming'), the rejection of the 'mind/spirit/body pollution' of patriarchy and reclaiming of 'life-loving female energy' which is 'Gyn/Ecology', but also a new *naming* of this experience. Hence women's 'new space' must be semantic as well as cognitive and physical, and one of Daly's major projects becomes that of subverting patriarchal language. To do this she employs a number of tactics, investing familiar (usually abusive) descriptions of women ('hag', 'crone', 'spinster') with new, positive meanings, 'unmasking deceptive words by dividing them and employing alternative meanings for pre-fixes' ('a-maze', 're-cover', 're-sister'), coining new words and reclaiming 'archaic' dictionary definitions. A series of 'double-edged pairs of words' establish the terms of her reversal: patriarchy–Otherworld; necrophilia–Biophilia; (patriarchal) foreground–Background; tame–Wild. The last of these examples indicates that the negative term in Daly's paired opposites does not always describe patriarchal practice; it may also describe those women ('token women/torturers', 'fembots', 'Painted Birds', 'mutants') who choose to remain within 'femininity', at the service of patriarchy. There is no place for these, the 'majority of women' under patriarchy, in the 'Celebration of Ecstasy' which closes *Gyn/Ecology*.

Daly's later books extend both her arguments and her methodology (which she describes in *Pure Lust* as 'Methodicide'). *Pure Lust* (1984) repeats the call to abandon the patriarchal Foreground, whose three 'Spheres' are here described as the 'sadosociety', the 'plastic passions, potted feelings, and victimizing "virtues" and "vices"'', and the false 'belonging', 'befriending' and 'bewitching' held out by patriarchy as traps for women in their journey to Elemental Be-ing. Far more emphasis is given here, however, to the reversals, or transvaluations, which Daly seeks to effect. Lusty Women, who have eschewed 'plastic and potted passions', are rooted in the Earth and the Elements; released by Female Fury, they both reclaim their Original Selves and break through to 'radiant powers of words' with which to name this experience. Daly's use of language in *Pure Lust* goes further than before, therefore, in attempting to overcome what she describes as 'the dualism between abstract and mystical/poetic/mythic thought'; thus the 'Index of New Words', begun in *Gyn/Ecology*, is greatly expanded, to be fully realized in her next book, *Websters' First New Intergalactic Wickedary of the English Language* (1987). Daly's most recent book, *Outercourse* (1993), charts her own exemplary journey towards such transcendence.

Daly's *Gyn/Ecology* has been described as 'probably the most important and influential single work to come out of the American women's movement since Kate Millett's *Sexual Politics*' (Morris, p.28). Its importance lies first in its inclusiveness: it combines a critique of patriarchal history and myth with a theory of language and a female-centred value system and guide for living. Its description of the global nature of patriarchy and its assertion of an authentic and unitary female Self, connected spiritually with other women and with nature, has created, it can be argued, a position from which women both can and must speak. Secondly, its subversion of patriarchal language empowers women both to speak and to act ('I could not say, "I am a Positively Revolting Hag" without trying to live up to this challenging eruption of words'). Within feminist theory, however, Daly's vision has also been much criticized. There are three main grounds for criticism. First, its totalizing vision ignores the material conditions of women's lives, minimizing the cultural and material differences in forms of oppression and claiming the right to speak for, and as, all women. Such a strategy, it is argued, in refusing to engage with the social and political, is also without any power to effect change. Secondly, its value structure is based on an essentialism both biological (men are by definition excluded from grace) and spiritual (Revolting Hags are essentially different from 'fembots'). Thus its concept of female autonomy, while making a powerful appeal to women, is founded on the concept of a unitary Self beyond contradiction and fragmentation, as it is beyond cultural specificity. Finally, Daly's attack on language has been seen as itself the product of a kind of linguistic essentialism. Her attack on *words*, the subversion of isolated signs, does not, it is argued, constitute a transformation of *discourse*, or language in use. Indeed, the discourse she adopts, with its emphasis on authenticity, self-creation and transcendence, remains – for all its exhilarating power – firmly within a religious absolutism which excludes, as she herself admits at times, 'the majority of women'.

Main works

The Church and the Second Sex (1968). New edition with Feminist Postchristian Introduction and New Archaic Afterwords, Boston, MA: Beacon Press, 1985.

Gyn/Ecology: The metaethics of radical feminism, London: The Women's Press, 1979.

Pure Lust: Elemental feminist philosophy, London: The Women's Press, 1984.

Beyond God the Father: Towards a philosophy of women's liberation, London: The Women's Press, 1986.

Websters' First New Intergalactic Wickedary of the English Language, Conjured in Cahoots with Jane Caputi, London: The Women's Press, 1988.

Outercourse: The be-dazzling Voyage, London: The Women's Press, 1993.

Further reading

Lorde, Audre, 'An open letter to Mary Daly', in *Sister Outsider*, New York: The Crossing Press, 1984.

Morris, Meaghan, 'A-mazing grace: notes on Mary Daly's poetics', in *The Pirate's Fiancée: Feminism, reading, postmodernism*, London: Verso, 1988.

Ramazanoglu, Caroline, *Feminism and the Contradictions of Oppression*, London: Routledge, 1989.

Segal, Lynne, *Is the Future Female? Troubled thoughts on contemporary feminism*, London: Virago, 1987.

Spender, Dale, *For the Record: The making and meaning of feminist knowledge*, London: The Women's Press, 1985.

Tong, Rosemarie, *Feminist Thought: A comprehensive introduction*, London: Unwin Hyman, 1989.

Debord, Guy (1931–94)

Political theorist, film-maker and self-styled 'last revolutionary' Guy Debord was the leading member of the Situationists, a group of political activists, writers and artists who played a significant role in the May '68 events in Paris, where thousands of students and millions of workers took to the streets and organized occupations to make an enormous range of political and economic demands, from improvements in working conditions to the reform of the university system.

The events themselves were one of the high points of postwar political radicalism, bringing about a near-revolutionary situation in France and sparking off similar protests, especially among students, in the majority of Western countries. At this time, Situationist theories and practices played a role in both student and worker protests throughout the West, in particular Debord's analysis of postwar capitalism and, based upon this, a powerful and dramatic use of propaganda and media manipulation.

The Situationists were founded in Italy in 1957 and included Debord, the brilliant artist Asger Jorn and the writer Raoul Vaneigem. Their aim was nothing less than the transformation of everyday life. In this they were consciously pursuing a project begun by the Dadaists and Surrealists, artistic movements that had most influenced the Situationists. Debord edited the group's journal from 1957 until its demise in 1969. It carried articles on Vietnam, urban geography, cultural and political issues, and was full of examples of the Situationists' distinctive and influential approach to graphic design, using political slogans and doctored images from the popular press and advertising.

Debord's political theory – to be found most cogently in his *Society of the Spectacle* (1967), a series of 221 paragraphs on unnumbered pages – was the Situationists' most important theoretical document. With political consciousness running extremely high at the time of its publication, and with a rejection of many conventional answers for social transformation, its influence went beyond the confines of the intellectual avant-garde to inform political discussion on a broader scale.

The importance of *Society of the Spectacle* lies in its analysis of postwar capitalism. Debord takes theories from **Marx** and **Lukács** on alienation and commodity use, and applies them to the postwar period of mass consumption and communication.

Marx had explained how work under capitalism had become alienating; the tasks we perform in the productive process are without real meaning, and we have little or no control over what is produced. Everything produced becomes a commodity to be sold and exchanged and, as Lukács noted, capitalism attempts to satisfy all needs in terms of commodity exchange. Debord suggests, following Lukács, that this will include not just the exchange of commodities, but our very relations with one another; commodity relations now extend into all aspects of life, including our understanding of ourselves and others.

With the massive growth in the electronic media, we now live in what Debord memorably called 'the Society of the Spectacle'; for him, 'the spectacle is the moment when the commodity has attained the *total occupation* of social life' (Para. 42), but he notes that 'the spectacle is not a collection of images; it is a social relation among people, mediated by images' (Para. 4), for 'in societies where modern conditions of production prevail, all of life presents itself as an immense accumulation of *spectacles*. Everything that was directly lived has moved away into a representation' (Para. 1). Lived reality is materially invaded by the spectacle, where people become spectators of their own lives. Leisure time is spent consuming the things produced during worktime. Freedom is the freedom to choose one commodity over another.

Debord suggests that we accept the spectacular world because (in a formulation that echoes the **Barthes** of *Mythologies*) it presents itself as natural; it 'makes history forgotten within culture'. Lived experience is commodified and sold back to us in forms that reproduce the dominant ideology. It is in the nature of the spectacle that no one stands outside it, which immediately presents Debord with a fundamental problem: if life has been colonized by the spectacle, how could there be a space from which to criticize it, much less bring about revolutionary transformation of society? According to Debord, critical thinking must come from inside the very system to which it is opposed; there is no simple 'outside' from where a critique could position itself. Inevitably, critical thought will be tainted by and implicated in 'spectacular' logic, but for Debord this does not mean that critique cannot take place. Quoting Hegel, he writes: 'truth is not like a product in which one can no longer find any trace of the tool that made it' (Para. 206).

Towards the end of his book, Debord freely draws upon the dialectical concept of 'contradiction'. Derived from Hegel and Marx, Debord's dialectics suggests that any system (be it natural, economic or ideological) will produce contradiction from within; Debord sees the possibility of subverting the logic of the spectacle by, for instance, pushing it as far as it will go, so that its contradictions are exposed and its ideological 'gloss' is shattered. Against the spectacle, he argues dialectically that reality is not fixed, not even the critique that suggests so; critical theory is a 'scandal' (Para. 205) because although its concepts are concrete, it is aware of the fluidity of reality itself. Debord's writing, gnomic, epigrammatic and allusive, his 'insurrectional style' (a term he takes from early Marx), sees itself a challenge to the self-naturalizing discourses of the spectacle.

While Debord's theoretical work provided the foundation for much of the Situationists' practice, especially in the cultural field, it is these practices that provide concrete examples of the critique of the spectacle. The Situationists had a number of key concepts, such as *détournement* and the *dérive*, which they felt were ways of both appropriating and subverting 'spectacular' thinking. *Détournement*, which means 'diversion' or 'subversion', is a much-used technique devised by Asger Jorn in the late 1950s. For Jorn this meant taking cheaply purchased second-hand conventional artworks and 'over-painting' them – that is, adding a new image over the top of the old, though importantly, the old was still visible. Jorn, and the many who used this technique on comic books and advertising material after him, hoped to challenge the accepted artistic and moral codes of the day. By distorting the original meaning of the work by over-painting or adding new words or images, they attempted to lay bare its ideological assumptions; defamiliarizing images from everyday life was a way of giving the spectacle a history, and therefore suggesting the possibility of political change. *Détournement* is also a suggestive metaphor for the possibility of a critical theory in Debord's terms, as it raises all kinds of interesting questions about the position of criticism in relation to the dominant social value system.

Détournement became popular with activists during May '68; advertising hoardings were 'over-written' with political slogans and comic books were plagiarized for their images, the speech-bubbles rewritten with political propaganda. It had a lasting effect on the production of the Undergound and anarchist presses from the late 1960s to the punk explosion of the mid 1970s; the style of the many album covers and photocopied fanzines that appeared at this time can be traced back to the Situationists. More directly, the artwork and style of the the most influential punk group, the Sex Pistols, was mainly the creation of their manager and publicity designer, who had been students in '68 and have acknowleged the influence of Debord and others.

The early work of both **Lyotard** and **Baudrillard** bears the marks of Situationist thought. Baudrillard's concept of hyperreality has a good deal in common with Debord's spectacle, and the Situationists' concept of the *dérive*, a psycho-geographical 'drift' through an urban landscape, becomes the philosophical 'drifting thought' of Lyotard. Debord and the Situationists had much more of a cultural impact than a political or philosophical one. As Debord rejected the notion of a Leninist-style vanguard party, it is hard to see how he hoped to bring about fundamental social change, beyond the admittedly powerful consciousness-raising device of *détournement*.

Fredric **Jameson**'s citing of Debord in his introduction to Lyotard's *The Postmodern Condition* (1984) marks the start of a resurgence of interest in the Situationists' work with the debate around post-modernism and its concern with various types of mediation. It is easy to see that much of what is labelled postmodern art echoes Situationist practices of *détournement* and appropriation, but often without the critical zest, although American photographer/artists such as Cindy Sherman and Barbara Kruger are exceptions.

The political pessimism in art practice is to be found in Baudrillard's work too; although it is superficially similar to Debord in some respects, there is a crucial difference. For Baudrillard, hyperreality is just the way things are; for Debord, it is the way things are under capitalism; therefore, because of dialectical contradiction, there is always the space for some kind of critique and the possibility of political change. While Raoul Vaneigem warned of the spectacle's power to neutralize dissenting voices through absorption, in Baudrillard's work dissent is a form of 'inoculation' against the possibility of any real change; dissent becomes a structural part of the system.

Debord and the Situationists' influence was at its height when there was the possibility of revolutionary social change. It seems in retrospect that it could have been the very failure to turn that possibility into actuality that may have given us postmodernism in its various forms.

Main works

Society of the Spectacle, Detroit: Black & Red, 1970.

Comments on the Society of the Spectacle, trans. Malcolm Imrie, London: Verso, 1990.

Panegyric, trans. James Brook, London: Verso, 1992.

Further reading

Blazwick, Iwona (ed.), *An endless adventure . . . an endless passion . . . An Endless Banquet: A Situationist Scrapbook*, London: Verso/ICA, 1989.)

Knabb, Ken (ed.), *Situationist International Anthology*, Berkeley, CA: Bureau of Public Secrets, 1981.

Marcus, Greil, *Lipstick Traces*, London: Secker & Warburg, 1989.

Plant, Sadie, *The Most Radical Gesture*, London: Routledge, 1992.

Reader, Keith, *Intellectuals and the Left in France since 1968*, London: Macmillan, 1987.

Wollen, Peter, 'The Situationist International', *New Left Review*, 174 (1989): 67–95.

Deleuze, Gilles (1925–) and Guattari, Félix (1930–92)

Gilles Deleuze, who has taught philosophy at Vincennes, Paris, since the 1960s, has been one of the driving forces behind post-structuralism in France. Author of distinctive but conventional scholarly studies of writers such as Hume, Proust, Bergson and Spinoza, he found his vocation as an apostle of **Nietzsche**, developing his own Nietzschean philosophy in his first two original works of philosophy: *Différence et Répétition* (1968) and *Logique du Sens* (1969), to wide critical acclaim. It was, however, *Anti-Oedipus* (1972), written with Félix Guattari, which achieved international notoriety, with its iconoclasm and inventiveness (it is arguably the first major work of specifically *postmodern* theory). This collaboration, begun after the '68 events, continued until Guattari's death in 1992; during the 1970s, both authors were exemplary political intellectuals of the French radical left, involved in many political struggles.

Félix Guattari was for many years a member of **Lacan**'s Ecole Freudienne, and has been a leading figure in radical psychiatry in France. Guattari was an important political activist (ten years in the Communist Party and thereafter as a libertarian **Marx**ist), playing an influential part in the Italian 'Autonomist' movement, whose anti-authoritarian struggles were ruthlessly suppressed by the state during the late 1970s and early 1980s.

The explicit (indeed, somewhat melodramatically proclaimed) objective of all Deleuze and Guattari's work, to subvert and disorganize Western philosophy and all its categories, is meant to create the possibility of *thinking differently*. This radicality, this understanding of what it is to be radical, is probably the common denominator of the whole battalion of French philosophers who have risen to prominence since the 1960s; in the case of Deleuze and Guattari the project is directed principally towards the 'liquidation of the principle of identity', to destroy the very category.

Deleuze's early book *Nietzsche and Philosophy* (1962) provides the guiding principle of all his later work: Nietzsche's concept of the will-to-power is appropriated as the central interpretative concept. In Deleuze this leads to the equation between 'meaning' and 'force', and a whole new theorization of language and its materiality: 'meaning' is something to be not discovered, but produced. Deleuze's version of Nietzsche is, however, selective, and arguably superficial. He finds in Nietzsche a way of rejecting Reason and dialectics in favour of a philosophy of desire based on the will-to-power, whereas Nietzsche sees Reason as essentially about the will-to-power.

Desire is the central theme in Deleuze and Guattari, and the way it is transformed is so striking as to make its meaning quite incommensurable with other, earlier usages of the same word. Desire is not to be conceived in 'negative' terms, as being driven by a lack of something; nor is it even desire 'for' an object. It is, on the contrary, a *productive* force.

Anti-Oedipus (Capitalism and Schizophrenia, volume I) defies summary: on one level a hilariously iconoclastic denunciation of the Oedipus complex (seen as a neurosis inflicted by psychoanalysis itself), written from the standpoint of the libido, it is at the same time a deadly serious work of social and ethical theory. The book itself is a sustained, subversive rewriting of both psychoanalysis and Marxism, where the common point of reference is found in **Freud**'s 'economic' metaphors (the 'thermodynamic' model of libidinal energy; the notion of dream-work, etc.) and in Marx's use of bodily metaphors and his rhetorical personification of 'capital', and so on. It is not at all, as sometimes represented, directed against Marxism. The 'anti-Oedipus' in the title echoes Nietzsche's *Antichrist*, and it is obvious that not only psychoanalysis is being subverted in the same spirit that Nietzsche subverted Christianity, but also the figure of Oedipus itself – Freud's myth of the inevitably crucified libido. But Deleuze and Guattari are producing far more than just a critique of the theory of the Oedipus complex, or even of psychoanalytic theory as a whole; they have constructed an alternative, an entirely different way of thinking of the unconscious, of the 'individual', and of the body.

The ethics (**Foucault** calls it this in his preface) is explicit in the injunctions and implicit in the conceptual oppositions: Deleuze and Guattari affirm *desire* as creative energy and a value in itself (but conceived not as something individual, and not valued for what it creates); they affirm 'life' (but not as understood biologically); they affirm 'movement' as such (*deterritorialization, lines of flight*) against all attempts to capture and fix things, of which the state is the exemplary instance, and above all the various *flows* of which, in their perspective, the universe is really made up. The politics they uphold is not one of opposition and struggle in the conventional, dialectical, sense, but one of *difference*: they urge a strategy of experimental 'becoming-different', which amounts to an encouragement to continual self-reinvention. In a rhetoric intended to appeal to contemporary social and cultural tendencies, they uphold all the movements called 'minor' (*molecular* versus *molar* [pertaining to the mass]).

What can be seen at work in this text is a productive conjunction of Deleuze's Nietzschean theory of interpretation, which sees in 'objects' and 'concepts' the *forces*, the desires which constitute them, with Guattari's politically charged, 'military' assault on psychoanalysis, with the aim of transforming its language into a critical theory of society. There are in fact discernible differences between the vocabularies invented by Deleuze and those of Guattari. The more 'philosophical' terms come from Deleuze, while Guattari has a penchant for the physical and spatial: desiring-machine, molar/molecular, and so on. Among the much-misunderstood new concepts produced is the unconscious as a 'desiring machine' (which they later reformulate simply as 'assemblage') and the 'body-without-organs', which is an attempt to recover the potentialities of the pre-sexed and pre- 'socialized' state.

Their rewriting of psychoanalysis replaces it with what they call '*schizoanalysis*', a notion which goes beyond (but does entail) a glamorization of schizophrenia. Heavily influenced by Lacan – who, like Marx, seems to escape direct stricture in this book – Deleuze and Guattari give a positive meaning to madness: 'delirium' [*délire*] is the universal actually existing state of affairs; a collective schizophrenia is the revolutionary alternative they pose to the dominant fascistic paranoia of the ego, the 'private individual', which they see as produced by capitalism. Schizoanalysis, as a subversive theory at both social and psychological levels, is meant to describe (and reconstruct) the mechanisms by which desiring machines become 'paranoid' and persecute the body without organs – in other words, how we produce our own repression.

Volume II of *Capitalism and Schizophrenia, A Thousand Plateaus*, is even more far-reaching, a literary 'Tower of Babel', plundering and rewriting the vocabulary of every discipline from linguistics and biology to anthropology and military strategy. In this volume Deleuze and Guattari take their dismantling of hierarchical discourse further in a text which, its authors declare, 'has neither object nor subject; it is made of variously formed matters. . . . To attribute the book to a subject is to overlook this working of matters.' Repudiating linear development in the text, the authors advise the readers to pursue their own pathways. The metaphor of the *rhizome* (counterposed to the *tree*) is meant to signify the anti-hierarchical, undisciplined form of lateral, multi-branching growth. The precepts for rhizome-thinking are derived, point for point, from a simple inversion of the rules of the *Discourse on Method* of Descartes, the founding father of Rationalism. One of the other major concepts in this book is the idea of *nomad* thought, counterposed to the 'sedentary' thinking of the normal disciplines whose centralized, hierarchical logic links them with the state (for Deleuze and Guattari this link is real and psychological, not merely metaphorical). 'Nomadology', by contrast, elaborated through a rewriting of the pre-history of the state, involves a different relationship to territoriality. Deleuze and Guattari do not stay long in one place: their thought has always-already moved on.

Of all the 'New French Theorists' who swept into prominence in Britain and North America during the 1980s, Deleuze remains the least widely known, whilst the influence of his thought behind the scenes has been enormous. Foucault's claim that this century will be known as 'Deleuzian' reflects the extent to which contemporary thought is foreshadowed explicitly in Deleuze: the conceptual demolition of the 'individual' and the 'universal'; the repudiation of Western reason; and the movement to the outside and the marginal.

The torrent of conceptual innovations in *Anti-Oedipus* (mostly attributable to Guattari) has, to be sure, deposited many new terms on stony ground, but several key ideas have flowed directly into the mainstream of contemporary cultural theory. It is seen most clearly in the writings of Foucault, with whom Deleuze has worked so closely that many of their ideas may be considered to be joint productions. Just as it was Foucault's own history of madness (1961) that inspired Deleuze and Guattari to take psychoanalysis apart, so in turn it was Deleuze's appropriation/interpretation of Nietzsche that had a profound influence upon Foucault (they went on to collaborate in supervising the French translation of Nietzsche's writings). It is largely through Deleuze that *power* became a key category for Foucault, and from Guattari came '*micropolitics*'. From Deleuze's Nietzsche, Foucault adapted the concept and method of *genealogy*, replacing his earlier usage of *archaeology*. The 'break' between Deleuze and Foucault around 1977 can be deciphered in Foucault's shift towards an ethics of *pleasure* (as against Deleuze and Guattari's politics of *desire*). That this break however, was, more political than personal can be seen from the fact that Deleuze delivered the oration at Foucault's funeral.

Main works

Deleuze and Guattari:
Anti-Oedipus, trans. Robert Hurley, Mark Seem and Helen Lane, New York: Viking, 1977.

Rhizomes, trans. Paul Patton and Paul Foss in *I&C* journal, 1981. A reworked version forms part of *A Thousand Plateaus*, trans. Brian Massumi, Minneapolis: University of Minnesota Press, 1987.

What is Philosophy?, trans. Graham Burchell and Hugh Tomlinson, London and New York: Verso, 1994 (1991).

Deleuze:
Nietzsche and Philosophy, trans. Hugh Tomlinson, London: Athlone Press, 1983 (1962).

Différence et Répétition, Paris: Presses Universitaires de France, 1969a.

Logiques du sens, Paris: Editions de Minuit, 1969a.

Cinema I: The Movement–Image, trans. Hugh Tomlinson and Barbara Habberjam, London: Athlone Press, 1986.

Cinema II: The Time–Image, trans. Hugh Tomlinson and Robert Galeta, Minneapolis: University of Minnesota Press, 1989.

The Fold: Cerbnig and the Baroque, London: Athlone Press, 1993.

Guattari:
Psychanalyse et transversalite, Paris: Maspero, 1972.

La Révolution moléculaire, Paris: Editions Recherches, 1977. (Essays from both these books have been translated by Rosemary Sheed as *Molecular Revolution* Harmondsworth: Penguin, 1984.

Further reading

Bogue, Ronald, *Deleuze and Guattari*, London: Routledge, 1989.

Descombes, Vincent, *Modern French Philosophy*, Cambridge: Cambridge University Press, 1980.

Foss, Paul, and Meaghan Morris (eds), *Language, Sexuality and Subversion* Darlington, Australia: Feral Publications, 1978.

I&C journal, ed. Graham Burchell *et al.*, 8 (1981), Power and Desire: diagrams of the social, 1981: introductory essay by Colin Gordon and Notes for a Glossary by Paul Patton.

Massumi, Brian, *A User's Guide to Capitalism and Schizophrenia: Deviations from Deleuze and Guattari*, Cambridge, MA: MIT Press, 1992.

Patton, Paul, 'Deleuze and Guattari: ethics and post-modernity', in *Leftwright*, Sydney, NSW: Intervention Publications, 1986.

Glossary

Assemblage [agencement]: This refers to a combination of independent and heterogeneous things in such a way that they function together. Their disposition creates lines along which power flows. This is Deleuze and Guattari's conception of a social 'machein' e.g. **Desiring-Machein**], which is not really 'mechanical' or 'organic' in the sense of being made up of interdependent components designed to work in a specific fashion. In contrast to the concept of a 'system', for example, a Deleuzian 'machine' can be disassembled. Books are machines, philosophy is a machine, and so on.

Body-without-organs: By this is meant, among other things, the actual experience of one's own body, which does not correspond to the way biology represents how it is organ-ized. Deleuze coined this expression (from Artaud) in opposition to Freud's concept of the death instinct.

Desire: Deleuze and Guattari repudiate the pessimistic way desire is conceived in psychoanalysis as both regressive (determined by past investments) and imaginary (desire for images), and even the Lacanian version, which defines desire by a 'lack' (*manque*) of its object. They make desire into a positive and productive force in its own right – indeed, *the* productive force in both psychic and social life. They assimilate it with the Marxist idea of 'force of production' (which, for Marx, was *labour*) to assert its role as a kind of fundamental energy from which society is produced. The concept/phrase 'desiring machine' is meant to emphasize this productive activity of desire.

Nomadic: As early as the 1960s Deleuze was using this term for an as-yet-unrealized an-archistic philosophy which would accord equal ontological status to everything in the world of 'being'. Just as a nomadic people distributes itself over a territory without dividing it up among different individuals, so such a philosophy would have no supreme principle.

de Man, Paul (1919–83)

Paul de Man was born into the Flemish bourgeoisie, part of an established, educated and cultured Belgian family, the second son of a manufacturer. As the nephew of Hendrik de Man – one of the key socialist thinkers in the West in the interwar period, and the leader of the Belgian socialist party in 1939 – he was educated early in the shifting ground of socialist thought characteristic of the time. When he received what was the equivalent of a Bachelor's degree from the Free University of Belgium in 1937, de Man was enjoying a close relationship with his uncle. This relationship was arguably reflected in his early involvement with two journals, *Les Cahiers du Libre Examin* (as chief editor) and *Le Soir* (as a columnist in charge of literary criticism) – one an overtly 'democratic, anticlerical, antidogmatic, antifascist' enterprise, the second Nazi. The interval between these two events witnessed the German Occupation of Belgium, and a failed attempt by de Man and his wife to escape these forces by fleeing to the Spanish border. His involvement with *Le Soir* lasted for two years, between 1940 and 1942 (later he alleged that his resignation was a protest against German control, and despite the posthumous surfacing of some damning anti-Semitic articles, he was cleared of collaborative activities); he then became employed by a publishing company called Agence Dechenne, where he worked on translations of *Moby Dick* and Goethe until 1945. After the war de Man, along with some other contemporaries, made an unsuccessful attempt to enter the publishing industry, and in 1948 he emigrated to America.

De Man's plans to become a publisher/critic (in particular with the *Partisan Review*) in America never materialized, although the academic connections he acquired during this time eventually led him to teaching posts in New York and Boston, and to the Society of Fellows at Harvard University, where he became a Junior Fellow, gained his PhD and subsequently taught with the New Critic Reuben Brower. Turned down in a bid for a tenured post at Harvard, de Man taught at Cornell University, the University of Zurich, Johns Hopkins University, and finally Yale, where he made his reputation as a leading member of the Yale School of literary studies, becoming Sterling Professor of Comparative Literature and French in 1979. When he died of cancer in 1983, he was declared both an 'extraordinary intellectual authority' (J. Hillis Miller) and 'a liberator' (Shoshana Felman).

De Man's intellectual trajectory is often divided into three periods: his early cultural aestheticism of the 1940s, which culminates in the literary criticism published primarily in *Le Soir* (some of which has anti-Semitic undertones); the essays of the 1950s (considered by some to originate in autobiography), which are an attempt to construct a poetics of becoming based on the separation between subjectivity and subjectivism, and are born out of and delimited by an epistemic horizon of French phenomenology; and a final turn to rhetoric, a deconstructive phase in which he recognizes that the failure to know is not an epistemological problem linked to a phenomenological subject, but a problem endemic to language as a fundamentally tropological structure. Indeed, a definitive break does exist between the 'political aestheticism' of his wartime years and his later attempt to deconstruct an 'aesthetic ideology'.

In his early thinking de Man still maintains a belief in the referential power of literature – its ability to act in relation to an outside, however unsubstantive that 'no thing' may be. Poetic language is in fact defined in terms of action: it is not the eruption of nature into consciousness, or consciousness into language, but a continued attempt to figure a void, rather than face the 'nothingness of being'. In 'Criticism and crisis' he asserts that

> [p]oetic language names this void with ever-renewed understanding and, like Rousseau's longing, it never tires of naming it again. This persistent naming is what we call literature. (*Blindness and Insight*)

His later work, however, which drops its commitment to **Sartre**an Existentialism and engages more fully with contemporary semiotics, indicates an anxiety of reference, a reluctance to view reference as anything more than a linguistic function, one amongst many. Grammar, for de Man, operates machine-like, without regard for position or the body, with pathos emerging as a mere effect of language. The creative potential of language which might be made available in what **Greimas** calls a *zone of entanglement*, or in what **Kristeva** calls *signifying practice*, is not possible from de Man's point of view because the complicated link between logic and grammar is compromised, finally, by rhetoric: 'Considered as persuasion, rhetoric is performative but when considered as a system of tropes, it deconstructs its own performance' (*Allegories of Reading*).

The final phase of de Man's thinking is everywhere concerned with the question of the status of the self: its complex insinuation into language, and the structure of a knowledge produced and internalized from this desire for a 'human' principle of unity. For de Man, criticism has traditionally overlooked the problem of the structure of self-understanding by remaining blind to the absolute gulf between signifier and signified. In 'The rhetoric of temporality', a ground-breaking essay written in 1969, de Man mounted a formidable challenge to the mainstream English and American historians of Romanticism. Beginning from this insight that there is no necessary link between sound images and concepts – and, indeed, that conceptual categories themselves do not correspond across linguistic and discursive boundaries, that they are especially subject to temporal displacement – he effectively deconstructed the assumptions that lay behind what have been taken as the self-evident constructs of that 'period'. Coleridge's efforts in theorizing a precise referential relationship between self-consciousness and nature are seen as having succeeded only retrospectively, since this assumption survives un-examined in modern criticism.

Hence de Man's late work focuses on the materiality and self-reflexivity of language, its repeated attempt to give a shape to a self which culminates in ever more sophisticated figurations standing in place of a failure to do so. Whereas in his earlier work de Man was concerned to undermine the theological impulse behind traditional criticism (a criticism still controlled by Romantic mythologizing) by showing how Romantic texts indicate a new insight regarding the relationship between consciousness and nature – a relationship defined not by a clear distinction between inside and outside, but by a tension which exists internal to a structure of intentionality – his later work focuses on figures relating to selfhood (prosopopoeia, for example) and how a self is produced by them. This phase is strongly influenced by the work of Walter **Benjamin**, in particular *The Origin of German Tragic Drama*.

Like Walter Benjamin and Theodor **Adorno**, de Man finds the most appropriate expression for his habit of thought in the form of the essay. His use of the essay, however, is idiosyncratic: whereas Benjamin and Adorno champion a paratactical and fragmentary style which might mimetically reproduce a 'thinking in fragments', finding 'unity in and through the breaks rather than glossing over them' (Adorno, *Notes to Literature*, 1991, p.16), de Man remains sceptical about the felicity of such an approach:

> I feel myself compelled to repeated frustration in a persistent attempt to recuperate on the level of style what is lost on the level of history. By stating the inevitability of fragmentation in a mode that is itself fragmented, one restores the aesthetic unity of manner and substance that may well be what is in question in the historical study of romanticism. (*Rhetoric of Romanticism*, 1984)

The insight that reconciling the phenomenal and psychic with the world and the word is an inevitable impossibility, yet the ethical necessity of continuing this attempt even despite the knowledge that language will always strive to efface the signs of its failure to achieve such a correspondence, is the driving impulse behind de Man's writing. Reading, rather than being a journey through the materiality of the letter which at some point produces a flash of insight, a promise of totality in which the meaning of a text is revealed in all its cohesiveness, is in fact, for de Man, the arduous confrontation with aporias, conflicts and contradictions which inevitably 'add up to nought'. Thus, it can be nothing more than an allegory of the process of signification which stops short of thematic or narrative recovery by dint of constant negation.

De Man's influence in every area of literary study has been and continues to be considerable, especially in the United States, even despite the 1987 discovery of his wartime writings: his work on the 'text' of Romanticism has effectively transformed our reading of what has become one of the most important moments in literary history. He has been dubbed the 'godfather' (Lentricchia, *After the New Criticism*) of the Yale 'boa-deconstructors', a label that registers the authority of his disposition and tone, as well as his place as arguably the most important postwar literary critic working in America, but not the genuine esteem in which he was held during his lifetime.

Main works

Blindness and Insight: Essays in the rhetoric of contemporary criticism, New York: Oxford University Press, 1971.

Allegories of Reading: Figural language in Rousseau, Nietzsche, Rilke, and Proust, New Haven, CT: Yale University Press, 1979.

Rhetoric of Romanticism, New York: Columbia University Press, 1984.

The Resistance to Theory, ed. and intro. Wlad Godzich, Minneapolis: University of Minnesota Press, 1986.

Critical Writings 1953–1978, ed. and intro. by Lindsay Waters, Minneapolis: University of Minnesota Press, 1989.

Romanticism and Contemporary Criticism: The Gauss Seminar and other papers, ed. E.S. Burt, K. Newmark and A. Warminski, Baltimore, MD and London: Johns Hopkins University Press, 1993.

Aesthetic Ideology, Minneapolis: University of Minnesota Press, forthcoming.

Further reading

Brooks, Peter, Shoshana Felman and J. Hillis Miller (eds), *The Lesson of Paul De Man, Yale French Studies*, 69 (1985).

Derrida, Jacques, *Mémoires for Paul de Man*, trans. by Cecile Lindsay, Jonathan Culler and Eduardo Cadava, New York: Columbia University Press.

Diacritics (special issue devoted to Paul de Man), 20, 3 (1990).

Norris, Christopher, *Paul de Man: Deconstruction and the critique of aesthetic ideology*, London: Routledge, 1988.

Rosiek, Jan, *Figures of Failure: Paul de Man's criticism 1953–1970*, Aarhus: Aarhus University Press, 1992.

Waters, Lindsay and Wlad Godzich (eds), *Reading De Man Reading*, Minneapolis: University of Minnesota Press, 1989.

Derrida, Jacques (1930–)

One of the most controversial thinkers of his generation, Derrida has held academic appointments as a philosopher in both France and America at the École Normale Supérieure, Yale University, the University of California at Irvine, and Cornell University. He has also been a key figure in the development of the International College of Philosophy in Paris. Derrida's work is part of a wider cultural phenomenon called post-structuralism, a French-led cross-disciplinary cultural movement calling into question many of the foundations and assumptions of modern thought, such as those held to underpin the structuralist paradigm.

Derrida's reputation rests mainly on his work developing the theory of deconstruction, a form of textual analysis applicable to all modes of writing which seeks to demonstrate the inherent indeterminacy of meaning. There is no such thing as stable or absolute meaning for Derrida, who maintains that meaning is instead marked by the eternal play of difference (which is to say that it always suggests something other than itself at any one moment) and perpetually in a state of flux. This belief puts him at variance with a Western philosophical tradition which is based on precisely the assumption that meaning *is* stable and determinate, and communicable as such by words – the phenomenon known as logocentrism. Derrida further contends that this same tradition is committed to a belief in speech being closer to the supposedly stable and complete meaning present in one's mind than writing is (phonocentrism). Neither position is sustainable in Derrida's view, and he is dedicated to revealing the shaky foundations – the so-called 'metaphysics of presence', where meaning is held to be present in its entirety in the individual's mind, on which both logocentrism and phonocentrism rest.

   Saussure is a major point of departure for Derrida's philosophical inquiry, particularly the former's identification of the sign as arbitrary, which provides ammunition for Derrida's arguments about linguistic indeterminacy (although it is important to note that Saussure himself drew back from the unsettling implications of arbitrariness to a compromise position of 'relative arbitrariness'). Another major source of Derrida's ideas is the phenomenological movement, particularly the work of Husserl and Heidegger, who provide Derrida with the basis for some of his key concepts (the term 'deconstruction' itself is adapted from Heidegger). Derrida argues that it is not until the work of Heidegger that the notion of presence is systematically challenged, and he feels himself to be extending this aspect of the Heideggerean project in his own work. In the argument against the metaphysics of presence

Derrida reveals himself to be an anti-essentialist thinker, and his critique of structuralism is motivated by the desire to disclose the essentialist nature of that enterprise, with its acknowledged dependence on underlying structures and patterns of thought. **Lévi-Strauss's** structural anthropology is attacked for its belief that myths can be reduced to a common structure, since this requires the existence of an originary myth of which all others are simply variations. In Derrida's view to assume such essences is to be totalitarian and authoritarian, and to limit the creation and proliferation of new meanings. Structuralism is also heavily dependent on the principle of binary opposition (*langue/parole*; signifier/signified; synchronic/diachronic; syntagmatic/paradigmatic), which Derrida is always concerned to call into question for what he considers to be its authoritarian connotations. His contention is that Western thought in general is structured on a series of such oppositions, and that in each case one term of the opposition is privileged over the other (speech over writing, or man over woman, for example) such that a hierarchy of authority is established. Dismantling this hierarchy is a major concern of the deconstructive enterprise, which in this respect has liberationist and anti-authoritarian ideals.

Derrida has been accused of essentialism in his own thought – of being no less reliant than any other philosopher on a group of concepts to make his critical points, but he has devised some ingenious strategies to evade such charges. He denies that what opponents call his 'concepts' actually have the status of concepts, arguing instead that they are always to be regarded as *sous rature*, under erasure; that is, as being deployed without the author feeling himself bound to their having a fixed meaning. The idea is drawn from Heidegger, and has been criticized as making Derrida almost impossible to attack: if whatever he says is self-cancelling, opposition to his arguments is perpetually frustrated at source, and his discourse takes on an air of invulnerability that is philosophically very problematical. *Différance* is probably the best-known of these 'concepts', and its dual meaning of 'difference' and 'deferral' (derived from the fact that the two French words for 'difference' and 'deferral', *différence* and *différance*, cannot be distinguished from each other in speech) is taken to bear out Derrida's point about the general indeterminacy of meaning and arbitrariness of the sign: *différance* is never one thing or the other, but always both simultaneously.

Deconstruction is probably best approached as a form of radical scepticism, and Derrida's project has been variously compared to those of such other famous sceptics as Hume, **Nietzsche** and the later Wittgenstein. In common with philosophical scepticism in general, Derrida seeks out the weak points in discourses, and there is much talk in his writings of gaps, paradoxes and abysses (he can sound quite apocalyptic on occasion). Derrida is anti-foundationalist in his philosophical outlook, and his critique of the metaphysics of presence is effectively a critique of the notion of identity, one of the cornerstones of Western rationality. In Derrida's version of things the sign is never identical to itself, but always contains a trace of the other ('half of it always "not there" and the other half always "not that"', in **Spivak**'s formulation). Difference – the *play* of difference – is inevitably, inescapably, part of the equation. This line of argument, the source of much of Derrida's liberationist appeal in the way that it appears to free meaning from the constraints imposed by specific discourses, has its drawbacks, however, in that it renders Derrida's arguments just as problematical as those he is attacking – an irony that all relativists ultimately have to face. If all truth is relative, then so too is the 'truth' that truth is relative.

At once an extremely subtle and dauntingly obscure thinker, Derrida is famed for the difficulty and sheer eccentricity of his style ('elegant opacity', as his supporter Geoffrey **Hartman** has defined it), in which punning and wordplay, those staples of the deconstructive critical repertoire, are important elements in a strategy to locate gaps (aporia) in our discourse. The deconstructionist self-consciously plays with texts rather than subjecting them to analysis, with the objective being to provide a supplement to rather than a reading of a text. This leads to such practices in Derrida's case as works with parallel columns of text running the whole way throughout (*Glas*), or footnotes which last for the entire text and take on a life of their own in the process ('Living on-border lines'). The end result is a style of philosophy which is much more reminiscent of game-playing or creative writing than of traditional philosophical discourse, but as it is a key part of Derrida's overall project to break down the divisions between philosophy and other forms of writing such as literature, as well as to draw attention to what he considers to be the inescapably textual nature of philosophical writing, this has to be considered part of the plan. Philosophy is above all a form of writing to Derrida and, as such, cannot aspire to any condition of purity (of argument) uncontaminated by rhetoric and its many figures, as the analytical tradition would so often seem to be assuming it can. Punning and wordplay therefore become tactical weapons in a bid to undermine Western metaphysics, its methods and assumptions.

Not content with challenging stylistic canons, Derrida has also shown an obsessive concern with what most textual interpreters take to be highly marginal details of the text, such as borders, margins and authorial signatures. Not surprisingly, this approach has led to accusations of intellectual irresponsibility against Derrida and his followers, particularly from the Anglo-American analytical tradition, with its firm commitment to logical structures of argument, methodical interpretation and rationally conducted *explication de texte*.

Derrida's work tends to arouse extreme reactions, and by any standards he is one of the most controversial voices in twentieth-century philosophy. Deconstruction has been both reviled and heralded as a revolution in thought with emancipatory implications (French feminism has drawn widely on its methods for just that latter reason), but certainly never ignored. Although its influence is perhaps now on the wane, deconstruction has effectively set the terms of reference for cultural debate in Europe and America for much of the last couple of decades. It is no overstatement to claim that it has changed the face of cultural studies, and even now little can be written in the field without some account being taken of Derrida's theories. What Christopher **Norris** has spoken of as the 'deconstructive turn' to academic discourse in recent years is perhaps most noticeable in American intellectual life, where Derrida's theories have had a particularly powerful impact. There is a recognizable school of American deconstruction – the Yale Critics, for example – which, interestingly enough, Derrida feels has misrepresented his ideas to some extent, and made him sound more anarchic a thinker than he considers himself to be. In recent years Derrida has argued that he has never sought the downfall of philosophy, and that he views himself as having been always 'true' to the subject; in fact, of late, he has taken to presenting deconstruction as the heir to **Marx**ism. One has to balance such sentiments against the more iconoclastic, as well as apocalyptic, pronouncements of his earlier career, but presumably one is to assume that it has been Derrida's goal to shake the philosophical establishment and call into question some of its unexamined assumptions rather than to bring about the end of the subject as such. This would suggest that Derrida is perhaps not part of the more extreme wing of the post-philosophical movement, and that his real concern has been to disabuse philosophy of some of its pretensions and redraw its terms of engagement with other discourses.

In general Derrida's theories have met with a more enthusiastic response in the English-speaking world among literary and cultural theorists than philosophers (with a few honourable exceptions, such as Richard **Rorty** and David Wood); indeed, the philosophical establishment hardly credits what Derrida is doing most of the time as coming under the heading of philosophy at all. For one who has set out to problematize the boundaries of philosophy and other forms of writing, however, this fate is not necessarily an undesirable one.

Main works

'Speech and Phenomena' and Other Essays on Husserl's Theory of Signs, trans. David B. Allinson, Evanston, IL: Northwestern University Press, 1973.

Of Grammatology, trans. Gayatri Chakravorty Spivak, Baltimore, MD and London: Johns Hopkins University Press, 1976.

Edmund Husserl's 'Origin of Geometry': An introduction, trans. J.P. Leavey, New York: Hays, 1978a.

Writing and Difference, trans. Alan Bass, Chicago: University of Chicago Press, 1978b.

Spurs: Nietzsche's Styles, trans. Barbara Harlow, Chicago and London: University of Chicago Press, 1979.

Dissemination, trans. Barbara Johnson, Chicago: University of Chicago Press, 1981a.

The Truth in Painting, trans. Geoff Bennington and Ian McLeod, Chicago and London: University of Chicago Press, 1981b.

Margins of Philosophy, trans. Alan Bass, Chicago: University of Chicago Press, 1982.

Glas, trans. J.P. Leavey and R. Rand, Lincoln, NA and London: University of Nebraska Press, 1986.

The Post Card, trans. Alan Bass, Chicago and London: University of Chicago Press, 1987.

Spectres of Marx: The state of the debt, the work of mourning, and the New International, trans. Peggy Kamuf, Routledge: London, 1994.

Further reading

Llewelyn, John, *Derrida on the Threshold of Sense*, Basingstoke and London: Macmillan, 1986.

Norris, Christopher, *Derrida*, London: Fontana, 1987.

Ryan, Michael, *Marxism and Deconstruction*, Baltimore, MD and London: Johns Hopkins University Press, 1982.

Sallis, John (ed.), *Deconstruction and Philosophy: The texts of Jacques Derrida*, Chicago and London: University of Chicago Press, 1987.

Staten, Henry, *Wittgenstein and Derrida*, Lincoln, NA: University of Nebraska Press, 1984.

Wood, David and Robert Bernasconi, *Derrida and Differance*, Evanston, IL: Northwestern University Press, 1988.

Glossary

Differance: The play of difference within words such that they can never be pinned down to one particular meaning at any one time.

Derrida plays here on the similar sound-quality, but different meanings, of the French words *différence* and *différance*.

Erasure: Self-cancelling concept.

Metaphysics of presence: The assumption that the meaning of a word or concept can be present in its entirety in the individual's mind. In Derrida's view, given the action of *différance*, this is impossible.

Dollimore, Jonathan (1948–)

Cultural critic Jonathan Dollimore is a Professor in the School of English and American Studies at the University of Sussex. Through his own publications and his editorial work with his Sussex colleague Alan **Sinfield**, he was one of the leading exponents of 'cultural materialism', which became the most significant development in Renaissance studies in the 1980s.

Dollimore arrived at Sussex in the mid 1970s, when the university faculty began to feel the effect of continental critical theory, which had gained a new impetus after the student and worker uprisings in the late 1960s. The impact of continental theory and new interpretations of **Marx** and of **Freud** on Dollimore was, by his own account, 'a revelation'. Coming before the rise of the right in Britain, which brought with it a long period of political and cultural reaction, left intellectuals like Dollimore saw their role and the role of the institution as oppositional – that is, critical of the subtly repressive nature of liberal democracy. This criticism often took the form of 'ideological critique', a method of analysis developed at Birmingham University by Stuart **Hall** and others.

Also at this time, Raymond **Williams** was beginning to publish his more explicitly Marxist work. It was these critics, along with the European post-structuralist and post-Freudian writers then being published in Britain, who encouraged Dollimore to turn from more traditional research to the examination of subjectivity, power and ideology in the drama of the early modern period.

The term 'cultural materialism', the critical approach most associated with Dollimore and Sinfield, was originally coined by Raymond Williams in the early 1980s and defined by him as 'the analysis of all forms of signification, including quite centrally writing, within the actual means and conditions of their production'. Dollimore and Sinfield adopted Williams's term 'because it seemed to insist that culture was material rather than ideal, and because it implied a determined radical politics' (1990, p. 91). 'Materialist' criticism in this cultural context is opposed to 'idealism', which for Dollimore is the belief that there is an essential, irreducible self that exists before entering human social relations; and, following from this, that there are transhistorical truths that can be about the human self, and that these can be found in great literary works.

Drawing on concepts of ideology and subjectivity found in the work of **Foucault** and **Lacan**, and **Althusser**'s rereading of Marx, Dollimore's materialist criticism claims, quite contrary to idealism, that the human self is a social construct; for Dollimore, the individual cannot transcend the material forces and relations of production. Idealist criticism, in its attempt to find truths beyond the social, elides or erases cultural, racial and sexual difference, the very subjects that are the focus of cultural materialism's attention.

If, for Williams and Dollimore, culture is material, then Dollimore also follows Williams by taking an oppositional role in relation to the dominant culture: 'cultural materialism does not pretend to political neutrality. It knows that there is no cultural practice that is without political significance' (1985, p.viii).

If Dollimore's political position is different from that of the majority of critics of the Renaissance, then no less so is his textual approach and understanding of history. Cultural materialism is often seen as signalling a new 'historicist turn' in critical analysis, and it is has become something of a critical commonplace, though still instructive, to compare it to the older historicist approach of E.W.M. Tillyard, in his influential *The Elizabethan World Picture* (1943). As his title suggests, Tillyard takes what Stephen **Greenblatt** has called a 'monological' approach to the texts of history, finding there a single, shared vision. We find in Tillyard's version of the period what Dollimore calls 'a metaphysic of order' (1994, p. 10), a positive social cohesion characterized by harmony, stability and unity that seem to transcend sectional interests. This shared vision then becomes the background against which we can read the really important work; the literary text, which in turn reflects this world picture. Seen in its day as a useful counter to the more formalist approach of the dominant new criticism, for a materialist critic Tillyard's work is firmly in the idealist camp. Dollimore points out that this world-view was really the ideological cement of a ruling section of society who represented their interests as universal, the ideological legitimation of the existing social order.

Importantly, the literary text does not simply 'reflect' a world-view in the realm of ideas, but plays a part in the making of meaning, and for Dollimore, the most interesting drama of the period stages these struggles over meaning. For him, philosophical, historical and political texts do not form a 'background' for the real business of explicating the literary text, as they did for Tillyard; these works, taken together, form a network of meanings that require the close-reading skills that have been developed on literary texts, along with a form of ideological critique that sees texts as sites of political and cultural struggle, where the critic will attempt to locate what Dollimore calls its 'internal dissonance', or what Pierre **Macherey** describes as the text's difference from itself, its ideological contradictions.

Althusser's concept of ideology is important for Dollimore's work because it presents a theory of the construction of human identity: how we become subject beings. Dollimore's work – and cultural materialist work in general – focuses on the early modern period in Britain precisely because – along with the cultural materialists' interest in the growth of capitalism and British colonialism – the period sees the beginning of the formation of the modern human subject. Dollimore sees questions of subjectivity and subjection as inseparable from issues of gender. With his politically committed interest in 'the subordinate, the marginal, the excluded and displaced' (Wells, p. 409) he sees – drawing on the work of anthropologist Barbara Babcock – that the culturally peripheral turn out to be symbolically central. Like his American counterparts, the New Historicists, Dollimore finds in Jacobean drama a similitude between statecraft and stagecraft; the interaction between state power and cultural forms; the deeply theatrical nature of power and the theatre as a prime location for the representation and legitimation of power. In Jacobean drama's self-conscious artifice, its cross-dressing, and the like, he sees an exploration of the construction of subjectivity, and he pursues these issues in his book *Radical Tragedy*, first published in 1984.

Dollimore's first book argues that in the Renaissance, God was in trouble; the most interesting Jacobean drama subverts the idea of an ordered, providential universe and its corollary, the unified human subject. Religion and the law are demystified by a radical relativism. This idea is pursued through a range of texts, and each close reading of a play is preceded by a section of general theoretical reflection. For Dollimore, Jacobean tragedy is radical not in the sense of being politically 'progressive', but in the way the drama opens up the concept of the essential self to reveal its historical conditions. He finds that the radical nature of Jacobean tragedy 'is not a vision of political freedom, so much as a subversive knowledge of political domination' (1989, p. xxi), a knowledge that interrogated prevailing beliefs, radical in the special sense of going to their roots (*ibid.*, p. 22).

Such is self-reflexive nature of contemporary criticism that much has already been written on the differences between British cultural materialism and American New Historicism. These perceived differences revolve around the ideology of Renaissance drama, and can be summed up in the question formulated by Dollimore: did these plays reinforce or subvert the dominant order? Dollimore suggests, 'according to a rough and ready guide' (1989, p. xxi), that New Historicists tend towards the former and cultural materialists towards the latter. This is because the New Historicists, with their more Foucauldian orientation, see states as self-regulating structures that use and then contain subversive elements; authority produces resistance as its difference; in the dramas, subversion is rehearsed all the better to be contained, rather like **Barthes**'s notion of the ideological inoculation.

Dollimore finds the New Historicist argument salutary: 'It is too easy to appropriate the resistance of others for optimistic theoretical narratives' (1990, p. 94). It is indeed true that these dangerous knowledges were contained, and that subversion may be a ruse of power to consolidate itself (in a similar fashion to the figure of Goldstein in Orwell's *1984*), but this is a very dangerous game. To contain a threat by rehearsing it at least gives it a voice. A materialist has to say finally that it is only a necessary possibility, not inevitable, that subversive elements will be appropriated or contained, and therein lies their danger.

Dollimore pursues Babcock's insight about the symbolically central peripheral figure in *Sexual Dissidence* (1991), a term that refers to the gender-related unsettling of the opposition between dominant and subordinate. A major concern of the book is this very relationship, often fraught and sometimes violent, between dominant and subordinate cultures, groups and identities, and the forms resistance to it takes. Although the book ranges over texts from the early modern period to the contemporary, it develops and enlarges on the concerns of Dollimore's previous book.

As Catherine **Belsey** has pointed out, all texts are written from the present to the present, but for Dollimore this does not mean that he is arguing for some kind of spurious 'relevance' in the texts he studies, as many liberal critics often do. Taking **Brecht** at his word, Dollimore appropriates the past for the present while remaining committed to the past as different. He can also avoid the charge of valorizing or essentializing 'subversion' itself, for the term is not offered in that way; for Dollimore it is not an essentialist concept, because 'nothing is intrinsically or essentially subversive independent of its articulation and context' (1989, p. 22).

Dollimore's has been an influential approach, and its impact can be gauged by the sheer number of critical works that offer such a formula as their critical method. Dollimore and Sinfield have contributed to this process by editing a series of books for Manchester University Press under the general title 'Cultural Politics'. The many references in Dollimore's work to its oppositional or dissident nature may seem, in a bourgeois democracy, like self-aggrandizement, but the initial resistance to the publication of the path-breaking and agenda-setting *Political Shakespeare* (1985) and the dropping by the publishers of a book on gay issues in the 'Cultural Politics' series, for fear of contravening Section 28 of the Local Government Act, gives cause for thought.

Main works

'The Challenge of Sexuality', in *Society and Literature 1945–1970*, ed. Alan Sinfield, London: Methuen, 1983.

Radical Tragedy: Religion, ideology and power in the drama of Shakespeare and his Contemporaries, Harvester Brighton, 1984.

'History and Ideology, masculinity and miscegenation: the instance of *Henry V*' (with Alan Sinfield) in *Alternative Shakespeares*, ed. John Drakakis, London: Methuen, 1985.

'Introduction: Shakespeare, cultural materialism and the new historicism' and 'Transgression and surveillance in *Measure for Measure*', in *Political Shakespeare: New essays in cultural Materialism*, ed. Jonathan Dollimore and Alan Sinfield, Manchester: Manchester University Press, 1985.

'Subjectivity, sexuality and transgression: the Jacobean connection', *Renaissance Drama*, XVII (1986).

'The dominant and the deviant: a violent dialectic', in Colin MacCabe (ed.), *Futures for English*, Manchester: Manchester University Press, 1988.

'Critical developments: cultural materialism, feminism and gender critique, and New Historicism', in Stanley Wells (ed.) *Shakespeare: A bibliographical guide, new edition*, Oxford: Oxford University Press, 1990.

'Culture and textuality: debating cultural materialism', *Textual Practice*, 4, 1 (1990) (with Alan Sinfield).

Sexual Dissidence: Augustine to Wilde, Freud to Foucault, Oxford: Clarendon Press, 1991.

'Desire is death', in Margreta De Grazia and Peter Stallybrass (eds), *Material Culture in the Early Modern Period*, Cambridge: Cambridge University Press, 1994.

Further reading

Greenblatt, Stephen, *Shakespearean Negotiations*, Oxford: Oxford University Press, 1988.

Holderness, Graham (ed.) *The Shakespeare Myth*, Manchester: Manchester University Press, 1988.

Howard, J. and M. O'Connor (eds), *Shakespeare Reproduced: The text in history and ideology*, London: Methuen, 1987.

Wilson, R. and R. Dutton (eds), *The New Historicism and Renaissance Drama*, Harlow: Longman, 1992.

E

Eagleton, Terry (1943–)

Terry Eagleton's academic career has been spent mainly at the University of Oxford, where he is now Warton Professor of English. He has published widely on the subject of literary theory and aesthetics, as well as on authors as disparate as Shakespeare, Samuel Richardson, and the Brontë sisters, and is the leading representative of his generation of the **Marx**ist tradition in English literary studies. He is also a playwright and novelist of some note, and has been involved with Field Day, the Northern Ireland theatre group. Another recent project has been to write the script for Derek Jarman's film on Wittgenstein. Among his range of influences from the Marxist critical tradition is his one-time teacher Raymond **Williams**, whose debt Eagleton frequently acknowledges despite some critical points of difference between their respective theoretical positions.

Eagleton has been instrumental in introducing the ideas of several continental theorists into English critical discourse, most notably perhaps those of Pierre **Macherey**, author of the highly influential *A Theory of Literary Production* and disciple of the French structuralist Marxist philosopher Louis **Althusser**. He has also been a champion of the German Marxist critic Walter **Benjamin** – in Eagleton's reading a model of the open-minded Marxist willing to construct a dialogue with other modern theoretical discourses. Like Macherey, Eagleton's major concern has been with the ideology of literature: 'Marxist criticism' he notes, 'is part of a larger body of theoretical analysis which aims to understand *ideologies* – the ideas, values and feelings by which men experience their societies at various times. And certain of those ideas, values and feelings are available to us only in literature.'

Eagleton's main contribution to structural Marxist thought is *Criticism and Ideology*, probably his most challenging – certainly his most complex – theoretical work overall. *Criticism and Ideology* sets out to make the case for a materialist criticism (Eagleton is adamant that criticism can never be an ideologically neutral activity) and puts forward several categories by which this can be prosecuted: General

Mode of Production (GMP), Literary Mode of Production (LMP), General Ideology (GI), Authorial Ideology (AuI), Aesthetic Ideology (AI), and Text. The text is seen to be the product of the interaction of these various structures within a given social formation, and it is taken to be the critic's role to spell out the ideological processes that are involved in its production – the procedure known as 'reading against the grain'. The clear source of inspiration for the categories is to be found in the philosophy of Althusser and notions such as 'Ideological State Apparatus' (ISA) and 'Repressive State Apparatus' (RSA). One of the criticisms of Eagleton's adaptation of Althusserian concepts to criticism is that it shares the highly abstract nature of its source, suggesting as it does a world in which the human dimension is largely absent – 'history without a subject', as it has been called in Althusser's case.

Eagleton's concern to establish a science of materialist criticism runs into some difficulties over the issue of a Marxist aesthetic theory of value. Acknowledging that this has traditionally been a source of some embarrassment to Marxist critics, he espouses a **Brecht**ian aesthetic based on the text's ability to 'make us think' (Brecht had contended that working-class audiences were prone to reject any play that 'no longer made one think', and argued that an aesthetic could start from there), while ultimately conceding that perhaps we have not yet achieved the right social conditions for a true Marxist aesthetic theory of value to be possible. The problem is the usual one for Marxist theorists of trying to find a basis for an aesthetic theory of value in art itself rather than in politics (which latter source inevitably raises the spectre of a state-controlled socialist realism and a curbing of the artistic imagination, as had notoriously occurred in Soviet Russia), but Brecht–Eagleton's 'makes you think' criterion fails to resolve the issue entirely. Eagleton contends that the poetry of Wordsworth retains the capacity to make us think in the late twentieth century, whereas that of Walter Savage Landor does not, but it is by no means clear why this is so – or even if it *is* always so. The argument that Wordsworth's poetry is of a higher order of 'contradiction and complexity' than Landor's merely begs the question as to whether these terms are unambiguous enough to function as criteria for an aesthetic theory of value. Overall, the argument lacks conviction, and suggests just how intractable a problem on aesthetic theory of value poses for Marxist thought. One also wonders what Eagleton would make of a work of literature that spurred an audience on to having fascist, racist or sexist thoughts.

Walter Benjamin, or Towards a Revolutionary Criticism involves a noticeably less formalistic approach to theory than is found in *Criticism and Ideology*, and seeks to open up a dialogue between materialist criticism and the feminist and post-structuralist discourses that were beginning to call Marxist forms of textual analysis into question by the early 1980s. It is a trend in Eagleton's development that is continued in his study of Samuel Richardson, *The Rape of Clarissa*. But undoubtedly the most substantial theoretical work of Eagleton's later career is *The Ideology of the Aesthetic*, an analysis of the ideological role of the category of the aesthetic in modern Western thought which makes considerable claims for the importance of aesthetics in the development of modern consciousness, and is eventually highly critical of the postmodernist movement (**Lyotard** in particular coming in for some rough handling). Aesthetics is seen to constitute a site for articulation of some of the critical issues involved in the middle class's struggle for political hegemony in Europe from the Enlightenment onwards – issues such as freedom and legality, spontaneity and necessity, self-determination, autonomy, particularity and universality, for example – hence its importance for the cultural historian. Reading against the grain of this history, however, the aesthetic can also be made to provide the basis for a challenge to the dominant ideological orthodoxy, being, in Eagleton's words, 'an eminently contradictory phenomenon', and therefore a prime target for dialectical analysis. Thus Kant can be praised for the generosity of vision involved in his construction of an aesthetic realm of freedom and autonomy, even if this realm lies beyond any possibility of material realization, and Schopenhauer for unwittingly revealing to us the aridity of the bourgeois conception of the aesthetic as a form of moral redemption.

As the leading Marxist literary critic of his generation in England, Eagleton has exercised considerable influence on the direction of literary studies in this country, and has helped to turn 'reading against the grain' into one of the major analytical methods of the last few decades – even if his original dream of a science of criticism now looks more than a bit dated. Despite a degree of *rapprochement* with other theoretical discourses he has generally taken a fairly sceptical attitude towards the claims of post-structuralism and postmodernism, which in his opinion often take a cavalier attitude towards the political implications of their theorizing, and accordingly should be treated with suspicion by the left. In this sense Eagleton's work has constituted something of a rallying point for the left-wing reaction against post-structuralism and postmodernism in English literary-critical circles: an insistence that the ideological must always be kept at the forefront of the critic's concerns, and that there should be no lapse into subjectivism or an apolitical cultural relativism.

Main works

Shakespeare and Society, London: Chatto & Windus, 1967.

Exiles and Émigrés, London: Chatto & Windus, 1970.

Myths of Power: A Marxist study of the Brontës, London: Macmillan, 1975.

Criticism and Ideology, London: NLB, 1976a.

Marxism and Literary Criticism, London: Methuen, 1976b.

Walter Benjamin, or Towards a Revolutionary Criticism, London: Verso, 1981.

The Rape of Clarissa: Writing, sexuality and the class struggle in Samuel Richardson, Oxford: Blackwell, 1982.

Literary Theory: An introduction, Oxford: Blackwell, 1983.

The Ideology of the Aesthetic, Oxford and Cambridge, MA: Blackwell, 1990.

Further reading

Frow, John, *Marxism and Literary History*, Oxford: Blackwell, 1986.

Regan, Stephen (ed.), *This Year's Work in Critical and Cultural Theory, 1991*, Part II, 'Barbarian at the Gate: Essays in Honour of Terry Eagleton', Oxford: Blackwell, 1994.

Rorty, Richard, 'We anti-representationalists', *Radical Philosophy*, 60 (1992): 40–42.
Slaughter, Cliff, *Marxism, Ideology and Literature*, London and Basingstoke: Macmillan, 1980.

Glossary

General Mode of Production (GMP): Dominant mode of production in a given society. This is the major determinant of that society's social relations.

Literary Mode of Production (LMP): The form that literary activity takes within a given society. There can be several such modes operating at any one time (popular, serious, etc.), all of them influenced by the particular form of the GMP.

General Ideology (GI): Dominant ideological discourse in a given society.

Authorial Ideology (AuI): The author's ideological beliefs, which can either conform to or diverge from the GI.

Aesthetic Ideology (AI): Beliefs concerning the role and value of the arts in a given society.

Eco, Umberto (1932–)

Umberto Eco was born in Alessandria in Piedmont, Italy, in 1932. He studied philosophy at the University of Turin, and wrote a thesis on Thomas Aquinas (his interest in the Middle Ages has remained constant, even when he is immersed in the analysis of postmodern society). He taught at numerous Italian institutions – the University of Turin (1956–64); the University of Milan (1964–65) and the University of Florence (1966–69) – before his appointment as Professor of Semiotics at the University of Bologna in 1971. He has taught extensively in the United States, and has been Visiting Professor at Yale, Columbia, New York and Northwestern Universities. Eco became internationally famous in the 1980s with the publication of his bestselling novel *The Name of the Rose*, and has since been much in demand as a media commentator.

Riddle: what's the difference between a closed text and an open one? A closed text is one which is open to every possible reading, whereas an open text is closed to certain readings. According to Umberto Eco, anyway, in 'The poetics of the open work'. Eco is a man to whom paradox is a delight, as is evident in the following quotation:

> A work of art, therefore, is a complete and *closed* form in its uniqueness as a balanced organic whole, while at the same time constituting an *open* product on account of its susceptibility to countless different interpretations which do not impinge on its unadulterable specificity. (*Role of the Reader*)

Eco introduces the open/closed distinction in *The Role of the Reader*, a collection of essays originally published between 1959 and 1971. Here he explores the differences between those works written without regard for how they are decoded, and those constructed with a specific readerly response in mind. A book such as Eugène Sue's *Les Mystères de Paris*, for instance, may well aim for a readership of dandies, but ends up missing the target altogether by arousing revolutionary feelings in a public it never meant to address. This 'closed' text was therefore open to an aberrant reading. James Joyce's *Finnegans Wake*, on the other hand, is an 'open' text, one which lexically and syntactically forestalls misreadings because of its many idiosyncrasies. Few possibilities of aberration there. As Eco says, the ideal reader of *Finnegans Wake* cannot be from another century or a casual peruser of the text, but must indeed be the scholarly insomniac who devotes his entire life to studying Joyce and Joyce alone.

In *The Role of the Reader*, Eco combines the two things he does best: the generation of semiotic theory in densely packed, sometimes algebraic studies of models of language (see 'On the possibility of generating aesthetic messages in an Edenic language' and 'Lector in fabula: pragmatic strategy in a metanarrative text') and the application of some of these ideas to a wide range of literary and cultural artefacts.

The most notorious of these applied scrutinies are discussions of two durable heroic myths from the West, James Bond and Superman. In 'Narrative structures in Fleming', Eco reveals that the dozen or so 007 books from *Casino Royale* to *The Man with the Golden Gun* are a game in which the fundamental rule is that 'Bond moves and mates in eight moves'. The foreplay before this inevitable outcome involves the assignment of the mission by M, the first encounter with the Villain, meeting the Woman, and so on. Throughout the stories, Eco suggests, characters and values are opposed in fourteen 'dichotomies', such as the contrast between Bond and the Villain, the Villain and the Woman, the Free World and the Soviet Union, Excess and Moderation. The permutation of these core elements drives the narrative, to make Fleming's work a contemporary *ars combinatoria*.

The implications of Eco's reductive, **Propp**-like approach are twofold. First, by parsing the text into its constituent parts, Eco lays bare a very particular narratological grammar underlying the Bond saga, one which may well have repercussions for other types of fiction. Secondly, by choosing to analyze works from mainstream culture with the same rigour as would formerly have been accorded to, say, the high priests of modernism, Eco makes a polemical point about the inclusiveness of the critical gaze.

Superman, like Bond, has a double identity. In his civilian guise he is Clark Kent, mild-mannered and bespectacled; almost, at times, the fool. Once in the phonebooth he rips off his shirt and turns into the Man of Steel, who can fly faster than the speed of light and fell forests with a single blow. The comic strips in which these miracles take place embody a contemporary confusion about the nature of time, argues Eco's 'The myth of superman'. Unlike the archetypal heroes from Greek and Nordic myth, such as Hercules or Thor, Superman's story is not one which has already been told, but evolves with each new episode. This iteration prevents Superman from ageing, and offers an escapist entertainment strangely consonant with the atemporal worlds of Jorge Luis Borges or Alain Robbe–Grillet.

Superman is Eco's pet pop icon, and it is now almost a commonplace to see an echo of Eco in the man from Krypton. After all, he too is mild-mannered and bespectacled as he chats amiably to talk-show hosts about *feuilleton* and futons. Yet peel off the media personality, and underneath is an intellectual Superman, theorizing faster than the speed of light and felling fallacies left, right and centre in tomes such as *A Theory of Semiotics*, *Semiotics and the Philosophy of Language*, and *The Limits of Interpretation*.

There is something of the James Bond about Eco, too: a double agent, equally at home at the football match or in the senior common room. This dual allegiance was shaken, but not stirred, by the phenomenal success of *The Name of the Rose*, a metaphysical detective story set in a fourteenth-century monastery, featuring William of Baskerville, a Franciscan monk, and his sidekick, Adso of Melk. The book's meshing of Thomas Aquinas and Thomas Pynchon polarized opinion sharply. The highbrows thought it too middlebrow; the middlebrows thought it too highbrow; the lowbrows bought it in droves. In fact, during the mid 1980s the book became an index of cultural chic, to be displayed on black metal shelving next to the wok and Vivaldi cd box-set. Bringing semiotics to the sitting-room, as it were, caused some befuddlement – so much so that Eco published not one but two explanatory follow-ups, *Reflections on The Name of the Rose* and *Postscript to The Name of the Rose* (neither of which explains anything much).

To paraphrase what Eco has said about metaphor, his work probably defies every encyclopaedic entry. Suffice it to say that in addition to substantially increasing the academic understanding of sign-systems, Eco has done much to popularize some very abstruse ideas about literary and critical theory, especially in books such as *Faith in Fakes*. He has therefore helped to bring about the very breakdown between 'low' and 'high' culture which he himself has so assiduously described. In may ways he is the Italian Barthes, seeing signification in striptease or the furrowed brow of Humphrey Bogart (see 'Casablanca: cult movies and intertextual collage' for a discussion of the latter). Or perhaps we should say that Barthes was the French Eco? Another riddle.

Main works

'Casablanca: cult movies and intertextual collage', in *Modern Criticism and Theory*, ed. David Lodge, London: Longman, 1978.

A Theory of Semiotics, Bloomington, Indiana University Press, 1979.

The Role of the Reader, London: Hutchinson, 1981.

Semiotics and the Philosophy of Language, London: Macmillan, 1984a.

The Name of the Rose, trans. W. Weaver, London: Picador, 1984b.

Postscript to The Name of the Rose, trans. W. Weaver, San Diego, CA: Harcourt Brace Jovanovich, 1984c.

Reflections on The Name of the Rose, trans. W. Weaver, London: Secker & Warburg, 1985.

Faith in Fakes, trans. W. Weaver, London: Secker & Warburg, 1986.

The Limits of Interpretation, Bloomington: Indiana University Press, 1990.

Further reading

Cancogni, Anna and David Robey, *The Open Work*, Cambridge, MA: Harvard University Press, 1989.

Daddesio, Thomas C., 'Semiotics and the limits of interpretation', *Romance Languages Annual*, 3 (1991): 186–8.

Luke, Allan, 'Open and closed texts: the ideological/Semantic analysis of Textbook narratives' *Journal of Pragmatics: An Interdisciplinary Bi-Monthly of Language Studies*, 13, 1 (1989): 53–80.

Richter, David H., 'Eco's echoes: semiotic theory and detective practice in *The Name of the Rose*', *Studies in Twentieth-Century Literature*, 10, 2 (1986): 213–36.

Robey, David, 'Umberto Eco', in *Writers and Society in Contemporary Italy*, eds Michael Caesar and Peter Hainsworth, New York: St Martin's 1984.

Viegnes, Michael, 'Interview with Umbert Eco', *L'Anello Che Non Tiene*, 2, 2 (1990): 57–75.

Empson, William (1906–84)

Empson came to literary criticism through an oblique route, for he spent his first three years as a Cambridge undergraduate studying mathematics. In 1928 he reverted to English literature and was tutored by I.A. **Richards**, who was at that time expounding progressive theories for the conduct of the discipline, involving close textual study and a more hard-edged scientific approach to the resolution of issues such as literary meaning. Empson was a student of unusual precocity, and an essay written for Richards was subsequently worked up into his most influential and acclaimed book, *Seven Types of Ambiguity*. He spent several years teaching at universities in Japan and China before becoming a professor of English at the University of Sheffield. As well as being a critic, he produced two volumes of poetry, strongly influenced by Donne and the metaphysicals, though he ceased writing creatively in his mid-thirties. In addition to writing books, Empson was an indefatigable reviewer and rode a succession of unconventional hobbyhorses in the pages of learned journals. An inveterate maverick, he was dismissive of every emerging theoretical movement as well as being in a state of more or less open warfare with the literary critical 'establishment', which he branded loosely as 'neo-Christian'.

In one sense, Empson was not a theoretical critic: he was distrustful of abstractions, and as a critic he is best known not for the articulation of general precepts but for a fleet-footed virtuosity in attending to particular works or passages. On the other hand, however some of his works, such as *Seven Types of Ambiguity* and *The Structure of Complex Words*, are breathtakingly schematic, and show Empson importing into literary studies methods of argumentative formulation that are clearly derived from mathematics. Empsonian criticism is not a formalized set of precepts so much as a technique; and while this technique may be based on a worked-out rationale, Empson never troubled himself to expound this in any abstract way. Despite his early association with Richards, Empson rejected his belief that the truths vouchsafed by literary texts should be firmly demarcated from those yielded by non-literary discourse. Richards had categorized poetry as an emotive form of utterance, devoid of any truth-telling capacity or veridical force, in which apparent assertions of truth were, in reality, only 'pseudo-statements' serving the ulterior purpose of stimulating and organizing the reader's emotions. Empson's criticism differs from this in always insisting that the problem of interpreting literary texts be seen as continuous with the business of 'sense-making' in every other domain of human communication. As well as distancing him from Richards, this belief separates him from the New Critics, whose stress on rarefied terms like 'irony' and 'paradox' supported the notion that poetic meanings were insusceptible to any plain prose paraphrase. Empson's criticism always supposes that the divination of meaning, while it is invariably tricky, does represent a practical aspiration, the best way towards it being through plain paraphrase; and that any statement of 'meaning' is a statement of meaning as intended by the author: another belief antithetical to New Critical doctrine.

Empson's critical career begins with the precocious *Seven Types of Ambiguity*, essentially a project in close reading. In Empson's terminology, an ambiguity occurs wherever a piece of language can be understood in more than one way. Moreover, where multiple meanings derive from a single bit of text, the relation between these meanings may itself be of interpretative consequence. *Seven Types* helped to create the Empsonian stereotype of an indeflectible close reader, but his later criticism as a rule links literary texts with phenomena external to them: intellectual and cultural history, lexicography and authorial biography. The later criticism also sees a curious bent towards viewing literary works through polarities and equations. *Some Versions of Pastoral* considers pastoral not as a body of works mapping on to a common subject matter, but as a device or 'trick' operative across a range of works which are ostensibly very different from each other. This device Empson describes as putting 'the complex into the simple', and it involves him in a series of ingenious readings showing how literature can harmonize competing forces and interests that are at play within individuals and within society as a whole. The texts that demonstrate Empsonian pastoral are subject to some kind of internal division, such as those caused by double plots, the presence of mock-heroic, or the gap between surface and depth meanings. *Some Versions* is probably the work that best exemplifies Empson's relation to theory, for though a general theory of pastoral is worked out, this eventually gets outstripped by the sheer virtuosity of its own illustrations. This syndrome is less apparent in *The Structure of Complex Words*, the book which was Empson's most thoroughgoing work of interpretative theory as well as his least successful critical undertaking. This work explores semantic 'equations' latent within some ambivalent words. These equations are generated by the relation existing between the most current sense of a word and the sense called for by the immediate context of its usage. Such equations then give rise to implied arguments, and where a complex word is used persistently within a text, the 'argument' contained within it can become a key to the thematics of the work as a whole.

Empson would have scorned being thought of as a theorist. He never allowed that theory could have a value intrinsic to itself, though it could become useful by giving the critic practical assistance towards saying how a piece of literature worked and what its author meant by it. To judge the cogency of Empson's 'theorizing', then, is to miss the point; for what really matters are the practical critical insights that the scaffolding of general ideas merely helps into being.

Empson's impact on the cultural scene has been smaller than his intellectual gifts might have warranted. This circumstance probably owes much to the critical hegemony, during much of his career, of the Leavisite school: **Leavis** – a contemporary in Cambridge, as well as another early disciple of I.A. Richards – created an influential and stongly moralistic critical method that had the effect of marginalizing Empson's more idiosyncratic one. Moreover, Empson's critical method does not lend itself to any set of easy-to-follow rules, so it is hard to reproduce in the absence of the sort of searching intelligence that Empson himself possessed. In spite of this, there is currently a marked revival of interest in Empson's achievement, though his devotees split into two somewhat opposed camps. Some critics, the most eminent among whom is Christopher Ricks, have absorbed from his work a technique of minutely detailed close reading. Another critical group, including Christopher **Norris**, has been attracted not so much by Empson's method as by his theoretical assumptions: his dogged but sophisticated positivism, as well as his preparedness to allow his criticism to be coloured by strong beliefs, especially those of his far-left politics. The present moment sees the Empsonian legacy being fought over by both parties: the one seeing him as a dazzling critical technician, the other as the purveyor of a socially committed criticism that can stand as a bulwark against the value relativism of recent postmodern theorizing.

Main works

Seven Types of Ambiguity: A study of its effects on English verse, London: Chatto & Windus, 1930.

Some Versions of Pastoral, London: Chatto & Windus, 1935.

The Structure of Complex Words, London: Chatto & Windus, 1951.

Milton's God, London: Chatto & Windus, 1961.

Using Biography, London: Chatto & Windus, 1984.

Argufying: Essays on literature and culture, ed. John Haffenden, Iowa City: University of Iowa Press, 1987.

Further reading

Fry, Paul, *William Empson: Prophet against sacrifice*, London: Routledge, 1991.

Gill, Roma (ed.), *William Empson: The man and his work*, London: Routledge & Kegan Paul, 1974.

Kermode, Frank, 'William Empson: the critic as genius', in *An Appetite for Poetry: Essays in literary interpretation*, London: Collins, 1989, pp. 116–35.

Norris, Christopher, *William Empson and the Philosophy of literary Criticism*, London: Athlone Press, 1978.

Norris, Christopher and Nigel, Mapp (eds), *William Empson: The critical achievement*, Cambridge: Cambridge University Press, 1993.

F

Fanon, Frantz (1925–61)

Frantz Fanon was born and grew up on the island of Martinique in the French Antilles. He served for the Free French forces in Europe in 1944–5, and was awarded the Croix de Guerre for heroism in combat. Fanon returned to France after the war to train as a doctor, specializing in psychiatry. Soon after qualifying he was appointed Head of the Psychiatric Department at the Blida-Joinville Hospital in Algeria, where he worked for three years between 1953 and 1956. He resigned from the post because he felt compromised as an employee of the French colonial regime with whom the FLN (National Liberation Front) had been engaged in guerilla warfare since 1954. From 1956 he devoted himself increasingly to the cause of Algerian liberation from French colonization, and to African nationalism more generally. He took up an editorial post on the FLN newspaper, *El Moudjahid*, in Tunis, and in 1960 he was appointed Ambassador of the Algerian Provisional Government to Ghana. In the same year, having survived assassination attempts on his life, he was diagnosed as suffering from leukaemia, and despite medical treatment in the USSR and the United States, he died in hospital in Washington, DC in December 1961.

Fanon's first book was *Black Skin, White Masks* ([*BSWM*]; first published in 1952). Although it is less politically engaged and less clearly focused than his later work, *BSWM* lays the foundations of several important themes in Fanon's *œuvre*. The title refers to the psychology of racial division, which Fanon identifies in Manichaean terms. He argues that the social pressures deriving from a white, racist, colonial culture force the black man to identify his colour with negative and demeaning associations. The resulting desire to identify with his white oppressor, that is, to adopt a white mask, is therefore both inevitable and paradoxical. Fanon's frequently aphoristic and declamatory style in *BSWM* draws attention to the dehumanizing contradication to which his title alludes. He refers to the work of **Marx**, **Nietzsche**, **Freud** and **Lacan**, but the dialectical underpinning of his argument derives from the Hegelian tradition, as mediated by **Sartre**. In its attempt to resist static, essentialist categories, the book can also be seen as a critique of contemporary assessments of the colonial predicament. First, Fanon takes issue with the idea of 'Négritude' articulated by Francophone black writers (including the poet Aimé Césaire, who taught Fanon at the *lycée* in Martinique, and Leopold Senghor of Senegal) during the 1940s and 1950s. The essentialist notion of blackness offered by proponents of 'Négritude' is seen by Fanon as a product of a colonial characterization of the Negro as 'other'; as such, 'Négritude' simply panders to the white colonizers' racism. Fanon's attack on Mannoni's *Psychologie de la colonisation* (Paris, 1950, translated in 1964 as *Prospero and Caliban: The psychology of colonization*), is launched from a similar perspective. Mannoni, a psychologist by professional training, attempted to explain the colonial predicament in Madagascar by purporting to identify a 'dependency complex' among the colonized and a 'Prospero complex' among the colonizers. While he himself was interested in performing a psychological exploration of the colonial condition, Fanon exposed Mannoni as providing an abjectly apolitical account which appeared to offer a means of justifying colonial oppression.

Fanon's second published work, *Studies in a Dying Colonialism* ([*SDC*]; first published in 1959), is a collection of five essays examining aspects of the Algerian revolution against the French. The essays, on a variety of cultural and political issues which had arisen during the five-year war in Algeria between the FLN and the French, have a common strategic aim which derives from Fanon's sense that he is witnessing a genuinely revolutionary situation. Indeed, the original (i.e. French) title pointedly marks the events in Algeria as a stage in a revolutionary struggle which parallels the chronological typology of the French Revolution. The tone of *SDC* is markedly optimistic: 'We want to show in these pages that *colonialism has definitely lost out in Algeria, while the Algerians, come what may, have definitely won.*' The first – and in some ways most powerful – essay, 'Algeria unveiled', deals with the attempt by French colonial society to defuse nationalist sentiment by trying to persuade Algerian women that the wearing of the veil was a form of oppression. Fanon analyzes this manoeuvre instead as part of the official administration's attempt 'to bring about the disintegration of forms of existence likely to evoke a national reality directly or indirectly'. This attempt to win over Algerian women by persuading them that European ways signalled freedom, and that their own national culture was oppressive, is initially resisted through 'counter-assimilation', or the 'maintenance of a cultural, hence national originality'. Fanon's argument is typically subtle: the veil both protects and identifies the colonized woman, but at the same time the colonizers' unveiling imperative is an opportunity to fool the adversary by making unveiled, and therefore apparently Europeanized (i.e. 'safe'), women carry munitions and guns for the Resistance. Once this deception is discovered, the veil is once again adopted. Fanon thus identifies an infinitely powerful dynamic in the semiotic significance of the veil: 'Removed and reassumed again and again, the veil has been manipulated, transformed into a technique of camouflage, into a means of struggle.' The occupier's attempt to co-opt the Algerian woman to his side is turned on its head: from being a sign of national identity, the veil becomes literally a means of carrying forward the armed revolutionary struggle. In 'This is the voice of Algeria', Fanon describes the mobilizing effect of the nationalist radio station despite the frequently successful attempts of the French to jam its broadcasts. The war of the airwaves re-enacts the armed clash of the people and colonialism, foregrounding the idea of struggle in the minds of the audience. In each case, the attempt to break the people has, instead, the effect of uniting them.

The Wretched of the Earth [WE] was written in ten weeks in the last year of Fanon's life, after he had been diagnosed as suffering from leukaemia, and was published in French in 1961. *WE* is probably Fanon's most celebrated and influential as well as his most quotable work, in which he explicitly embraces the idea that the colonized can liberate themselves only through violent struggle. The first chapter of *WE*, 'Concerning Violence', begins with the assertion that 'decolonization is always a violent phenomenon'. However, Fanon asserts that while 'decolonization, which sets out to change the order of the world, is obviously a programme of complete disorder', it is, by definition, 'a historical process'. He elaborates this idea of the historical form and content of decolonization through a dialectical proposition: 'it is the settler who has brought the native into existence and who perpetuates his existence'. The idea that colonizer and colonized are mutually enforcing categories, and that colonization itself can be transcended only through violence, appears to owe something to the quasi-Hegelian and Manichaean model for considering colonialism evident in *BSWM*: the two terms of dialectical opposition, colonizer and colonized (or settler and native), are to be synthesized by a third, overarching term: violence. Violence, which is used to oppress and police the native, will be claimed and taken over by the native at the moment when, 'deciding to embody history in his own person, he surges into the forbidden quarters'. Violence, for Fanon, thus occupies both a material and a metaphysical status. Fanon's thesis is that through revolutionary violence, the colonized native gains the freedom to become human: 'decolonization is the veritable creation of new men . . . the "thing" which has been colonized becomes man during the same process by which it frees itself'. Echoing the theatrical metaphors of the opening paragraphs of **Mark**'s 'Eighteenth Brumaire', Fanon states that decolonization 'transforms spectators crushed with their inessentiality into privileged actors, with the grandiose glare of history's floodlights upon them'. For Fanon the settler has deprived the native of history, 'the settler makes history and is conscious of making it', but 'the history which he writes is not the history of the country which he plunders but the history of his own nation in regard to all that she skims off, all that she violates and starves'. The native puts an end to the history of colonization by bringing into existence the history of a nation, the history of decolonization. Colonialism is violence in its natural state, and it will yield only when it is confronted with greater violence.

Running through *WE* is a triadic structure (which clearly borrows from Hegel, Marx and Sartre). In the most anthologized section of the book, the chapter 'On National Culture', Fanon meditates on the role of the intellectual and the artist in the process of decolonization. He identifies three stages of native writing in the colonies: in the first the nativist writer wishes to assimilate the colonists' culture; in the second comes a reaction, a movement towards finding what is believed to be the authentically 'native' but which is in fact an overly sentimental search for 'roots'; third is the 'fighting' stage of revolutionary literature where the writer goes to the people, learns from them and teaches them to identify with the struggle. In this analysis, Fanon continues his vehement attack on Négritude, which he sees as stuck at the second of these stages in an essentialist negation of the colonized. Accompanying his focus on revolutionary intent is his scepticism of the bourgeois intellectual and, by contrast, his faith in the revolutionary possibilities of mass culture. Fanon is concerned that the native intellectual becomes complicit with the bourgeois intellectuals of the colonized culture and their faith in individualism, his guardianship of 'the Graeco-Latin pedestal' crumbling only when he comes into contact with the masses. This hostility to the bourgeoisie extends to his view that national consciousness in the hands of (bourgeois) nationalist politicians is in danger of becoming corrupted, since they are interested solely in espousing nationalism to further their own interests through negotiation and compromise with the settlers. In a typically dialectical shift of argument, Fanon suggests that at this stage only a transnational notion of liberation can achieve revolution; the only class with the awareness to achieve this goal is the masses. It is clear that towards the end of his life Fanon envisaged the war in Algeria as part of the liberation of the African continent as a whole from colonialism, not just one colony's struggle for freedom.

Toward the African Revolution (first published in 1964) comprises political essays, articles and notes unpublished in Fanon's lifetime. It includes his letter of resignation from the Blida-Joinville hospital, and essays on the wider question of Africa's liberation from colonialism.

Fanon's work has obviously had a profound impact on Third World political theory, and on theories of the relationship between race and class. His iconic status as a Che Guevara of black Africa was particularly potent in the 1960s; it was said after the Newark and Chicago riots of 1967 that 'every brother on the rooftops can quote Fanon'. More recently, in literary and cultural studies, Fanon's work has been seen as a cornerstone of debates within theories of colonialism and 'post-colonialism'. **Said**'s work, especially the insight in *Orientalism* that the separate identities of colonizer and colonized are ironically bound together in a mutually dependent way, owes much to Fanon's Manichean ideas (the insight in *WE* that 'Europe is literally the creation of the Third World's is one that underpins Said's own work). **Bhabha**'s more sophisticated reading finds in the split identity discussed in *BSWM* the basis of a radical, destabilizing strategy which can assist understanding of the 'post-colonial' predicament.

Main works

Black Skin, White Masks, trans. Charles Lam Markmann, Foreword Homi Bhabha (London: Pluto Press, 1986).

A Dying Colonialism, trans. Haakon Chevalier (London: Writers and Readers Publishing Co-operative, 1980).

The Wretched of the Earth, trans. Constance Farrington, Preface Jean–Paul Sartre (Harmondsworth: Penguin, 1967).

Toward the African Revolution, trans. Haakon Chevalier (London: Writers and Readers Publishing Co-operative, 1980).

Further reading

Bhabha, Homi, Foreword to *Black Skin, White Masks*, London: Pluto Press, 1986.

Bhabha, Homi, 'Interrogating identity: Frantz Fanon and the post-colonial prerogative', in *The Location of Culture*, London: Routledge, 1994, pp. 40–66.

Caute, David, *Fanon*, Fontana Modern Masters series, London: Fontana/Collins, 1970.

Feuchtwang, Stephan, 'Fanonian spaces', *New Formations*, 1 (1987): 124–130.

Said, Edward, in *Culture and Imperialism*, London: Chatto & Windus, 1993.

Taylor, Patrick, in *The Narrative of Liberation: Perspectives on Afro-Caribbean literature, popular culture, and politics*, Ithaca, NY: Cornell University Press, 1989.

Fish, Stanley (1938–)

Stanley Fish is the leading American proponent of reader-orientated criticism. He is Arts and Sciences Distinguished Professor of English and Professor of Law at Duke University, and has previously taught at the University of California, Berkeley and at Johns Hopkins University.

Fish's highly sophisticated criticism is based on the simple contention that the role of the reader in generating the 'end product' of reading (meaning or understanding) has usually been neglected or ignored. Fish redresses the balance in favour of the reader, provocatively declaring that criticism should address the effects of literature rather than examining the text as a thing in itself.

For much of his career, Fish's work has addressed the experience of reading Renaissance literature. His early emphasis on authorial psychology (evident in *John Skelton's Poetry*) was abandoned in *Surprised by Sin: The reader in Paradise Lost* which, as its subtitle suggests, is preoccupied with the position of the reader, a theme systematized in *Self-Consuming Artifacts* notion of 'affective stylistics', an analytical methodology which addresses the process of interpretation. Aspects of this methodology are defended, developed and in very significant ways recanted in the essays collected in *Is There a Text in this Class?*, where Fish introduces his concept of 'interpretive communities'.

John Skelton's Poetry claims to examine Skelton's 'relationship with that which is outside time', employing a New Critical methodology in which the literary artefact transcends the circumstances in which it was originally produced. Though historically specific analysis should not be completely abandoned, conventional literary historians are attacked for concentrating 'reductively' on context. Instead – and here Fish is borrowing from phenomenological criticism – the 'accidents of history' offer 'the raw material for a drama which is essentially interior'; Skelton's poetry must be addressed in terms of the 'psychological . . . history of its protagonist'.

In contrast, *Surprised by Sin* examines the reader's experiential patterns rather than the author's, the 'psychological effects' of literature rather than the psychological history of the authorial voice. These effects are often traumatic, as Milton 'consciously' offers a 'programme of reader harassment'. His 'purpose' is to 'educate the reader', and *Paradise Lost* is a *Bildungsroman* with the inexperienced protagonist the reader rather than a fictional character. The poem is coercive, offering encoded instructions as to how it should be read correctly. The narrative betrays its reader into assumptions which, later in the reading process, are shown to be mistaken; reading the story of the Fall enacts a similar psychological drama for the reader who, like Adam, comes to realize that he is 'fallen'. And, as in the best devotional writing, humiliation leads to repentance and a consequent ethical improvement; Milton has achieved his purpose. Fish's Milton is not very appealing, a stern moral disciplinarian inscribed in an overwhelming authorial presence analogous to the voice of God himself. Though *Surprised by Sin* instigates an emphasis on the importance of the position of the reader which has become significant in modern American literary studies, here the position of the reader is abject in relation to the coercive power of the text.

Fish is not afraid at this stage in his career to indulge in what **Wimsatt** famously labelled the 'intentional fallacy', and the key essay in *Self-Consuming Artifacts*, 'Literature in the reader: affective stylistics', is a prolonged assault on New Critical values. Wimsatt and **Beardsley**'s essay 'The affective fallacy' attacks 'a confusion between the poem and its results (what it *is* and what it *does*)', but Fish embraces the affective fallacy, recommending a method of analysis which focuses on the effects of a poem upon the 'informed reader' who possesses both linguistic and literary competence and 'does everything within his power to make himself informed'. The informed reader must attempt to approximate to a Renaissance man in order to interpret Renaissance writings; he must filter out what is 'personal and idiosyncratic and 1970sish' in his response. Again working against New Critical doctrine, Fish declares this a 'radically historical' methodology. He also quarrels with New Criticism's spatial model. Works of art are not immobile self-sufficient objects; they are available to us only in the temporal process of reading. 'Literature in the reader' is a manifesto for affective stylistics, and the rest of *Self-Consuming Artifacts* gives practical demonstrations of its experiential techniques. Fish details the process of reading 'one word after another', offering close readings of reading. This temporal model resembles a 'slow-motion camera', its analyses detailed to the point of laboriousness. Fish, like the New Critics, offers microscopic analysis, but here the emphasis is on the impact of poetic language rather than the language itself.

Fish has been described as a pure subjectivist who argues that the reader alone determines textual meaning. However, though *Self-Consuming Artifacts* declares, in terms that would lead some to argue that it celebrates the hegemony of the reader over the text, that 'the experience of an utterance . . . is its meaning', it should be registered that the text itself determines that experience, tells the reader how to read. Fish's position resembles that of **Iser**'s *The Act of Reading* (which examines how a text manipulates its reader) rather than of **Barthes**'s *S/Z* (which offers a textually productive reader). However, while Iser prefers literature characterized by 'gaps' (fragmentary narratives such as *Tristram Shandy*) which leave something to the reader's imagination, Fish chooses texts where 'the evidence of control is overwhelming'.

Only in *Is There a Text in this Class?* does Fish become one of the 'most radical of the "negative" hermeneuticians' (Suleiman, 1980). The book is the best introduction to Fish's work, charting his progress from textually determinate affective stylistics to a radical literary relativism, and finally to the synthesizing notion of interpretative communities. 'Interpreting the *Variorum*' rejects Fish's previous argument that texts encode instructions for their own interpretation; intention, rather than being something 'in' texts before the reader comes to them, is actually the product of interpretation. Its offspring essay, 'Interpreting "Interpreting the *Variorum*"', goes even further along the relativist path, dismissing the problematically monological implications of the earlier version of affective stylistics and arguing that the reader makes meaning, 'creates new texts' (echoing Barthes's notion of the reader as a 'producer of the text'). The essay repudiates *Surprised by Sin*'s ritual humiliation of the reader and, conversely, apotheosizes the reader. Affective criticism is a 'superior fiction' and, aware of its own subjective nature, is thus relieved 'of the obligation to be right (a standard which simply drops out)'. Instead, it must only 'be interesting'.

The later essays in *Is there a Text in this Class?* move away from the potentially solipsistic implications of such fearless subjectivism. 'Literature in the reader' prefers 'an acknowledged and controlled subjectivity' to an ultimately illusory objectivity and *Is There a Text in this Class?* attempts to describe how this controlled subjectivity might be attained. Confronted by the impasse between the objectivity of *Surprised by Sin* (which deals in correct interpretations) and the subjectivity of 'Interpreting "Interpreting the *Variorum*"' (which denies the possibility of correct interpretation), Fish uses the concept of interpretative communities to escape this subject/object dilemma. If 'authority' is not to be found in the text, and is available only as a product of interpretation, does this mean that it now lies with the reader? Not quite, for the reader is not an independent agent but a member of an interpretative community, a set of readers with shared norms and values. Our interpretative strategies are not uniquely ours, and our meanings are 'not individual specific or idiosyncratic but communal and conventional'. Authority is invested within the interpretative community 'made up of those who share interpretive strategies' rather than in the objective text or subjective reader. The possibility of objectively correct interpretation disappear; readings are 'good' readings when they meet with community acceptance. Fish subtly rescues reader-response theory from the charge of interpretative anarchy, but at the same time he rejects the possibility of claims to hermeneutical objectivity. Critics must acknowledge that the validity of their interpretations is sanctioned by the authority of the community of which they are members.

Though Fish is too much of an iconoclast to be the founder of a school or movement, his work (along with that of his continental peers Iser and **Jauss**) has been significant in contemporary Anglo-American literary theory in registering the importance of the role of the reader in constructing literary meaning and value.

Main works

John Skelton's Poetry, New Haven, CT and London: Yale University Press, 1965.

Surprised by Sin: The reader in Paradise Lost, London: Macmillan, 1967.

(ed.), *Seventeenth Century Prose: Modern essays in criticism*, New York: OUP, 1971.

Self-Consuming Artifacts: The experience of seventeenth century literature, Berkeley: University of California Press, 1972.

The Living Temple: George Herbert and Catechising, Berkeley: University of California Press, 1978.

Is There a Text in this Class? The authority of interpretive communities, Cambridge, MA: Harvard University Press, 1980.

Why Not Say What Happened?: Change, rhetoric, and the practice of theory in literary and legal studies, Oxford: Clarendon Press, 1988.

Further reading

Holub, Robert C., *Reception Theory: A critical introduction*, London and New York: Methuen, 1984.

Suleiman, Susan R. and Inge Crosman, *The Reader in the Text: Essays on audience and interpretation*, Princeton, NJ: Princeton University Press, 1980.

Tompkins, Jane, *Reader Response: From formalism to post-structuralism*, Baltimore, MD: Johns Hopkins University Press, 1980.

Fiske, John (1939–)

John Fiske was born in Bristol, and studied at Cambridge University. He has taught Communication Studies at Sheffield Polytechnic, the Polytechnic of Wales, and Curtin University, Perth, Australia. He is currently Professor of Communication Arts, University of Wisconsin-Madison, USA.

The central point in John Fiske's approach to cultural theory is the contention that popular culture is what people actively *make* from the repertoire of cultural texts and practices produced by the cultural industries. If the texts and practices of the cultural industries 'do not contain resources out of which the people can make their own meanings of their social relations and identities, they will be rejected and will fail in the marketplace. They will not be made popular' (*Reading the Popular*). From a position which draws creatively on the work of Pierre **Bourdieu**, Michel de Certeau, Michel **Foucault** and Antonio **Gramsci**, Fiske argues against the view that 'the capitalist cultural industries produce only an apparent variety of products whose variety is finally illusory, for they all promote the same capitalist ideology' (*Television Culture*). He also rejects the view that ordinary people are 'cultural dopes', a helpless and passive mass unable to discriminate and always at the ideological mercy of the cultural industries.

Fiske's position is built on the thesis that the commodities from which popular culture is made circulate in two simultaneous economies: the financial and the cultural. The financial economy is primarily concerned with exchange value, whereas the cultural is primarily focused on use – meanings, pleasures, and social identities. Although they are separate, there is continual interaction between the two economies. Analysis of both economies is necessary for a full understanding of a cultural text or practice. However, if we wish to understand the meanings, the pleasures, the popularity of a text or practice, our focus must be the cultural economy.

'Hill Street Blues', for example, was made by MTM and sold to NBC. NBC then 'sold' the audience to Mercedes-Benz, the sponsors of the programme. These exchanges, which feature 'Hill Street Blues' as a cultural commodity, all occur in the financial economy. If we turn our attention to the cultural economy, however, the series changes from a commodity (to be sold to NBC) to a text for the production of meaning(s) by and for its audience. In this way, the audience changes from a commodity to be sold by NBC to Mercedes-Benz, to a producer of meanings and pleasures. Fiske argues that 'the power of audiences-as-producers in the cultural economy is considerable'. The power of the audience, in his view, 'derives from the fact that meanings do not circulate in the cultural economy in the same way that wealth does in the financial' (*ibid.*). By this he means that meanings cannot be possessed in the same way that wealth can be possessed in the financial economy. Moreover, the production of meaning does not presuppose the clear distinction between production and consumption which prevails in the financial economy. The circulation of meaning and pleasure (and the use made of cultural texts and practices) is thus very difficult to control and predict. The power of the consumer is demonstrated in the fact that over 80 per cent of cultural commodities fail to find an audience. In an attempt to offset the costs of failure, the cultural industries produce 'repertoires' of goods in the hope of attracting an audience. But audiences constantly engage in 'semiotic guerilla warfare', countering the attempts of the cultural industries to incorporate them as commodity junkies, seeking instead to excorporate texts and practices to their own desires and purposes. Fiske cites the example of Australian Aboriginal viewers who appropriated 'Rambo' as a figure of resistance, relevant to their own political and cultural struggles. He also cites the example of Russian Jews watching *Dallas* in Israel and reading it as a self-conscious critique of capitalism.

Fiske develops his position to argue that resistance to the power of the powerful by those without power in the Western capitalist democracies takes two forms, semiotic and social. Semiotic resistance is mainly concerned with meanings, pleasures and social identities; social resistance with attempts to transform the socioeconomic system. He contends that 'the two are closely related, although relatively autonomous'. Popular culture operates mostly, 'but not exclusively', in the domain of the semiotic. It is a terrain for the struggle between the forces of homogenization and the forces of heterogeneity. From this perspective, popular culture is a semiotic battlefield on which a conflict is fought out between the forces of incorporation and the forces of resistance, between an imposed set of meanings, pleasures and social identities and the meanings, pleasures and social identities produced in acts of semiotic resistance. In Fiske's semiotic war scenario, the two economies tend to favour opposing sides of the struggle: the financial economy tends to favour the forces of incorporation and homogenization, the cultural economy tends to be more favourable to the forces of resistance and difference. Semiotic resistance, he argues, has the effect of continually undermining capitalism's attempt to secure ideological homogeneity: dominant meanings are challenged by subordinate meanings, thus the dominant class's intellectual and moral leadership is challenged.

In his most recent work, *Power Plays, Power Works*, Fiske shifts his focus from semiotics and meaning to power, knowledge and the body (a consolidation of Foucault's influence on his work) as he analyzes the recent series of cultural debates – multiculturalism, political correctness, and so on – which have taken place in the United States over recent years.

Fiske is seen by others who study popular culture within cultural studies (especially advocates of the political economy of culture approach) as the epitome of a supposed uncritical drift into cultural populism. His work is said continually to sacrifice questions of economic and technological determinations in favour of an almost total focus on strategies of popular production-in-consumption. Rather than grounding his analyses in the economic and political relations of production, he is said to celebrate, instead, consumption as pleasure, empowerment, resistance and popular discrimination. The implication of such critiques is that without attention to the mode of production, the determining site of cultural meaning, cultural analysis can have little of serious interest to say. This is based on the assumption that the way the cultural industries produce cultural products (mass production) determines how they can be consumed (mass consumption). Despite such criticisms, Fiske's work has proved influential, both in the field of communication studies and in the recent international development of British cultural studies.

Main works

Reading Television (with John Hartley), London: Methuen, 1978.

Introduction to Communication Studies, London: Methuen, 1982.

Television Culture, London: Methuen, 1987.

Reading the Popular, London: Unwin Hyman, 1989a.

Understanding Popular Culture, London: Unwin Hyman, 1989b.

Power Plays, Power Works, London: Verso, 1993.

Further reading

Golding, Peter and Graham Murdoch, 'Culture, communications and political economy', in *Mass Media and Society*, eds James Curran and Michael Gurevitch, London: Edward Arnold, 1991.

Harris, David, *From Class Struggle to the Politics of Pleasure: The effects of Gramscianism on cultural studies*, London: Routledge, 1992.

McGuigan, Jim, *Cultural Populism*, London: Routledge, 1992.

Storey, John, *An Introductory Guide to Cultural Theory and Popular Culture*, Hemel Hempstead: Harvester Wheatsheaf, 1993.

Turner, Graeme, *British Cultural Studies: An Introduction*, London: Unwin Hyman, 1990.

Foucault, Michel (1926–84)

Michel Foucault studied philosophy at the elite Ecole Normale Supérieure, Paris in the late 1940s, during which time he was briefly a member of the Parti Communiste Français (PCF). Foucault held teaching positions in a number of universities in France and elsewhere. He was teaching at the University of Tunis when the events of May 1968 were unfolding in Paris. On his return to France in late 1968, Foucault was appointed Professor of Philosophy at the new University of Vincennes; he became involved in the intense and often violent political activity that occurred there during 1969. In 1970 he was elected to the Chair of History of Systems of Thought at the prestigious Collège de France. During the 1970s Foucault was politically very active, especially on behalf of the Group for Information about Prisons (GIP), which sought to make the voices of prisoners heard. In the late 1970s and early 1980s he found a new audience in West Coast North American universities, which he visited frequently. He died of AIDS-related complaints in 1984.

Michel Foucault's texts are both histories and theoretical critiques which address a remarkable variety of social and cultural concerns: the construction of madness; the means by which the configuration known in France as 'the human sciences' became epistemologically organized; the institutions of modern punishment; and human sexuality. These concerns are often addressed in a stylistically dazzling and unconventional manner. In the light of this diversity and rhetorical brilliance, Foucault's question 'What is an Author?' (posed in an essay of that title; see *The Foucault Reader*) can be asked in respect of the problem of classifying his own writings and assessing their academic validity. The usual mutually exclusive disciplinary labels such as 'philosopher' and 'historian' that are used to ascribe academic writings, thereby converting them into authorial *oeuvres*, are difficult to apply in Foucault's case.

Neither are Foucault's writings characterized by methodological homogeneity. While all his texts meditate on the complex relationship between historically situated modes of discourse – which for Foucault are material practices which produce power – and forms of knowledge and subjectivity, Foucault's writings conceive of this relationship in different ways at different stages of his project.

Foucault's early writings focus on the primacy of discourse; this is to contest the Kantian transcendental notion of 'man' as a knowing, willing and judging subject *and* object of 'the human sciences'. In *Madness and Civilisation* (1961) his concern is with the 'mad', or those who have been deemed by the human science of psychiatry to be incapable of knowing, willing and judging in line with the protocols of reason. Far from being a transcendental given, Foucault argues that 'man' was an effect of history and discourse. Included in this effect was the emergence, during the classical age (the seventeenth and eighteenth centuries), of a new discourse on madness, which created new institutions enabling powers of confinement and restraint to be used against those who became subjected to 'reason's monologue on madness'. *The Order of Things* (1966) was a wider-ranging archaeology of the knowledges comprising the human sciences which, from being unthinkable during the Renaissance, emerged during the classical episteme and transformed themselves again during the modern episteme (nineteenth and twentieth centuries). From these distanciating archaeological investigations Foucault concluded that 'man' was a relatively recent invention. Balanced on the theshold of what seemed, in mid-1960s France, to be an intellectual revolution grounded in structural linguistics, which claimed that there could be no notion of 'man' which transcended discourse, Foucault famously proclaimed 'the death of man'. This obituary was aimed at the figure of 'man' inscribed within an apparently all-powerful discourse of modern rationality, a discourse which, for Foucault, was responsible for the oppression of those marginalized by its relentless desire to exclude difference.

During the 1970s Foucault's interests in marginalized groups extended to prisoners; he founded the GIP. *Discipline and Punish*, a history of the structures of modern punishment, was published in 1975. Foucault argues that between the eighteenth and nineteenth centuries the elements comprising the system of punishment practised by Western societies were redistributed. Whereas in the Renaissance and classical periods punishment was practised as a public display, during which the body was hideously mutilated so as to inscribe a sign of the sovereign's awesome power, in the modern period punishment has been taken inside the penitentiary or prison. The body is no longer the object of punishment; instead, the moral reform of the deviant is the desired end, which is to be brought about by means of surveillance and a disciplinary regime. To the standard argument that the modern state of affairs constitutes enlightenment in the administration of punishment, Foucault replies: power has simply transferred its sphere of operation – from the body to the 'soul' of the deviant.

It is possible to draw conclusions from this claim that point to subtle but important shifts in Foucault's methodology. First, Foucault argues that there is no relationship which exists outside the anonymous and continuous operations of power; a premise of *Madness and Civilisation* was that the 'truth' of madness could be unshackled from the monolithic power of the discourse of reason which silenced it, enabled to 'speak' and thus be liberated from domination. *Discipline and Punish* marks the point where Foucault formulates the 'power/knowledge' couplet: there is no 'truth', and all knowledge is a will to power – including Foucault's own writings. Second, Foucault is less of an archaeologist and more of a genealogist; if an archaeologist works as an austere positivist attempting to uncover the total relations that unite the discursive practices comprising an episteme, the genealogist has abandoned such totalizing intellectual ambitions. Instead, the genealogist is disturbing the received wisdom surrounding the relations between specific practices of past and present – such as punishment – for strategic local aims which are highly political – for instance, enabling prisoners to speak against the conditions in which they are held captive. Third, discourse – which shapes the conceptual horizons of a subject – is no longer the primary object of analysis; instead, the genealogist is equally concerned with non-discursive, institutionalized 'political technologies' – such as surveillance – and the way in which they shape and discipline the body of the individual subject.

Foucault's last major writings – three volumes known as *The History of Sexuality* (1976–84) – focus on the part played by sexuality in constructing the individual subject through networks of power and knowledge. To some extent the methodology is still that of *Discipline and Punish*: in Volume 1, *Introduction* (*La Volonté de Savoir* in the French), Foucault clears the ground for his forthcoming project by arguing against 'the repressive hypothesis'. According to this hypothesis, the nineteenth century was a period of sexual repression; this repression was lifted when **Freud**ian psychoanalysis enabled the 'deep truth' of the subject's sexuality to be spoken again. Foucault argues against this: even during the nineteenth century, the *medicalization* of sex ensured that its taboo status was voluminously committed to discourse, and monitored through surveillance and the practice of confession. The taboo on sex was a productive as opposed to a repressive form of power, and it actively created new forms of subjectivity. However, *The History of Sexuality* was clearly a difficult project to complete: originally planned as six volumes when the first part appeared in 1976, it changed shape considerably so that in the end it was to consist of four volumes, two of which appeared eight years later (1984) and one of which remained unpublished at Foucault's death. These last volumes have been seen as a new direction in Foucault's work. As commentators such as Peter Dews have pointed out, Volume 3, *The Care of the Self,* which examines the ethics of male friendship and homosexual practice in classical Roman culture, has a very different focus to Foucault's other writings. It is concerned with the fashioning of subjectivity as an aesthetic practice, but in being concerned with the self – other relation it is also a philosophy of ethics. Moreover, in being plainly written and scrupulously attentive to the scholarly conventions of intellectual history, it is markedly different to Foucault's other work.

Even so, intellectual and social historians have tended to reject Foucault's histories, claiming that they are under-researched and draw weighty conclusions from insufficient evidence. But Foucault playfully described his writings as 'fictions', and his challenges to the conventions of scholarship were clearly related to the searching questions he asked about the contingencies attached to the organization of knowledge. The critique levelled at him by philosophers of the critical theory tradition is more pressing. While Foucault's work is quite clearly calculated to function as a source of critique enabling subjects to resist systems of domination, it is hostile to **Marx**ist politics and philosophy. For Foucault during the 1960s and 1970s, political resistance had to be specific, localized and free from universal claims grounded in reason and appeals to justice. The latter would lead to totalitarianism, and Marxism was one such totalitarian form of power/knowledge which forged the institutional tyranny of the PCF (which the young Foucault had left, embittered) and the Soviet Gulag. However as Christopher **Norris** and Peter Dews have argued, Foucault's refusal to ground his theory of subjectivity in Kantian conditions of possibility, and his concommitant failure to follow **Adorno** and Horkheimer in discriminating dialectically between instrumental rationality and the promise of a benevolent reason, fatally disabled the viability of his project. For there are no rational grounds on which to communicate and seek support for ethically based political actions which resist systems of domination. Norris has argued that Foucault's return to Kant in late life (see the essay 'What is Enlightenment?') partially recognizes this, and Dews argues that Foucault came closer to the Frankfurt School's critique of instrumental rationality at the time when the ethics of *The Care of the Self* were being formulated.

Apart from Edward **Said**'s use of Foucault in *Orientalism*, Foucault's main impact on literary studies has been filtered through the movement known as the New Historicism, which has predominantly reread Renaissance texts and cultural practices in terms of the networks of power, or circuits of social energy, within which they were transacted.

The introductory chapter to Stephen **Greenblatt's** *Shakespearean Negoti- ations* (1987) gives a sense of the way in which Foucault has contributed to New Historicist methodology; and in *Power on Display* (1986) Leonard Tennenhouse utilizes Foucault's genealogical reading of punishment as a public display of sovereign power in the early modern era to reread Shakespearean drama as a parallel spectacle imitating and displaying political power. Tennenhouse also uses Foucault to assess critically the way in which history has produced a discourse and institutional space in which he can adopt a position as a Shakespearean critic. This points to the way in which, in some quarters, the institution of literary pedagogy has come to see itself in Foucauldian terms – that is to say, as a system of normalizing techniques grounded in power/knowledge. Ian Hunter's *Culture and Government* (1988), which draws on *Discipline and Punish* and *The History of Sexuality*, is exemplary in this respect. Hunter argues that British literary education has historically been concerned to make the pupils that it teaches not so much better selves, but more administrable subjects. In addition, Hunter's study is a genealogy in that it disturbs the continuity of the story that the cultural studies tradition of literary teaching – exemplified by F.R. **Leavis** and Raymond **Williams** – told about itself and its historical mission of liberating subjectivity.

Main works

Madness and Civilisation: A history of insanity in the age of Reason (1961), trans. Richard Howard, London: Tavistock, 1967.

The Order of Things: An archaeology of the human sciences (1966), trans. Alan Sheridan, London: Tavistock, 1974.

Discipline and Punish: The birth of the prison (1975), trans. Alan Sheridan, Harmondsworth: Pelican, 1977.

The Foucault Reader, Paul Rabinow, Harmondsworth: Peregrine, 1986; contains 'What is an author?', 'Nietzsche, genealogy, history', 'What is Enlightenment?'

The History of Sexuality: Volume One: An introduction (1976), trans. Robert Hurley, Harmondsworth: Penguin, 1990.

The History of Sexuality: Volume Three: The care of the self 1984, trans. Robert Hurley, Harmondsworth: Penguin, 1990.

Further reading

Dews, Peter, 'The return of the subject in late Foucault', *Radical Philosophy*, (1989): 37–41.

Dreyfus, Hubert and Paul Rabinow, *Michel Foucault: Beyond structuralism and hermeneutics*, Brighton: Harvester, 1982.

During, Simon, *Foucault and Literature: Towards a genealogy of writing*, London: Routledge, 1992.

Macey, David, *The Lives of Michel Foucault*, London: Hutchinson, 1993.

Norris, Christopher, ' "The undefined work of freedom": on Foucault and philosophy', *Southern Review*, 26, (1993): 270–75.

Glossary

Archaeology: – concept in Foucault's earlier work; a method of analyzing a discourse – either from the past, or active in the present – which suspends all questions of its truth and meaning, and seeks to grasp the discourse as an object displaying systematicity and rules of formation.

Episteme: – concept in Foucault's earlier work; the *total* set of relations which unite, at a given period, the discursive practices that give rise to epistemological figures, sciences and discursive regularities.

Genealogy: – concept in Foucault's later work derived from the philosophy of Nietzsche; genealogy is a historical method which seeks out locality, discontinuity and groundlessness in practices where conventional methods of interpretation have located universality, continuity and essence.

Freud, Sigmund (1856–1939)

Born in 1856 in Freiburg, Sigmund Freud first qualified as a Doctor of Medicine. After studying the use of hypnosis in the treatment of hysteria in Paris with Jean Martin Charcot, he set up a private practice in Vienna. With his interests moving away from neurology to psychopathology, he gave up hypnosis in favour of free association and what one of his patients named 'the talking cure'. His project is to study the unconscious, which he pursues through publications which include *The Interpretation of Dreams* (1900); *Three Essays on the Theory of Sexuality* (1905); *Totem and Taboo* (1914); *Introductory Lectures* (1917); *Beyond the Pleasure Principle* (1920); *The Ego and the Id* (1923); *Civilization and its Discontents* (1930). After the Nazis seized power he was forced to leave Vienna for London in 1938. He died there on 23 September 1939, leaving posterity to interrogate his lifetime's work in the founding of psychoanalysis.

'WOMAN FAINTS EVERY TIME SHE HEARS WORD SEX': on 5 July 1993 the London *Daily Mirror* reported a Cincinnati court case involving just what the headline said. The story poses vividly the possibility that normal, everyday human consciousness depends upon something radically other – not just 'subconscious', as popular usage prefers, but *unconscious*, such that it can be observed only in its effects and traces: in stories told by patients on the psychoanalyst's couch, in jokes, everyday verbal slips, memories of dreams, the well-attested phenomenon of hypnosis. If there were such an unconscious, how might it be rendered the object of a coherent study consistent with the usual methods of science?

Consider: while awake I am aware of a 'stream of consciousness' continuing in my mind without ever being spoken. That consciousness has been called as 'inner speech', yet it cannot be studied except when you talk about it, in which case it is something else, its mode transformed from inner to outer speech or writing. Inner speech is conscious: how much more challenging then to wish to analyze thought which is always unconscious! Where *is* the unconscious? How is it related to instincts, which clearly arise from the body?

For the seemingly impossible project of studying the pathways followed by the unconscious, Freud's point of departure was Darwin's materialist account of species and instincts. Freud approaches the unconscious as an effect derived from bodily instinct [German *Instinkt*] but differing from it in that it operates as drive [*Trieb*]. His repeated position is that drive [*Trieb*] 'appears to us as a concept on the frontier between the mental and the somatic, as the psychical representative [*Repräsentant*] of the stimuli originating from within the organism and reaching the mind' (*SE* 14). Whereas instinct links the human species to nature and the body, drive is specifically human, claiming the species for culture (it is unfortunate that the *Standard Edition* generally translates both *Instinkt* and *Trieb* as 'instinct'). Instinct compels an infant to seek milk so as to survive, but for the pleasure of the breast to be recalled – imagined – it must take the form of a *sign* for the bodily organ. Freud therefore tends to deconstruct the inherited Cartesian body/mind opposition, taking as his object of study the network of representations deriving from but always exceeding mere physical instinct.

The Darwinian argument is that in order to succeed, a species must develop not only instincts for survival – which (as many people know) Darwin monumentalized in *The Origin of Species* (1859) – but also instincts for reproduction, which (not so well known) he wrote up in

The Descent of Man and Selection in Relation to Sex (1871). Corresponding to these two instincts [German *Instinkt*] Freud began by theorizing narcissism and sexual desire as forms of drive [*Trieb*]. It is often thought that he was concerned only with sexuality, but this ignores his insistence that self-love is always involved in love for the other. (In his later work Freud grouped narcissism and desire together as life drives, and theorized that they were opposed to the death drive – see *Beyond the Pleasure Principle*).

Anthropology confirms that for the human species the incest taboo is universal, though the particular objects of its prohibition vary from culture to culture. As psychic correlative to the incest taboo, in the unconscious (and one main reason for its existence), Freud proposes that all human subjects must negotiate the Oedipus complex, though he remarks how few do so unscarred. The little boy takes (an image of) the mother as object of his drive but, pursuing this, becomes threatened with the prohibition on incest from law and the (image of the) father, a threat expressing itself in the idea of 'the worst thing in the world', symbolic castration. Acceding to that threat, he redirects his desire (if he does) from the mother to another adult woman, in the process identifying with the father. Freud constantly affirmed, however, that the human species was characterized by 'constitutional bisexuality' (*SE* 19), so that there is simultaneously a 'positive' and 'negative' pathway opened up – positive (for the boy) in his heterosexual desire for the mother/other woman; negative in his homosexual desire to become, like the mother, object of his father's desire.

At first Freud hoped that the same model would explain the development of female sexuality, but he soon found that it didn't – or didn't adequately. He pursued the topic in essays including 'Some psychological consequences of the anatomical distinction between the sexes' (1925) and 'Female sexuality' (1931), but without achieving a solution which has won general acceptance. It might be, as Freud suggested, that femininity originates earlier in the human subject and so is harder to analyze; or that – as Juliet Mitchell says in the preface to her book *Psychoanalysis and Feminism* – 'psychoanalysis is not a recommendation *for* a patriarchal society, but an analysis *of* one'. Debate continues.

For Freud, human culture necessarily represses and redirects the forceful effects of natural instincts in a process of gain and inevitable loss which renders us human and, potentially, civilized. He writes that 'the finding of an object is in fact a refinding of it' (*SE* 7); it is a consequence of the Oedipus complex that a predominantly heterosexual man, surrendering his first object, the symbolic mother, should try to refind her in another woman. Originating in the substitution of the real by a sign, drive always swerves through a series of replacements –

in place of the breast there is the thumb, then chocolates, chewing gum, cigarettes (alas), gin and tonic, kissing. No object ever makes good what provokes the process of refinding.

Phantasy (spelt thus to indicate its unconscious sources) is one major mode for this attempt to replace – dreams, for example. In phantasy dreams exhibit a manifest and a latent form: manifest being what we remember of a dream, its absurd little narrative, which conceals at the latent level a wish, both together making up the dream-work as an expression of the unconscious. This mechanism of concealment works variously by: (1) representing wishes in visual images and narratives; (2) displacing key features into marginal positions; (3) repeating and condensing motifs; (4) subjecting the whole to a revision acceptable to waking consciousness. Nightmares? But then not all wishes are nice ones, so there can be a troubling conflict between good and bad wishes, perhaps one strong enough to wake us.

Enjoyment of the aesthetic for Freud is essentially the pleasure of dreamlike phantasy initiated by a formal organization (Freud says the work/play of the signifier in itself gives 'fore-pleasure'). In 'Creative writers and day-dreaming' (1908) he argues that children begin by playing roles ('You be the mummy and I'll . . .') until, at a certain stage, actual role-playing is replaced by telling stories. Adults go on imagining themselves as main actors in wish-fulfilling scenarios, but just because those daydreams are so obviously self-concerned, we would be embarrassed to narrate them publicly. However, the artist knows how to link such phantasies to formal pleasures and, disguising any over-personal features, transmute them into acceptable public images and narratives.

Freud anticipated Roland **Barthes** in proclaiming the death of the author. In his later work, turning away from the personal towards the collective and cultural, he reiterates in his *Introductory Lectures* (1917) that aesthetic texts are like a daydream, worked over so as to 'lose what is too personal about them', toned down so they do not 'betray their origin from proscribed sources', shaped formally with a particular material 'until it has become a faithful image' of that phantasy, yielding pleasure (*SE* 16). The artist thus drops out of the picture, for his or her text 'makes it possible for other people once more to derive consolation and alleviation from their own sources of pleasure in their unconscious which have become inaccessible to them' (*ibid.*). We, the public, refind our pleasures in the text. On this showing, presumably, Shakespeare's *Hamlet* offers a handful of phantasy pleasures – of identifying with an effortlessly eloquent and superior hero who struggles with his oedipal problems yet wins through to die nobly; two heroines who (as in the patriarchal scenario) suffer for love; a villain we might like to be, but one whose evil is finally destroyed for us in the working out of the plot. There are also the pleasures of an endlessly inventive narrative, delight in the high formality of the poetry as well as a rich plurality of comic characters and jokes, both tasteful and indecent (isn't this Shakespeare's funniest play?). And overall a dark intangible 'atmosphere', the realized 'world of Denmark', full of players and ghosts, raging seas and pantomime gravediggers. As Freud notes regarding *Hamlet* in *The Interpretation of Dreams*: 'all genuinely creative writings are the product of more than a single motive . . . and are open to more than a single interpretation' (*SE* 4).

It would be hard to exaggerate the enormous impact of Freud's writing on literary and cultural theory. Three strands of thought may be distinguished, concerned with the level of signified meaning; form and the operation of the signifier; and, third, the value of psychoanalysis as a model for textual interpretation.

A first application of psychoanalysis targeted the artist and his or her particular unconscious and phantasies. In 1910 Freud pioneered this approach in his book on *Leonardo da Vinci*. He also wrote in 'Some character-types met with in psychoanalytic work' (1916) about stage characters as if they were patients on the couch, psychoanalyzing Lady Macbeth and, even more suggestively, Rebecca in Ibsen's *Rosmersholm*. During the 1960s psychoanalysis re-entered the domain of textual theory in association especially with post-structuralism. Attention now shifts to the text/reader relationship, and the formal work of textuality in affording an unconscious position and points of identification for the reader.

English theorists grouped around the film journal *Screen*, including Stephen Heath and Colin **MacCabe**, set out to theorize the contrasted textual effects of realism and modernism. In a series of essays from the early 1970s Stephen Heath, leaning on Barthes, initiates an analysis of the process of transformation and closure enacted by narrative as an effect in and for the subject. And this line of inquiry is brilliantly worked through by Peter Brooks in *Reading for Plot: Design and intention in narrative* (Oxford, 1984) as an endless interaction of closure and process, the death drive and desire.

Psychoanalysis, more perhaps than any other theoretical project, poses the question of gender. It renders inescapable the issue of gendered reading, and specifically the possibility that forms of textuality and organizations of the signifier may themselves be inscribed in terms of masculine and feminine. Hélène **Cixous** and Luce **Irigary** draw heavily on psychoanalysis for a dazzlingly suggestive set of writings exploring the notion of *écriture féminine*, 'feminine writing'.

These are applications of psychoanalysis to the text. Yet perhaps psychoanalysis may count most because it holds out a paradigm for textual interpretation and theorization. In principle, for psychoanalysis nothing is neutral, nothing immune to unconscious charge of some degree. So in the aesthetic text no feature, no detail, can be set aside as disinterested, undifferentiated, non-signifying. Like the split which instates opposition between conscious and unconscious, or that between manifest and latent content in the dream-work, what orders the aesthetic text is on the surface an avowed project (Hamlet must avenge his father) effacing a volume of meanings which are a condition for that 'official' project. In *Theory of Literary Production* (1966) Pierre **Macherey** seized on the psychoanalytic model to argue that the literary text is always incomplete, always divided from itself, so that what it says depends upon what must remain unspoken – an account followed through by American deconstruction (see **de Man**, **Bloom**, and the work of the Yale School).

Psychoanalytic interpretation is endless, as is the reading and rereading of the text. Freud introduced the concept of 'deferred interpretation', as when the very young child, passing from the oral to the genital phase, reinterprets the earlier experience of weaning and loss of the breast in the context of the subsequent encounter with castrating threat. In his essay 'Freud and the scene of writing', **Derrida** takes up deferred interpretation to argue that subjectivity is thus without point of origin and without destination, its causes, as it were, existing only in its effects. In default of a truth or transcendental signifier which might bring aesthetic reading and textual theorization to an end once and for all, psychoanalysis may be the least inappropriate model for textual analysis.

Main works

The Standard Edition of the Complete Psychological Works (SE), trans. James Strachey, 24 vols, London: Hogarth Press and the Institute of Psycho-Analysis, 1953–74; see also *Penguin Freud Library*, 15 vols, Harmondsworth, Middlesex, 1974–86.

Further reading

Brennan, Teresa, *The Interpretation of the Flesh: Freud and femininity*, London: Routledge, 1992.

Lacan, Jacques, *Ecrits: A selection*, London: Tavistock, 1977.

Laplanche, J. and J-B. Pontalis, *The Language of Psycho-Analysis*, trans. Donald Nicholson-Smith, London: Hogarth Press and the Institute of Psycho-Analysis, 1980.

Mitchell, Juliet, *Psychoanalysis and Feminism*, Harmondsworth: Penguin, 1975.

Sulloway, Frank, *Freud: Biologist of the mind*, London: Fontana, 1980.

Weber, Samuel, *Legend of Freud*, Minneapolis: University of Minnesota Press, 1982.

Frye, Northrop (1912–91)

Northrop Frye was born in Quebec in 1912; he was educated at Victoria College in Toronto and Merton College, Oxford. After Oxford he returned to Victoria, where he spent the rest of his career as, successively, Lecturer, Professor, Principal and Chancellor. He died in 1991.

Northrop Frye once called **Freud** a 'great genius, with his colossal simplifying vision'. The description fits Frye himself. His *Anatomy of Criticism* attempts to explain the organizing principles of literature as a whole. Anglo-Saxon literature and high modernism, *The Decameron* and *Huckleberry Finn* – all are slotted neatly into its schemata. This dazzlingly erudite work offers a homogenizing (and ultimately tendentious) account of the whole history of (Western) literature. Frye grants literary criticism the status of a science. Science emphasizes the principle of causality, and so does Frye; literature's roots lie in myth. The *Anatomy* is the classic work of the archetypal criticism which challenged the New Criticism's hermeneutical hegemony during the 1950s and 1960s.

Frye's first book, *Fearful Symmetry: A study of William Blake*, was instrumental in rescuing Romantic studies from a critical neglect inspired by T.S. Eliot and **Leavis**. It registers the importance of myth to literature, dismissing the argument that Blake, dissatisfied with Classical and orthodox Christian myth, constructs a new, supposedly 'private' mythology. Frye repudiates the very possibility of 'private symbolism'; Blake's iconoclastic, supposedly chaotic, mythopoetical work is actually carefully ordered. It also possesses a large number of similarities to other poetry; the most 'individual' and 'original' poetry participates in the ordered conventions of a wider 'literary universe'.

The *Anatomy* is a systematic attempt to map the contours of this universe, investigating the modes, symbols, myths and genres which make up its 'total form'. Appropriately, this anatomizing of the body imaginative is described as a 'science'. In a procedure analogous to scientific method, Frye's 'inductive survey' lets the general postulates of criticism develop from the experimental data (poems, plays and novels) which it studies. Classification is the first principle of the natural sciences, the means of discovering order and unity in the world, and Frye draws up a complex set of taxonomic structures: seven categories of imagery, five structures of narrative, four archetypal narratives, and so on. (His attempt to identify the underlying system which informs individual works has sometimes led him to be classed as a structuralist.) 'Theory of modes' begins by classifying the literary world according to a (descending) scale: 'myth', 'romance', 'high mimetic', 'low mimetic' and 'ironic'. Each 'mode' successively dominates the 'five epochs' of literature since the Dark Ages: Celtic and Teutonic epic, the medieval period, the Renaissance, the eighteenth and nineteenth centuries, and the modern.

'Theory of symbols' examines the concept of 'archetypes'. Just as individual myths link together in a mythology, so literature has archetypes, recurring symbols which connect one work with another. Archetypal criticism, in addressing these 'associative clusters', is able to 'fit poems into the body of poetry as a whole'. Archetypes are thus the key to the system, the means whereby the fundamental unity of the literary universe can be demonstrated. How archetypal criticism works in practice is exemplified in an extended simile in which looking at a painting illustrates different critical approaches. Standing near a painting and analyzing its brushwork is analogous to New Critical close reading. 'At a little distance back', the picture is read for its 'content'. The archetypal critic is positioned still further away, to the point where the painting's figurative content blurs. Here 'organizing principles' are more apparent than specific subject: 'At a great distance from, say, a Madonna, we can see nothing but the archetype of the Madonna.' The same applies to literature: 'If we "stand back" from Spenser's *Mutabilitie Cantoes*, we see a background of ordered circular light and a sinister black mass thrusting up into the lower foreground.' 'Standing back' allows a work's archetypes to become apparent, and the critic to notice its associative clusters. Thus Spenser's 'sinister black mass' is 'much the same archetypal shape we see in the opening of the Book of Job'. Myth predates literature and then merges into it, becoming its key structural principle. Archetypal analysis can track the operation of 'displaced' myth in the most realistic narrative. Standing back from *Germinal*, for example, reveals its dependence on myth (its 'archetypal organization'). Conversely, moving closer towards Zola's text illustrates the process of displacement; the mythical modulates back into the realistic.

Frye attempts to demystify the study of literature, replacing the 'mystery-religion without a gospel' of contemporary criticism with an egalitarian and coherent methodology which any 'intelligent nineteen-year-old' can understand. Criticism is not about an elite set of 'sensitive' initiates evaluating the 'greatness' of a particular writer; the *Anatomy* offers the idea (startling in its time) that value judgements are irrelevant to literary criticism. They are simply documents in the history of taste: 'To say Shakespeare was a great poet is a value-judgement and not a shred of systematic criticism can ever be attached to it.' This is part of Frye's repudiation (in his benign, 'well-tempered' critical manner) of certain key tenets of New Critical orthodoxy. Instead of attending to linguistic minutiae, he offers a synoptic approach. Poems are part of the literary universe rather than self-contained verbal icons. Dismissing New Criticism's autotelic focus, Frye insists that literature should be contextualized. This context is not historical or sociological; Frye addresses 'poetic society', not social context. His 'historical approach' involves 'a general history of literature, and not simply the assimilating of criticism to some other kind of history'. He dismisses literary critics who import the 'conceptual framework' of non-literary disciplines. A poem's context is to be found 'within literature itself'. Literature 'shapes itself, and is not shaped externally'. There is a close analogy between Frye's account of the literary universe and post-**Saussurean** views of language; both are self-referring systems.

Though Frye quarrels with New Criticism, his work often develops from its positions (and sometimes anticipates those of its truculent offspring, deconstruction). In one sense archetypal criticism is New Criticism writ large, examining the massive 'self-contained literary universe' rather than the self-contained verbal icon. Frye worries that perhaps the *Anatomy* 'merely restore[s] the aesthetic view on a gigantic scale'. Archetypal criticism also participates in the New Critical project of banishing the author from the central place in critical discourse. And, like the deconstructors, the great Romanticist Frye has little time for the Romantic concepts of originality and the creative subject. The 'onlie begettor' of Shakespeare's sonnets is not 'Shakespeare himself', but 'the form of the poem itself'. Seeing the author as the authentic source of meaning is an illusion. Frye notes that what classical authors call the Muse is actually the 'universal spirit of poetry', the circumambient literary universe which shapes individual poems. More recent critics might call it intertextuality and, for Frye, a poet's work is intertextually conditioned: 'Poetry can only be made out of other poems'.

Paradoxically, the *Anatomy*'s 'Tentative Conclusion' seems to problematize the scientific paradigms which inform and organize the work. Is science a 'verbal' structure which is 'informed by the same kinds of myths or metaphor' which condition literature? The point has wider philosophical significance; as 'all structures in words are partly rhetorical', it follows that a 'philosophical verbal structure free of rhetorical elements is an illusion'. Claims to knowledge are, in part, dependent upon metaphor. If that is so, then 'our literary universe has extended into a verbal universe'. Is there anything outside this textual universe? In his discussion of the 'informing of metaphysical and theological constructs by poetic myths', Frye hovers close to deconstruction.

However, he finally shies away from his own implications and argues that a rhetorical analysis which contends that 'theology, metaphysics, law' are based upon 'metaphors or myths' is ultimately reductive.

As most of his later work simply offers practical demonstrations of the *Anatomy*'s theoretical concerns, it is upon *Fearful Symmetry*, which finally admitted Blake to the Romantic canon and was crucial to the revival of Romantic studies, and the *Anatomy*, which remains archetypal criticism's finest hour, that Frye's critical reputation ultimately depends. More generally, his professional, 'scientific' approach was instrumental in making academic literary criticism seem a vital, intellectually respectable activity.

Main works

Fearful Symmetry: A Study of William Blake, Princeton, NJ: Princeton University Press, 1947.

Anatomy of Criticism: Four essays, Princeton, NJ: Princeton University Press, 1957.

The Educated Imagination, Toronto: CBC, 1963a.

Fables of Identity: Studies in poetic mythology, New York: Harcourt, Brace & World, 1963a.

T.S. Eliot, New York and Edinburgh: Oliver and Boyd, 1963b.

The Well-Tempered Critic, Bloomington, IN: Indiana University Press, 1963c.

A Natural Perspective: The development of Shakespearean comedy and romance, New York: Columbia University Press, 1965.

The Return of Eden: Five essays on Milton's epics, Toronto: University of Toronto Press, 1966.

The Modern Century, Toronto: Oxford University Press, 1967a.

Fools of Time: Studies in Shakespearean tragedy, Toronto: University of Toronto Press, 1967b.

A Study of English Romanticism, New York: Random House, 1968.

The Stubborn Structure: Essays on criticism and society, London: Methuen, 1970.

The Bush Garden: Essays on the Canadian imagination, Toronto: Anansi, 1971a.

The Critical Path: An essay on the social context of literary criticism, Bloomington, IN: Indiana University Press, 1971b.

The Secular Scripture: A study of the structure of romance, Cambridge, MA and London: Harvard University Press, 1976.

Spiritus Mundi: Essays on literature, myth and society, Bloomington, IN: Indiana University Press, 1977.

The Great Code: The Bible and literature, Toronto: Toronto Academic Press, 1982.

Further reading

Denham, John D., *Northrop Frye and Critical Method*, University Park, PA and London: Pennsylvania State University Press, 1978.

Hamilton, A.C., *Northrop Frye: An Anatomy of his Criticism*, Toronto, Buffalo and London: University of Toronto Press, 1990.

Krieger, Murray (ed.), *Northrop Frye in Modern Criticism*, New York: Columbia University Press, 1966.

G

Gadamer, Hans-Georg (1900–)

Gadamer studied philosophy and classics at Marburg, West Germany, and received his doctorate in 1922. He then taught philosophy successively at Marburg (1922–37), Leipzig (1938–47), Frankfurt (1947–9) and Heidelberg (1949–68). His first mentor was the philosopher Heidegger, and in many ways Gadamer's work has been an ongoing debate with and development of Heidegger's thought.

Gadamer's ideas, as articulated in his *magnum opus, Truth and Method* (1975), owe their origin and form to a debate within idealist philosophy that begins with the work of Schleiermacher and Dilthey, both of whom sought to challenge the model of neutral, objective 'explanation' of phenomena characterized by the natural sciences. The social and human sciences, in Dilthey's view, were not susceptible to the same certainty of explanation or reliability of method as natural science. Hermeneutics, from being associated with the elucidation of ancient texts or the teasing out of legal complexities, becomes in the late nineteenth century a more effective model of understanding (for the 'Human Sciences') than the explanatory models that had proved so useful to science. Both Schleiermacher and Dilthey were concerned to articulate an epistemology and a method that would give clear guidelines to the social scientist or interpreter of texts. E.D. **Hirsch**, who has sought to reinstate 'intentionality' as a key element of the hermeneutic process, is a contemporary follower of this line of thinking.

It is in opposition to this search for a method of validating one's interpretations that Gadamer's reflections have been directed. For Gadamer, 'Truth' and 'Method' are in opposition. Any allegiance to or adoption of a particular 'method' necessarily precludes other possible ways of coming at the 'truth', of arriving at an understanding; and any understanding arrived at will always be incomplete, unfinished. For Gadamer, the question of 'understanding' [*Verstehen*] is an ontological question, for in his view it is our nature as human beings that we are defined and limited by our entrapment in language and time. Like translation, all attempts to understand anything involve us in the subjective process of 'interpreting', using our partial and prejudiced personal language to render things meaningful. No method can ever guarantee that we have arrived at a complete or finite understanding: there will always be something that we have overlooked or which, by virtue of our entrapment in time and place, may yet come to light to modify our grasp or meaning. For Gadamer, the 'hermeneutic circle' (the dialectical relation between parts and wholes) is an existential condition: as historical beings we are part of a process which is incomplete; we cannot stand 'outside' of time to see it whole. The most we can do is to strive for an ever greater awareness of our own 'prejudices' (those preconceptions which we carry with us as linguistic and historical beings) and a preparedness to be 'open' to other ways of understanding things.

What Gadamer rejects is the idea that we can adopt a position of objectivity outside of the language or the time that determines us. He is thus challenging one of the most cherished of assumptions about knowledge that have held sway since the Enlightenment: that knowledge should be impartial, neutral, objective. He is perhaps being deliberately provocative in identifying what he calls 'prejudice' as the primary and inescapable element in the hermeneutic process. Not only should we become conscious of all the prejudices that affect our understandings, but prejudice can and should be utilized in a positive manner. As many feminist interpreters have recognized, our gender constitutes a prejudice which can afford us vital insights as well as create difficulties and inhibit understanding. Our 'prejudices' may be obstacles to knowledge, but they cannot be thought away, and in Gadamer's hermeneutic project they serve as the substance through which we come to understand the other, be it other minds or beings that speak to us through texts and across time.

Two concepts closely linked in Gadamer's work are 'fusion of horizons' and 'effective history'. The former represents the goal towards which the hermeneut strives – and it is Gadamer's alternative to the more determinate outcomes of Diltheyan or Hirschean hermeneutics. Thus, rather than being able to assert that something has been understood 'as it is in itself' – a kind of Platonic ideal – Gadamer promotes the idea that the understanding of the other or the past is a process of accommodation whereby our enlarged understanding brings us closer to that which we seek to know, but that knowledge also involves a movement towards us of our subject. Where Schleiermacher, Dilthey and Hirsch retain a clear sense of the subject devising means of understanding the object, Gadamer repudiates the possibility of such a clear subject–object split. Effective history is his term for the process which renders the past understandable; but understandable not as an object to be known 'as it is in itself', but in terms of the effects or influence which enable things to be known. It is, once again, the hermeneutic circle that makes things meaningful in terms of their relationships, their contingency and contiguity – and we can never step outside this circle.

Gadamer's impact has been profound – not only within the philosophical domain of phenomenology and hermeneutic theory itself, but markedly in his influence on the debates concerning interpretative social science and literary theory and practice (his influence on Hans Robert **Jauss**'s reception-theory, for example, has been substantial). The term 'hermeneutic' has become a commonplace in literary critical discussion and commentary – so much so that it is in danger of becoming a mere synonym for 'interpretation' or 'interpretative method'. Gadamer's reflections on hermeneutics have begun to have an impact on literary theory and promise to continue to do so, particularly in the light of the re-emergence of the historical in interpretative studies. His debate with **Habermas** signals the ongoing challenge his hermeneutic (idealist) reflections pose to any theories which recognize language and history as determinates of meaning. At least two aspects of Gadamer's work have proved contentious. One is his reliance on a notion of 'tradition' which finds him falling back on a rather conservative and, surprisingly, uncritical sense of history. His own sense of the historical or artistic past, which serves to provide him with most of his examples, seems very much a product of an haut-bourgeois, classical education. This, coupled with his apparent inability to conceive of a position which would allow the hermeneut to recognize ideology (Habermas's critique), remains a vulnerable area. The other issue, his persistent refusal to see his own work as proffering anything like a methodology, has recently been taken up by G.B. Madison who has argued, persuasively, that it is possible to derive from Gadamer's writings a set of methodological guidelines which might usefully serve future generations of textual interpreters.

Main works

Truth and Method, trans. G. Barden and W.G. Doerpal, Sheed & Ward, 1975; 2nd edn 1979.

Kleine Schriften (3 vols; Tübingen: J.C.B. Mohr, 1967–72: vol.1: *Philosophie und Hermeneutik*; vol.2: *Interpretationen*; vol. 3: *Idee und Sprache*). A number of these essays have been collected in English translation in *Philosophical Hermeneutics*, trans. and ed. David E. Linge, Berkeley, Los

Angeles and London: University of California Press, 1976; and in *The Relevance of the Beautiful and Other Essays*, trans. Nicholas Walker, ed. Robert Bernasconi, Cambridge: Cambridge University Press, 1986. Gadamer's response to Habermas's criticism of 1967 appeared in *Kleine Schriften*, vol. 1., trans. Jerry Dibble as 'Rhetoric, hermeneutics, and the critique of ideology: metacritical comments on *Truth and Method*', this essay can be found in *The Hermeneutics Reader*, ed. Kurt Mueller–Vollmer, Oxford: Blackwell, 1986, pp. 274–92.

Hegel's Dialectic, trans. P. Christopher Smith, New Haven, CT: Yale University Press, 1976.

Dialogue and Dialectic: Eight hermeneutical studies on Plato, trans. and intro. P. Christopher Smith, New Haven, CT: Yale University Press, 1980.

Reason in the Age of Science, trans. F.G. Lawrence, Cambridge, MA: MIT Press, 1981.

Lectures on Philosophical Hermeneutics, Pretoria: Universiteit van Pretoria, 1982.

Philosophical Apprenticeships, trans. Robert R. Sullivan, Cambridge, MA: MIT Press, 1985.

The Idea of the Good in Platonic–Aristotelian Philosophy, trans. P. Christopher Smith, New Haven, CT: Yale University Press, 1986.

Further reading

Bleicher, Josef, *Contemporary Hermeneutics: Hermeneutics as method, philosophy and critique*, London: Routledge & Kegan Paul, 1980.

Hoy, David Couzens, *The Critical Circle: Literature, history, and philosophical hermeneutics*, Berkeley, Los Angeles and London: University of California Press, 1982.

Madison, G.B., *The Hermeneutics of Postmodernity: Figures and themes*, Bloomington and Indianapolis: Indiana University Press, 1990.

Mendelson, Jack, 'The Habermas–Gadamer debate', *New German Critique*, 18 (1979): 44–73.

Newton, K.M., *Interpreting the Text: A critical introduction to the theory and practice of literary interpretation*, Hemel Hempstead: Harvester Wheatsheaf, 1990.

Palmer, Richard E., *Hermeneutics: Interpretation Theory in Schleiermacher,*

Dilthey, Heidegger, and Gadamer, Evanston, IL: Northwestern University Press, 1969.

Gates, Henry Louis Jr (1950–)

Henry Louis Gates Jr, Professor in the Humanities and Chair of the Afro-American Studies Department at Harvard University, is – along with Houston A. Baker Jr – the most prominent male theorist of African-American literature of his generation and, with a number of colleagues, among the first to use the insights of continental critical theory, from structuralism to more recent developments, to examine black American literature. He has argued that black texts need a critical method of close reading that is alive to their structural, rhetorical and deeply figural nature which, for Gates, is the distinguishing feature of black literary language. Along with his own writings, he has edited the two most influential collections of essays on black literature and literary theory.

Gates has also has been both an important critic of the American literary canon and instrumental in expanding it through his articles, his books, and especially through his general editorship of the Schomburg Library, a huge series of nineteenth-century texts by black women, with over thirty in print at the most recent count, and through his involvement with the new *Norton Anthology of Afro-American Literature*. Furthermore, in a number of articles in both academic and mass-circulation journals since the mid-1980s, he has made a significant contribution to the fraught debate in America on 'multiculturalism'. His most recent book is an eloquent defence of the concept.

Gates took a degree in history at Yale and, at 22, became a correspondent at the London bureau of *Time* magazine, but finally he studied for a doctorate on black literature at Cambridge and began an academic career in the late 1970s.

As an expert on black literature schooled in what many radical black writers would call a 'white' tradition, that of contemporary critical theory, Gates's work takes the form of a meditation not just on what theory has to say to about black texts, but also on what these texts already know about the nature of signification, a notion that is at the heart of his theory of 'signifyin(g)'. Gates wonders whether it is possible or legitimate 'to apply' simply theorical concepts to black texts and, more importantly, what these theories would have to say about such essentialist concepts as the 'black experience' or blackness itself? In his introduction to *Figures in Black* (1987), he asks: 'can it be a legitimate exercise to translate theories drawn from a literary tradition that has often been perpetrated by white males who represent blacks in their fiction as barely human?'. For Gates, '*any* tool that enables the critic to explain the language of a text is an appropriate tool. For it is language, the black language of the black text, that expresses the distinctive quality of our tradition'.

In 'Criticism in the jungle' (1984), he suggests that the application of modes of reading found outside the black tradition to black texts can transform both theory and text, and that the black literary tradition needs, for its own sustenance and growth, the sorts of readings that the contemporary literary critic can render. In an interview, Gates says that he had noticed a resistance, among critics of Afro-American literature, to the most exciting developments in literary analysis; they were dismissed as 'white', and therefore alien, an affront to the putative integrity of black literature. He found it strange that anyone would want to turn such impure, relational and cross-fertilized writing into 'a sump of essentialism' (Ward, 1991).

We can see a potential contradiction, impossible for Gates finally to resolve, between the sceptical anti-essentialism of contemporary critical theory and the American black tradition of unearthing a repressed, authentic black voice in the face of slavery, and its historical consequence: racism, institutional and otherwise. For Gates, 'race' is not an essence or a thing in itself. Ethnic identity is a social construction; you learn, as did Gates himself, how to be 'black', for instance, through reading people of colour writing precisely about discovering that they were black (Ward, 1991), while never forgetting that you will be perceived as essentially black by many of the dominant systems of meaning.

A good deal of criticism has revolved around a similar question of representing blackness – or, more broadly, the black experience – and both Houston A. Baker Jr and Gates have argued that it ultimately fails to address texts as texts – complex organizations of language – and it is the peculiarities of this language that critics should examine. This project has a central place in Gates's work; in 'Criticism in the jungle' he suggests that because criticism of black texts has concentrated on their polemical, mimetic and social functions, their structure has been repressed and treated as if it were, in Gates's phrase, 'transparent . . . invisible . . . a one-dimensional document'. This is mainly because the black text's most important function has been seen as its ability to contain 'black experience'. Texts were analyzed in terms of their content, 'as if a literary form were a vacant enclosure that could be filled with this or that matter' (Gates, 1987).

Although this was understandable in claiming an essential humanity for people of colour in the context of a predominantly racist society, it ignores the way a whole range of African-American oral and written texts operate, and this can be seen by examining the black tradition of figuration, of 'saying one thing to mean something quite other', a technique cultivated by the American slave and an important tactic of survival in oppressive Western cultures (Gates, 1984). Gates has a very different approach in which, rather than applying literary theory to black texts, there is a form of dialectical play between figural, rhetorical criticism and the black figural tradition he calls signifyin(g). In an important formulation in 'Criticism in the jungle', Gates suggests that black literary criticism's challenge is to derive its principles from the black tradition itself, using the idiom of critical theory 'but also in the idiom which constitutes the 'language of blackness', the signifyin(g) difference which makes the black tradition our very own'.

The kernel of Gates's theory in its most influential form is expressed in his much-anthologized essay 'The blackness of blackness: a critique of the sign and the Signifying Monkey', which first appeared in the prestigious literary journal *Critical Inquiry* in 1983. 'Signifyin(g)' is Gates's term; it refers both to the African-American tradition, with its roots in African folk myth, and to contemporary critical theory which has its roots in the linguistic theories of **Saussure**. 'Signifyin(g)' is a form of critical parody; it has been a term in black vernacular for at least two centuries, and refers to the verbal skill to parody, reverse and revise another's language. The figure of the Signifying Monkey can be found in folktales from Africa, the Caribbean and the Americas. It is a creature which is a 'mediator', and these 'mediations' are tricks of language in which a story is first heard, then twisted and related to a third party, repeated but with trouble-making differences. Gates suggests that a type of signifyin(g) is characteristic of African-American literature, and his essay gives an example of it in the work of a number of black novelists.

Signifyin(g) or critical parody is repetition with a critical difference. Gates shows how Ralph Ellison's modernist *Invisible Man* (1952) 'signifies' on the titles of two earlier, more naturalistic works by Richard Wright, *Black Boy* (1945) and *Native Son* (1940). Wright's titles suggest a powerful racial identity. Ellison's title, however, is an ironic, anxious response signifying the problematical nature of race and identity. Ishmael Reed's post-modern novel *Mumbo Jumbo* (1972) plays variations on these and other novels in the black tradition, its very title the English-language parody of black language itself, but also a Swahili greeting. For Gates, *Mumbo Jumbo's* 'double-voicedness' represents the use of 'standard' or 'Western' traditions along with the vernacular black tradition. Reed is signifyin(g) upon 'blackness' itself, refusing it as a 'transcendent signified' (an irreducible essence) and showing how it must be 'produced' in various cultural forms such as music, language and religion – precisely Gates's critical project.

Gates's work represents the most sustained attempt yet to theorize Afro–American writing. A number of critics, especially from the black feminist tradition, feel that he dispenses too quickly with the notion of black identity, and find his theory of the black text too narrow. Barbara T. Christian, for example, feels that the need for the kind of alienating theoretical discourse Gates attempts is exaggerated, and can only ever have a very narrow audience. For his part, Gates is under no illusion about who reads his work (see Ward), but he certainly feels a responsibility to translate academic jargon into language accessible to a larger audience – which, as he says, is why he writes so much literary journalism. His *Loose Canons* is a defence of multiculturalism during a decade when the concept was under sustained attack from a conservative backlash. His own critical work is part of that defence, but Gates may have a much larger cultural impact not just as a polemical journalist (his first vocation) but, more importantly, as an editor, by making new and neglected texts available.

Since the late 1970s, radical critics have been arguing about the literary canon. As a large proportion of teaching in colleges in America is done through the ubiquitous Literary Anthology, actually producing new anthologies that revise and contextualize the canon – questioning the boundaries of the 'literary', as the recent *Heath Anthology* does – becomes a project of some cultural significance. Gates's general editorship of Norton's Afro–American Anthology is a project of a similar order, and the chance to think through the concept of 'blackness' again. Gates's own signifyin(g) practice is, of course, that of the 'mediator' or trickster. His work is not the repetition of contemporary theoretical tropes upon the benighted black text; recent theory would question that very notion of mastery. Gates wishes to explicate black writing in a way which 'changes both the received theory and received ideas about the text' (Gates, 1984).

Main works

'Criticism in the jungle' and 'The blackness of blackness: a critique of the sign and the Signifying Monkey', both in *Black Literature and Literary Theory*, ed. Henry Louis Gates Jr, London: Routledge, 1984.

The Slave's Narrative, ed. Henry Louis Gates Jr and Charles T. Davis, Oxford: Oxford University Press, 1985a.

'*Race*'. *Writing and Difference*, ed. Henry Louis Gates Jr, Chicago: University of Chicago Press, 1986; previously a special issue of *Critical Inquiry*, 12 (Autumn 1985b).

Figures in Black: Words, signs and the 'racial' self, Oxford: Oxford University Press, 1987.

The Signifying Monkey: A theory of Afro-American literary criticism, Oxford: Oxford University Press, 1988a.

The Schomburg Library of Black Women Writers, general editor Henry Louis Gates Jr, New York, 1988b.

'Authority, (white) power, and the (black) critic; or, it's all Greek to me', in *The Future of Literary Theory*, ed. Ralph Cohen, London: Routledge, 1989.

Loose Canons: Notes on the culture wars, Oxford: Oxford University Press, 1992.

Further reading

Bucknell, Brad, 'Henry Louis Gates, Jr and the theory of signifyin(g)', *Ariel* 21, (1990) 65–84.

Christian, Barbara T., 'The race for theory', *Cultural Critique*, (1988).

Joyce, Joyce A., 'The black canon', *New Literary History* 18 (1987): 335–44.

McDowell, Deborah E., 'The changing same', in *New Literary History* 18, 2 Winter 1987 281–302.

Showalter, Elaine, 'A criticism of our own', in *The Future of Literary Theory*, ed. Ralph Cohen, London: Routledge, 1989.

Ward, Jerry W., 'Interview with Henry Louis Gates, Jr', *New Literary History* 22, 1991: 927–36.

Genette, Gérard (1930–)

Narratologist and rhetorician Gérard Genette teaches at the Ecole des Hautes Etudes in Paris, and has taught at both Columbia and New York universities. His work has covered a large range of topics (Baroque poetry, European and American fiction, mimetic theories of language) using a large number of methodological tools, but it is his work on the rhetoric of fictional narrative which has made his reputation both in Europe and in the English-speaking world.

Genette began writing during what turned out to be some of the most fruitful years for the study of narrative in France, when the structuralist work of **Barthes** and **Todorov**, and Todorov's translations of Russian Formalist criticism, were beginning to appear. Between 1966 and 1972 Genette published the volumes of essays *Figures I, II,* and *III.* Teaching in American in the 1970s, he gave a landmark paper on time and narrative in Proust, which was translated by Paul **de Man** in 1970. His important essay 'Frontières du récit' was published as 'Boundaries of narrative' in *New Literary History* in 1976, but it was with the publication in 1980 of *Narrative Discourse* (a translation of 'Discours du récit: essai de Méthode', itself a portion of *Figures III*), that Genette made his greatest impact in Britain and America; it has become one of the standard works on the poetics of fiction, and a text with which any serious student of narrative must grapple.

Narrative Discourse begins with some considerations of narrative in general, and the text Genette uses for the majority of his examples, Proust's novel *Remembrance of Things Past* (*A la recherche du temps perdu*). He suggests – using a linguistic metaphor that 'shouldn't be taken too literally' – that all narratives can be viewed as the expansion, 'monstrous if you will', of a verb; Proust's enormous novel becomes the expansion of the statement 'Marcel learns to write'. Genette is careful not to treat Proust's novel as a mere example of narrative in general; the specificity of the Proustian narrative is 'irreducible . . . the *Recherche* illustrates only itself. But, on the other hand, that specificity is not *undecomposable*'. Genette insists that all fiction uses the same fundamental elements, but each work is distinctive in the way it combines them. For him, the general is at the heart of the particular, and the knowable is at the heart of the mysterious.

Genette sets before us the paradoxes of his chosen method, one that refuses the mastery of theory and criticism over its subject; theory will be at the service of criticism, it seems, but also – and inevitably – he puts criticism at the service of theory. He hopes to use Proust to illustrate aspects of narrative theory, while he is aware that Proust will also be called upon to explain heretofore unexplained aspects of the rhetoric of fictional discourse.

In *Narrative Discourse*, Genette suggests that in order to discuss narrative with any clarity, we need to be able to distinguish between three aspects of narrative: to study the relationship between (1) the text; (2) the events it recounts (the old Russian Formalist distinction between the plot, the 'fabula', and the story as it is presented in discourse, the '*syuzhet*'); and (3) the act of narrating itself. Genette calls these three aspects of narrative '*histoire*', '*récit*' and '*narration*'. Using Rimmon-Kenan's mild revision of the English translation of these terms, we can call them 'story', 'text' and 'narration'.

The story, for Genette, is the signified or narrative content. The text consists of the signifiers, the verbal representation of events; what we actually read. All written texts imply a writer or speaker, and Genette calls this the act of narration. Although we only ever have the text in front of us, he points out that for it to count as a narrative, the text needs the other two aspects – both a story and a narrator.

Narrative Discourse is essentially the analysis of the manipulation of time and what used to be called point of view in narrative, using a more precise and productive terminology which, in important ways, supersedes Anglo-American discussion of these topics. Genette examines three aspects of time in narrative: order, frequency and duration; broadly, 'when?', 'how often?' and 'for how long?'. 'Order' is the relation between the assumed sequence of events – the story, and the order of events as they are found in the text. The story is always chronological, while the text may not be; for instance, according to Genette most fictions begin in 'in medias res' and contain flashbacks and, to a lesser extent, flashforwards. Genette calls these 'analepses' and 'prolepses'. While analepses give us informaton from the past of the story, the much rarer prolepses tell us about what is to come, creating an effect of anticipation. An example would be Tim O'Brien's story 'The Things They Carried' (1990), where we learn early in the story of a character's later death.

The character's death is narrated a number of times, and thus falls into Genette's second aspect of narrative time – frequency, defined as a relation of repetition between story and text – that is, how often an event is narrated. Among the most familiar permutations are single events narrated a number of times (B.S. Johnson's *House Mother Normal* [1971] narrates the same event seven times in seven chapters) and repeated events narrated once ('Every morning I walked to work . . .'). The third aspect of narrative time is duration, which Genette admits to be the most problematic of his categories because 'no one can measure the duration of a narrative'. Duration is the ratio between the duration of the story and the number of pages devoted to it. As all readers read at differing speeds, and we can break off when we like, Genette discusses duration in terms of relative speed and pace inside the individual text; so while, for example, Nicholson Baker's novel *The Mezzanine* (1989) takes takes place in a single lunch hour, the pace within the text accelerates and decelerates. The fastest speed is an omission, an event unnarrated (see Virginia Woolf's *Between the Acts* [1941]); the slowest is the pause (see the extensive descriptions in Baker's novel).

The last two chapters of *Narrative Discourse* deal with 'mood' and 'voice' and have, perhaps, been the most discussed aspects of Genette's work in the English-speaking world, because here he is intervening in an Anglo–American debate that has its origins in Henry James's criticism. Mood, for Genette, is the regulation of narrative information, and it has two aspects, 'distance' and 'perspective'. For example, one can tell more or tell less, and tell it in a more or a less direct way (distance), or tell from one point of view or another (perspective). This concept of perspective, of 'focalization', has been one of Genette's most influential ideas.

As he saw it, Genette had exposed a confusion in concepts of 'point of view', which had been the cornerstone of Anglo-American criticism for many years. For him, a writer's decision to narrate from the point of view of one or more of the characters is a question of narrative perspective. Who actually narrates is a question of 'voice'. In other words, it is the difference between who sees and who speaks, of confusing the question 'who is the character whose point of view orientates the narrative perspective? with the very different question 'who is the narrator?'; who focalizes and who narrates? For Genette the author imagines, but the narrator knows.

Genette is a prolific writer, and his work since the early 1970s has taken off in a number of directions; *Mimologiques* (1976) is the study of writings that see a mimetic relationship between word and thing; while *The Architext: An introduction* (first pub. 1979; trans. 1992) discusses types of textuality and variations in narrative modes, and goes beyond structuralist notions of the text as a self-enclosed linguistic entity. More recent work includes a text on **Bachelard** and the development of the concept of textuality in such a way as to deal with writer/text/reader relations.

Anglo-American writers on narrative have praised Genette for his elegant analysis of temporal relations in Proust, and for its general applicability; for showing that a broadly structuralist analysis of narrative need not be limited to the simplest of narrative forms; and for providing a terminology that is more precise, and therefore more useful, than that which had gone before. In his afterword to *Narrative Discourse*, Genette expects his self-confessedly 'barbaric' terminology to date; it is a mark of his influence that terms such as 'focalization' and 'iteration' are still part of the currency of narratology rather than its history; although they have been adapted and criticized, a number of Genette's coinages have yet to be superseded. Genette has sometimes been seen as a critic who has not responded to post-structuralism, yet as a careful reader of rhetoric – and in his work on the history of narrative, written in the mid 1960s – he displayed the ability to trouble the binary oppositions upon which critics of narrative had hitherto relied; writing on mimesis and diegesis, for instance, in a way which foreshadowed some of the later work written under the sign of deconstruction.

Main works

Figures I, Paris: Editions du Seuil, 1966.

Figures II, Paris: Editions du Seuil, 1969.

'Time and narrative in Proust' trans. Paul de Man, in *Aspects of Narrative,* ed. J. Hillis Miller, New York: Columbia University Press, 1971.

Figures III, Paris: Editions du Seuil, 1972.

Mimologiques, Paris: Editions du Seuil, 1976a.

'Boundaries of narrative', in *New Literary History,* 1976b.

Introduction a l'architexte, Paris: Editions du Seuil, 1979.

Narrative Discourse, trans. Janes E. Lewin, Oxford: Blackwell, 1980.

Figures of Literary Discourse, trans. Alan Sheridan, Oxford: Blackwell, 1982.

The Architext: An introduction, trans. Jane E. Lewin, Berkeley: University of California Press, 1989.

'The Gender and genre of reverie', with Thais E. Morgan, *Critical Inquiry,* 20, 2 (Winter 1994).

Further reading

Bennington, Geoff, 'Genette and deconstruction', *The Oxford Literary Review,* 4, 2 (1980).

Culler, Jonathan, *Structuralist Poetics,* London: Routledge, 1975.

Martin, Wallace, *Recent Theories of Narrative,* Ithaca, NY: Cornell University Press, 1986.

Rimmon-Kenan, Shlomith, *Narrative Fiction: contemporary poetics,* London: Methuen, 1983.

Gilbert, Sandra (1936–) and Gubar, Susan (1944–)

Sandra Gilbert is an American poet, literary critic and Professor of English at the University of California at Davis. Her collections of poetry include *The Summer Kitchen* (1983) and *Poems in Blood Pressure* (1988), and she has published a number of critical essays. Susan Gubar is also a literary critic and Professor of English at Indiana University; she had edited and published critical work on women's writing. They began collaborative work when they were both teaching at Indiana University in the 1970s, and their main published works are *The Madwoman in the Attic: The woman writer and the nineteenth-century literary imagination*: and *No Man's Land: The place of the woman writer in the twentieth century*, which is published in two volumes with a third volume forthcoming. They have also edited *Shakespeare's Sister: Feminist essays on women poets*; *The Norton Anthology of Literature by Women: The tradition in English*: and *The Female Imagination and the Modernist Aesthetic*.

In 1979 Gilbert and Gubar published *The Madwoman in the Attic*, one of a growing number of critical reappraisals of women's writing which appeared in the 1970s and included Ellen Moers's *Literary Women* (1976) and Elaine Showalter's *A Literature of Their Own* (1979). This growing interest in women as writers became known as gynocriticism, and took its place in a burgeoning tradition of feminist poetics which found its roots in Kate **Millett**'s feminist classic *Sexual Politics* (1969).

The focus of *The Madwoman in the Attic* is canonical nineteenth-century women writers such as Jane Austen, Charlotte Brontë, George Eliot and Emily Dickinson, and the reactions of these writers against the invisibility which had been imposed upon them by a patriarchal literary tradition. What Gilbert and Gubar find in these texts are related themes and images such as enclosure, escape, doubles of self, frozen landscapes, disease and claustrophobia. Taking this evidence in hand, they conclude that nineteenth-century women writers are overwhelmingly faced with confinement, both literal and figurative, and that this confinement is a result of the social, political and economic position of women, and of the literary tradition they have inherited.

The task of *The Madwoman in the Attic* becomes one of exploring women writers' redefinitions of selfhood, art and society through the prism of a gendered experience which frequently identifies the author with characters, and also as the source of the meaning in the text. Beginning the opening chapter with the then controversial but now ubiquitous question 'Is the pen a metaphorical penis?', Gilbert and Gubar argue that under patriarchy artistic creativity is seen as an essentially male preserve, and that the male writer 'fathers' his text; the woman writer, in contrast struggles against the metaphor of literary paternity which imprisons her, and on the journey towards literary autonomy she must transcend the pernicious images of angel and monster. By mapping Harold **Bloom**'s literary reading of **Freud**'s Oedipus complex – which deals with the anxiety of writers in the path of their predecessors, known as the 'anxiety of influence' – on to a feminist poetics, they deal with the woman writer's 'anxiety of authorship', which manifests itself in a number of ways which both conform to and subvert patriarchal literary standards. In the search for their own literary genealogy they argue that women often write palimpsestic works which conceal something much deeper than surface readings may imply. A common feature of all the chosen texts is the exploration of the mad double; the figure of the madwoman, as the title suggests, is inspired by Charlotte Brontë's Bertha Mason, who represents women's rage against the patriarchal society and literary tradition which confines her, but she is also the author's double, and is representative of a sophisticated literary strategy which is both revisionary and revolutionary.

Moving away from the gender-specific focus of *The Madwoman in the Attic*, the next major pieces of work are the two volumes of *No Man's Land*; the first volume, *The War of the Words* (1988), deals with both male and female writers from the middle of the nineteenth century to the present; the second, *Sexchanges* (1989), deals specifically with the period 1880 to 1930.

The War of the Words begins with another controversial question: 'Is the pen a metaphorical pistol?'; this foregrounds the prelude to a description of the interaction between male and female writing as one of sexual battle. Modernist texts are identified as particularly interesting examples of anxiety about male impotence and female potency, and the rise of Modernism can be attributed to male fear of the feminine. For women writing at the turn of the century, Gilbert and Gubar identify a symptom of the presence of an identifiable female literary history which they term the 'female affiliation complex'. Women writers feel obliged to affiliate with both maternal and paternal traditions, and by mapping a Freudian theory of primary sexuality on to literature, Gilbert and Gubar chart the various routes for the female affiliation complex. Dealing with the question of language, they assert that the battle of the sexes is also a battle over words. By engaging with feminist theory on women's relationship to language, they conclude that the view that language is patriarchal avoids the possibilities for female linguistic primacy through the role of the mother in the symbolic contract, claiming that the womb is a metaphorical mouth.

The work of Gilbert and Gubar, particularly *The Madwoman in the Attic*, has received much critical attention since publication, not all of it positive. Indeed, aspects of their approach seem naive in the light of the developments in post-structuralist theory, notably the shift in interest from the text to the reader, and work on language and ideology which makes a simple understanding of subjectivity increasingly difficult to maintain. Their readings of nineteenth-century realist texts assume that literature has a mimetic relationship to the society from which it emerges, and although in *The War of the Words* Gilbert and Gubar respond in part to this criticism, they continue to maintain an entirely author-orientated approach. The consequences of this are that as meaning is seen to be determined by authorial intention, they have been charged with performing reductive readings which oversimplify the complex relationship between author, text and reader. This debate is part of the bifurcation of gendered theoretical discourse which locates Gilbert and Gubar in the Anglo-American feminist theoretical tradition in contrast to the French feminist tradition. As representative of the early stages of development in this critical tradition, their work takes a broadly liberal humanist position which presents the author as unified self and patriarchy as a monolithic totality, and the notion of the unity and organicism of the text is also arguably closer to Romantic theory than the influences drawn upon by the French feminist tradition.

However, the impact of *The Madwoman in the Attic* in particular cannot be overestimated – it is a monumental and erudite piece of scholarship, which on publication paved an entirely new direction for feminist literary criticism and is now accepted as a feminist classic. It offers a radical reinterpretation of canonical works by women writers, and the part it has played in the development of a woman-centred critical practice has been instrumental in shifting the focus on to the distinctiveness of female experience. *No Man's Land* also plays an important role in the debate about the inherent elitism and masculinity of Modernism, and the exploration of the linguistic primacy of women contributes to contemporary discussions concerning gender and language. The collaborative nature of Gilbert and Gubar's work is an explicit example of the efficacy and benefit of 'sisterhood', which their writing seeks so hard to explore and encourage.

Main works

The Madwoman in the Attic: The woman writer and the nineteenth-century literary imagination, New Haven, CT: Yale University Press, 1979a.

Shakespeare's Sisters: Feminist essays on women poets (eds), Bloomington: Indiana University Press, 1979b.

The Norton Anthology of Literature by Women: The tradition in English, (eds), New York: W.W. Norton, 1985.

The Female Imagination and the Modernist Aesthetic (eds), London: Gordon & Breach, 1986.

No Man's Land: The place of the woman writer in the twentieth century. The

War of the Words, vol.1 New Haven, CT: Yale University Press, 1988; *Sexchanges*, vol.2 New Haven, CT: Yale University Press, 1989.

Further reading

Abel, Elizabeth (ed.), *Writing and Sexual Difference*, Chicago: University of Chicago Press, 1982.

Belsey, Catherine and Jane Moore (eds), *The Feminist Reader: Essays in gender and the politics of literary criticism*, London: Macmillan, 1989.

Mills, S. *et al.*, *Feminist Readings/Feminists Reading*, Hemel Hempstead: Harvester Wheatsheaf, 1989.

Mol, Toril, *Sexual/Textual Politics: Feminist literary theory*, London: Methuen, 1985.

Todd, Janet, *Feminist Literary History: A defence*, Oxford: Polity, 1988.

Weedon, Chris, *Feminist Practice and Poststructuralist Theory*, Oxford: Blackwell, 1987.

Gilroy, Paul (1956–)

Paul Gilroy, who is currently Senior Lecturer in Sociology at Goldsmiths' College, University of London, is one of the most interesting and influential young black critics in Britain today. In addition to his academic career he has worked as a journalist, musician and disc jockey.

Gilroy's work encompasses an impressive diversity of concerns, ranging across issues of 'race' and anti-racism, class, nation, ethnicity, the law, and all forms of black British – more recently, black Atlantic – culture. He is one of the co-authors of the influential collection *The Empire Strikes Back*, produced from Birmingham's Centre for Contemporary Cultural Studies during Stuart **Hall**'s directorship, but is probably better known for his book *There Ain't No Black in the Union Jack*. The book's subtitle, 'The cultural politics of race and nation', is significant in its insertion of culture where one would not usually expect to find it. This is typical of Gilroy's approach, and something to which we shall return later.

Along with a number of other writers (including those, like Robert Miles, with whom he would otherwise only partially agree), Gilroy has attacked the insufficiency of existing approaches and paradigms such as race relations and ethnic studies. Briefly, the race relations position is inadequate because it treats races as fixed and separate groups, in a way which risks reproducing the bases of racist categorizations. More provocatively, Gilroy has repeatedly criticized the concept of ethnicity, which all too easily hardens into what he terms 'ethnic absolutism', where belief in an essential ethnic identity paradoxically unites black people with the ideologues of the far right.

In addition, Gilroy has insisted on the need to rethink the question of 'race' in a number of important contexts, including the relation between 'race' and class. Disagreeing strongly with those – including some black **Marx**ists – who would make 'race' subordinate to class, he argues for a complex and non-hierarchical articulation between them. He goes on to identify related but separable processes of race and class formation, where the former has an important economic dimension but is far from being reducible to it. Also, 'the fact that "race" can become a distinctive feature at the level of economic development' (*Ain't No Black*) means that for Gilroy, class theory needs an even more fundamental rethink than race.

If Gilroy's attitude to theories of class seems inconoclastic, then his analysis of racism and British nationalism is particularly uncomfortable for many on the left. Raymond **Williams**, E.P. Thompson, Anthony Barnett and Michael Igantieff are among those whose model of the nation (unproblematized, according to Gilroy) places them in far too close proximity to the position of the 1980s New Right, and their 'new racism', whose 'capacity to link discourses of patriotism, nationalism, xenophobia, Englishness, Britishness, militarism and gender difference into a complex system . . . gives "race" its contemporary meaning' (*ibid.*). The particular relation of nationalism and racism is seen – in a way which recalls Stuart Hall's arguments – as a feature of postwar national decline; while the failure of the left in general to produce an adequate understanding of their model of nationality and identity is replicated in one of its academic flagships – Cultural Studies – whose domestic radicalism takes no account of the racial or racist components of the tradition to which it is heir.

One particular problem in all this is how to grant appropriate importance to race without risking a relapse into fixed or essentialist ways of thinking. Gilroy therefore suggests that ' "Race" has to be socially and politically constructed, and elaborate ideological work is done to secure and maintain the different forms of "racialization" which have characterized capitalist development' (*ibid.*). 'Race' formation, like class formation, is the product of various historically specific struggles, both political and cultural. One of the most visible of these – and one which has by no means been black-led – is that known as anti-racism. Here again, the British left and certain of its black allies are seen as having failed, not least through an inability to understand that, for instance, anti-racism and black liberation are distinct, and may even conflict. The Greater London Council's commendable efforts at municipal anti-racism, for example, were flawed, among other things, by a lack of involvement by black people, and a lack of attention to their perception of political needs and priorities. On the other hand, Rock Against Racism's degree of success was attributable to its incorporation of the aims of black people.

The latter fact is significant, since Gilroy locates many of the most important contemporary struggles of black people at the cultural level, and it is here, perhaps, that the major force of his writing lies. While he is clearly an important theorist of race, class, and so on, Gilroy's subtle and intelligent analyses of black popular and 'expressive' cultures, as well as his insistence on their value, has given them a standing which had previously largely eluded them, and cannot be wished away. On the one hand, this is a challenge to dominant Eurocentric or high cultural biases; but on the other hand it is also a problem for certain purist views of 'African' culture, since the popular cultural forms are inescapably mixed or hybrid.

This hybridity is the result of the historical situation of black people in the diaspora, and is one of the issues which Gilroy examines in his more recent work, especially *The Black Atlantic*. The image of a connected black culture spanning the Atlantic, transmitting ideas and cultural forms in a version of the antiphonal call-and-response structures of black music, is a powerful antidote both to the priority still regularly (and unthinkingly) acorded to national cultures, and to the idea that diaspora necessarily equals irremediable separation and cultural fragmentation. In no way does Gilroy want to minimize the importance of diaspora, however, he regards it as a way to break out of constraining categories such as the nation, culture or ethnicity. In this view, the fashionable Afrocentricity popularized by writers like Molefi Kete Asante can be as retrogade as any particularist centripetal European nationalism – not least because both attempt to ignore contemporary reality: European nationalism refuses to accept that, as a result of the inmixing of black cultures, it is irretrievably syncretic; while Afrocentricity forsakes the uncomfortable facts of present-day Africa for the glories of a distant and frequently romanticized past.

Yet another of Gilroy's ideas which unsettles established ways of thinking is the contention that black peoples and black cultures, far from belonging in some zone of underdevelopment as the Other to a relentlessly modernizing West, belong at the heart of modernity. The fact that their position there is as a counter-culture in no way detracts from its importance. As Gilroy had written earlier: 'Black expressive cultures affirm as they protest', and protest here could not just include opposition to histories of servitude, or the daily pains of racism, but encompass rejection of the West's universalizing assumptions; while affirmation could include both the celebration of positive aspects of black life and a commitment to a better future. To that extent, black culture remains resolutely loyal to the kind of *'grands récits'*, narratives of emancipation, which postmodernism has declared definitively out of date.

Ideas and arguments like these make Gilroy a disturbing presence for some, so it is no surprise that he comes in for criticism. What is perhaps surprising, given the importance of his cultural analysis, is that the criticism has largely been at the theoretical level. Robert Miles, for example, criticizes what he sees as Gilroy's vague or contradictory conceptions of 'race', which apparently claim that it is both a descriptive and an analytical term (something that Miles cannot accept). Anthias and Yuval–Davis are rather more in sympathy with Gilroy, but feel that his rejection of the category of ethnicity creates difficulties for his ability to analyze racial phenomena fully. The black writer Kobena Mercer has criticized Gilroy for arguing that black cultural politics should adopt anti-state strategies (since this is apparently old-fashioned and economistic); and this is all the more surprising, since it is precisely Gilroy's move away from **Marx**ist-type positions which worries people like Miles. Certainly at times it can feel as if it is very hard to pin down some of Gilroy's central concepts, especially 'race', but then he would no doubt say that that is precisely the point – that they are not fixed, stable entities, and need to be continuously re-examined and redefined.

Main works

The Empire Strikes Back, London: Hutchinson, 1982 (as co-author).

There Ain't No Black in the Union Jack, London: Hutchinson, 1987.

Problems in Anti-Racist Strategy, London: Runnymede Trust, 1988.

'Cultural studies and ethnic absolutism', in Grossberg, Treichler and Nelson (eds), *Cultural Studies*, London: Routledge, 1991.

The Black Atlantic, London: Verso, 1993a.

Small Acts, London: Serpent's Tail, 1993b.

Further reading

Anthias, Floya and Nira Yuval–Davis, *Racialized Boundaries*, London: Routledge, 1993.

Helmreich, Stefan, 'Kinship, nation, and Paul Gilroy's concept of Diaspora', *Diaspora*, 2, 2 (1992).

Miles, Robert, *Racism after 'Race Relations'*, London: Routledge, 1993.

Goldmann, Lucien (1913–70)

Lucien Goldmann was the son of a rabbi, his first university studies were in law in his native city of Bucharest, followed by a year's philosophy in Vienna. Following his arrest for activities as part of a clandestine **Marx**ist group, he fled in 1934 to Paris, where he gained French degrees in Law and Politics. In the early 1940s he worked as an assistant to the Swiss psychologist Jean Piaget, having fled to neutral Switzerland following an escape from wartime internment by the Vichy authorities. There he was awarded his first doctorate, by the University of Zurich, for a dissertation on Kant. He returned to France after the Liberation, and joined the Centre National de la Recherche Scientifique. A dissertation on Pascal and Racine earned him his second doctorate, from the Sorbonne in 1956. In 1958 he became Directeur d'Etudes in the VIth section of the Ecole Pratique des Hautes Etudes; and then in 1961 he became director of his own research institute, the Centre des Recherches de Sociologie de la Littérature at the Université Libre de Bruxelles, a post he held until his comparatively early death.

In common with his senior and mentor, Gyorgy (Georg) **Lukács**, also a Central European Jewish Marxist, Lucien Goldmann sought to explain the connections between literary works and the societies that gave rise to them. His most sustained attention to a particular body of literary texts was the study of the works of Racine and Pascal, initially undertaken for his Sorbonne doctorate and eventually published as *Le Dieu caché* (1955). This project compelled him to systematize his thinking on the relationship of a specific historical period to a specific literary deposit. But whereas Lukács praised the novels of early-nineteenth-century 'realism' as furnishing a full and adequate aesthetic 'form' to represent the social totality, Goldmann proposed an inter-mediate term between society and the work: that of social class, or *social group*.

Racine and Pascal are associated with a particular class grouping in seventeenth-century France, the 'noblesse de robe'. This social group comprised court officials, marginalized by the increasing appropriation of power to the person of the monarch and increasingly overtaken by an up-and-coming urban mercantile bourgeoisie. Racine and Pascal had connections with the Jansenist sect, which sought to reconcile acknowledgement of the absolute authority of a concealed godhead ('le dieu caché') with the growing cultural authority of human rationality. Goldmann immersed himself in the study of Jansenism, which extended to editing a collection of the letters of Martin de Barcos, the Jansenist Abbé de Saint Cyran. He considered Jansenism to be the ideological expression of the 'noblesse de robe', performing the social tensions of their class position in theological form. In turn, Pascal's philosophy – where the famous wager constitutes an attempted accommodation between absolute uncertainty over God's existence and human rational calculation – and Racine's dramatic work – where the protagonists' 'tragedies' pivot around the inability to reconcile divine arbitrariness with human yearning – are the expression in letters of the ideological tensions of Jansenism. The nature of this expression of the 'world-view' of a particular class group is thus not direct and substantive – the subject of Racine's drama was, after all, wholly pagan on the surface. Rather, the deep thematic structures and their mode of literary embodiment are similar to the 'mental structures' of the class from which the author is drawn. These similarities Goldmann called 'homologies'.

Goldmann differs from Lukács in that the great literary work need not reflect a whole society; it is not necessarily 'reflective' at all in the sense of depicting the contemporary or historical reality of a society. But it does constitute, often unconsciously, the adequate and coherent literary expression of the 'world-view' of a particular social segment, caught within the class contradictions of their particular historical moment. His approach is thus more properly and orthodoxly sociological than Lukács's, and it is as a sociologist of literature that Goldmann received recognition within conventional academic divisions: the research institute he headed was dedicated to the sociology of literature.

In line with aspects of the classical tradition of sociology, Goldmann is preoccupied with the issue of the social nature of consciousness. He treats literary masterpieces as providing some of the most detailed and sophisticated historical evidence of consciousness for a given social faction at a given conjuncture. The author is the one able to transpose what are the 'trans-individual mental structures' of his group into an appropriate literary form. This is often seen by commentators as meeting unsatisfactorily the question of criteria for aesthetic value, because artistic stature is simply taken as already established when selecting the texts deserving of attention for a particular historical period.

Goldmann's research on Racine and Pascal was his single most profound and thorough piece of scholarly investigation. (He was to continue to publish on Racine with his popular introduction *Racine* [1956] and his posthumous *Situation de la critique Racinienne* [1971].)

In his early 1960s work, gathered into the volume *Pour une sociologie du roman* – which surprised him by a degree of popularity that occasioned three reprints in France – he covered, *inter alia*, the work of the contemporary French novelists of 'le nouveau roman'. He regarded the intensive description of objects in the work of Alain Robbe-Grillet and others as cultural indicators of the increased reification generated by the renewed round of capital accumulation in the advanced industrial societies of the West during the postwar period. Several commentators have seen Goldmann's later work as returning to a more mechanical base–superstructure model of the social determinants of the literary work.

Although *Le Dieu caché* was translated as early as 1964, Goldmann's influence in the Anglophone academy has never been substantial. It was at its zenith immediately following his death, in the early to mid 1970s, as part of the renewed attention to Marxism that followed the social upheavals of the late 1960s on Western campuses and elsewhere. Goldmann shared something of the **Marcus**ean displacement of socialist hopes onto the agency of students and sub-proletariat, because of the perceived incorporation of working-class consciousness into Western capitalist ideology during the postwar boom, and he greeted the May 1968 Paris *événements* with enthusiasm. (Marcuse's appreciative comments on Goldmann are available in *Cultural Creation in Modern Society*, 1976.)

In England Goldmann addressed the notorious 1968 London Roundhouse Conference, whose proceedings were published in an influential widely selling paperback edited by David Cooper, *The Dialectics of Liberation*. The memorial lecture given by Raymond **Williams** in Cambridge in 1970 (published both in *New Left Review* and as the introduction to the 1972 English translation of *Racine*) also contributed to focusing some attention on Goldmann within circles in Britain concerned to develop a progressive approach to literary studies. This attention peaked with the English translation, in 1975, of *Pour une sociologie du roman*.

Already, by the time of his *Marxism and Literature* in 1977, Williams – while still registering that with the publication of translations of Goldmann, later Lukács and other continental figures 'an argument that had drifted into deadlock . . . in the late thirties and forties, was being vigorously and significantly reopened' – acknowledged that he found Goldmann's theory of 'homology' unsatisfactory, vitiated by a residual mechanical materialism. He detected a circular self-confirming methodology, in which only evidence upholding the purported 'homology' was advanced and other evidence was neglected. Similarly, Terry **Eagleton**'s resistance to Lukácsian neo-Hegelianism extended to

Goldmann's work, which he judged as 'too trimly symmetrical' in its expressive chain of social class – social consciousness – literary text. In general, the rapid absorption into the Anglophone academy in the early and mid seventies of a structuralism which tended to suspend questions of real social agency meant that Goldmann's more humanistic and sociological approach failed to capture lasting attention. The general waning of the political and intellectual prestige of Marxism since the early 1980s continues to leave Goldmann's work with some historical respect, but little current following. The implicit repudiation of his position in the intervening years by Goldmann's most celebrated student, fellow Romanian Julia **Kristeva**, sharply illustrates this contemporary neglect.

Main works

The Hidden God: A study for tragic vision in the Pensées of Pascal and the tragedies of Racine, trans. Philip Thody, London: Routledge & Kegan Paul, 1964.

The Human Sciences and Philosophy, trans. Hayden V. White and Robert Anchor, London: Jonathon Cape, 1969.

Towards a Sociology of the Novel, trans. Alan Sheridan, London: Tavistock, 1975.

Cultural Creation in Modern Society, trans. Bart Grahl, St Louis, MO: Telos Press, 1976.

Lukács and Heidigger: Towards a new philosophy, trans. W. Boelhower, London: Routledge & Kegan Paul, 1977.

Essays on Method in the Sociology of Literature, Oxford: Blackwell, 1981.

Further reading

Cohen, Mitchell, *The Wager of Lucien Goldmann: Tragedy, dialectics and a hidden God*, Princeton, NJ: Princeton University Press, 1994.

Evans, Mary, *Lucien Goldmann: An introduction*, Brighton: Harvester, 1981.

Leavell, Terry, 'Weber, Goldmann and the Sociology of Beliefs', *European Journal of Sociology*, Vo. XIV, no. 2, 1973.

Routh, Jane, 'A reputation made: Lucien Goldmann', in J. Routh and J. Wolff (eds), *The Sociology of Literature: Theoretical approaches*, University of Keele Sociological Review Monographs, no.25, 1977.

Slaughter, Cliff, *Marxism, Ideology and Literature*, London: Macmillan, 1980.

Williams, Raymond, 'From Leavis to Goldmann: in memory of Lucien Goldmann', *New Left Review*, 67 (1971).

Glossary

Genetic structuralism: A 'structuralism' – a focus on the ensemble of inter-relationships (which are their defining characteristics) among the elements making up the object under scrutiny (a society, a language, a personality) – qualified by simultaneous attention to the processes of change, development and historical transformation to which such ensembles and their constituent elements are necessarily subject. This is a methodology that seeks to overcome the one-sidedness of structuralism by synthesizing the synchrony of structures with the diachrony of historical development.

Gramsci, Antonio (1891–1937)

Antonio Gramsci was born in Ales, Sardinia, and educated at the University of Turin. He joined the Italian Socialist Party in 1913, and helped found the socialist newspaper *L'Ordine Nuovo* in 1919. In 1921 he became a founder member of Italian Communist Party. In 1924 he was elected to the Italian parliament. Arrested and imprisoned by Mussolini's fascist regime in 1926, he remained a prisoner until six days before his death in April 1937.

Antonio Gramsci's contribution to cultural theory is, in essence, the concept of hegemony. This concept is an expansion of the Marxist concept of ideology, found especially in the work of **Marx**, Lenin and **Lukács**. Hegemony, for Gramsci, is a political concept developed to explain the absence of socialist revolutions (given the exploitative and oppressive nature of capitalism) in the Western capitalist democracies. Gramsci uses the concept of hegemony to refer to a condition in process in which a dominant class (in alliance with other classes or class factions) does not merely *rule* a society but *leads* it through the exercise of moral and intellectual leadership. In this sense the concept is used to suggest a society in which, despite oppression and exploitation, there is a high degree of consensus and social stability; a society in which subordinate groups and classes appear *actively* to support and subscribe to values, ideals, objectives, cultural and political meanings, which bind them to and incorporate them into the prevailing structures of power. Throughout most of the twentieth century, for example, general elections in Britain have been contested by what are now the two main political parties, Labour and Conservative. On each occasion the contest has circled around the question of who can best administer capitalism (usually referred to by the less politically charged term 'the economy'): less nationalization, more nationalization; less taxation, more taxation, and so on. And on each occasion, the mainstream media have concurred. In this way the parameters of political debate within each election are ultimately determined by the needs and interests of capitalism. However, these needs and interests are always articulated as the interests and needs of society in general. This is clearly an example of a hegemonic situation in which the interests of one powerful section of society have been 'universalized' as the interests of the society as a whole – so much so that the situation – the parameters of debate – seem perfectly natural (culture presented as nature, as 'common sense'); virtually beyond serious contention. But it has not always been like this. Capitalism's hegemony is historical rather than natural. It is the result of a series of profound political, social, cultural and economic changes that have taken place over at least the last three centuries. In fact, until as late as the second half of the nineteenth century, capitalism's hegemony was by no means secure. Only in the twentieth century has capitalism become hegemonic.

Although hegemony implies a society with a high degree of consensus, it should not be understood to refer to a society in which all conflict has been drained away. What the concept is meant to suggest is a society in which conflict (including class conflict) is contained and channelled into ideologically safe harbours. That is, hegemony is maintained (and must be continually maintained: it is an ongoing process) by dominant groups and classes 'negotiating' with, and making concessions to, subordinate groups and classes. Hegemony is always the result of 'negotiations' between dominant and subordinate groups; it is a process marked by both 'resistance' and 'incorporation'; it is never simply power imposed from above. There are, of course, limits to such negotiations and concessions. As Gramsci makes clear, they can never be allowed to challenge the economic fundamentals of class power:

> Undoubtedly the fact of hegemony presupposes that account be taken of the interests and the tendencies of the groups over which hegemony is to be exercised, and that a certain compromise equilibrium should be formed – in other words, that the leading group should make sacrifices of an economic-corporate kind. But there is also no doubt that such sacrifices and such a compromise cannot touch the essentials. (*Selections From Prison Notebooks*)

Moreover, at times of crisis, when moral and intellectual leadership is not enough to secure continued authority, the 'normal' processes of hegemony are bolstered, temporarily, by the coercive power of the state. But even here, as Gramsci maintains, 'the attempt is always made to ensure that force will appear to be based on the consent of the majority' (*ibid.*).

Hegemony is 'organized' by those whom Gramsci designates 'organic intellectuals'. According to him, intellectuals are distinguished by their social function. That is to say: all men and women have the capacity for intellectual activity, but only certain men and women have the function of intellectuals in society. Each class, as Gramsci explains, creates 'organically' its own intellectuals. Organic intellectuals function as class organizers (in the broadest sense of the term). They give a class 'homogeneity and an awareness of its own function not only in the economic sphere but also in the social and political fields. The capitalist entrepreneur [for example] creates alongside himself the industrial technician, the specialist in political economy, the organizers of a new culture, of a new legal system, etc.' (*ibid.*). It is the task of the organic intellectuals of the dominant class to 'determine and to organize the reform of moral and intellectual life' (*ibid.*). They are, in short, the dominant class's 'deputies', striving to secure and sustain its hegemony. Gramsci tends to speak of individuals, but the way the concept of the organic intellectual has been mobilized in cultural studies, following Louis **Althusser**'s barely acknowledged borrowings from Gramsci, is in terms of *collective* organic intellectuals: what Althusser refers to as the 'Ideological State Apparatuses' of, for example, the family, education, the media, organized religion, the culture industries, and so on. Again, like Althusser after him, Gramsci sees the winning of consent as only part of the strategy of dominant groups and classes; when consent can no longer be won, there is always the coercive force of the 'Repressive State Apparatus': the army, the police, the prison system, and so forth.

For the student of cultural studies, hegemony has proved a very fruitful concept. From the perspective of hegemony theory, the field of culture is seen as an area of exchange between dominant and subordinate forces in society; a structured terrain of continuous negotiation between the forces of incorporation and the forces of resistance; the site a struggle between the attempt to universalize the interests of the dominant against the resistance of the subordinate. This can be analyzed in many different configurations – gender, generation, race, and so on – for the field of culture always contains a contradictory mix of competing interests and values: neither middle class nor working class, neither racist nor anti-racist, neither sexist nor anti-sexist, neither homophobic nor anti-homophobic, and so on, but always a shifting balance ('a compromise equilibrium') between the interests of the dominant and the resistance of the subordinate. Culture (especially the culture provided by the cultural industries) is continually redefined, reshaped, relocated and redirected in strategic acts of selective consumption and productive acts of reading and 'articulation', often in ways not intended or even foreseen by its authors and producers. From a Gramscian perspective, culture (elite and popular) is what men and women make from their active consumption of the texts and practices of the cultural industries (both elite and popular).

For the student of popular culture, youth subcultures are perhaps the most spectacular example of the processes of hegemony within the field of culture. What has come to seem one of the defining features of youth subcultures is the way in which they appropriate and articulate for their own purposes and meanings, through transformation or unexpected combination, the commodities of everyday existence. Examples include: teddy boys wearing Savile Row Edwardian jackets; mods wearing Italian suits; punks using bin-liners and safety pins. Through these acts of appropriation (and through patterns of behaviour, ways of speaking, taste in music, etc.) youth subcultures engage in symbolic forms of resistance to both dominant and parent cultures. Sooner or later, however, the shifting equilibrium tilts in favour of the interests of the dominant. The moment of symbolic resistance gives way to commercial incorporation and ideological defusion as the culture industries eventually succeed in marketing subcultural resistance for general consumption and profit.

The most common criticism made against the use of the concept of hegemony in cultural studies is that it explains too much. Whether this is true or not, the concept of hegemony allows the student of cultural studies to see the field of culture as a 'political' terrain: a negotiation mix of intentions and counter-intentions, stategies and counter-strategies, both from 'above' and from 'below', from the 'commercial' and the 'authentic'; a shifting balance of forces between resistance and incorporation. Gramsci's concept of hegemony has been central to the formation of cultural studies, especially the influential work emanating from the Centre for Contemporary Studies in the 1970s. Gramscianism continues to be the main theoretical orientation within the field of British cultural studies.

Main works

Selections From Prison Notebooks, ed. and trans. Q. Hoare and G. Nowell Smith, London: Lawrence & Wishart, 1971.

Selections From Political Writings 1910–1920, ed. Q. Hoare, trans. J. Matthews, London: Lawrence & Wishart, 1977.

Selections From Political Writings 1921–1926, ed. and trans. Q. Hoare, London: Lawrence & Wishart, 1978.

Selections From Cultural Writings, eds D. Forgacs and G. Nowell Smith, trans. W. Boelhower, London: Lawrence & Wishart, 1985.

A Gramsci Reader, ed. D. Forgacs, London: Lawrence & Wishart, 1988.

Further reading

Harris, David, *From Class Struggle to the Politics of Pleasure: The effects of Gramscianism on cultural studies*, London: Routledge, 1992.

Holub, Renate, *Antonio Gramsci: Beyond Marxism and postmodernism*, London: Routledge, 1992.

Mouffe, Chantal, *Gramsci and Marxist Theory*, London: Routledge, 1979.

Ransome, Paul, *Antonio Gramsci: A new introduction*, Hemel Hempstead: Harvester Wheatsheaf, 1992.

Sassoon, Anne Showstack (ed.), *Approaches to Gramsci*, London: Writers & Readers, 1982.

Simon, Roger, *Gramsci's Political Thought: An introduction*, London: Lawrence & Wishart, 1982.

Greenblatt, Stephen

Stephen Greenblatt is Class of 1932 Professor of English Literature at the University of California, Berkeley. Greenblatt is commonly identified as the central figure in American 'New Historicism' – or 'cultural poetics', to use his preferred terminology. H. Aram Veeser has argued that New Historicism, a term coined by Greenblatt in 1982, is a 'phrase without an adequate referent', but one might describe it as old-fashioned historical contextualization of the literary artefact with new-fashioned anthropological and Foucauldian trimmings. It is a movement closely aligned in literary studies with what J. Hillis **Miller** famously, and somewhat disparagingly, identified as the turn towards history evident in the literary theory of the 1980s.

The implicit premiss for New Historicism is that the American theoretical orthodoxies of the 1970s, notably deconstruction, were as ahistorical in their methodologies as the orthodoxies – New Criticism and myth criticism – which they challenged and replaced. Greenblatt rejects criticism which addresses a work of art as a self-sufficient textual object divorced from its historical contexts and cultural antecedents; texts are not simply iconic objects which encapsulate their meanings in their own formal structures. However, addressing literature in its historical context is nothing new; what distinguishes Greenblatt from what might be called 'old' historicist Renaissance scholars such as Tillyard or Dover Wilson is his problematizing of their division between literary foreground and political background. In addition, Greenblatt borrows from sources alien to traditional historical criticism: anthropology (notably Geertz), **Lacan**ian neo-**Freud**ianism (especially in his earlier work) and, in particular, **Foucault** (especially in his recent work).

Greenblatt, following Foucault, foregrounds the concept that 'history' is itself textually mediated, and problematizes the mimetic model of previous historicist criticism which views a text as simply reflecting the history around – and thus still outside – it. Representations are not simply the products of an age; they are themselves productive, engaging with and often subsequently altering the forces which brought them into being. Nor is history the stable and incontrovertible backdrop to the work of literature assumed by monological historical scholarship. Non-literary texts are not simply neutral transcriptions of reality; instead, historical fact and experience are available to us only in what Greenblatt calls the 'textual traces' of the dead, with all the concomitant rhetorical strategies which characterize textuality.

Whereas American deconstruction found nineteenth-century literature (especially the novel and Romantic poetry) most amenable to its purposes, the New Historicism has concentrated on Renaissance literature (though it has spread to British Romanticism – see **McGann**). *Renaissance Self-Fashioning*, which examines More, Tyndale, Wyatt, Spenser, Marlowe and Shakespeare, is the pioneering example of this New Historicist concern with Renaissance literature. It takes issue with the presuppositions of New Criticism's close-reading techniques. Art cannot pretend to autonomy, and textual traces are 'self-consciously embedded in specific communities, life situations, structures of power'. Simultaneously, Greenblatt rejects reductive generalizations about his authors' relationship to their culture. Shakespeare's plays do not offer a 'single timeless affirmation or denial of legitimate authority'. Instead of viewing Shakespeare as an apologist for the hierarchies of Tudor society, or as an author whose work mirrors some Elizabethan World Picture, Greenblatt argues that English Renaissance culture was not homogeneous, and that Shakespeare's work enacts its ideological struggles, relentlessly exploring the manifestations of power in his particular culture. As he says in the Preface to *The Power of Forms in the English Renaissance*, Renaissance literary works are not 'a stable set of reflections of the historical facts that lie beyond them'; they are 'places of dissension' and 'occasions for the jostling of orthodox and subversive impulses'.

Though some New Historicists have taken issue with the ahistorical orientation of the *nouvelle critique*, *Renaissance Self-Fashioning* owes much to deconstruction, borrowing some of its terminology ('origins', 'rupture', 'inscription', and so on) and arguing that there is no grand originating consciousness available in Shakespeare's plays, which have no 'central, unwavering authorial presence'. All Greenblatt's chosen authors address the concept of the construction of identity, and his ideas are often heavily influenced by deconstructive notions of human subjectivity. For instance, Othello's self-fashioning is seen as discursive, produced by external rhetoric; his innermost self is dependent 'upon a language that is always necessarily given from without and upon representation before an audience'. *Renaissance Self-Fashioning* is, in part, an attempt to reclaim postmodernist ideas about the nature of the human subject from their allegedly timeless setting for a culturally specific, historicist methodology.

Shakespearean Negotiations employs Foucault's genealogical methodology, refusing to privilege canonical Renaissance literature and dwelling upon what Greenblatt calls writings from the 'borders'. This strategy raises issues of canonicity, politicizing major/minor literary argument and, in particular, problematizing orthodox historiography. Greenblatt, like Foucault, is unafraid of connecting supposedly non-literary historical texts with the literary artefact – a legitimate strategy if history is available to us only in the form of narrative. Considerations of canonical literature are introduced by writings from the borders. 'Invisible bullets' meshes a police report of Marlowe's allegedly blasphemous conversation with *Henry IV* and *Henry V*, and 'Fiction and friction' uses an anecdote about transvestism in the 1580s to initiate a reading of *Twelfth Night*. Such juxtapositions have become mannerisms in New Historicist writing, but can be defended as part of what Joel Fineman called 'anecdotal historiography'. Employing anecdotes – or 'petites histoires', as Greenblatt has called them – rejects the integrated and teleologically progressive conventions of orthodox historiography (with its coherent narratives of beginning, middle and end). Such an approach is not without its attendant paradoxes. As Jean E. Howard has argued, Greenblatt's influence has led New Historicist critics to use such anecdotes to reintroduce their own grand narrative. Anecdotes become paradigmatic moments which 'sketch a cultural law'.

Shakespearean Negotiations is also Foucauldian in its concern with power, especially in its close attention to the concepts of subversion and containment. 'Invisible bullets' examines how ideologies – to use a New Historicist keyword – 'co-opt' subversive discourses, thereby assimilating or neutralizing them. Sixteenth-century 'rogue' narratives about contemporary criminals – or, indeed, Shakespeare's portrayal of Falstaff – are indicative of 'a carefully plotted official strategy whereby subversive perceptions are at once produced and contained'. The gloomy message for the radical is that subversive voices are 'produced by and within the affirmations of order; they are powerfully registered, but they do not undermine that order'.

Learning to Curse brings together some of Greenblatt's uncollected essays written between 1976 and 1990, including the provocative and important essay 'Psychoanalysis and Renaissance culture' (1986). This argues that psychoanalysis was the outcome of certain historical conditions evident during the early modern period and that, consequently, psychological interpretations of Renaissance texts are problematic in that they manifest 'the curious effect of a discourse that functions *as if* the psychological categories it invokes were not only simultaneous with but even prior to and themselves causes of the very phenomena of which in actual fact they were the results'. Despite its attention to alienated forms of consciousness, Freudianism still presupposes a stable self which is capable of being alienated. Psychoanalytic interpretation is therefore of little use when it is applied to early modern discourses which do not recognize the proprietary rights to selfhood which are prerequisite to its project.

Marvelous Possessions, heavily indebted to **Todorov**, is Greenblatt's most sustained discussion of the concept of alterity. It develops *Renaissance Self-Fashioning*'s examination of how selfhood is often constructed by the identification of an (often demonic) other. *Marvelous Possessions* addresses the textual traces of encounters between Europeans and the inhabitants of the New World. How did the one read the signs of the other? The Spanish, when they first glimpse Mexico, react with a sense of wonder. Thus in the face of the 'undreamed', there is a crisis of representation; how does one address the absolutely other? In the face of this radical alterity, one can adopt a discursive strategy of self-estrangement which articulates the sameness in opposed ways of being: 'you *are* the other and the other is you'. Or one can, with Columbus, rename, transform and appropriate in a strategy of terroristic estrangement. The other is made an alien object, a thing that can be either destroyed or subtly incorporated and contained through linguistic colonialism.

Greenblatt's work, notably *Renaissance Self-Fashioning* and *Shakespearean Negotiations*, and the journal *Representations*, which he edits, have set the tone for the New Historical strand within contemporary literary theory. Greenblatt has also been highly influential as a propagandist for Foucault in American literary theory, and his work is central to the new brand of Renaissance studies which began to reclaim the critical high ground from Romanticism during the 1980s.

Main works

Renaissance Self-Fashioning: From More to Shakespeare, Chicago and London: University of Chicago Press, 1980.

The Power of Forms in the English Renaissance (ed.), Norman, OK: Pilgrim Books, 1982.

Representing the English Renaissance (ed.), Berkeley, CA: University of California Press, 1988a.

Shakespearean Negotiations: The circulation of social energy in Renaissance England, Oxford: Clarendon Press, 1988b.

Learning to Curse: Essays in early modern culture, New York and London: Routledge, 1990.

Marvelous Possessions: The wonder of the New World, Oxford and New York: Clarendon Press, 1991.

Further reading

Kinney, Arthur F. and Dan S. Collins (eds), *Renaissance Historicism: Selections from English Literary Renaissance*, Amherst, MA: University of Massachusetts Press, 1987.

Veeser, H. Aram (ed.), *The New Historicism*, New York and London: Routledge, 1989.

Wilson, Richard and Richard Dutton (eds), *New Historicism and Renaissance Drama*, London and New York: Longman, 1992.

Greimas, Algirdas Julien (1917–)

A.J. Greimas is a linguist specializing in semantics and semiotics; he was born in Zula, Russia but acquired much of his higher education in Western Europe: he obtained his Licence-ès-lettres in 1939 from the University of Grenoble, and a Doctorat-ès-lettres in 1948 from the University of Paris. In 1965 he became Professor of Semantics and Semiotic Theory at the Ecole des Hautes Etudes en Sciences Sociales in Paris, and continues to be an associate of that school. He is arguably the most comprehensive theorist to have participated in what has come to be known as the 'structuralist revolution' of the mid 1960s. Structuralism – evolving out of a reading of Ferdinand de **Saussure**'s *Course in General Linguisitics*, which emphasized the dependence of meaning on the diacritical (or differential and hence structural) relations between elements in a semiological system, over and above its historical dimensions – was an attempt to establish a science of meaning that would apply to culture and its representation in the narrative structures of literature. In its development it would give scientific status to the study of what was traditionally known as the humanities by producing a vocabulary purportedly operating at the metalinguistic level. Following Saussure, structuralism came to view language as essentially dualistic – a complex system consisting of parts and wholes which work reciprocally to produce meaning, one that communicates messages and its own code: this insight became the basis for a revival of the study of semiotics (sometimes known as semiology), which was grounded in the view of language as system. Greimas's own semiotic orientation is related to Louis Hjelmslev's *glossematic* model of linguistic analysis, in that its rigorously deductive method aims to fund communication in what Kant calls 'the conditions of possibility'.

In keeping with the need to develop a theory of human culture and a method of analysis that could aspire to scientific status, Greimas's thinking about the nature of signification unfolds in three stages, the components of which become recontoured as they develop. The first stage (beginning in 1956), for example, is concerned with lexicology, or the classification of words, an enterprise that contradicted the Saussurean tradition (Saussure denied that the word had fundamental linguistic unity). This orientation is reconfigured in 1966, when Greimas moves into the area of semantics and the analysis of logical systems, in particular as they are understood in the binary phonological model of Roman **Jakobson**. Here, Jakobson's bifurcation of the expression plane of language into an immanent sphere of organization (the ordering of elementary units of expression, bundles of distinctive features or *phemes*) and a sphere of manifestation (the actual expression of complex phonological units or *phonemes*) is applied to the content plane of language: immanent elementary units of content (these minimal units of signification which are not substantive but acquire existence in relation to other units are called *semes*) are organized and manifest as complex units of content (*sememes*). This new model displaced lexicology and its axiological directive by replacing word classification with the study of *lexemes*, or configurations of sememes. In 1970, when it was clear that semantics could not provide an exhaustive scientific description of all linguistic forms because 'a natural language is coextensive with the culture of a community' (Greimas, interview in *Pratiques*, 11/12 (1976)), and hence circumscribed by a system or constellation which reflects back upon its own internal organization, Greimas moved into the area of semiotics.

What distinguishes Greimas's system, then, as outlined in his book *Sémantique Structurale*, is the emphasis he places on the phenomenal aspect of reception – the actual experience of meaning which exceeds the limits of the sentence (in other words, is not reducible to the bipolar reciprocity between parts and wholes), but is nevertheless explicable within the terms of the system as a whole, rather than by metaphysics. In other words, he attempts to move structuralism from the focus on the 'pure syntax' of binary oppositions into the context of *semantics*. Working through what he calls the 'duplex' structure of language (its ability to contrast and combine, disjunctively choose between different elements and conjoin elements in a series on what Saussure calls respectively the paradigmatic and the syntagmatic planes), Greimas identifies a *zone of entanglement*, a 'complex elemental structure', the concept of which takes the form of the *semiotic square*. The semiotic square includes three logical relations between binary oppositions: contrary, contradictory and complementary. For example, the opposition man/woman would be mapped as follows:

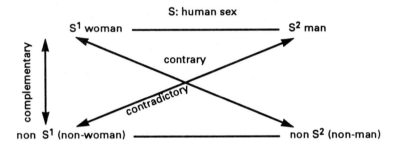

Contrary relations are both conjunctive and disjunctive; that is, they are different but united by some shared feature, in this case human sex. *Contradictory* relations, however, are joined and divided according to a shared function; here the absence or presence of the male reproductive function, or the absence or presence of the female reproductive function. *Complementary* relations complicate the logic of this easy scheme by allowing in other associations which do not follow the positive/negative pattern: woman implies non-man, but it also implies such discursive meanings as nurturing and domesticity. It is precisely these complementary relations that exceed the logic of the square and constitute the zone of entanglement; and it is here that the ideological function and the creative potential of language lie. If, for example, we were to change the contrary relations in this square from human sex to human gender, the cultural and political significance of what is left out becomes apparent.

The semiotic square, then, is an attempt to map the differential structure of meaning at its deepest level. The perception of differences between semes allows a world to form before us; but more than that – it allows for the formation of language, not only its syntax but the larger narrative structures which are articulated through this perception. This *double articulation* of meaning structure is constituted by the planes of immanence and manifestation in content and expression: whereas **Chomsky**, for example, uses the dichotomies competence/performance, deep structures/surface structures, *langue/parole* to account for two *levels* of meaning structure, Greimas locates semiotic and narrative structures on the same level.

In other words, Greimas's theory 'attempts to account for verbal meaning of all kinds . . . to formulate rules and concepts to account for meanings produced when they combine in sentences or in complete texts' (Culler, 1975). To this end, then, he argues for a 'grammar' of narrative, where narrative structures are generated by a finite number of semantic elements, analyzable at the level of the sentence: 'the content of the actions', he says, 'changes all the time, the actors vary, but the enunciation-spectacle [narrative grammar] remains always the same, for its permanence is guaranteed by the fixed distribution of the roles' (1983a). Hence Greimas describes his own semiotic project as one which tries to discover the relations between discourse and the sentence, a discursive linguistics and a sentential linguistics: his project is to articulate a semiotics that would 'theoretically mediate between narrative forms and linguistic forms of sentential dimensions' (1983b). For this he develops what he calls an 'actantial model' of narrative grammar, and uses the terms *actants, actant roles*, and *functions* in his description of the relationship between these two dimensions. *Actants* are abstract agencies, a grammar or structure of agency effects in discourse. They are defined reciprocally in relation to one another in terms of their actant roles and in relation to their 'spheres of action' or 'narrative functions'.

Like Vladimir **Propp** [*Morphology of a Folktale* (1928)] before him, Greimas attempts to work out the conditions for possible combination in the production of narrative, the elemental ground for the generation of semantic structures. In this he reconfigures Propp's seven 'spheres of action' (villian, donor, helper, sought-for person and her father, dispatcher, hero, false hero) into actantial categories, emphasizing the oppositional and relational aspects of these spheres (subject versus object, sender versus receiver, helper versus opponent): correspondingly, he organizes Propp's thirty-one functions into binary oppositions presupposed in the logical relations of the semiotic square. Combining actantial categories and functions in various ways makes it possible for him to isolate distinctive structural paradigms for the generation of narrative.

Despite the comprehensiveness of Greimasian linguistics, when the structuralist enterprise was at its zenith his work received little attention in the English-speaking West, though it was very important in France. His classification of characters in terms of actions rather that essential characteristics underpinned Roland **Barthes's** structural analysis of narrative (Barthes, 1977). However, this very sophisticated semiotics, which focus on enunciation rather than the utterance, have been considered, in the aftermath of structuralism, as an address to the crisis in semiotics which has produced the radical scepticism of 'post-structuralist' semiotics, or deconstruction. As such, his work continues to be relevant in current theoretical debates.

Main works

'The interaction of semiotic constraints', with Francios Rastier, *Yale French Studies* 41 (1968a): 86–105.

Dictionnaire de l'Ancien Français: jusqu'au milieu du XIV siècle Paris: Librairie Larousse, 1968b.

Du Sens, Paris: Editions du Seuil, 1983b.

Maupaussant La Sémiotique du texte: Exercises practiques, Paris: Editions du Seuil, 1976a.

Sémiotique et Sciences sociales, Paris: Editions du Seuil, 1976b.

Semiotics and Language: An analytical dictionary, with J. Courtes, trans. Larry Crist, Danielle Patte *et al.*, Bloomington: Indiana University Press, 1979.

Structural Semantics: An attempt at a method, trans. Daniele McDowell, Ronald Schleifer and Alan Velie, Lincoln: University of Nebraska Press, 1983a.

Du Sens, vol. 2, Paris: Editions du Seuil, 1983b. (with Teresa Mary Keane) *Aesthetics: A semiotic approach*, Minnesota: University of Minnesota Press, 1994.

Further reading

Armstrong, Nancy, 'Inside Greimas's square: literary characters and cultural restraint', in Wendy Steiner (ed.), *The Sign in Music and Literature*, Austin: University of Texas Press, 1981, pp. 52–66.

Barthes, Roland, *Image, Music, Text*, trans. Stephen Heath, London: Fontana, 1977.

Culler, Jonathan. *Structuralist Poetics*, Ithaca, NY: Cornell University Press, 1975.

Hawkes, Terence, *Structuralism and Semiotics*, London: Methuen, 1977.

Jameson, Fredric. *The Prison-House of Language*, Princeton, NJ: Princeton University Press, 1972.

Jameson, Fredric, *The Political Unconscious*, Ithaca, NY: Cornell University Press, 1981.

H

Habermas, Jürgen (1929–)

Habermas is currently Professor of Sociology and Philosophy at the Goethe University in Frankfurt, and has been described as the most important living intellectual in Germany, and certainly the most internationally renowned social theorist of the twentieth century since Max Weber. He reached maturity in the aftermath of the Second World War. As with many Germans of his generation, the traumatic discovery of what he calls the 'collectively realized inhumanity' taking place during his childhood years has endowed his writing with serious moral purpose. As assistant to **Adorno** in the 1950s, Habermas was schooled in the German philosophical tradition from Kant, through Hegel and **Marx**. His vocation today as critical conscience of the Federal Republic derives from commitment to the ideals of _'Enlightenment'_ in its radical sense of the constant interrogation of socially accepted norms to determine their validity through rational argument. It is this concept of 'rationality', and the attempt to define its meaning, which is central to Habermas's work, which has developed through a series of major academic controversies with significant public and political implications, including the confrontation with the student revolt of 1968, the debate with Hans-Georg **Gadamer** in 1971 over the relationship between ideology-critique and hermeneutics, and the attack on Postmodernist theory in the early 1980s.

The origin of Habermas's project lies in the perceived impasse reached by the so-called Frankfurt School, whose 'critical theory of society' had failed, according to Habermas, to provide either the normative foundations for its critique of modern capitalism or an adequate way of conceptualizing the mechanisms for its political transformation. Habermas's aim since the beginning of his enterprise in the 1960s is to reconstruct critical theory to rescue it from the exorbitant historical pessimism of Adorno on the one hand and reversions to Marxist 'orthodoxies' on the other.

For Habermas, social theory is neither a game nor 'science' in the narrow sense, having a larger social purpose; he sees the *raison d'être* of the social sciences in terms of the goal of human emancipation. Identifying himself with the dialectical tradition, he treats the knowledge social theory produces as *reflexive*: its subject matter includes the conditions for its own existence. Habermas's own social theory may be approached through his historical analysis of the bourgeois *public sphere* developed at the very beginning of his career. It becomes reformulated during the 1970s in his analysis of the 'crisis tendencies' in late capitalism and his reconstruction of Marxism into a more general theory of social evolution.

By the term 'public sphere' Habermas means the social world in which public opinion emerges. The public sphere, he argues, is a historically specific cultural institution as well as an imperfect prefiguration of a much larger, as yet unrealized, ideal. It represents the idea of a space, or an arena of democratic deliberation. The first forms of this public sphere are, of course, not 'open' at all: it is literally a bourgeois sphere in that it not only excluded those who did not own property, but is also defined in opposition to the 'private' sphere. Habermas's account of the structural transformation of this public sphere in the twentieth century follows the classic arguments of the Frankfurt School in seeing a concentration and centralization of power by parties and mass media increasingly displacing and distorting public debate. Manipulation and pseudo-communication have, he suggests, dominated politics.

In his subsequent analysis of late capitalism he tries to draw out the tensions and contradictions to which modern society is subject by a careful analysis of the concept of crisis in terms of system theory. While the central contradictions and conflicts of capitalism continue to be economic, these are no longer, as in Marx's time, capable of directly producing a crisis of the system itself, because the state and the political-administrative system has to a large extent modified the working of the economic system, so that crisis tendencies become, so to speak, displaced elsewhere, and take different forms. Habermas's revisions of Marxist theory are fundamental in this respect. Accepting much of Marx's critique of the way capitalism subjects society to its irrational and uncontrolled dynamics, he does not regard the class conflict between capital and labour as any longer the mechanism for its transformation. In Habermas's theory this is replaced by a more complex tension between what he calls the 'system' and the 'lifeworld', in which the latter is described as being 'colonized' by the former.

The lifeworld corresponds to the 'social' world as ordinarily understood: the everyday world in which social action and interaction occur. Habermas analyses it into three structural components: first, the stock of 'knowledge' – which he names culture – on which people draw; secondly, the social norms which regulate the institutional order – he calls this society – within which people act; and thirdly, the socially developed capabilities and skills – which he calls personality. For each of these there are corresponding processes of reproduction: cultural reproduction (whereby the culture furnishes knowledge and interpretive schemes sufficient for people to understand their situation); social integration (which legitimizes their social roles); and socialization (which equips people with the motivations for their social activity). These reproduction processes, when disturbed, are related to three corresponding forms of crisis: loss of meaning, anomie and psychopathology respectively. These social pathologies, Habermas suggests, are symptoms of the colonization of the lifeworld by the system of late capitalism.

The very existence of a 'system' (he is referring to the capitalist economy and the modern state appararatus) in modern society is grounded in an incomplete and constrained 'rationality', for a system can be said to exist only when purposive, or goal-directed action has, so to speak, insulated itself from the need for continual discursive justification. Once instrumental action is 'uncoupled' from communicative action in this way, it becomes possible for all the apparently automatic 'mechanisms' of economic and political institutions to regulate and dominate society. Habermas's analysis of the conditions for the functioning of the mechanisms of social reproduction arrives at the conclusion that one of the central problems that can be expected to be faced by modern societies is that of the need for *'legitimation'*. Contemporary society increasingly requires that its further development be morally accepted and actively supported by its members, and this requirement cannot be automatically guaranteed or artificially manufactured. It is this that underpins Habermas's analysis of the nature of communicative action. His theory of communication is directly linked with his social theory.

In the 1970s, through a 'linguistic turn', Habermas sought to develop the grounds for both critical social theory and democratic politics in a theory of language. His conception of language differs sharply from the way it has been treated by structuralist and post-structuralist theorists; for the latter, it is language as a *system* or code, or as *signifying practices*, which is the focus of interest. For Habermas, language is examined as a medium of *communication*, and communication as a social process whose political and, crucially, ethical dimensions are his central concern. Communicative action, as he calls it, is as fundamental to human society as material production; indeed, the latter cannot take place without it. He counterposes communicative action – by which he means 'action oriented to reaching an understanding' – with instrumental or strategic action, which is orientated towards the attainment of ends which may not be shared by the other participants, and may even be concealed from them. Habermas's concept of 'communicative rationality' is meant to define what he sees as the rational potential inherent in everyday communication.

Every time we speak, we are implicitly but necessarily subscribing to an idea of the possibility of communication; there are, he argues, basic norms involved even in the most elementary act of saying something to someone else. Habermas calls these 'validity claims': what you are saying has meaning; (if it is a statement of fact) it is true; it is justifiable or appropriate to say it (since speaking is a social act, it is subject to social norms), and you are being sincere, and not deceiving your listener. These norms provide the criteria by which actual communicative actions may be criticized through communicative action itself. His specification of the conditions for communicative rationality – for what he calls the liberation of the rational potential in everyday communication – makes it clear that he is reformulating the whole idea of 'emancipation' as conventionally understood: rather than thinking in terms of the individual subject, Habermas is trying to define emancipation in intersubjective terms. The theory of communication is part of a larger social theory.

Habermas's writings span the whole of social theory and the philosophy of the social sciences and have included several notable interventions in political affairs in Germany. The central aim of all his work is to demonstrate the possibility of a society that is both free and just. Modern capitalism, he insists, poses massive institutional obstacles to the realization of this through the domination of society by money, bureaucracy and, above all, by what he calls the 'systematically constrained and distorted communication' arising from the impact of power upon language. He claims that the way to achieve an emancipated society can be found through furthering the process of what he calls communicative rationality. A good deal of Habermas's sociological theorizing is devoted to systematically clarifying just what this 'rationality' (derived from the Classical conception of Reason) means.

Habermas has been a major figure in debates in North America on the philosophy of the social sciences, in political philosophy, and in sociological theory in Britain since the 1970s; his ideas have been drawn upon by writers such as Bauman, Giddens, Lash, and Keane in discussions of such issues as the nature of modernity, the rise of new social movements, the politics of science and technology, and the nature of democracy. In the early 1980s his involvement in the debates over postmodernism brought his ideas into the orbit of Anglo-American literary and cultural theory. This began with an attack upon the neo-conservative writers who had blamed aesthetic and cultural modernism for the social pathologies of modern life, and his argument took the form of a defence of the 'unfulfilled project' of modernity itself, in which, he claims, aesthetic modernism and avant-garde art, contrary to their own ambitions, can play only a limited and specific progressive role. This argument was the subject of a critique by **Lyotard**, who presented Habermas as a conservative figure seeking to 'liquidate the heritage of the avant-garde', whose philosophy of communication implied a totalitarian demand for universal consensus.

It is Habermas's allegiance to – and painstaking efforts to vindicate – the ethical and political implicit in the idea of enlightenment that has given his work, in the eyes of many cultural theorists today, the aura of a deeply unfashionable rationalism and moralism.

Main works

The Theory of Communicative Action, trans. T. McCarthy, Cambridge: Polity, 1987.

The Philosophical Discourse of Modernity, trans. F. Lawrence, Cambridge: Polity, 1987.

The New Conservatism, trans. S.W. Nicholsen, Cambridge: Polity, 1989.

Structural Transformation of the Public Sphere, trans. T. Burger and F. Lawrence, Cambridge, Mass.: MIT Press, 1989.

Knowledge and Human Interests, trans. J.J. Shapiro, Boston: Beacon Press, 1971.

Legitimation Crisis, trans. T. McCarthy, Boston: Beacon Press, 1975.

Moral Consciousness and Communicative Action, trans. C. Lenhardt and S.W. Nicholsen, Cambridge: Polity, 1990.

Autonomy and Solidarity: Interviews, ed. P. Dews, London: Verso, 1986.

Further reading

Brand, A., *The Force of Reason: An introduction to Habermas' theory of communication*, London: Allen & Unwin, 1990.

Holub, Robert C., *Jürgen Habermas: Critic in the public sphere*, London: Routledge, 1991.

Pusey, Michael, *Jürgen Habermas*, London: Tavistock/Ellis Horwood: Key Sociologists series, 1987.

Rasmussen, David, *Reading Habermas*, Oxford: Blackwell, 1990.

Ray, Larry J., *Rethinking Critical Theory: Emancipation in the age of global social movements*, London: Sage, 1993.

White, Stephen K., *The Recent Work of Jürgen Habermas*, Cambridge: Cambridge University Press, 1990.

Glossary

Rationality: Habermas draws a distinction between instrumental or purposive rationality and communicative rationality. It is the former, definable as the methodical and efficient utilization of things and people as means towards some end, which underlies Weber's theory of **rationalization**, as a historical tendency (characteristic of modernity) for human action to be subject to increasing calculation, measurement and control. Habermas distinguishes this from another meaning of 'rationality', as when one demands that 'reasons' be given when one is given orders. This sense of rationality is what he has elaborated with his concept of 'communicative rationality'.

Hall, Stuart (1932–)

Stuart Hall was born in Kingston, Jamaica, and educated in Jamaica and at Merton College, Oxford (Rhodes Scholar). He was a founding editor of *New Left Review*, Research Fellow and then Director of the Centre for Contemporary Cultural Studies, University of Birmingham. He is currently Professor of Sociology, The Open University.

Stuart Hall's work is defined by a dialectic of structure and agency. In a paraphrase of **Marx**, his critical focus is the way in which 'we make history in conditions not of our making'. In a series of critical engagements with the work of major European thinkers – including Louis **Althusser**, Roland **Barthes**, Umberto **Eco**, Antonio **Gramsci**, Claude **Lévi-Strauss**, Ferdinand de **Saussure** and Valentin **Voloshinov** – Hall has defined the theoretical concerns of British cultural studies, establishing ideology and ideological struggle as its central concepts.

In the 1970s Hall developed the encoding/decoding model of media productions. This model posits two moments of meaning production: the meaning made in production and the meaning made in consumption. 'Messages' are encoded, using a variety of codes, conventions and discourses, to produce a 'preferred' meaning, but there are no guarantees that this meaning will be taken up by an audience, 'decoding' itself is also an act of producing meaning. However, it is a situated form of production, constrained by the discursive positions available to the viewer. Hall (borrowing from Raymond **Williams**) suggests three possible positions: 'dominant', 'negotiated' and 'oppositional'. Occupation of the dominant position is taking the message at the level of the preferred meaning, understanding it as it is intended to be understood. A negotiated reading entails an acknowledgement and acceptance, in general terms, of the legitimacy of the preferred meaning, but a refusal, on the basis of a logic of 'exception to the rule', to accept it. Finally, an oppositional reading is one in which the preferred meaning is recognized and understood, but nevertheless rejected.

In the 1980s Hall increasingly embraced the work of Gramsci to formulate what has become the dominant cultural studies position on ideology. Rejected is the view that ideology is a form of concealment, a process of masking the the real nature of struggles taking place elsewhere; instead it takes on a specificity of its own, a 'relative autonomy', requiring analysis on its own terms. No longer the immaterial expression of forces operating elsewhere in the social formation, ideology is now seen as a material force in its own right: that is, material in its effects. Ideological struggle is still related to other struggles. To win consent to 'Black is Beautiful', for example, required more than words and images. However, a class which neglects ideological struggle will quickly find its economic interests under threat.

Within the framework of Gramsci's concept of hegemony, Hall developed a theory of 'articulation' and 'disarticulation' to explain the processes of ideological struggle. (Hall's use of 'articulation' plays on the term's double meaning: to express, to utter, to speak forth, but also to connect, as in 'articulated lorry'.) He argues that cultural texts and practices are not inscribed with a meaning guaranteed once and for all by the intentions of production. Meaning is always the result of an act of 'articulation' within particular social relations. Articulation is the active process of production in use. Culture is both the site and the result of a struggle over meaning: a process of articulation and disarticulation. Cultural texts and practices are not inscribed with particular politics – texts and practices have to be articulated for particular politics. The meaning of a cultural text or practice, or its place or status in the cultural field, is not inscibed in its form, nor is its meaning, place or status in the cultural field fixed for all time. 'This year's radical symbol or slogan will be neutralized into next year's fashion; the year after, it will be the object of profound cultural nostalgia' ('Notes on deconstructing "the popular"').

The cultural field is defined by this struggle to articulate and disarticulate texts and practices for particular ideologies, particular politics. Hall contends that 'meaning is always a social production, a practice. The world has to be *made to mean*' ('The rediscovery of "ideology"'). If this is so, it leads to the question of which kinds of meaning are systematically and regularly constructed around particular events. Moreover, because meaning is always a production, a practice, different meanings can be ascribed to the same events. But some meanings achieve the status of 'common sense', acquire a certain taken-for-granted quality. What makes this process ideological is the will to win credibility for a particular and partial account of social reality, but ideologies do not belong to particular classes or group.

This does not mean that particular ideologies do not have a particular historical relationship with a specific class or group, but such ideologies are always open to disarticulation and rearticulation in the interests of other groups and classes. Ideological struggle, therefore, consists of attempts to win new meanings for particular concepts or practices, and attempts to dis-articulate other concepts and practices from their location in competing discourses. Although Hall sees the mass media, and the cultural industries generally, as a major site of ideological production, constructing powerful images, descriptions, definitions, frames of reference for understanding the world, he rejects the view that working people who consume popular culture are 'cultural dopes', victims of 'an up-dated form of the opium of the people':

> That judgement may make us feel right, decent and self-satisfied about our denunciations of the agents of mass manipulation and deception – the capitalist cultural industries: but I don't know that it is a view which can survive for long as an adequate account of cultural relationships; and even less as a socialist perspective on the culture and nature of the working class. Ultimately, the notion of the people as a purely *passive*, outline force is a deeply unsocialist perspective. ('Notes on deconstructing "the popular"')

In contrast, the field of culture is for Hall a major site of ideological struggle, a 'constant battlefield' in which there is 'a continuous and necessarily uneven and unequal struggle, by the dominant culture, constantly to disorganise and reorganise popular culture; to enclose and confine its definitions and forms within a more inclusive range of dominant forms' (*ibid.*). The cultural field is one of the sites where hegemony is to be won or lost: a terrain of 'consent' and 'resistance', marked by attempts to secure relations of domination and subordination, and the processes by which these relations are articulated. The logic of Hall's position, clearly influenced by the work of Pierre **Bourdieu**, is that cultural power, as an aspect of the struggle between dominant and subordinate classes in society, depends on a constant and vigilant policing of the boundaries between dominant and popular culture. Moreover, the distinction between dominant and popular culture is one of 'form' rather than 'content'. What is significant, what must be policed, is the categories, the categorical differences. The content of these categories can change, and does change; it is the distinction between them – and, more importantly, the distinction between their occupants (for these are, ultimately, social rather than cultural categories) – which is of crucial importance, and must be policed at all costs.

From the late 1980s, onwards Hall's work has focused more and more on the politics of identity; on an attempt to theorize identity as always 'formed at the unstable point where the "unspeakable" stories of subjectivity meet the narratives of history, of a culture' ('Minimal selves', *Identity*). He has written about his own 'long, important education of discovery that I am "black"' (*ibid.*). But in keeping with his earlier work, Hall rejects the view that identity is an 'accomplished fact', arguing instead that identity is always a '"production", which is never complete, always in process, and always constituted within, not outside, representation' ('Cultural identity and diaspora').

Stuart Hall is one of the founding figures of British cultural studies. His name carries enormous authority in the field – he has been a leading figure in cultural studies for almost thirty years. In fact, in the internalization of British cultural studies, Hall seems at times to *be* the field. His influence on British cultural studies has therefore been immense. More than any other writer, he has defined and redefined the field of British cultural studies.

Main works

The Popular Arts (with P. Whannel), London: Hutchinson, 1964.

Resistance through Rituals (ed. with T. Jefferson), London: Hutchinson, 1976.

Policing the Crisis (with C. Chritcher, T. Jefferson, J. Clarke and B. Roberts), London: Macmillan, 1978.

Culture, Media, Language (ed. with D. Hobson, A. Lowe and P. Willis), London: Hutchinson, 1980.

'Notes on deconstructing "the popular"', in R. Samuel (ed.), *People's History and Socialist Theory*, London: Routledge, 1981.

'The rediscovery of "ideology": return of the repressed in media studies', in M. Gurevitch *et al.* (eds), *Culture, Society and the Media*, London: Methuen, 1982.

Politics of Thatcherism (with M. Jacques), London: Lawrence & Wishart, 1983.

The Hard Road to Renewal: Thatcherism and the crisis of the left, London: Verso, 1988.

New Times (with M. Jacques), London: Lawrence & Wishart, 1989.

'Cultural identity and diaspora', in J. Rutherford (ed.), *Identity*, London: Lawrence & Wishart, 1990.

Further reading

Brantlinger, Patrick, *Crusoe's Footsteps: Cultural Studies in Britain and America*, London: Routledge, 1990.

Harris, David, *From Class Struggle to the Politics of Pleasure: The effects of Gramscianism on cultural studies*, London: Routledge, 1992.

Journal of Communication Inquiry, 10, 2 (1986), 'Special Issue on the Work of Stuart Hall'.

McGuigan, Jim, *Cultural Populism*, London: Routledge, 1992.

Turner, Graeme, *British Cultural Studies: An introduction*, London: Unwin Hyman, 1990.

Hartman, Geoffrey H. (1929–)

Geoffrey Hartman was born in Frankfurt-am-Main, Germany, into a Jewish family. His family fled from Germany in the late 1930s because of the persecution of the Jews, and Hartman came to England, where he received his secondary education. In 1946 he left England to join his mother in New York and completed his BA there at Queens College in 1949. After graduation he went to Yale University, where he studied Comparative Literature under Rene Wellek and Erich Auerbach, amongst others. He was awarded his PhD in 1953, and from 1955 he taught at Yale, then at the University of Iowa, and from the mid 1960s again at Yale, where he is currently Karl Young Professor of English and Comparative Literature. Hartman's career is characterized by several concerns: a broad interest in Romantic and modern European literature and philosophy; influential contributions to Wordsworth studies; meditations on the role of the critical essay in contemporary literary and cultural studies (including the idea of 'criticism as answerable style'); a notable receptivity to the work of Jacques **Derrida** and, most recently, contributions to the field of Jewish studies.

The methodology of Hartman's early books, especially *The Unmediated Vision* [*UV*] (1954) and *Wordsworth's Poetry 1787–1814* (1964), shows him to be independent of the prevalent critical orthodoxy of the time in North America, the New Criticism. Hartman was educated within the

European tradition of Comparative Literature, and his early critical thinking seems to have been influenced by phenomenology, which to him meant 'describing one's responses and feelings as directly as possible'. In terms of his early work, Hartman has insisted that his reading of Kant, Hegel and Husserl was intuitive rather than a matter of a conscious awareness of, or identification with, contemporary schools of critical thought. *UV*, a revised version of his PhD, appears loosely phenomenological in its examination of four 'modern' poets, Wordsworth, Hopkins, Rilke and Valéry, each of whom, in different ways, breaks from Judaeo-Christian traditions in his quest 'for a pure representation through the direct sensuous intuition of reality'. Hartman's view of Romanticism as the negotiation of the relationship between consciousness and nature within a new, secular context, and his related insight that 'the aggrandizement of art' in the Romantic period can be seen most profitably in terms of a new-found freedom from religion or religiously inspired myth, places his work within an identifiable relationship to other North American Romanticists influential in the 1950s and 1960s, including Abrams, Hillis **Miller**, **Bloom** and even **Frye**.

Hartman's most singular contributions to Romantic studies within the American academy are to be found in his essay 'Romanticism and anti-self-consciousness' (1962), and the highly influential book *Wordsworth's Poetry* [*WP*]. These works place him at the forefront of a North American tradition of understanding English Romantic poetry through the language of German Romantic philosophy, a tradition to be sharply differentiated from the work of certain British critics, including Raymond **Williams** and Marilyn Butler, for whom Romanticism demands location within a historical and material context. Cynthia Chase's elegant summary of 'Romanticism and anti-self-consciousness' captures well the paradoxical nuances it explores: 'Hartman describes art as conceived by the Romantics as a remedy for the ills of thought, a cure drawn from consciousness itself for the disintegrative effects of self-consciousness.' The idea of describing the interaction between mind and nature in terms of a triadic function, 'Nature, Self-Consciousness, and Imagination – the last term . . . involving a kind of return to the first' displays Hartman's implicit debts to both Kant and Hegel. The second part of *WP*, 'Synopsis: The *Via Naturaliter Negativa*' is a further working-out of this movement whereby there is a consistency in what seems to be the 'negative way of nature': 'It can be shown, via several important episodes of *The Prelude*, that Wordsworth thought nature itself led him beyond nature' (*WP*). Hartman thus provides an account of the relationship between consciousness and nature, both in Wordsworth's poetry and in Romanticism generally, which opens up the way for the reflexive concerns of deconstruction. Though he was to deny any unity of outlook in the so-called 'Yale School', his institutional affiliations with **de Man**, Hillis Miller and Bloom, and his essay in (and Preface to) *Deconstruction and Criticism* (1979), indicate his instrumental role in this important development in Romantic criticism in the United States.

The 'Romanticism' essay is reprinted in *Beyond Formalism* [*BF*] (1970), a collection of essays on various themes, which inaugurates Hartman's continual attempt to mediate between 'the Continental style of criticism', in which literary form is often neglected and art dissolved 'into a reflex of consciousness, technology, or social process', and an Anglo-American respect for literary form. Contrary to what might reasonably be assumed, the title essay of *BF* is preoccupied with 'how hard it is to advance "beyond formalism" in the understanding of literature' (*FR* [*The Fate of Reading*]), rather than with offering an alternative to it. In this regard, Christopher **Norris** is close to the mark in his assertion that Hartman's 'criticism moves not so much "beyond formalism" as round and about its ambiguous fringes'. Nevertheless, *BF* is concerned with moving beyond what Hartman sees as a narrowness of approach in the brand of formalism bequeathed by the New Critics, towards a mode of criticism which will 'lead to an understanding of the intrinsic role of the arts in all culture'. His interest in the larger gestures of interpretation rather than the finer, narrower ones of exegesis or explication, is already articulated here in terms of the great models of interpretation within the biblical tradition. From 'The interpreter: a self-analysis', the opening essay in *The Fate of Reading* (1975), onwards, Hartman's own style begins to adopt a wilfully allusive, punning, ironic tone in contradistinction to the severity and restraint of the British tradition inaugurated by Matthew Arnold and T.S. Eliot. There are parallels with Bloom in this refusal of the polite civilities of British criticism (as there are in many other features of Hartman's work). From *FR* to *Minor Prophecies* [*MP*] (1991), Hartman's pre-eminent concern is with meditating on the activity of criticism and interpretation, and in promoting his own favoured medium, the essay. The summation of this self-conscious fascination with the critical enterprise is *Criticism in the Wilderness* [*CW*] (1980), which consolidates his attempt to 'to view criticism, in fact, as within literature, not outside of it looking in'. The idea that criticism needs to be expressed in a language which is answerable to the art with which it engages means that Hartman, as Norris puts it, 'makes a virtue and even a vocation of pushing his critical style to the edge of sheer self-indulgence'. But there is also, arguably, an ethical dimension to Hartman's enterprise. The essay is seen as the most fitting medium of criticism for our time because 'All occasions inform the essayist . . . but in a purely secular way' (*CW*), and 'the secularism of critical prose' serves during the totalitarian phases of the twentieth century as a mode of resistance against 'the mere substitution of politics for religion' (*MP*).

The quest to blur the conventionally sharp distinction between critical and creative writing, and to challenge the normative hierarchy of 'primary' and 'secondary' reading in the study of literature, reflects Hartman's reading of Derrida, which began to influence his work from the mid 1970s. The idea (expressed in *CW*) that 'there is no absolute knowledge but rather a textual infinite, an interminable web of texts or interpretations' can also be seen to share Bloom's contemporary preoccupation (in his tetralogy) with interpretation rather than notionally stable texts. *Saving the Text* (1981) is Hartman's most sustained engagement with Derrida, and it takes the form not of an exposition but, rather, of an assessment of 'Derrida's place in the history of commentary, and with *Glas* as an event in that history'. *Glas* was the first of Derrida's texts to compel Hartman, and clearly it is Derrida's engagement with the question of the status of commentary which is of fundamental interest in terms of Hartman's wider consideration of the role of criticism (a question which also informs his more recent interest in the study of Hebrew traditions of interpretation).

Hartman's most striking contribution to contemporary theory has been his desire to elevate the role, and the language, of literary criticism. This can be seen within several contexts: a hostility to the traditional (especially British) view of the secondary role of the critic; a receptivity to the work of Derrida, de Man and others in extending rhetorical inquiry beyond primary texts; and an interest in the creative forms of commentary within the Jewish tradition. Hartman's celebrated promotion of the essay form has also generated a significant momentum in contemporary American criticism (see, for example, the work of G. Douglas Atkins).

Main works

The Unmediated Vision: An Interpretation of Wordsworth, Hopkins, Rilke, and Valéry, New Haven: Yale University Press, 1954.

André Malraux, London: Bowes & Bowes, 1960.

Wordsworth's Poetry, 1787–1814, New Haven: Yale University Press, 1964.

Beyond Formalism: Literary essays, 1958–1970, New Haven: Yale University Press, 1970.

The Fate of Reading and Other Essays, Chicago: University of Chicago Press, 1975.

'Words, Wish, Worth, Wordsworth', in Harold Bloom *et al.*, *Deconstruction and Criticism*, London: RKP, 1979.

Criticism in the Wilderness: The study of literature today, New Haven: Yale University Press, 1980.

Saving the Text: Literature, Derrida, philosophy, Baltimore: Johns Hopkins University Press, 1981.

Easy Pieces, New York: Columbia University Press, 1985.

(ed. with Sanford Budick), *Midrash and Literature,* New Haven: Yale University Press, 1986.

The Unremarkable Wordsworth, Foreword by Donald G. Marshall, London: Methuen, 1987.

Minor Prophecies: The literary essay in the culture wars, Cambridge, Mass.: Harvard University Press, 1991.

Further reading

Atkins, G. Douglas, *Geoffrey Hartman: Criticism as answerable style,* London: Routledge, 1990.

Chase, Cynthia (ed.), *Romanticism,* Harlow: Longman, 1993, pp. 4–8, 43–54.

Norris, Christopher, *Deconstruction: Theory and practice,* London: Methuen, 1982, pp.92–9.

Salusinszky, Imre, Interview with Geoffrey Hartman in *Criticism in Society,* London: Methuen, 1987, pp. 75–96.

Sprinker, Michael, 'Aesthetic criticism: Geoffrey Hartman,' in Jonathan Arac, Wlad Godzich and Wallace Martin (eds), *The Yale Critics: Deconstruction in America,* Minneapolis: University of Minnesota Press, 1983, pp. 43–65.

Hirsch, E.D. Jr (1928–)

E.D. Hirsch, who has held professorships of English at the universities of Yale and Virginia, has been the most forceful advocate in American academe of the methodology of traditional literary scholarship. His early work is devoted exclusively to the Romantic period, consisting of studies of Wordsworth and Schelling and of Blake, but in 1967 he produced *Validity in Interpretation,* a far-ranging defence of conventional protocols of literary interpretation. He continued this project, though in a work more slanted towards the task of aesthetic evaluation, with *The Aims of Interpretation* (1976). Before *Validity in Interpretation,* the case for traditional literary history had, to some extent, gone unstated. Its exponents had been content to repose on a corpus of somewhat pious truisms: that literary meaning is an essentially knowable and shareable commodity; that is is identical to, or closely linked with, an authorial intention; and that there are valid and invalid procedures through which meaning can be ascertained. For the most part Hirsch goes along with such tenets, while he also makes the radical contribution of putting at their disposal a comprehensive hermeneutic rationale, culled in large part from theological and philosophical sources.

The cogency of *Validity in Interpretation* owes much to Hirsch's willingness to concede ground to (what might seem) sceptical assumptions in order to fight his case on more favourable territory. Even the book's title is concessive: nowhere does Hirsch seek to argue that the 'truth' of an interpretation can be demonstrated, only that an interpretation can gain 'validity' by being arrived at through a normative and consensually-agreed procedure. Several of his particular standpoints also seem, at face value, to coincide with broadly sceptical assumptions: for example, he refuses to accept that 'meaning' can be intrinsic to an utterance or word-sequence, arguing instead that it arises from the interrelation between an utterance and an intending consciousness. The argument, then, is sinuous, and in no sense 'commonsensical'; indeed, the book's arguments are hard to dislodge simply because they themselves incorporate sceptical positions.

Validity in Interpretation begins with an attack on a series of then modish critical standpoints, all of them conspiring to downgrade the importance of the author's intention to the act of interpretation. Most of the polemic is turned on two distinct schools of thought. First, there is the New Critical dogma that an utterance (or a literary work) possesses intrinsic meanings that exist autonomously of any intention belonging to its author: Hirsch thinks this argument is merely a smokescreen for the critic to impose his own meaning on the text and then claim that it is objective to the work itself. Second, there is the highly subjectivist notion that the meaning of a text varies with each successive reader, so that the pertinent question is not what a text *means* but what it *means to* an individual reader. Hirsch's response to this subjectivist challenge is far-reaching for his entire project, and involves both ethical and taxonomic judgements. It should be stressed that nowhere does he claim that there is an absolute intellectual sovereignty of one philosophy of interpretation over any other; no logically unassailable case exists for taking the author's intention (rather than the reader's response) as the locus of meaning.

Hirsch's valorization of authorial meaning is thus an ethical decision: to try to procure an authorial meaning is, for him, to interpret in a way that respects all language as an extension into the social domain of an individual human consciousness, and to work on the assumption of objective meaning is to posit a community of readers who can share its perceptions and co-operate towards deeper understanding. These values come to the fore intermittently in *Validity in Interpretation*, and are elaborated in a later essay, 'Three dimensions of hermeneutics' (reprinted in *The Aims of Interpretation*). On the basis of them, Hirsch makes probably his most influential hermeneutic distinction: that between meaning and significance. 'Meaning' is equated with an authorial intention incarnated in an utterance or word-sequence; 'significance' is a reader's relation to a work's meaning or, indeed, the relation authors may have to their own meanings. This distinction, though elementary, has been useful as an antidote to critical fuzziness. For example, it helps us to see Matthew Arnold's public renunciation of his poem 'Empedocles on Etna' not as an attempt to restate the poem's meaning but as an expression of the changed significance that the original meaning had acquired for the author.

By proposing that meaning arises from the relation between a word-sequence and a mental intention, Hirsch poses for himself a theoretical conundrum: how is it that something ostensibly so nebulous, and by its nature relational, can be conveyed from one person to another? Hirsch goes to some lengths to claim that verbal meanings are, in fact, determinate, and both shareable with and reproducible by those to whom they are transmitted. How this becomes possible owes much to his concept of 'typification'. All verbal meanings – so Hirsch claims – are instances of 'types'; types, indeed, are basic to how we construe our experience, since to understand any phenomenon is to understand it with regard to the 'type' of which it is an instance. You can, for example, understand what an owl is only if you have a prior familiarity with the type of 'bird'; similarly, you cannot understand 'love' without reference to the larger type of 'human emotion'. All verbal meanings, then, are resoluble to type; and it is the fact of their typologicality that makes them objective and therefore capable of being conveyed to, and understood by, others. The typological system that is most closely bound up with literature is that of genre, and Hirsch proposes that literary interpretation will often conform to the following pattern: first a reader encounters the particulars of a work, and from these recognizes the type to which the work belongs (realist novel, tragic play, etc.); having grasped the type, he then repairs back to the text's particulars, construing them in the light of the high-level type they exemplify.

Hirsch's hermeneutic theory proved serviceable mainly as a theoretical rationale for what was, even in the 1960s, a long-standing literary historical methodology: in other words, his work never attempted to instigate some radically new method of interpreting literary texts. For this reason, his theoretical project is vulnerable to being seen as essentially backward-looking. Moreover, simply because

Hirsch has tried to rest a case on strenuous argumentation, his enterprise is badly compromised where particular arguments do not seem to hold up. The argument about typification, for example, has more than a whiff of expedience about it: are *all* verbal meanings really instances of types? But Hirsch's work does retain the merit of putting itself on the line, and of making itself available to all refutations that might be forthcoming.

To some extent, Hirch's has been an isolated voice. His project for an objectivist criticism was unfortunate in that it coincided with a general movement towards critical subjectivism – one, indeed, which *Validity in Interpretation* was unable to arrest. The chief effect of Hirsch's two major theoretical works was probably to put heart into those engaged in traditional literary scholarship, who suddenly discovered that their activity, which some thought obdurate to theorization, could actually be accounted for and justified in theoretical terms. The present moment sees increasing intolerance of extremities of critical subjectivism and relativism, to which Hirsch himself was doggedly opposed, but it is not clear that his work is gaining prominence even in this new context. This is, perhaps, a pity. Although he is always seen as a 'conservative' critic, Hirsch anticipates the commitment of many current critical 'radicals' in believing that protocols of interpretation should be accountable to the social values and practices we would like to see nurtured and upheld in the world around us.

Main works

Wordsworth and Schelling: A typological study of Romanticism, New Haven, CT: Yale University Press, 1960.

Innocence and Experience: An introduction to Blake, New Haven, CT: Yale University Press, 1964.

Validity in Interpretation, New Haven, CT: Yale University Press, 1967.

The Aims of Interpretation, Chicago: University of Chicago Press, 1976.

Cultural Literacy: What every American needs to know, Boston, MA: Houghton Mifflin, 1987.

Further reading

Eagleton, Terry, *Literary Theory: An introduction*, Oxford: Blackwell, 1983, pp. 67–71.

Fowler, Alastair, *Kinds of Literature: An introduction to the theory of genres and modes*, Cambridge, MA: Harvard University Press, 1982.

Meiland, Jack, 'Interpretation as a cognitive discipline', *Philosophy and Literature*, 2 (1978): 23–45.

Nehamas, Alexander, 'The postulated author: critical monism as an ideal', *Critical Inquiry*, 8 (1981): 133–49.

Selden, Raman, *Criticism and Objectivity*, London: Allen & Unwin, 1984.

Hoggart, Richard (1918–)

Richard Hoggart was born in Leeds, and educated at local schools and at the University of Leeds. He has been staff tutor and then senior staff tutor in the Department of Adult Education, University of Hull, lecture in English at the University of Leicester, and Professor of English and Director of the Centre for Contemporary Cultural Studies (which he founded in 1963) at the University of Birmingham. He was Assistant Director-General for UNESCO from 1970 to 1975, and Warden of Goldsmiths' College, University of London, from 1976 until his retirement in 1984.

Although Richard Hoggart has written a great deal on matters of culture, from his early work on the poetry of W.H. Auden to his later work on society and the mass media, his reputation continues to be founded on *The Uses of Literacy*. Therefore, any discussion of his contribution to cultural and literary theory tends, in effect, to be a discussion of this book.

The Uses of Literacy is a book about working-class culture, but it has also become, for the student of cultural and literary theory, a book about the break with the **Leavis**ite tradition of cultural analysis. Hoggart locates the working class in two historical moments; the 1930s and the 1950s. His aim is explore how one kind of working-class culture has given way to another. The first part of the book describes the working-class culture of Hoggart's youth. This is seen as a 'traditional' culture. The second part describes the culture under threat from new forms (especially from America) of mass entertainment. Dividing the book in this way produces a 'before and after' effect, an inevitable sense of cultural fall: the good traditional popular culture of the 1930s gives way to the bad inauthentic mass culture of the 1950s. At times Hoggart is aware that a certain nostalgia might be colouring his account of the 1930s, and thus darkening his perception of the 1950s. He is also conscious of the way his decision to divide his account in this way underplays the amount of continuity between the two periods. However, his argument is not that the working class suffered a 'moral' decline from one period to the other, but that there is a clearly identifiable decline in what he calls the 'moral seriousness' of the culture provided for the working class.

Hoggart breaks with the Leavisite tradition in that he does not view the working class as the passive and hopeless victims of a manipulative culture. On the contrary, he argues that there is something about the working-class response to mass culture which protects it from total manipulation. It is always partial: 'with a large part of themselves they are just "not there", are living elsewhere, living intuitively, habitually, verbally, drawing on myth, aphorism, and ritual. This saves them from the worst effects.' Moreover, the working class, according to Hoggart, operate (this is especially true of the period before the 1950s) with a popular aesthetic marked by a taste for culture that 'shows' rather than 'explores', an aesthetic which seeks not 'an escape from ordinary life' but its intensification, premised on the belief 'that ordinary life is intrinsically interesting'. The problem with the mass culture becoming available in the 1950s is that it is a culture 'full of corrupt brightness, of improper appeals and moral evasions'. As if this were not bad enough, it is also a culture which actively threatens 'a gradual drying-up of the more positive, the fuller, the more cooperative kinds of enjoyment, in which one gains much by giving much'. In this way, the new mass culture threatens to destroy the very fabric of the older and, for Hoggart, much more 'healthy' working-class culture of the 1930s.

Hoggart's fear is that 'we are moving towards the creation of a mass culture; that the remnants of what was at least in parts an urban culture "of the people" are being destroyed; and that the new mass culture is in some important ways less healthy than the often crude culture it is replacing'. For Hoggart, the working-class culture of the 1930s expressed what he calls 'The rich full life', marked by a strong and active sense of community. He sees this as a culture made by the people; a popular culture that is both communal and self-made: a culture 'of the people' rather than 'for the people'. The first half of *The Uses of Literacy* consists of example of communal and self-made entertainment. The analysis is often in considerable advance of Leavisism. For example, Hoggart defends working-class appreciation of popular song, against the dismissive hostility of Leavisite longings for the 'purity' of folk music, in terms which were soon to become central to the project of cultural studies. Songs become successful, he argues, 'no matter how much Tin Pan Alley plugs them', only if they can be made to meet the emotional requirements of their popular audience. When, in the second part of the book, Hoggart turns to consider the popular culture of the 1950s, the self-making and communal aspect of working-class culture is mostly kept from view. The popular aesthetic, so important for an understanding of the working-class culture of the 1930s, is now forgotten in a breathless rush to condemn the popular culture of the 1950s. Instead of a discussion of the popular aesthetic, and the active audience, we are taken on a guided tour of the manipulative power of mass culture. Hoggart decribes a culture which no longer offers the possibility of a full rich life. The traditional working-class culture of his youth (as perceived and understood by Hoggart the middle-aged academic) is under threat and in retreat from the 'commercial' onslaught of the 'shiny barbarism' of a new mass culture.

This is an attack to which the young are most vulnerable. These 'barbarians in wonderland' demand more, and are given more, than their parents or grandparents had or expected. But such mindless hedonism, according to Hoggart, leads only to a cycle of debilitating excess. The pleasures of mass culture do not so much 'debase taste', 'they over-excite it, eventually dull it, and finally kill it'. Hoggart offers many examples of what he takes to be instances of cultural decline, but perhaps the most striking portent of the decline into a 'candy-floss wonderland' is the habitual visitor to the new milk bars, the so-called 'juke-box boys' (Hoggart's term for the teddy boy). Milk bars are themselves symptomatic: they 'indicate at once, in the nastiness of their modernistic knick-knacks, their glaring showiness, an aesthetic break-down so complete'. Patrons are mostly 'boys between fifteen and twenty, with drape-suits, picture ties, and an American slouch'. Night after night they 'put copper after copper into the mechanical record-player'. The music is played loud: it 'is allowed to blare out so that the noise would be sufficient to fill a good-sized ballroom. . . . The young men waggle one shoulder or stare, as desperately as Humphrey Bogart, across the tubular chairs.' Hoggart describes the culture of the juke-box boys as 'a peculiarly thin and pallid form of dissipation, a sort of spiritual dry-rot'. To Hoggart, they are 'a depressing group', and although 'they are not typical', they are an ominous sign of things to come. The juke-box symptomatically bears the prediction of a society in which 'the larger part of the population is reduced to a condition of obediently receptive passivity, their eyes glued to television sets, pin-ups, and cinema screens'.

Hoggart's approach to popular culture has much in common with the approach of Leavisism. Hoggart shares with Leavis a belief in a fall from a healthy popular culture to a manipulative and corrupting mass culture. He also shares with Leavis the belief that this can be resisted by education in discrimination. However, what marks the difference between Hoggart and Leavis is the former's detailed preoccupation with – and above all, his clear commitment to – working-class culture. The distance between the two positions is most evident when we consider Hoggart's 'good past/bad present' binary opposition. Instead of Leavis's organic community of the seventeenth century, Hoggart's 'good past' is the working-class culture of the 1930s. The culture he celebrates is the very culture the Leavisites are 'armed' to resist. This alone makes Hoggart's approach an implicit critique of – and advance on – Leavisism.

Main works

Speaking to Each Other (volume I): About society, London: Chatto & Windus, 1970a.

Speaking to Each Other (volume II): About literature, London: Chatto & Windus, 1970b.

Only Connect: On culture and communication, London: Chatto & Windus, 1972.

The Future of Broadcasting, London: Macmillan, 1982.

Liberty and Legislation, London: Cass, 1989.

The Uses of Literacy, Harmondsworth: Penguin, 1990.

Further reading

Clarke, John *et al.* (eds), *Working Class Culture: Studies in history and theory*, London: Hutchinson, 1979.

Corner, John, 'Studying culture: reflections and assessments. An interview with Richard Hoggart', *Media, Culture and Society*, 13 (1991).

Hall, Stuart, 'Cultural studies at the Centre: some problematics and problems', in *Culture, Media, Language*, ed. Stuart Hall *et al.*, London: Hutchinson, 1980.

Johnson, Lesley, *Cultural Critics*, London: Routledge & Kegan Paul, 1979.

Laing, Stuart, *Representations of Working-Class Life 1957–1964*, London: Macmillan, 1986.

Williams, Raymond, 'Fiction and the writing public', *Essays in Criticism*, 7 (1957).

Holland, Norman N. (1927–)

Norman Holland was the James H. McNulty Professor of English and Director of the Center for the Psychological Study of the Arts at the State University of New York in Buffalo. He completed a programme for non-medical candidates at the Boston Psychoanalytic Institute, and is a member of the Boston and Western New York psychoanalytic societies. The author of over one hundred articles and reviews, as well as three books on Shakespeare, Holland is the leading psychoanalytic interpreter of reader response.

Holland can be credited with providing a systematic framework for the psychoanalytic approach to reader response, a form of critical theory which focuses on the reader and her experience of the text. His approach is derived from 'ego-psychology' (in particular the work of Heinz Lichtenstein, whom Holland acknowledges as a seminal influence), which postulates that all of us receive the imprint of our 'primary identity' from our mother. As adults we have what Holland calls our own 'identity theme', a 'continuing core of personality' which we bring as individuals to each new experience. Although it is capable of some degree of variation (Holland defines personal identity as 'a theme and variations' on the model of musical composition), this 'continuing core' holds throughout the individual's life – Holland following Lichtenstein in believing that the mother-child relationship establishes a stable identity which informs all the individual's subsequent transactions, including her transactions with texts. Texts are read in accordance with that identity theme, Holland believes: in effect, we use texts to meet the psychological needs of our identity themes.

Holland proceeds to develop this theory of the identity theme in studies such as *Poems in Persons* and *Five Readers Reading* by examining the responses of various readers to H.D.'s poetry and William Faulkner's fiction. In the case of the five student readers in the latter text, for example, it is concluded that the meaning of Faulkner's short story 'A Rose for Emily' is determined by the particular identity theme of each of the readers, Holland noting how his subjects react in very different ways to key words or phrases in the text as they relate them to their own life experience ('fathered' being one such word that sets up very different responses across the group of readers being monitored). Such experiments lead Holland to claim that 'interpretation is a function of identity'.

In the article 'Hamlet – my greatest creation', Holland goes on to investigate how his interpretation of *Hamlet* mirrors his own personal identity theme. Equally, Poe's 'The Purloined Letter', a text Holland first encountered at the age of 13, is read through the critic's personal history of adolescent fears and fantasies, and his subsequent adult response to these.

Holland's earlier work emphasizes the role played by fantasy in the reading process. Thus in *The Dynamics of Literary Response* he is concerned to demonstrate that the reader of a text responds to that text as a socially acceptable, and also highly pleasurable, transformation of unconscious fantasy to a conscious level. This fantasy is to be regarded as the source from which all readings of the text are produced. Holland posits a 'dictionary of fantasy', based on the **Freud**ian phases of infantile development, arguing that one or other of these phases will dictate the manner in which fantasy functions in the text. Literary meaning is therefore held to consist of the transformation of content from the unconscious to the conscious level, and the text becomes a site where author and reader collude in a 'core-fantasy' shared by each.

Holland views reading as a 'transactive' process on the analogy of a feedback loop, where the reader is engaged in a constant search for reassurance from her many anxieties and fears. There are four stages in the transaction process whereby 'we involve texts in the creative variation of our identities': 'expectation' (the reader's initial approach to the text), 'defence' (selection from the text), 'fantasy' (projection of wish-fulfilments on to the text), and 'transformation' (translation of wish-fulfilments into identity themes). This process, whereby the reader adapts the author's identity theme to her own purposes, is collectively referred to by the acronym DEFT, and is modelled on the psychoanalytic phenomenon of 'transference', which Holland treats as an inescapable part of our existence (as the title to one of his articles puts it, 'Why this is transference, nor am I out of it'). In Holland's conception of the process the text functions as the analyst, generating responses in the reader/analysand which s/he must examine in turn, thus ultimately becoming both patient and analyst in a complex game of transference and countertransference which answers our deep-seated psychological needs.

True to the reader-response mode of approach, Holland's concern invariably remains the process of reading itself rather than issues of textual content or context, and he has in fact gone so far as to claim that 'psychoanalysis has nothing, nothing whatsoever, to tell us about literature *per se*'.

Holland has been criticized – by Elizabeth Wright among others – for failing to discriminate between subjective and intersubjective readings of texts; thus the readings of the five guinea-pig students in *Five Readers Reading* are implicitly taken to be as valuable as Holland's own critical readings of texts. Holland himself differentiates between his early concern with 'the real responses of real readers' in *Poems in Persons* and *Five Readers Reading* and his later, more theoretical writings (regarding them as two different models of the reading process), but he does seem to treat reading and criticism as essentially the same activity – in each case the interpretation is an expression of an identity theme brought to the text by the individual reader. Wright also argues that it is a drawback of reader-response theorists in general that they never ask themselves why readings should be communicated at all: 'according to the dictates of his theory', she notes, 'Holland should be quietly transacting in private instead of flooding the market with his own, often remarkably persuasive readings'.

Holland is also very much open to attack from post-structuralist and postmodernist theorists, few of whom would be persuaded by his now highly unfashionable conception of personal identity as a fixed and stable entity holding over time – indeed, 'ego-psychology' would appear unacceptably essentialist to such thinkers.

Holland's impact has been on reader-orientated theory and practice, but different in kind from that represented by German theoreticians such as Wolfgang **Iser** or Hans Robert **Jauss**, who draw upon phenomenology or hermeneutics for their models of the reading process. Holland's emphasis relates to the psychological needs of the reader, and however curious some of the outcomes of this process, there is little doubt that they have substantially modified the text-orientated theories of New Criticism and Formalism. It is virtually impossible nowadays to discuss textual meaning without taking reader response into account, and Holland's importance lies in his provision of a systematic framework for psychoanalytic approaches to the topic.

Main works

Psychology and Shakespeare, New York: McGraw-Hill, 1966.

The Dynamics of Literary Response, New York: Oxford University Press, 1968.

Poems in Persons: An introduction to the psychoanalysis of literature, New York: Norton, 1973.

Five Readers Reading, New Haven, CT: Yale University Press, 1975a.

'Hamlet – my greatest creation', *Journal of the American Academy of Psychoanalysis* 3 1975b: 419–27.

'Literary interpretation and three phases of psychoanalysis', *Critical Inquiry* 3 1976a: 221–3.

'Transactive criticism: re-creation through identity', *Criticism* 18 1976b: 334–52.

'Literature as transaction', in Paul Hernadi (ed.), *What is Literature?*, Bloomington: Indiana University Press, 1978.

'Reading and identity: a psychoanalytic revolution', *Academy Forum* (American Academy of Psychoanalysis) 23 1979: 7–9.

'Unity identity text self', in Jane P. Tompkins (ed.), *Reader–Response Criticism: From formalism to post-structuralism*, Baltimore, MD and London: Johns Hopkins University Press, 1980a.

'Re-covering "The Purloined Letter" ', in Susan R. Suleiman and Inge Crossman (eds), *The Reader in the Text: Essays on audience and interpretation*, Princeton, NJ: Princeton University Press, 1980b.

Laughing, a Psychology of Humour, Ithaca, NY and London: Cornell University Press, 1982a.

'Why this is transference, nor am I out of it', *Psychoanalysis and Contemporary Thought* 5 1982b: 27–34.

Holland's Guide to Psychoanalytic Psychology and Literature-and-Psychology, New York and Oxford: Oxford University Press, 1990.

The Critical I, New York: Columbia University Press, 1992.

Further reading

Hartman, Geoffrey (ed.), *Psychoanalysis and the Question of the Text*, Baltimore, MD: Johns Hopkins University Press, 1978.

Newton, K.M., *Interpreting the Text: A critical introduction to the theory and practice of literary interpretation*, Hemel Hempstead: Harvester Wheatsheaf, 1990.

Skura, Meredith Anne, *The Literary Uses of the Psychoanalytic Process*, New Haven, CT and London: Yale University Press, 1981.

Sulieman, Susan R. and Inge Crossman (eds), *The Reader in the Text: Essays on audience and interpretation*, Princeton, NJ: Princeton University Press, 1980.

Tompkins, Jane P. (ed.), *Reader–Response Criticism: From formalism to post-structuralism*, Baltimore, MD and London: Johns Hopkins University Press, 1980.

Wright, Elizabeth, *Psychoanalytic Criticism: Theory in practice*, London and New York: Methuen, 1984.

hooks, bell

bell hooks (born Gloria Watkins) was raised in a Southern black community in the United States. She uses the pseudonym bell hooks, which was the name of her maternal great-grandmother, and has stated that the use of the pseudonym enabled her to 'claim an identity that affirmed for me the right to speech'. She draws an opposition between her assumed identity and her given identity, which is characterized by the difference between the 'strong, creative and wild woman' and the 'sweet southern girl, quiet, obedient and pleasing'. The use of the pseudonym can be perceived as emblematic of hooks's work as she makes a shift away from 'personality, from self, to ideas . . . that address issues rather than identity'. It also raises the tropes of empowerment, subjectivity and identity which are crucial aspects of her project.

---

bell hooks is arguably the foremost black feminist critic of her generation. Best known as a cultural theorist, she has published a large body of work, her writing spanning a broad range of categories including plays, novels, short stories and poems, together with the cultural theory for which she is most famous. Her writing is predominantly devoted to the interrogation of the politics of domination, with a particular focus on the deconstruction of racism, sexism and homophobia within the parameters of a postmodernist framework. She has argued forcibly against the limiting possibilities enforced by notions of essentialism; consequently, much of her work addresses the political and ideological problems concomitant with the forging of new intellectual and cultural spaces for the construction of a radical black subjectivity. hooks's work also strives to bridge the gap between the theoretical discourse of academia and people's real-life experiences. Thus one of the much-noted features of her work is the fusion of subjective and objective knowledges. This strategy, whereby she highlights her personal experiences as a black woman within a white supremacist culture, calls into question and places in jeopardy the notion of scientific 'objective' knowledge, breaking down the artificial separation between the personal and the political.

Hooks has made important critical interventions in the field of cultural theory, exploring the 'radical potential' of black cultural forms, particularly within the realm of popular culture. Her best-known text to date is the path-breaking polemical work *Aint I a Woman*. In this text it is possible to locate the genesis of hooks's thinking around the issues of race, gender, sexuality, identity and subjectivity, all of which are framed within a political, economic and cultural interface which she refers to as the 'politics of domination'. The text is significant in terms of its position in the African–American women's literary and theoretical tradition which traces its roots back as far as Sojourner Truth, after whose famous question the book is titled. The text also received a substantial amount of critical attention, and, as hooks states, her work was met with an astonishing amount of resistance and hostility, as its main premise challenged the ideological basis of Western bourgeois feminist theories and practice. The text also draws attention to black women's double marginalization from the liberatory discourses of both race and gender. Hooks argues forcibly that 'When black people are talked about the focus tends to be on black men; and when women are talked about the focus tends to be on white women.'

Hooks's main project, then, was to trace the historical roots of African–American women's silence within American culture, forcibly creating a space in which the African–American woman could come to voice. She argues in the introduction to the text that black women's silence was: 'the silence of the oppressed, that profound silence engendered by resignation and acceptance of one's lot'. To this end the text critiqued various Western feminisms which posited the notion that 'women share a common plight'. She argued that both the cultural and political effects of slavery and the inherent patriarchal nature of modern America invalidated and sought to eradicate a black female voice. hooks's extensive research indicated that in actual fact white women and black women had always been forced to compete against one another and this competition had, since the days of slavery, been lived out in the arena of sexual politics, as white men had exercised their economic power to gain access to the bodies of black women.

The impact of the text was no less notable in terms of its challenge to essentialism. At the time when it was written the issues of class, sexuality and race had not been sufficiently addressed by the feminist movement; in this climate *Aint I a Woman*, challenged the 'whole construction of white woman as victim, or white woman as the symbol of most oppressed . . . or woman as the symbol of the most oppressed'. At the same time it drew attention to the effects of sexism in the black community on black women's lives. hooks's understanding of the exclusion of black women from the black liberation struggle recognizes the fact that diversionary issues such as class, gender or sexuality might only serve, at a time of intense political upheaval, to split the focus of the movement. She has argued that black leaders, both male and female, were unwilling to acknowledge the complexity surrounding issues of oppression, since to do so would have meant to recognize that black men's oppression in a white supremacist culture did not mean that they were automatically excluded from the ability to oppress women, both white and black. In hooks's political vision the exploration of sexism and racism in *Aint I a Woman* underlines the proposition that to make these issues separate 'would be to deny a basic fact of our existence, that race and sex are both immutable facets of human identity'.

Thus, while hooks foregrounds the issues of race and gender in her work, she also draws attention to the complex nature of the subjectivity and identity of oppressed peoples. As a result in her later works, both fictional and theoretical, hooks has focused upon the facets of postmodern theory and culture which make possible a recognition of the broader frameworks of oppression in which sexism, racism, homophobia and class struggle are located. She argues that radical postmodernist practice, conceptualized in her work as a 'politics of difference', should 'incorporate the voices of the displaced, marginalized, exploited and oppressed . . .'. This argument is pursued by positing the notion that the gaps within ideology that postmodernist practices and theory expose, 'make space for oppositional practices'. Hooks is very aware that the exclusive nature of postmodern critical discourse means that it is unlikely that it will filter down to the grass roots of the African–American community. Thus while she advocates a policy of unmitigated intervention on the part of African–American intellectuals, in the same process she critiques the role of all academics, suggesting that they have a responsibility to 'translate the jargon' of complex theory so that it is more accessible to the community. Primarily, her engagement with postmodernism focuses on the reconstruction and representation of black identity with the black underclass, through the medium of popular culture, acting as the source for political and social regeneration.

---

hooks states that postmodernism allows for a critique which can 'affirm multiple black identities, varied black experience'. This model challenges Eurocentric constructions of black identity, which is represented to a white public through popular cultural forms (such as hip-hop). These representations serve to reinforce racism which is located within the paradigm of Western metaphysical dualism, but hooks argues that by abandoning essentialist notions of identity, African-American peoples can forge a political identity characterized by heterogeneity. In this way it may be possible to construct identities that are oppositional and liberatory. At the same time hooks emphasizes the significance of the 'authority of experience'. Unlike much feminist writing, however, this does not mean privileging of the voices of black people over the voices of non-black people on issues of race. It is simply a recognition that 'black identity has been specifically constituted in the experience of exile and struggle'. hooks's work has been extremely influential. It has informed and enriched/feminist debates, and rigorously interrogated and challenged received ideas on African–American identity.

Main works

Aint I a Woman, Pluto Press, 1983.

Feminist Theory: From margin to centre, South End Press, 1984.

Talking Black: Thinking feminist, thinking black, South End Press, 1989.

Yearning: Race, gender and cultural politics, Turnaround, 1990.

Black Looks: race and representation, Turnaround, 1992.

Sisters of the Yam: Black women and self recovery, Turnaround, 1993.

Further reading

Re-Search, 13 (1991): *Angry Women*.

Gilroy, Paul, *Small Acts*, Serpent's Tail, 1993.

I

Irigaray, Luce (1932–)

Luce Irigaray is a French philosopher and psychoanalyst whose feminist critique of psychoanalysis led to her expulsion from the Department of Psychoanalysis at Vincennes, headed by Jacques **Lacan**. Best known for her work on language and sexual difference, particularly 'Ce Sexe qui n'en est pas un' ('This sex which is not one') and 'Quand nos lèvres s'écrivent' ('When our lips speak together'), both included in *Ce Sexe qui n'en est pas un* (1977), Irigaray is often bracketed with Julia **Kristeva** and Hélène **Cixous** as an advocate of 'écriture féminine' (female writing). This grouping of the three as representatives of French feminist theory, however, should not conceal what are considerable theoretical and political differences between them.

As a feminist theorist of sexual difference, Luce Irigaray seeks to challenge, and to change, what she sees as the patriarchal foundations of Western metaphysics. She argues that women have been denied the status of subject within Western culture, and that in order to produce change and make possible women's access to subject positions in language, culture and society, a fundamental change in the symbolic order must be effected. Irigaray's project is therefore twofold. First, from within frameworks provided by and yet radically challenging both psychoanalysis and philosophy, she seeks to analyze the processes by which women and the feminine have been excluded from philosophy/discourse/culture. Secondly, she addresses the question of how to make possible, and how to enact, an autonomously defined female position within the symbolic and social order.

Irigaray's *critical* project has been seen as a deconstruction of psychoanalysis and a psychoanalysis of Western culture and metaphysics, since she employs both deconstructive and psychoanalytic methods to reveal the patriarchal structure of both. Psychoanalysis, she argues, accurately *describes* what it finds; the theory it constructs from these findings, however, unaware of its own determinants, attempts to impose as universal, immutable and politically neutral what is in fact the product of a particular (patriarchal) cultural order. If it is read symptomatically, psychoanalysis can itself be seen to be governed by unconcious male fantasies, and to be founded on a repression of the debt owed to the maternal. Freud's account of psychic development, then, is in fact a *single*-sex model; femininity is simply seen in relation to the male model: as lack, absence, negativity. Similarly, Lacan's account of the beginnings of the subject in the 'mirror stage' is an exclusively masculine account. The separation effected by the perception of difference, which for Lacan is an essential prerequisite for entry into the symbolic, is an exclusively masculine perception; the separation envisaged is that of the *male* child from the mother. The idealized body image which the mirror reflects is therefore implicitly male; Lacan's concept of the imaginary is of a masculine imaginary, his symbolic a masculine symbolic.

The primacy of the phallus, of a *masculine* imaginary, is not, however, central only to Lacanian theory; it underlies the whole of the Western symbolic and social order. Western discourse and culture, including the meta-discourse of philosophy, is a hom(m)osexual economy which does not recognize sexual difference. In it, women have no identity *as women*. Its representational systems correspond to the morphology, the imagined form or structure, of the male body, and its requirements and desires. Western discourse, then, privileges unity, the oneness of the self, the visible; Western rationality is characterized by the principles of identity, of non-contradiction, and of binarism, (e.g. nature/reason, subject/object, matter/energy). Attempts to deconstruct this structure, and its inevitable privileging of the 'male' term in the structure of binary oppositions, are not, however, enough for Irigaray. The deconstruction of the 'masculine' position, or the adoption of a 'feminine' position – in the work of **Derrida**, for example – in divorcing 'the feminine' from the state of *being a woman*, represents merely another gesture of appropriation, another strategy for remaining the master of discourse. In claiming for himself the 'feminine' position, Derrida in effect robs women yet again of a position from which to speak. What is needed, therefore, is a specifically *female* imaginary and *female* symbolic, with structures corresponding to the morphology of the female body.

It is this second, *constructive* aspect of Irigaray's project which has aroused most controversy. Since she is arguing that Western thought, informed by an imaginary which has the morphology of the male body, has left women with no possible position from which to speak *as a woman*, consigned as she always is to the place of the other, or to a role as object of symbolic exchange, Irigaray's concern must then be that of creating a place from which women *can* speak as subjects. At the same time, to attempt to speak from this place is to claim a position which does not yet exist. This constructive aspect of her theory has, therefore, two elements: to attempt to shift the position of the speaking subject so that women *can* occupy it; and to theorize the conditions necessary for a socially embodied sexual difference.

Of Irigaray's images and representations of a *feminine* morphology, her image of the 'two lips' is the best known. Female sexuality, characterized as multiple, ambiguous, fluid and excessive, can be represented by the metaphor of the 'two lips'. The two lips are neither one nor two, but both; where one identity ends and the other begins is unclear; the contact of *'at least two* [lips]' keeps woman in touch with herself, but without any possibility of distinguishing what is touching from what is touched. What must be found is a language capable of expressing such female pleasures and corporeality. It is difficult to know how to read this and other expressions of Irigaray's constructive vision. While it has been criticized as essentialist, her metaphor can be read as strategic, an attempt to intervene in discourse at the level of cultural representation, to produce a *different* model of female sexuality, a female imaginary through which women might speak. Elsewhere, she advocates the strategy of 'mimesis', the deliberate assumption of a 'feminine' position to produce *'disruptive excess'*, with the aim not of producing a new theory of woman but of 'jamming the theoretical machinery itself'. Her 'visionary' texts are thus deliberately difficult, shifting and ambiguous.

Irigaray's advocacy of a specifically female symbolic leads her also to argue the case for a maternal genealogy and an ethics of sexual difference. Western culture, she argues, has repressed its debt to the mother and left unsymbolized the mother–daughter relationship. As a result, women can have no identity that is not tied to the maternal function; the place of the mother becomes a single place to be competed for. Until the identity of *woman* can be separated from that of *mother* and the relationship between women can be symbolized, and until a maternal genealogy is established which would coexist with the paternal, then women will remain outside the symbolic order. Similarly, if women are to attain the status of subject, then they must have access to a *female* transcendent, or divine, an ideal which would represent the horizon of possibility for women, as the male God has for men. Such a divine would make possible both the relationship between women, who would share this horizon, and an ethics of sexual difference. Released from the sexed division material/ideal, both women and men would have access to both – to a 'sensible transcendental' which would form the basis of a new ethics. Finally, in her most recent work, Irigaray has turned to the social and material changes necessary for women's accession into the social and symbolic order. The struggle for equal rights, she argues, may be necessary as a first stage in the winning of specific women's rights. Social rights should be negotiated, however, on the basis not of equality but of *identity*.

Irigaray is a controversial figure within feminist cultural theory. Although her writings on sexual difference address issues fundamental to feminism, her position has frequently come under attack. From within psychoanalysis she can be attacked for her critique of its phallocentrism, while from a materialist perspective her debt to psychoanalytic concepts can be seen as positioning her still within its dualist, ahistorical framework. Her representation of patriarchy as a 'univocal, non-contradictory force' [*Moi*] is seen as leading to a failure adequately to conceptualize power, and therefore change. Most seriously, her emphasis on sexual difference has led to a charge of essentialism, whether biological or 'psychic', a charge which some of her formulations of the 'two lips' metaphor can seem to support. In addition, her difficult and ambiguous 'visionary' writings can lead to accusations of utopianism and, once again, of lack of concern for the social and political in her proposals for change. More recently, however, she has received much more sympathetic attention (from Braidotti, Grosz and Whitford, for example). In particular, Rosi Braidotti has argued that a feminism of sexual difference is essential both theoretically and politically if the specificity of the feminist project is not to be lost in the face of postmodernism's disembodying of sexual difference in a 'new' anti-essentialist subject.

Main works

Speculum of the Other Woman, trans. Gillian C. Gill, Ithaca, NY: Cornell University Press, 1985 [1974].

This Sex Which Is Not One, trans. Catherine Porter with Carolyn Burke, Ithaca, NY: Cornell University Press, 1985 [1977].

The Irigaray Reader, ed. Margaret Whitford, Oxford: Blackwell, 1991.

The Ethics of Sexual Difference, trans. Carolyn Burke, Ithaca, NY: Cornell University Press, 1993a [1984].

Sexes and Genealogies, trans. Gillian C. Gill, New York: Columbia University Press, 1993b [1987].

Je, Tu, Nous: Towards a culture of difference, trans. Alison Martin, London: Routledge, 1993c [1990].

Further reading

Braidotti, Rosi, *Patterns of Dissonance*, Cambridge: Polity, 1991.

Gallop, Jane, *Feminism and Psychoanalysis: The daughter's seduction* London: Macmillan, 1982.

Grosz, Elizabeth, *Sexual Subversions: Three French feminists*, Sydney: Allen & Unwin, 1989.

Moi, Toril, *Sexual/Textual Politics*, London: Methuen, 1985.

Silverman, Kaja, *The Acoustic Mirror: The female voice in psychoanalysis and cinema*, Bloomington: Indiana University Press, 1988.

Whitford, Margaret, *Luce Irigaray: Philosophy in the feminine*, London: Routledge, 1991.

Iser, Wolfgang (1926–)

Wolfgang Iser is a leading exponent of *Rezeption-aesthetik*, or 'reception theory', a theoretical school that can be seen as a response to the heavily text-centred methods of Russian Formalism and structuralism. Reader-reception theory, unlike those movements, sees meaning as arising not from significatory structures intrinsic to a text but from the relation of text and reader. Iser is a Professor of English and Comparative Literature at the University of Constance in Germany. Although his work has developed partly in parallel (and rivalry) with an American reader-response criticism that has its roots in philosophical *pragmatism*, the sources of Iser's thought are exclusively European: the phenomenological philosophy of Edmund Husserl and the aesthetic theories of Roman Ingarden are most important. Iser's view of reading is expounded at greatest length in *The Act of Reading: a theory of aesthetic response*, yet despite his prosecution of a large-scale theoretical project, he also has impressive credentials as a literary historian. He wrote an early monograph on Walter Pater, and his interest in the reading experience had drawn him repeatedly to eighteenth-century novelists, especially Sterne. Recent years have seen Iser's interest shifting from reading as an individual act to the role played by literary works in human culture: a turn from psychology to anthropology.

In 'The reading process: a phenomenological approach', his most frequently reprinted essay, Iser sets up a hermeneutic trichotomy of text, reader and literary work. The 'text', here, is constituted by the actual words on the page, whereas the 'literary work' is the text as brought to life, and invested with meaning, by the reader. The 'virtuality' of the text, the fact that it is realized only through a reading process, gives rise to its 'dynamic nature'. Iser's belief in the 'text' – his conviction, in other words, that there is something prior to the reading process that acts as the object of that process – separates him from the radical reader-response theory of the American critic Stanley **Fish,** who believes that the reader actually 'produces' the work rather than merely bringing it to fruition. Iser's reader-reception theory is principally concerned with a reader's psychological traversing of a text. His model for this traversing is a rigorously semiotic one: reading becomes a drive towards intelligibility, a relentless decoding, with the end in view being the most total construction of a work's meaning. This conception explains why Iser values second or subsequent readings of the same text over first ones, for successive readings are likely to produce an ever greater harvest of meaning. Forms of pleasure that might arise from reading books, but are unrelated to the production of meaning, form no part of his theoretical concern.

Iser sees the text as consisting of 'schematized views' (a term derived from Ingarden), which are the viewpoints that the text provides on its own subject matter. Such viewpoints might emanate from the narrator or the characters, and they will invariably change across the work's temporal span. Between these 'views' are indeterminate sections, or gaps, which, for Iser, form the basic elements of aesthetic response. They are not defects so much as opportunities for the reader to project reading. Indeterminacy gaps occur, according to Iser, in texts of all kinds: they figure prominently in experimental and cryptic modern texts such as Joyce's *Ulysses*, but they also occur in Victorian realist novels, especially through the phenomenon of serial publication. How the reader projects meaning on to the text's indeterminacies is regulated by the principle of consistency-building: the gaps have to be filled in such a way that all bits of the work appear consistent with each other. Also crucial to Iser's theory of reading is that it is not a present-second activity: it is, instead, always anticipative, involving the reader in forward speculation about how a work will ultimately resolve itself, speculation that consistently gets revised against the continuous flow of new knowledge vouchsafed by the work's 'schematized views'.

Iser's theory of reading has also been affected by the psychoanalyst R.D. Laing's ideas about interpersonal communication. All human interaction is dogged by the dilemma that we can never be privy to how people experience us, yet such interaction could never take place without our making some assumptions about the nature of that experience. This drive to understand interpersonal meanings can be seen as very analogous to the drive to construe meaning in works of literature. Where that analogy fails to hold up is that the social situation is more regulated: people can tell us what they think of us, whereas texts never talk back. The result is that no reading can ever fully 'know' a text: a single text will lend itself to an almost limitless number of different realizations, and no one realization will be able to do justice to a text's total significatory potential.

Iser's reading theory is really an attempt to slow down, and to render in full psychological complexity, the act of reading: it is not, then, a method for 'producing' readings or interpretations of texts. Moreover, unlike **Barthes**, who thought that different sorts of texts imposed different regimes of reading, Iser's model is offered as more or less applicable to all texts. One judgement on his work (although a severe one) might be that it theorizes, albeit with admirable sophistication, an entirely commonsensical proposition: namely, that an interpretation of a work depends partly on what is in the text and partly on what a reader brings to the text. Iser's theory, accordingly, is prone to attack from hermeneutical monists, like Stanley Fish, who do not accept that a text possesses any fully determined elements, and for whom, therefore, Iser's crucial distinction between textual determinacies and indeterminacies is meaningless. Fish, and other critics, have also expended more energy than Iser in trying to theorize the reading position rather than merely the reading act. Iser is largely indifferent to what might lead an individual reader to construe a text in a particular way: he has no counterpart to Fish's idea of the *'interpretive community'*, nor any concern for the sociological factors governing reading. While this is not necessarily a shortcoming of his work, it could be seen as one of its limitations.

Reviewing Iser's *Act of Reading* in 1981, Stanley Fish remarked that Iser is 'influential without being controversial', and a decade on, this still stands as a fair summary of his profile. Iser's reader reception, with its balancing of the determinate and indeterminate, the objective and subjective, seems to have spoken to a particular epoch in theoretical studies: the period between the demise of structuralism and the rise of more subjectivist, post-structuralist theories. The moment, then, of Iser's reader reception has probably now gone, and this seems evident from his own latest work, which has shifted towards anthropology: towards an understanding of the uses to which literature is put within cultures. While reader-reception studies of authors remain fairly commonplace, the fact that Iser's is not an hermeneutic theory – it does not tell us how to produce readings – has perhaps limited its vogue in a critical culture in which meaning-production is paramount.

Main works

The Implied Reader: Patterns of communication in prose fiction from Bunyan to Beckett, Baltimore, MD: Johns Hopkins University Press, 1974.

The Act of Reading: A theory of aesthetic response, Baltimore MD: Johns Hopkins University Press, 1978.

Walter Pater: The aesthetic moment, trans. D.H. Wilson, Cambridge: Cambridge University Press, 1987.

Laurence Sterne: Tristram Shandy, trans. D.H. Wilson, Cambridge: Cambridge University Press, 1988.

Prospecting: From reader response to literary anthropology, Baltimore, MD: Johns Hopkins University Press, 1989.

The Fictive and the Imaginary: Charting literary anthropology, Baltimore, MD: Johns Hopkins University Press, 1993.

Further reading

Fish, Stanley, 'Why no one's afraid of Wolfgang Iser', *Diacritics*, 11 (1981): 2–13.

Freund, Elizabeth, *The Return of the Reader: Reader-response criticism*, London: Methuen, 1987.

Holub, Robert, *Reception Theory: A critical introduction*, London: Routledge, 1984.

Glossary

Interpretive community: an expression coined by the American critic Stanley Fish to refer to groups of readers who share the same strategies for seeing (or, as Fish would have it, 'making') meanings in texts.

Pragmatism: a broad and miscellaneous movement in twentieth-century American philosophy. Its general contention is that we make sense of our experience of the world in ways that are governed by issues of expedience and utility. Accordingly, literary theorists of a pragmatic orientation stress that our interpretations of texts are not objective, but are motivated by the reader's desires and aptitudes.

J

Jakobson, Roman (1896–1982)

Roman Osipovich Jakobson was born in Russia in 1896. He was a founder-member of the Moscow Linguistic Circle (1915–16), a group which incubated Russian Formalism. He was Professor at the Higher Dramatic School in Moscow between 1920 and 1923. After his move to Czechoslovakia in the 1920s, he formed the Prague Linguistic Circle. Jakobson was forced out of Czechoslovakia by the Nazis in 1939, and settled in the United States. Here he taught at the University of Columbia between 1943 and 1949, at Harvard between 1949 and 1967, and at MIT from 1957 to 1967. Jakobson was a crucial figure in the rise of structuralism, and in promoting the application of linguistics to literature.

'The object of study in literary science is not literature, but "literariness", that is, what makes a given work a literary work.' Here we have the pith of Roman Jakobson's contribution to modern literary theory. The remaining juice of his research is collected in the eight volumes and six thousand pages of his *selected* writings. His bold (some would say bald) assertion about literariness is from an early work on Russian Futurist poetry. It can be matched by an equally famous remark from his 'Concluding statement: linguistics and poetics', presented during a 1958 conference at Indiana University: 'Because the main subject of poetics is the *differentia specifica* of verbal art in relation to other arts and in relation to other kinds of verbal behavior, poetics is entitled to the leading place in literary studies.' Both sentences convey clearly Jakobson's belief in the critical distance of the literary scientist, who should wear the protective gloves of an objective discipline when handling (with care) the mess of literature.

Jakobson was an early member of the Moscow Linguistic Circle alongside thinkers such as Victor **Shklovsky** and Yuri Tynyanov. When he moved to Czechoslovakia he became a leading figure in the Prague Linguistic Circle, which included René Wellek and Jan Mukarovsky. Both the Moscow and the Prague schools insisted upon the wide

aperture between practical and literary language. Shklovsky familiar-
ized us with the concept of defamiliarization, whereby the writer,
through words, exiles ideas from their habitual homes and forces them
to wander around strange landscapes. Mukarovsky foregrounded
foregrounding as the systematic means by which language draws
attention to itself in poetry and fiction.

Jakobson pursued similar ideas in a different direction by focusing
upon deviant language. His seminal essay 'Two aspects of language
and two types of aphasia' deals with the verbal problems of aphasics,
who defamiliarize and foreground language in unusual ways. In
Wernicke's aphasia, or similarity disorder, there is an inability to deal
with the 'vertical' or paradigmatic axis of language. In the sentence 'The
cat sat on the mat', for instance, the word 'cat' is chosen from the set of
words denoting a feline pet (pussy/kitten/moggy, and others), just as
the word 'sat' is selected from the verbs indicating a stationary posture.
An aphasic with similarity disorder would have problems substituting
terms for 'cat' and 'sat' in this way, and is unable to detect likenesses
between items from two different contexts. Conversely, Broca's
aphasia, or contiguity disorder, leads to a breakdown on the 'horizontal' or syntagmatic axis of language. To take our example again, the
declaration 'The cat sat on the mat' is the simplest combination of
subject, verb and object. Because the aphasic with contiguity disorder
has difficulty combining units of language into higher orders of
complexity, he or she might have problems extending the sentence to
something like 'The cat, sitting on the mat, watches the mouse'. On the
basis of this clinical evidence, Jakobson – with intoxicating brevity –
asserts that metaphor (a vertical figure of speech) and metonymy (a
horizontal figure of speech) are fundamentally opposing principles of
language. Furthermore, all verbal behaviour tends towards one or
other of these poles:

> In normal verbal behaviour both processes are continually operative, but
> careful observation will reveal that under the influence of a cultural pattern,
> personality, and verbal style, preference is given to one of the two processes
> over the other. (*Fundamentals of Language*)

This dichotomy has proved influential to those eager to develop
Jakobson's contention that it can be applied to the widest manifestations
of culture. (David Lodge, for instance, constructs a poetics of twentieth-
century fiction in *The Modes of Modern Writing* around the metaphor/
metonymy opposition.)

Another of Jakobson's proposals which has intrigued both literary
and cultural theorists is the six-term model of communication discussed
in 'Linguistics and poetics'. Relying upon earlier technical work by
Shannon and Weaver, Jakobson states that in every communication an
addresser sends a message, by means of a contact, to an addressee
within a context, using a partially common code. There are therefore six

different functions to be considered in analyzing spoken or written texts. The emotive function is concerned with the expression of the addresser, and the conative function with the addressee towards whom the message is directed. The poetic function, on the other hand, concentrates on the message itself, while the referential function invokes the context of the message. The phatic function ensures that communication is ongoing, without necessarily relaying any message. Lastly, the metalingual function checks that both addresser and addressee are using the same code. Elegant and compact though this formulation is, it has limited application: the path of a literary utterance surely cannot be traced as if it were a simple electronic signal.

The bulk of Jakobson's work takes up questions of specialized grammatical and lexical interest, but with a Borgesian breadth: word pitch in Norwegian verse, Czech Gothic poetry, physiognomic indices, and so on. Other essays are less localized and have consequently achieved a far wider currency. 'Charles Baudelaire's *"Les Chats"* ', for instance, co-written with the anthropologist Claude **Lévi-Strauss**, is a textbook example of a certain kind of structuralist approach, one which reduces the poem to a pattern of phonetic parallelisms. Wellek questions whether the analysis, scrupulous as it is, enunciates anything about the aesthetic value of the poem. Perhaps it is inevitable that when the linguistic Bunsen burner heats the literary work for too long, cinders will be all that remain at the bottom of the test-tube. Similar criticisms have been made of Jakobson's scrutiny of Shakespeare's 129th sonnet. His vision is so acute that he can't see the meanings for the morphemes.

Jakobson's importance is unassailable. His involvement with two of the major theoretical movements of the twentieth century meant that he became an arch between Russian Formalism, with its emphasis upon 'literariness', and structuralism, which looked with X-ray eyes at cultural phenomena and found, beneath the social skin, combinations of arbitrary signs. His geographical move from Russia to Czechoslovakia, and then to the United States, mirrors his intellectual journey. Jakobson was nothing other than the 'addresser', 'message' and 'contact' between the Eastern European and Anglo-American 'addressees', 'contexts' and 'codes'.

Main works

Selected Writings, Vols I–VIII, The Hague: Mouton, 1966–85.

(with) Claude Lévi–Strauss, 'Charles Baudelaire's *"Les Chats"* ', in

Structuralism: A reader, ed. Michael Lane, London: Jonathan Cape, 1970, pp. 202–21.

(with) Morris Halle, 'Two aspects of language and two types of aphasia', in *Fundamentals of Language*, 2nd rev. edn (The Hague: Mouton, 1971), pp. 69–96.

'Concluding statement: linguistics and poetics', in *Modern Criticism and Theory: A reader*, ed. David Lodge, London: Longman, 1988, pp. 32–57.

Further reading

Bredin, Hugh, 'Roman Jakobson on metaphor and metonymy', in *Philosophy and Literature*, 8, 1 (1984): 89–103.

Lodge, David, *The Modes of Modern Writing: Metaphor, metonymy and the typology of literature*, London: Edward Arnold, 1977.

Pomorska, Krystyna and Stephen Rudy (eds), *Verbal Art, Verbal Sign, Verbal Time*, Minneapolis: University of Minnesota Press, 1985.

Pomorska, Krystyna *et al.*, *Language, Poetry and Poetics: The generation of the 1890s: Jakobson, Trubetzkoy, Majakovski*, The Hague: Mouton, 1987.

Riffaterre, Michael, 'Describing poetic structures: two approaches to Baudelaire's *"Les Chats"* ', *Yale French Studies*, 36–7 (1966): 200–42.

Stankiewicz, Edward, 'Linguistics, poetics, and the literary genres', in *New Directions in Linguistics and Semiotics*, Amsterdam: Benjamins, 1984, pp. 155–70.

Jameson, Fredric (1934–)

Fredric Jameson is the best-known **Marx**ist literary and cultural critic in the United States. His commitment and formidable publishing output have ensured a continuing presence for Marxist criticism in a country where it might otherwise appear a distinctly endangered species. Jameson has held a number of prestigious academic positions, and is currently William Lane Professor of Comparative Literature at Duke University. Among the most important influences on his thought has been the work of Georg **Lukács**, particularly such early studies as *The Theory of the Novel*.

The problems which would accompany the attempt to summarize the ideas of any prolific writer are increased when that writer's work encompasses as many areas of cultural production and as many theoretical debates as the books and articles of Fredric Jameson. The fact that many of his arguments resist easy précis merely compounds the difficulty. This discussion will therefore focus on two of Jameson's main works, both of which contain ideas which span his critical output.

The Political Unconscious is perhaps Jameson's most important book, as well as being for many the major work of contemporary Marxist criticism. It is typical of Jameson, not least in the boldness which characterizes it, from its famous opening injunction – 'Always historicise!' – to its concluding discussion of Utopia, a recurrent theme in Jameson's writing. The book's overall project is, if anything, even bolder in its attempt to assert the primacy of a politicized and historicized (i.e. Marxist) reading of texts. Other theories, such as semiotics, structuralism or post-structuralism, are not to be simply discarded, however. On the contrary, Jameson acknowledges their ability to provide useful – even important – knowledge, but in a more 'local' way than Marxism, since they lack the radical understanding of history which would allow them to explain the text more fully. Marxist criticism thus both appropriates and historicizes the partial insights of other critical methods, thereby achieving not some form of absolute truth but, rather, greater 'explanatory adequacy' than its rivals.

One of the ways in which other theories fall short is in adopting an 'immanent' approach – staying resolutely within the limits of the text. For Jameson, as for **Macherey**, this type of analysis is necessary but altogether insufficient, and in 'moving beyond' the text as Macherey does – though in a much more comprehensive manner – he proposes three 'horizons' of analysis. The first of these examines the text in detail, but not in a merely immanent way: even at this stage, the text is situated in its historical moment, not as an inert object but as a 'symbolic act', something which has an effect on the world. The second level is that of the social – in particular, society understood as structured by antagonistic class relations; and here the text is seen, by analogy with **Saussure**'s model of language, as an individual *parole* or utterance in the larger *langue* of class discourse. The third and final level is that of history viewed as a sequence of modes of production, with – in a way reminiscent of Raymond **Williams**'s formulation of dominant, residual and emergent aspects of social structure – any given society or historical period revealing a coexistence of elements from different modes of production. Here the text functions as a 'field of force', where the ideologies and sign systems appropriate to the different modes of production leave their traces. Having set out this ambitious interpretative model in a chapter which encompasses **Althusser**, Lukács, **Habermas**, **Baudrillard**, **Foucault**, **Lacan**, **Eco**, **Gadamer**, **Greimas** and **Frye**, among others, Jameson puts versions of it to work in a series of cumulatively difficult and impressive readings which focus on romance as a genre, and on the individual novelists Balzac, Gissing and Conrad.

After all the effort of demystificatory ideological criticism, Jameson ends the book with another bold – or, as he would see it, properly dialectical – move. Categorizing the ideological criticism as a Marxist 'negative hermeneutic', he argues for the need for a corresponding positive hermeneutic. This would consist of identifying and explaining the utopian element present in any ideology – even the most apparently dystopian – in so far as it included a version of a collectivity, a preferred social order. For Jameson, however, these other collectivities remain only 'figures' for the real Utopia of a future classless society, their achievements at best partial and anticipatory.

If *The Political Unconscious* is Jameson's major work, then the essay which provides the title for *Postmodernism, or the Cultural Logic of Late Capitalism* is perhaps his best known and certainly one of his most controversial works. Attacked from the left for conceding too much to postmodernism (accepting it as a 'cultural dominant', for example), or from other quarters for being too old-fashioned and suspiciously Marxist in his approach (for instance, in seeing it as indissolubly linked to the latest phase of capitalism, as the latter's 'cultural logic'), Jameson's essay nevertheless remains one of the best short analyses of this complex cultural phenomenon. Although *Postmodernism* is explicitly an attempt to periodize and historicize, using a three-phase model derived from Ernest Mandel's book *Late Capitalism*, it might seem as if the secure status of history had been shaken in the few years since *The Political Unconscious*. Among the central features of postmodernism which Jameson lists (new forms of temporality and space; the disappearance of the 'depth' model based on the difference between, for example, appearance and reality, or latent and manifest content; the decline of affect or emotion) there occurs a crisis of historicity. *The Political Unconscious* confronts the argument about the textuality of history by contending that while history is not itself textual, we can know it only via the mediation of texts. In *Postmodernism*, the situation has deteriorated, so that instead of texts representing the (real) historical past, they can now represent only our ideas and stereotypes about the past, and history as such becomes doubly distanced. This is the case even with left-wing writers such as E.L. Doctorow.

In a series of chapters covering, among other things, architecture, film, video, economics, theory, language and literature, Jameson examines some of the forms which postmodernism takes in contemporary society. Many of the features and processes which he lists are negative ones, and certainly life in late capitalism provokes none of the euphoria in him which it seems to generate in others – so much so that for some critics, such as Robert Young, Jameson has surrendered entirely to postmodernism, seeing it as an inescapable, all-embracing system. However, although Jameson's approach is unrepentant and unfashionably 'totalizing', he has consistently rejected the idea of a 'total system' (which he associates with Foucault and others, and pessimistic visions such as Orwell's *1984*). For Jameson, any system, no matter how complete and hermetic it aspires to be, is always permeable, penetrable, offering space for resistances and 'counter-forces'.

Jameson's use of terms such as totality and totalizing is typical of his method. On the one hand, they identify him as a Marxist in the Hegelian tradition (currently held to be one of the less acceptable forms, because of the problematic nature of categories inherited from Hegel – including totality – deemed to be universalizing). At the same time, Jameson is concerned to confront what he calls 'the war on totality' – and, rather than simply dismissing it, explaining why it occurs. Among its causes, he discerns the fragmentation of social forms (and ways of thinking associated with them) as capitalism extends its disruptive power across the globe – thereby, ironically, becoming the nearest thing we have to a totality, and simultaneously making totality harder to contemplate. Another reason for the 'war' is the mistaken assumption that the desire for a form of totality inevitably leads to totalitarianism: 'from Hegel's Absolute Spirit to Stalin's Gulag', as Jameson had earlier summarized it. Jameson, however, is happy to talk of 'the revolutionary, Utopian or totalising impulse', bringing several unfashionable concepts together in a way which clearly construes them positively.

Jameson's adoption of unfashionable positions is oddly related to his own situation as one of the most influential Marxist critics. It is certainly not true that Marxism somehow represents the last refuge of the theoretical dinosaurs: Terry **Eagleton**, for instance, has criticized Jameson's lack of attention to the question of gender; while Aijaz Ahmad has roundly denounced his approach to Third World literature. Other broadly left-wing critics, such as Robert Young and Peter Osborne, have variously attacked Jameson as the latest in a line of Marxists who have failed to produce a coherent concept of history, and as someone who inappropriately hijacks **Adorno** (in *Late Marxism*) in an attempt to produce 'a dialectical model for the 1990s' – in particular, one which would provide another rebuttal of post-structuralism (and, interestingly enough, its attack on totality). Perhaps the latter fact is no more than a timely reminder that the dialectic is a process whose closure in the form of synthesis is never more than temporary and provisional.

Main works

Marxism and Form, Princeton, NJ: Princeton University Press, 1971.

The Prison House of Language, Princeton, NJ: Princeton University Press, 1972.

The Political Unconscious, London: Methuen, 1981.

Late Marxism, London: Verso, 1990.

Postmodernism, or the Cultural Logic of Late Capitalism, London: Verso, 1991a.

Signatures of the Visible, London: Routledge, 1991b.

Further reading

Ahmad, Aijaz, 'Jameson's rhetoric of otherness and the "national allegory" ', in *In Theory: Classes, nations, literatures*, London: Verso, 1992.

Dowling, William C., *Jameson, Althusser, Marx*, London: Methuen, 1984.

Eagleton, Terry, 'Fredric Jameson: the politics of style', in *Against the Grain: Selected essays*, London: Verso, 1986.

Kellner, Douglas, *Postmodernism/Jameson/Critique*, Washington, DC: Maisonneuve Press, 1989.

West, Cornell, 'Ethics and action in Fredric Jameson's Marxist hermeneutics', in Jonathan Arac (ed.), *Postmodernism and Politics*, Manchester: Manchester University Press, 1986.

Young, Robert, 'The Jameson raid', in *White Mythologies: Writing history and the West*, London: Routledge, 1990.

Jardine, Alice (1951–)

Alice Jardine, a feminist literary theorist, holds an Associate Professorship in Romance Languages and Literature at Harvard University. In the early 1980s she wrote a number of articles on contemporary literary theory which culminated in her major work, *Gynesis: Configurations of woman and modernity*, which was published in 1986. She has also co-edited *The Future of Difference, Men in Feminism*, and *Shifting Scenes: Interviews on women, writing, and politics in post-68 France*, and she has also translated some of the work of Julia **Kristeva**. Jardine has already established a reputation as a sophisticated Francophile, and as a seminal critic of the relationship between feminism and postmodernism.

Jardine's *Gynesis* takes its place as an ambitious and erudite critique of feminism and postmodernism at a crucial and dynamic time in the development of post-structuralist literary theory. She creates the neologism 'gynesis' from the greek 'gyn', signifying woman, and 'sis', specifying process, to describe what she calls the 'putting into discourse of "woman"'. This process is intrinsic to the condition of what the French call modernity (known in the Anglo-American critical tradition as postmodernism), and the task of *Gynesis* is to consider the inter-presentation of four discursive elements; modernity, contemporary French thought, feminism and Anglo-American feminist theory. Using the work of French philosophers such as Michel **Foucault**, Jardine considers the possibility that epistemological breaks in Western thought may actually be a result of this coming into discourse of woman, and that as a process gynesis has always been marginally at work in Western tradition.

The reason for the requestioning of Western critical thought is a result of the breakdown of Western master-narratives which attempt to explain the world in terms of such concepts as Man, the Subject, Truth and Meaning. As such, what Jardine terms 'the seeds of the West's modernity', the death of the Cartesian subject, the default of representation and the loss of the authority of the father, need to be explained. Gynesis is the result of this collapse; thus it represents the postmodern crisis and offers new ways of explaining and articulating the spaces in discourse such as madness, the unknown and the unclean, for example, which have traditionally been associated with women, by offering new modes of inquiry. The recognition that woman has been an area of concern historically leads Jardine on to consider how the metaphor of woman operates in the work of writers like **Derrida** and **Lacan**, and she concludes that 'woman' has indeed become a new rhetorical space for these writers; Lacan's 'unconscious', Derrida's 'écriture' and Foucault's 'madness' are all abstract spaces which are gendered female.

Jardine considers that feminism and modernity are perhaps so far apart in their terms of reference that they may be oxymoronic. Feminism is the single narrative of woman, and this is a manifestation of a conceptual apparatus inherited from the nineteenth century; as modernity is about the loss of narrative, then in many ways the two are incompatible. But she points as they are both linked through an interest in new directions in contemporary thought, such as the re-definition of the Self, Representation and Truth, they may not be as inherently resistant to each other as they appear to be. Anglo-American feminist literary theory is criticized in *Gynesis* for failing to assimilate the crisis of modernity; rather than peeking at modernity it should, perhaps, discover some of the interconnections in order to forge new points of departure.

Jardine's work has had a significant impact on the development of critical theory, especially feminist literary theory, which has engaged with her ideas in a dynamic and sometimes controversial fashion. The main points of focus cluster around her critiques of essentialism and empiricism, which tend to pick up on the larger debate within feminism about the dichotomy between French and Anglo-American traditions. In Jardine's work, and most notably in *Gynesis*, the pursuit of a non-essentialist theory of *subjectivity* can take place in the space created by the coming into discourse of woman, and within that space the potential for liberation is great. The call to explore the boundaries and common spaces between postmodernism and feminism is an interesting move in contemporary epistemologies, and has engaged key figures in what have become somewhat polarized critical positions. However, some feminist critics, while applauding Jardine for the originality of her work, have felt uncomfortable with the lack of historical engagement in *Gynesis*. The replacement of real women by the 'woman in effect', and the evasion of the role of history in the construction of subjectivity, have created concerns about the metaphorized idea of woman, which seems somewhat detached from the experiences of women in a patriarchal society.

Main works

The Future of Difference, co-editor Hester Eisenstein, New York: Barnard College Women's Centre, 1980.

Gynesis: Configurations of woman and modernity, Ithaca, NY: Cornell University Press, 1985.

Men in Feminism, co-editor Paul Smith, London: Methuen, 1987.

Shifting Scenes: Interviews on women, writing and politics in post-68 France, co-editor Anne Menke, New York: Columbia University Press, 1991.

Further reading

Belsey, Catherine and Jane Moore (eds), *The Feminist Reader: Essays in gender and the politics of literary criticism*, London: Macmillan, 1989.

Humm, Maggie, *Feminist Criticism*, Brighton: Harvester, 1987.

Marks, Elaine and Isabelle de Courtrivon, *New French Feminisms*, Brighton: Harvester, 1980.

Moi, Toril, *French Feminist Thought*, Oxford: Blackwell, 1987.

Todd, Janet, *Feminist Literary History: A defence*, Oxford: Polity, 1988.

Jauss, Hans Robert (1921–)

Hans Robert Jauss, Professor of Romance Philology and Literary Criticism at the University of Konstanz in West Germany, is a German literary historian and theorist and a specialist in French literature. Having studied with Hans-Georg **Gadamer** in Heidelberg, he has taught at Columbia, Yale, and the Sorbonne. He is a leading member (along with, among others, Wolfgang **Iser**) of the Konstanz School of literary studies at the University of Konstanz. The members of this group practise a method of investigating and teaching literature known as *Rezeption-aesthetik* (in the English-speaking West this is called 'reception theory'), which has its roots in Russian Formalism, Prague structuralism, Gadamer's hermeneutics, Roman Ingarden's phenomenology, and the work of Löwenthal, Hirsche and Schucking in the area of the sociology of literature. *Rezeption-aesthetik* is often contrasted, in English institutions, with theories such as 'reader response' and 'affective stylistics', which foreground the constitutive element of the reading process: what distinguishes it from these theories, however, is an emphasis on aesthetic experience.

Since 1963 the proceedings of the yearly meetings of the Konstanz School have been published in *Poetik und Hermeneutik* (Poetics and Hermeneutics). The title of this publication appropriately signals not only the divergent interests of the group but its aim: to bring two distinct but interrelated disciplines together to form an understanding of the way a reader and a literary text interact. Paul **de Man**, in his introduction to a collection of essays by Jauss called *Toward an Aesthetic of Reception* [*TAR*], defines hermeneutics and poetics, and indicates the implications of conjoining these two terms: 'Hermeneutics', he says, is 'a process directed toward the determination of meaning; it postulates a transcendental function of understanding, no matter how complex, deferred, or tenuous it may be, and will, in however mediated a way, have to raise questions about the extralinguistic truth value of literary texts.' By contrast, poetics is 'a metalinguistic, descriptive or prescriptive discipline that lays claim to scientific consistency. It pertains to the formal analysis of linguistic entities as such, independent of signification; as a branch of linguistics, it deals with theoretical models prior to their historical realization' (*TAR*). In theory, all the aestheticians of reception are united in their aim to synthesize poetics and hermeneutics. In practice, the competence and discursive histories of each of its members have divided its emphasis. On the one hand, some members, who find their genealogy in the structural linguistics of the Prague linguistic circle and with the more technical aspects of phenomenology, focus primarily on poetics. On the other hand, some, like Jauss himself, turn to philosophers of history and interpretation (in particular Hans-Georg Gadamer), and hence focus on hermeneutics. What all members of the group share, however, is their starting point: the rejection of all 'essentialist' notions of literary art.

Jauss's own early work begins with an attempt to displace the fashionable critical methods – sociological, psychological, semiotic, aesthetic – and thereby restore literary history to the centre of literary study. He does not, however, advocate a return to old generic canons, or the life and works of authors; rather, he attempts to combine the historical dialectic found in Marxism and the aesthetic perception of Russian Formalism. This translates as a refusal to study the production or structure of a literary text at the expense of its reception: that is, at the cost of ignoring the individual or collective patterns of understanding that attend its reading and evolve in time. Jauss introduces the term *horizon of expectation* to account for the intersubjective system of references which contour a given individual's reception of the literary text, and it is the breaking and reconfiguring of this horizon that constitutes history. The value of a text is therefore determined in the distance between this horizon and the work itself.

Jauss later repudiates the aesthetic negativity implicit in his theory, because a reception theory based on the breaking of horizons of expectation does not allow for an affirmative social praxis, denying as it does 'identification with the social condition', and hence art's 'communicative', 'norm-constituting' function; therefore, it does not provide for an understanding of the historical function of art as aesthetic experience. In 'Literary history as a challenge to literary theory', he asks:

> [i]f on the one hand literary evolution can be comprehended within the historical change of systems, and on the other hand pragmatic history can be comprehended within the processlike linkage of social conditions, must it not then also be possible to place the 'literary series' and the 'nonliterary series' into a relation that comprehends the relationship between literature and history without forcing literature, at the expense of its character as art, into a function of mere copying or commentary?

The turn away from a strictly 'negative' aesthetic in Jauss marks the return to aesthetic experience conceived as both a surrendering of the ego to the charms of the object and then a creative sacrificing of the object to the realm of the imaginary in the interest of objectivity. This reformulation of aesthetics as experience allows for a 'back-and-forth' movement between the work and its reception in a way that keeps in place art's productive, receptive, and communicative functions (poiesis, aesthesis, catharsis). In contrast to the aesthetiticians of negativity, then, Jauss now seeks to understand patterns of identification in art. For Jauss, five patterns of interaction between the work and its reception are available in all societies: these include five modalities of identification – associative, admiring, sympathetic, cathartic, ironic – and five corresponding receptive dispositions. Hence Jauss provides a more comprehensive model for understanding the relationship between aesthetics and receptivity – one that that includes, but is not reduced to, the critical function of negativity.

The idiosyncratic development of Jauss's own thought has been received differently, at different stages, in America as in Germany. Nevertheless, *Rezeption-aesthetik*, as a mode of investigation and principle of pedagogy, has left its imprint on the study of literature in both Europe and North America. From its earliest articulation, the Konstanz School of literary theory attracted the attention of international scholars, such as Stanley **Fish** and Michael Riffaterre, to its colloquia; and the leading members of the group – such Wolfgang Iser, Jurij Strieder, and Jauss himself – have held teaching positions in American academic institutions.

Main works

'Paradigmawechsel in der Literaturwissenschaft', *Linguistische Berichte*, 3 (1969): 44–56.

Kleine Apologie der asthetischen Erfahrung, Konstanzer Universitätsreden, 59, Constance: Universitätsverlag, 1972.

'The idealist embarrassment: observations on Marxist aesthetics', *New Literary History*, 7, 1 (1975a): 191–208.

'Der Leser als Instanz einer neuen Geschichte der Literatur', *Poetica* 7, 3–4 (1975b): 325–44.

Toward an Aesthetic of Reception, trans. Timothy Bahi, intro. Paul de Man, Brighton: Harvester, 1982a.

Aesthetic Experience and Literary Hermeneutics, trans. Michael Shaw, intro. Wlad Godzich, Minneapolis: University of Minnesota Press, 1982b.

Further reading

Damrosch, Leopold Jr, 'Samuel Johnson and Reader-Response Criticism', *The Eighteenth Century, Theory and Interpretation*, XXI, 2 (1980): 91–108.

Fish, Stanley, *Is There a Text in This Class?*, Cambridge, MA: Harvard University Press, 1980.

Holub, Robert, *Reception Theory: A critical introduction*, London: Methuen, 1980.

Iser, Wolfgang, *The Act of Reading*, Baltimore, MD: Johns Hopkins University Press, 1978.

Iser, Wolfgang, *The Implied Reader*, trans. David Henry Wilson, Baltimore, MD: Johns Hopkins University Press, 1974.

The Reader in the Text: Essays on audience and interpretation, ed. Susan Suleiman and Inge Crossman, Princeton, NJ: Princeton University Press, 1980.

Jencks, Charles (1939–)

Charles Jencks, the architectural historian, theorist and designer, is an expatriate American living in London. He divides his teaching between the Architectural Association in England and UCLA in the United States. As well as touring the world interviewing architects, researching and debating architectural theory and photographing buildings, Jencks is a prolific author and editor of some twenty-five books, including influential studies of twentieth-century architecture.

Although he has written on a wide range of architectural subjects, he is best known for his characterization of post-modern architecture, most notably in *The Language of Post-Modern Architecture* (1977, sixth edn 1991). This book, its following editions and his other texts on postmodernism, are part of an ongoing project of definition, redefinition and updating that makes his work a starting point for many discussions of postmodernism; he is now part of a debate he initially sought to analyze.

The field of architecture has been a useful focus for debates on postmodernism for three main reasons. First, because the failure of modernist architecture has been so spectacular and so visible; we are surrounded by the forbidding state housing and office blocks of postwar modernism. Secondly, and as a consequence of this failure, the contrast between modern and postmodern architecture has been so stylistically marked, and its difference is therefore easy to 'read'. As Fredric **Jameson** has written: 'nowhere else has the death of modernism been felt so intensely', for in architecture, Jameson suggests, the political resonances of these seemingly aesthetic matters become inescapable. Finally, and as a consequence of this, the most important theorists of postmodernism, like Jameson and Jean–François **Lyotard**, have used architecture (with reference to Jencks's work on it) as an index of the 'postmodern condition', and have linked a critique of the built environment to larger cultural, political and economic changes.

Jencks began his career writing on modernist architecture, and his work charts a growing disenchantment with it. His early work at the end of the 1960s marks the introduction of semiotic analysis into architectural criticism. Using rhetorical, linguistic and grammatical categories in a sensibly loose way, Jencks 'read' buildings as forms of communication; by the mid 1970s, he had come to see modernism as a style with a very narrow language, one that has little to say to those outside the architectural profession. In *Le Corbusier & The Tragic Vision of Architecture* (1973), for instance, he calls the famous arch-modernist 'the greatest architect of the twentieth century', but – foreshadowing his later attack on modernism – he criticises the naivety of Corbusier's urban schemes, and the limited nature of his architectural themes.

By 1975, Jencks had begun to lecture and write on postmodern architecture, finally producing his most influential work, *The Language of Post-Modern Architecture*, in 1977. By this point he had crystallized what he thought was wrong with modernist architecture, but had yet to produce a positive definition of postmodernism; in 1977, it is a number of plural departures from modernism of a hybrid kind; – that is, architecture that used styles from the past as well as modernist techniques in which all architects were trained. While Virginia **Woolf** is credited with dating the beginning of literary modernism (December 1910; see Woolf), Jencks is noted for registering its architectural and ideological demise; it 'died in St. Louis, Missouri, on July 15th, 1972 at 3.32 p.m. (or thereabouts)' (Jencks, 1977), when part of the Pruitt–Igoe housing project was blown up because no one wanted to live in the crumbling, vandalized blocks.

Jencks was not alone in his criticism of both the narrow language and social consequences of what was called modernism's 'International Style', which ignored any kind of cultural, social or geographical difference; in an office block or a housing scheme, in Cardiff or Calcutta, modernism had lost any notion of 'decorum' or appropriateness to context 'as if Esperanto had been enforced everywhere' (Jencks, 1977). Since Jane Jacobs's work in the early 1960s, many writers had criticized modernist urban style, but Jencks's work, along with that of other architects and critics in the mid 1970s, signalled a disaffection that represented a shift in architectural practice itself.

'Postmodernism', then, for Jencks in 1977, had been 'a negative term, its very vagueness appealing' (Jencks, 1977). By 1978, and the second edition of *The Language of Post-Modern Architecture*, he offered a positive definition; his much-quoted and influential concept of 'double-coding': 'the combination of modern techniques with something else (usually traditional building) in order for architecture to communicate with the public and a concerned minority, usually other architects' (Jencks, 1989). It is not the revival of old styles, nor simply anti-modernist, for postmodernism has, according to Jencks, 'the essential double-meaning; the continuation of modernism and its transcendence' (*ibid.*). One example he uses is the British architect James Sterling's addition to the state gallery in Stuttgart. While obviously a contemporary building, it echoes and plays with past art and architecture, including classical and pop art. Postmodern architecture, for Jencks, is the opening up of the minimalist language of modernism to history, context and difference; a pluralist approach to cultural communication.

During the 1980s, Jencks began to expand his theory of post-modernism as double-coding to other areas of culture; his *What Is Post-Modernism?* (1986; 3rd edn 1989) is still the most useful and concise guide to his thought. As well as architecture, Jencks looks at painting, literature, and what will develop into a postmodern social criticism. His more polemical aim in this text is to investigate the burgeoning literature on postmodernism in which his work has an important place, and to draw, for him, a necessary distinction between the postmodern and the late modern.

For Jencks, postmodernism is both 'cultural movement and historical epoch' (Jencks, 1989), and he finds that his concept of double-coding explains the 'Postmodern turn' in other arts. He draws on the work of novelist John Barth to describe recent developments in fiction. Barth wrote in 1980 that while he neither repudiated nor imitated the experimental writers of the early part of the century, he hoped to go beyond the limited audience available to them, the circle of devotees of high art, by writing 'double-coded' fiction that gives us the traditional pleasures of plot in self-conscious abundance and works at a number of other levels too.

Linda Hutcheon's characterization of a particularly postmodern fiction (she takes Jencks as her starting point) has called these works 'historiographical metafictions' – that is, texts that deal with the past but are conscious of the fact that history is a text to be interpreted from a contemporary point of view. It is in relation to double-coding that Jencks (and, following him, Hutcheon too) make an interesting distinction between double-coded postmodernism and 'late modernism': works that take modernist techniques to an extreme – for example the novels of Samuel Beckett and Alain Robbe–Grillet, or the 'guts-on-the-outside', high-tech buildings of Richard Rogers: the Pompidou Centre and the Lloyds Building.

In art, Jencks sees the return of representational painting, self-conscious allegory, along with an eclectic, hybrid style, as signs of ubiquitous postmodern double coding, which amounts to the ability of the work (be it painting or text) to be doubly read in the way he outlines. This plurality of readings is not modernist work's much-vaunted difficulty or complexity (though it can be this too); this plurality implies a democratic notion of reading which is to do with speaking, in various ways, and at various levels, to as many people as possible.

Jencks shares with Lyotard a sense of the end of the Enlightenment or modern project with its (as he sees it) oppressive notion of 'progress' (Jencks, 1989); while Lyotard himself has been highly critical of Jencks's celebration of postmodern architecture, seeing it as an 'anything goes' anti-modernist 'realism' which accepts and panders to capitalism and commodified culture.

Jameson, too, sees postmodern architecture as a complacent eclecticism which cannibalizes styles 'without principle' (Jameson, 1984). For Jameson, too, Jencks is an anti-modernist. Jencks is clearly not simply anti-modernist, for 'all the creators who could be called Post-Modern keep something of a modern sensibility – some intention which distinguishes their work from that of revivalists' (Jencks, 1989).

Finally, Jencks's work on postmodernism *is* celebratory – he celebrates not 'anything goes' architecture but a democratic, plural, humanist approach to the built environment, which would align itself not to the post-structuralist, anti-humanist philosophy of Lyotard and similar thinkers, but to a post-modern politics of difference, dialogism and heterogeneity (as he calls it in his most recent book, *Heteropolis*) which, at the very least, would open up architectural language to previously marginalized accents.

Main works

(ed. with G. Baird) *Meaning in Architecture*, London: Barrie & Rockliff, 1969.

Le Corbusier & The Tragic Vision of Architecture, London: Allen Lane, 1973.

The Language of Post-Modern Architecture, London: Academy Editions, 1977.

What Is Post-Modernism? London: Academy Editions, 1986.

Post-Modernism: The new classicism in art & architecture, London: Academy Editions, 1989.

Heteropolis, London: Academy Editions, 1993.

Further reading

Hutcheon, Linda, *A Poetics of Postmodernism*, London: Routledge, 1988.

Jacobs, Jane, *The Death and Life of Great American Cities*, 1961, Harmondsworth: Pelican, 1964.

Jameson, Fredric, 'Postmodernism, or the cultural logic of late capitalism', *New Left Review*, 146 (1984): 53–92.

Jameson, Fredric, *The Ideologies of Theory*, vol. 2, London: Routledge, 1988.

Lyotard, Jean–François, *The Postmodern Condition*, trans. by Brian Massumi and Geoffrey Bennington, Manchester: Manchester University Press, 1984.

K

Kristeva, Julia (1941–)

Julia Kristeva is a Bulgarian-born literary critic, cultural analyst, linguist and psychoanalyst whose work in the 1970s and 1980s virtually revolutionized Western thinking about language and culture. Roland **Barthes** once noted that what makes Kristeva unique is that she 'subverts authority, the authority of monologic science' by destroying previous preconceptions, a habit of mind that helped to contribute to his own shift from 'a semiology of products to a semiotics of production'. In 1966, when she moved from Sophia, where she was a specialist in French literature at the Institute of Literature, to the University of Paris VII, she brought to the then fashionable structuralist studies of culture a uniquely Eastern perspective. Her educational background, materially grounded in catholicism and communism alike, included not only knowledge of **Marx** and Hegel, but a fluency in Russian that afforded her an intimate familiarity with Russian Formalism and 'postformalism', in particular the work of Mikhail **Bakhtin**. This intellectual background produced a natural resistance to the literary structuralism in France of the late sixties – its blindness to historical genesis and to the force of the writing subject. One year after beginning her work in Paris under the direction of Lucien **Goldmann** and Roland Barthes, whom she met through Tzvetan **Todorov**, she was publishing articles in many prestigious journals, including *Tel Quel*, which was run by her future husband, Philippe Sollers. In 1974 she received a Chair at the University of Paris VII for the publication of her doctoral thesis, *La Révolution du langage poétique*, and she has continued there as Professor of Linguistics since that time. The progressive importance of psychoanalysis – in particular the work of Jacques **Lacan** – for Kristeva's thinking is foregrounded by the fact that she has in the interim become qualified as a practising psychoanalyst.

Kristeva's work is both an assimilation and a critique of Marx, Hegel, **Lukács, Saussure, Jakobson**, Benveniste, **Chomsky**, Peirce, Bakhtin and **Freud**, not to mention **Derrida** and Lacan. Indeed, the power of her thinking derives from a stated desire to reinvest old philosophies of language with a sense not only of the historical and social function of language, but also of its dynamism and subversive potential. Her concern is to displace the positivism of traditional philosophical discourse by including the heterogeneous *speaking subject* in an equally heterogeneous signifying process. In the first phase of her inquiry she was concerned with producing a semiotic theory of the poetic dimension of language, or a way of understanding and speaking about the musical and rhythmical in language without reducing this dimension to just another way of communicating or conveying information. Here her intellectual debt to Formalism is clear. However, she moved beyond both Formalism and Saussurean linguistics in her theorizing of poetic language: for her, language was both a system and systematizing, a structure and structuring, and the 'poetic' became the most important site of disruption and change.

In her early work Kristeva makes broad claims for the poetic: it is theorized as having, since the end of the nineteenth century, 'deliberately maintained the balance between sociality and madness', signalling the advance of a new era. In *Le Texte du roman* for example, she is concerned mainly with the authority of a text, and she makes a case for a changed understanding of 'genre' such that the novel emerges as a mixture of heterogeneous verbal practices controlled by the 'ideologeme' (the organization of a system of relationships represented and functioning in a particular social and historical context) of the sign. Hence her inquiry initially took the form of an attempt to understand the 'force' underlying literary production, a force attributed solely neither to authorial intention nor ideological structures, but one that includes an understanding of *negativity* within its complexity.

Kristeva's work of the 1970s, the second phase of her development culminating in *Revolution in Poetic Language*, is concerned with the relationship between the development of subjectivity and the production of a symbolic order. It is here that negativity becomes important. Negativity, a concept she takes from Hegel, is not negation in the sense of a negative proposition (the tree is not green); rather, it is determinate and part of the substance of reality: she defines it as 'the cause and organizing principle of the [*thetic*] *process*' which 'figures as the indissoluable relation between an "ineffable" mobility and its particular determination . . . the logical functioning of the movement that produces the theses' (Kristeva, 1984a). For Kristeva, negativity is linked to body drives, which in negating themselves determine the semiotic process. So in this work she attempts to account for a linguistic performativity which is not strictly 'phenomenological', one that includes an understanding of a subject in process, always 'on the way' to becoming.

In other words, she attempts to give an account of what J.L. Austin called the constative and performative dimensions of language, which would reflect a dialectic between a *symbolic* order of signification and an unconscious and disruptive, *semiotic* disposition. Here, then, the revolution in poetic language is recontextualized in explicitly psychoanalytic terms, as the development of the subject coincides with the development of the signifying process. Underpinning this realm of signification are a series of biological/psychological processes: the semiotic *chora* (from the Greek for *receptacle*), which is articulated by energy charges and psychical marks, becomes the place of an ordering through the respective generating and constraining characteristics of these two forces. This chora is then split as signification moves into a two-stage *thetic phase*, which includes first the production of spatial intuition (mirror stage) and the capturing of a unified image (imago) through separation (castration); secondly, it involves the spontaneous initiation of semiotic motion and the emergence of the subject as available for signification. The perception of a lack moves the subject into the realm of signification, where the semiotic function is transferred on to the symbolic function. However, this resolution of what Freud would call the Oedipus complex does not altogether eliminate semiosis: rather, signification consists of two modalities: the semiotic process, which is linked to the signifier, and the symbolic process, which becomes the signified. These two operations are inseparable, and constitute the subject. The whole process might be mapped in the following manner:

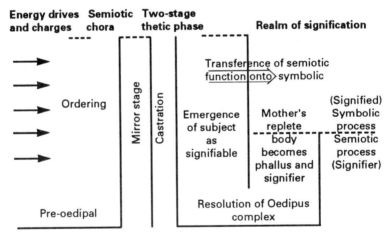

This view of language differs from a generative model by virtue of the fact that it refuses a phenomenological subject, positing instead a subject in process with identity constantly in question. Both the politics of social change and the semiotic/symbolic process of identity formation are made explicit in her theorizing of *signifying practice*, which she describes as 'the establishment and countervailing of a sign system'.

Identity is determined and structured by its placement within a social formation; nevertheless, signifying practice continually 'pulverizes' symbolic unity, in various ways.

Kristeva's work of the 1980s utilizes the direct experience of her psycholanalytic practice to inform an understanding of the modern experiences of horror, melancholy and love. In *Powers of Horror* the structuring of subjectivity – in both the experience of the individual and the constitution of culture – is described in terms of a theory of abjection: abjection is the act of severing or casting off, the act of separation which precedes transference into the symbolic order. It is a product of universal horror, the horror of being that is repressed. 'Abjection', says Kristeva,

> is the other facet of religious, moral, and ideological codes on which rest the sleep of individuals and the breathing spells of societies. Such codes are abjection's purification and repression. But the return of their repressed make up our 'apocalypse', and that is why we cannot escape the dramatic convulsions of religious crisis. (1982)

Her own 'dramatic convulsions of religious crisis' have taken, since the early 1980s, the form of an interest in the representation of motherhood in Western culture, particularly as it finds embodiment in the figure of the Madonna. Her most recent written works (*Tales of Love* and *Black Sun*) focus on aspects of love – including melancholia and depression – in the experience of Western culture.

Kristeva's influence is difficult to measure in terms of the number of practitioners utilizing her critical method and insights. For while she provides feminists with a linguistic theory that recovers unconscious forces in the production of language, thus making possible a conception of subjectivity as a construction in process, she refuses to essentialize the semiotic process by tying it to an objectified concept of woman. For Kristeva, semiosis is inscribed in the symbolic order through the very action of negativity; it cannot therefore exist independent of this order. The speaking subject includes both male and female gender, and cannot be reduced to just one; hence she has remained on the margins of feminism. Nevertheless, her work is unique in providing a semiotic theory that includes the unconscious as the very source of disruption and change. This orientation is now commonplace in all areas of cultural study.

Main works

Semeiotike, Recherches pour une sémanalyse, Paris: Editions du Seuil, 1969.

Le Texte du roman, Approche sémiologique d'une structure discursive transformationnelle, The Hague: Mouton, 1970.

La Traversée des signes (collective work), Paris: Editions du Seuil, 1975.

Folle vérité (collective work), Paris: Editions du Seuil, 1979.

Le Langage cet inconnu, Paris: Editions du Seuil, 1981.

Powers of Horror: An essay on abjection, trans. Leon S. Roudiez, New York: Columbia University Press, 1982.

Revolution in Poetic Language, trans. Margaret Waller, New York: Columbia University Press, 1984a.

Desire in Language: A semiotic approach to literature and art, trans. Thomas S. Gora, Alice Jardine and Leon S. Roudiez, Oxford: Blackwell, 1984b.

About Chinese Women, trans. Anita Burrows, New York and London: Marion Boyars, 1986a.

The Kristeva Reader, ed. Toril Moi, Oxford: Blackwell, 1986b.

In the Beginning was Love: Psychoanalysis and faith, trans. Arthur Goldhammer, New York: Columbia University Press, 1987a.

Tales of Love, trans. Leon S. Roudiez, New York: Columbia University Press, 1987b.

Language: The Unknown, trans. Leon S. Roudiez, New York: Columbia University Press, 1987c.

Black Sun: Depression and melancholia, trans. Leon S. Roudiez, New York: Columbia University Press, 1989a.

Strangers to Ourselves, trans. Leon S. Roudiez, New York: Columbia University Press, 1989b.

Nations without Nationalism, trans. Leon S. Roudiez, New York: Columbia University Press, 1993a.

The Samurai, trans. Leon S. Roudiez, New York: Columbia University Press, 1993b.

Further reading

Fletcher, John and Andrew Benjamin (eds), *Abjection, Melancholia and Love: The work of Julia Kristeva*, London and New York: Routledge, 1990.

Lechte, John, *Julia Kristeva*, London and New York: Routledge, 1990.

Payne, Michael, *Reading Theory: An introduction to Lacan, Derrida, and Kristeva*, Oxford: Blackwell, 1993.

L

Lacan, Jacques (1901–81)

Lacan qualified as a doctor and specialized in psychiatry, joining the French branch of the International Psychoanalytic Association in 1934 and practising as an analyst. He was involved in the first major split of the the French psychoanalytic institution in 1953, and the founding of a new society. In 1964, after expulsion from the IPA, he continued his influential seminars and formed his own school, l'ecole Freudienne de Paris, which he dissolved a year before his death.

Lacanian psychoanalysis mounts a concerted attack on the notion of the subject embodied in rationalist philosophy and humanism as well as the autonomous ego of traditional psychology. The Cartesian *cogito*, the 'I' which in thinking is conscious of its being, and the humanist self, the integral individual, do not, Lacan argues, compose a pre-existent, unified, whole or autonomous subject, the expressive and interior centre of the human being. Ex-centric, the subject of Lacanian psychoanalysis is an effect of unconscious processes and desires articulated in language. In the **Freud**ian terms on which Lacan's arguments are based, the ego is less the stable unity underlying systems of perception and consciousness and more a position uncomfortably pressed between the social and moral imperatives of the superego and the urgencies and uncertainties of the id.

Lacan's famous return to Freud was a return to the works of the founder of psychoanalysis from an entirely new perspective: it was a return by way of the differences integral to **Saussure's** notion of language, and involved serious recourse to the work of other structuralists, Roman **Jakobson** and Claude **Lévi–Strauss** in particular. Seen in the light of structural linguistics, the focus of Freudian psychoanalysis, with its many discussions of philology, was shifted by Lacan away from a discourse that was – albeit uncomfortably – associated with biology and medicine, and redefined with an emphasis on the role of language and culture. The unconscious, conventionally the locus of primal wishes and energies, was, Lacan repeatedly stated, 'structured like a language'. Its structure, moreover, was not simply that of Saussure's *langue,* since Lacan significantly reformulated the Saussurean concept of the sign by severing the unity of signifier and signified with a bar that established them as dissociated units of separate systems.

The signifier is privileged by Lacan: it determines the course of the subject's development and the direction of its desire; it constitutes the possibility of identity and relationship at the expense of the subject's alienation in language. In stressing the role of the signifier in the constitution of subjectivity, Lacan is not reiterating a nominalist position in which the name replaces the thing. Rather, the signifier stands as a mark of the symbolic differentiations and relationships that govern human activity: the topographical character of signification is the important factor, not its content. In this respect, for example, it is not the content of the oedipal triangle, but its structural relationships and effects.

The emphasis placed by Lacan on language as a system of signification problematizes conventional assumptions in rationalism, empiricism or humanism which assert that the determining factors of human development are mind, nature or self. Being is rendered other to itself, identity shaped and orientated externally, in relation to the effects of the signifier and the articulations of desire. Being, in the sense of unity, wholeness and self-presence, is lacking, a result of the separation between the animal needs of humans and the constitution of identity, relationships and values in culture and language: the subject is thus defined as the *manque-à-être,* the want-to-be, in which 'want' connotes both lack and desire. The exteriority of subjectivity, an exteriority which is within – in the form of structures that are internalized in the unconscious and remain inaccessible to the ego – is first manifested for Lacan in an early essay on the 'mirror stage'. It is in the mirror that the ego assumes its unified state, achieving a coherence that is other to itself because it exists only in the reflected image. This is the basis of the imaginary register. The ego misrecognizes or misapprehends the image in the mirror, assuming the other's unity as its own in an anticipation or projection of psychic and bodily integration. The 'I' emerges in this process of specular reflection and misrecognition, and enables the assumption of a different social 'I', an entry into the symbolic circuits of language involving identification with signifiers rather than images.

The symbolic register, language as the locus of signifying conventions, encodes the rules, mores and taboos of a given culture, operating as a system of exchange and differentiation which positions subjects with social identities. Constituting, articulating and alienating 'original' identity, the symbolic register serves as the dimension of law, and is presided over by the 'Name of the Father'. In a typically Lacanian pun, the name [*nom*] is also the no [*non*] of the father, connecting structures of symbolic differentiation with the prohibitive and regulative powers of law. The Name of the Father, a primal entity postulated in Freud's *Totem and Taboo*, is a purely symbolic figure, though its function, in the imaginary of particular subjects, can be embodied by actual figures, most obviously in institutions like the family or the Church. As a symbolic figure, a paternal metaphor, the Name of the Father is located in the Other, the locus of law and signification in which the subject is alienated and constituted. Freudian notions of castration are thus reformulated as the separation from any fundamental unity or wholeness and the subjection to the laws of desire and signification.

Consequently, desire emanates not from the interior of the subject but in the relation to the Other where identity is established in the articulation of signifiers. Desire is distinct from need, strictly biological in form, and demand, which describes the subject's call for recognition and love, a call that can never be satisfactorily answered because it is addressed not to a person but to the whole system, the Other. The lack of satisfaction, moreover, requires a reiteration that displaces demand in the movements of desire. In the oedipal triangle, for instance, the initial demand of the child for the mother's recognition and love is displaced because it encounters the prohibition of law against incest and the mother's desire for the father. Eschewing the direct approach of the demand, a detour is taken: identifying with the father, the object of the mother's desire, becomes a possible way of avoiding censure and belatedly satisfying the initial want. Desire is the desire of the Other, then, in two senses: the subject wants to be desired by the Other and its desire is located in the Other, in the structural relations rather than the individual.

The third register in Lacan's system is the Real. Distinguished from reality, which is shaped, perceived and understood in symbolic processes, the Real marks a fundamental absence, a hole, over and around which signifiers circulate. In psychoanalytic practice it designates a scene of trauma which can never be represented but continues to produce neurotic symptoms – signifiers – that attempt to fill the hole, the gap caused by anxiety. The three registers – Imaginary, Symbolic and Real – are not separable but interdependent systems: their relation takes the form of a Borromean knot in which the disconnection of one results in the disconnection of them all. As the leftover of – an excess that cannot be contained by – any symbolic system, the Real manifests a disruptive and anxiety-provoking force, condensed in what Lacan calls the object small 'a': the tears that this object makes in the imaginary and symbolic network require, in the therapeutic work of analysis, their reorganization. An impossible object in the sense that it is not a physical thing, the object small 'a' reopens the lack that motivates desire: it is thus the cause of – and object in – desire, the object around which signification circulates and in relation to which it is articulated and displaced. The relationship between the imaginary and symbolic registers is most evident at the level of meaning, at the point where the specular I is joined to the social I. Determined by a chain of signifiers, the desiring subject reaches a point where a particular signifier, the phallus, is (mis)recognized as the chain's signified. The 'anchoring point' of the metonymically organized chain arrests the sliding movements of signifiers by metaphorically substituting one term for another, thereby mapping the phallus on to the symbolic Name of the Father in the manner of the subject's misrecognition of the image as its self in the mirror stage.

The dynamic interrelation of the registers in Lacan's system and their topographical character make for a level of difficulty and opacity that is often criticized as unnecessarily obscure. The range of interdisciplinary reference, from psychoanalytic to linguistic, philosophical, anthropological and mathematical theories, exacerbates the complexity as well as indicating the extensive implications of Lacan's writings. The shifting nuances of the terms that are employed are also an effect of the intertextual variety, and display the continuing development and revisions undertaken by Lacan. From the 1950s to the 1970s, when many of the revisions are evident, Lacan held a fortnightly public seminar that became one of the major intellectual events in Paris. His published writings are generally based on material from these seminars, preserving the masterly manner of delivery – the rhetorical flourishes and erudite allusions – that both captivated and irritated audiences. For feminist detractors, this style confirmed suspicions about the patriarchal and phallocentric basis of psychoanalysis: that its concerns remained centred on male sexuality to the exclusion of female differences. In **Deleuze** and **Guattari**'s political critique of Lacan, *Anti-Oedipus*, the dependence on organic notions of the body and rigid symbolic structures was seen to be exceeded by the machinic and economic movements, flows and circulations of desire. In a similar vein, **Derrida** disclosed underlying phallogocentric assumptions, critiquing Lacan's undue insistence on full speech wherein the return to the meaning of Freud, as father of psychoanalysis, serves to contain and delimit issues of difference within a rigid, oedipal version of psychoanalysis.

For a theory developed specifically within and directed at the institution and practice of psychoanalysis, Lacan's work has been influential in a variety of other disciplines. Political philosophy – **Althusser**'s work in particular – significantly adapted the notion of the imaginary to analyze the internalization and reproduction of ideological state apparatuses. While challenging the predominance of patriarchal assumptions, much feminist theory has used and transformed ideas about subjectivity, sexuality and difference: work by **Irigaray** and **Kristeva** proposes a more fluid, plural and open conception of writing and identity, closer to female experience and the body. Literary, cultural and cinema studies have also been reshaped by notions of identification, signification and the role of social and symbolic processes in the constitution of identities, ways of seeing, interpreting and desiring: the focus of reading has shifted from an author- and character-centred practice to examinations of the positioning of textual figures in relation to unconscious structures of meaning; cultures are studied as effects of imaginary and symbolic differentiations that produce notions of otherness; film theory emphasizes the effects of desire and symbolic structures on perceptions of visual signifiers and images. In queer theory, notably in recent work by Judith Butler, psychoanalytic concepts of perversion have been reworked to address questions of gender and sexual performativities.

Main works

Ecrits, trans. Alan Sheridan, London: Tavistock, 1977a.

The Four Fundamental Concepts of Psychoanalysis, trans. Alan Sheridan, Harmondsworth: Penguin, 1977b.

The Seminar of Jacques Lacan: Book I, Freud's papers on Technique, 1953–1954, trans. John Forrester, Cambridge: Cambridge University Press, 1988a.

The Seminar of Jacques Lacan: Book II, The Ego in Freud's Theory and in the Technique of Psychoanalysis, 1954–1955, trans. Sylvana Tomaselli, Cambridge: Cambridge University Press, 1988b.

The Ethics of Psychoanalysis, 1959–1960: The seminar of Jacques Lacan, Book VII, trans. Dennis Porter, London: Routledge, 1992.

The Psychoses: The seminar of Jacques Lacan, Book III, 1955–1956, trans. Russell Grigg, London: Routledge, 1993.

Further reading

Benvenuto, Bice and Roger Kennedy, *The Works of Jacques Lacan: An introduction*, London: Free Association Books, 1986.

Clément, Catherine, *The Lives and Legends of Jacques Lacan*, trans. Arthur Goldhammer, New York: Columbia University Press, 1983.

Mitchell, Juliet and Jacqueline Rose (eds), *Feminine Sexuality: Jacques*

Lacan and the Ecole Freudienne, London and Basingstoke: Macmillan, 1982.

Nancy, Jean-Luc and Philippe Labarthe–Lacoue, *The Title of the Letter: A reading of Jacques Lacan*, trans. François Raffoul and David Pettigrew, New York: SUNY Press, 1992.

Roudinesco, Elisabeth, *Jacques Lacan & Co.: A history of psychoanalysis in France 1925–1985*, trans. Jeffrey Mehlman, London: Free Association Books, 1990.

Žižek, Slavoj, *Enjoy Your Symptom: Jacques Lacan in Hollywood and out*, New York and London: Routledge, 1992.

Leavis, F.R. (1895–1978)

F.R. Leavis was born in Cambridge, and educated at the Perse School and Emmanuel College, Cambridge, where he read History and English. He was the founder and editor of *Scrutiny* (1932–53); Fellow of Downing College, Cambridge (1937–62), University Reader in English (1959–62), and Honorary Fellow (1962–64).

To understand F.R. Leavis's approach to literature, we must first understand the cultural theory which underpins it. According to Leavis and the Leavisites (Leavis generated a body of followers around the journal *Scrutiny*), the twentieth century is marked by increasing evidence of cultural decline. What had been identified by Matthew Arnold in the nineteenth century had continued at an accelerated pace in the twentieth. The problem was the spread of 'mass' culture – marked, as it is, by 'standardisation and levelling down'. Against this 'the citizen . . . must be trained to discriminate'.

Leavis's analysis starts from the assumption that 'culture has always been in minority keeping'. It is always the minority who 'keep alive the subtlest and most perishable parts of tradition'; it is upon the minority that we must depend for 'the implicit standards that order the finer living of an age' (*Mass Civilization and Minority Culture*). However, the status of the minority had changed. Whereas in the past it could command cultural deference, the twentieth century has witnessed an increasing weakening – almost to the point of collapse – of its cultural authority. For the Leavisites it amounts to a 'revolution against taste' (Q.D. Leavis, quoting Edmund Gosse) which, according to Leavis, threatened 'to land us in irreparable chaos'. Against this threat Leavis proposes 'to introduce into schools a training in resistance [to mass culture]'; and outside schools, to promote a 'conscious and directed effort . . . [to] take the form of resistance by an armed [with the timeless values of the literary text] and active minority' (Q.D. Leavis).

The resistance of the Leavisites was fuelled by a mythic reading of the past. It was claimed by Leavis and others that prior to the nineteenth century, and certainly before the seventeenth, England had a vigorous common culture. As a result of the traumatic changes brought about by the Industrial Revolution, this common culture splintered into two cultures: on the one hand a minority culture; on the other a mass civilization. The minority culture is the embodiment of the values and standards of 'the best that has been thought and said' (Matthew Arnold), now – more or less – reduced by Leavis to the literary tradition. In opposition to this is the mass culture of mass civilization, 'commercial' culture consumed by the 'uneducated' majority. This includes cinema, radio, popular fiction, the popular press. But for Leavis and the Leavisites it is advertising, capitalism's cultural form *par excellence*, which is the main symptom of cultural decline. To understand why, we must understand Leavis's attitude to language. He argues that 'it should be brought home to learners that this debasement of language is not merely a matter of words; it is a debasement of emotional life, and the quality of living' (*Culture and Environment*). Advertising does not just debase the language, it debases the emotional life of the whole language community. He provides numerous examples (mostly written by himself to avoid copyright difficulties) to demonstrate this point.

Leavis looks back with longing to a cultural golden age before the fall – the lost 'organic community'. The Elizabethan period of Shakespeare's theatre is often cited as a time of cultural coherence. Leavis writes of Shakespeare belonging 'to a genuinely national culture, to a community in which it was possible for the theatre to appeal to the cultivated and the populace at the same time' (*For Continuity*). Q.D. Leavis's own comments on the relation between populace and cultivated in the Elizabethan period are very revealing of the general Leavisite position: 'the masses were receiving their amusement from above. . . . They had to take the same amusements as their betters. . . . Happily, they had no choice.' This is a cultural coherence built on foundations of authoritarian and hierarchical principles; a common culture which gives intellectual stimulation at one end, and affective pleasure at the other. This is a mythic world in which everyone knows their place, knows their station in life. Despite these obvious qualifications, Leavis insists 'that there was in the seventeenth century, a real culture of the people . . . a rich traditional culture . . . a positive culture which has disappeared' (*The Common Pursuit*). Most of this culture, according to Leavis, was destroyed by the changes brought about by the Industrial Revolution. A world of rural rhythms had been lost to the monotony and mediocrity of urban culture. Whereas in the organic community everyday culture was a constant source of – and support to – the health of the individual, in mass civilization one must make a conscious and directed effort to avoid the unhealthy influences of everyday culture. However, Leavis's account of the lost organic community is an account not so much of a lost historical moment as of a literary myth, a constructed memory of an old order to incite the creation of a new.

Although the organic community is lost, it is still possible to get access to its values and standards. It is here that Leavis's cultural theory embraces the literary. For Leavis and the Leavisites, literature is a cultural treasury embodying all that is to be valued in human experience. It is quite simply 'the best that has been thought and said'. Unfortunately, literature as the jewel in the crown of culture has, like culture itself, lost its full authority. Leavis hopes to remedy this by dispatching cultural missionaries, a small select band of literary intellectuals, to establish outposts of culture within universities, to maintain and nurture the literary tradition and encourage its 'continuous collaborative renewal'; and in schools, to arm students to enable them to wage war against the general barbarism of mass culture and mass civilization.

The Leavisite approach to literature is essentially moral criticism. Through a confrontation with the concrete reality of the text a 'training of sensibility' can be achieved. Literary study is privileged because 'It trains, in a way no other discipline can, intelligence and sensibility together, cultivating a sensitiveness and precision of response and a delicate integrity of intelligence – intelligence that integrates as well as analyses and must have pertinacity and staying power as well as delicacy' (*Education and the University*). Study of the the literary text is able to achieve this because in essence it is for Leavis a treasury of timeless moral truths, and thus a source of moral order. In short, the achievement of great writers is to give literary form to timeless moral truths. The responsibility of the critic is twofold: first, to ensure this process is understood; second, to bring about an understanding of literature's position of authority in English culture. The re-establishment of literature's authority will not, of course, herald the return of the organic community, but it will keep under control the expanding influence of mass culture, and thus help to preserve and maintain the continuity of England's cultural tradition(s), by producing an 'educated public' who will continue the Arnoldian project of keeping in hierarchical circulation 'the best that has been thought and said'.

It is very easy to be critical of Leavis and the Leavisite approach to literature and culture. Given the recent developments in the fields of cultural and literary theory, it is almost enough to present a narrative of the Leavisite approach to condemn it to ridicule. However, it has to be remembered that from a historical point of view, Leavis's work is absolutely central to the academic project of literary and cultural analysis. Much contemporary British analysis has its roots in a dialogue (often very critical) with Leavisism. As for the cultural impact of Leavis and Leavisism, it is undoubtedly true that from the 1930s to the end of the 1950s, Leavisism was in many respects the dominant paradigm in British cultural and literary theory and analysis. Indeed, it could be argued that it still forms a kind of repressed 'common sense' in certain areas of British academic and non-academic life.

Main works

Mass Civilization and Minority Culture, Cambridge: Gordon Fraser, 1930a.

D.H. Lawrence, Gordon Fraser: Cambridge, 1930b.

New Bearings in English Poetry, London: Chatto & Windus, 1932.

Culture and Environment (with Denys Thompson), London: Chatto & Windus, 1933a.

For Continuity, Cambridge: Minority Press, 1933b.

The Great Tradition, London: Chatto & Windus, 1948.

The Common Pursuit, London: Chatto & Windus, 1952.

Nor Shall My Sword, London: Chatto & Windus, 1972.

Further reading

Bell, M., *F.R. Leavis*, London: Routledge, 1988.

Bilan, R.P., *The Literary Criticism of F.R. Leavis*, Cambridge: Cambridge University Press, 1979.

Greenwood, E., *F.R. Leavis*, London: Longman, 1978.

Mulhern, F., *The Moment of 'Scrutiny'*, London: New Left Books, 1979.

Samson, A., *F.R. Leavis*, Hemel Hempstead: Harvester Wheatsheaf, 1992.

Thompson, D. (ed.), *The Leavises: Recollections and impressions*, Cambridge: Cambridge University Press, 1984.

Lévi-Strauss, Claude (1908–)

Although Claude Lévi-Strauss was born in Brussels, he was educated in France – first at the Lycée Janson de Sailly and subsequently at the University of of Paris, where he graduated in Law and Philosophy. After some years as a provincial schoolmaster, he joined the staff of the University of São Paolo. His interest in social anthropology stems from expeditions undertaken during this Brazilian stay (1934–9). His next appointment was at the New School for Social Research in New York. He became one of the founders of the Ecole Libre des Hautes Etudes de New York. Subsequent posts were Cultural Attaché at the French Embassy in Washington (1945–8), Associate Curator of the Paris Musée de l'Homme (1949), and Directeur d'Etudes at the Ecole Pratique des Hautes Etudes (1950–74). For the last thirty-one years he has occupied the Chair of Social Anthropology at the Collège de France. A member of the Académie Française since 1973, he has been honoured extensively at home and abroad, his latest award being the Great Cross of the Légion d'Honneur (1991).

Although Lévi–Strauss is widely regarded as a celebrated structuralist anthropologist, his influence has been much broader. He was a key figure in the initial stages of structuralism in France in the late 1950s and 1960s. Structuralism is concerned not with *meaning* but with how meaning is produced, the rules governing the production of meaning. It owes much to the structural linguistics of Trubetskoy, **Saussure** and **Jakobson**. During the war Lévi–Strauss had worked with Jakobson in New York. Saussure pioneered structural linguistics. He viewed language as a system, a linguistic paradigm whereby *langue* is the given, pre-existing language system, *parole* the individual utterance generated by the system. Similarly, culture equates with *langue,* just as an object in culture equates with *parole.* In both cases, it is the network of relationships between the two that produces meaning.

In *Les structures élémentaires de la parenté* (1949), Lévi–Strauss drew upon his preliminary work, 'Structural analysis in linguistics and anthropology' (1945). He proposed that all kinship systems are constructed in accordance with an elementary structure consisting of four patterned relationships: brother/sister; husband/wife; father/son; mother's brother/sister's son. These patterned relationships account for marriage/exchange rites and taboos. That patterning process is a mental operation. Some critics dispute his findings or complain of his failure to take sociological factors into account. Although his *Tristes Tropiques* (1955) is largely an autobiographical travelogue, he takes the opportunity to reinforce his particular view of kinship.

Lévi–Strauss later treated myths in a similar fashion – that is, as evidence of mental structuring operations. It is this work which literary scholars have found most stimulating. Again Lévi–Strauss makes use of a linguistic paradigmatic model. Myth is seen as a *langue*; individual myths are seen as *paroles*. Lévi–Strauss considers the Oedipus myth. **Propp** would have analyzed the functions and actions in the myth in a linear or syntagmatic manner; Lévi–Strauss began by dividing the story into episodes. For example, 'Cadmos seeks his sister Europa', 'Oedipus kills his father Laios', 'Oedipus kills the Sphinx'. He calls each episode a *mytheme*. Just as a *phoneme* is the minimal unit of sound which can distinguish two words, so a *mytheme* is the smallest possible unit of a myth. Such *mythemes* he placed in a new, non-chronological configuration. He maintains that the *mythemes* themselves do not produce meaning. Meaning is generated by the configuration, or the relationships between the *mythemes*. Furthermore, each time the myth is told, it is perceived against all the other versions of the myth. Lévi–Strauss's Oedipus myth paradigm reveals a four-term homology:

Column I : Column II : : Column III : Column IV

in which column I groups all the *mythemes* which speak of incest; column II contains those *mythemes* which concern parricide or fratricide; column III embraces those *mythemes* in which anomalous monsters are destroyed by men, and column IV refers to Labdacos (Laios's father), Laios (Oedipus's father) and Oedipus, who may all be regarded as anomalous in that they all have difficulty in walking straight; their names suggest this: 'lame', 'left-sided', 'swollen foot'. In support he cites some tribal myths in which characters are similarly afflicted.

The binary oppositions under the first and second columns are the overrating of kinship and the underrating of kinship respectively; those under columns III and IV are the negation of man's autochthonous origin and the affirmation of that origin respectively. Lévi–Strauss observes that although Greek religion claimed that man was autochthonous, human beings are produced through the sexual union of a man and a woman. The content of the Oedipus myth is of little importance as such, because the particular anomaly cannot actually be solved. However, the myth's form, its structure, are what counts, for just as this myth reveals the human mind in operation, so too all myths reveal the processes by which it tries to come to terms with problems, and by which it structures reality.

It follows from this that if myths reveal the mental processes of the human mind, and given that myths occur in all societies, then one cannot claim that the so-called civilized mind of Western man is superior to that of a so-called primitive man living in the jungles of Borneo, for example. In some respects – his appreciation of personal relationships, his closer ties to nature, his oral tradition – the primitive is to be admired. Lévi–Strauss took up some of these ideas in *The Savage Mind* and *Totemism* (1962). He distinguishes between a primitive 'logic of the concrete' (contrasts between raw and cooked, wet and dry, for example, and a sophisticated, modern 'logic of the abstract' (contrasts expressed by mathematical signs + and −) and suggests that they are both different ways of talking about the same thing. The logic of the concrete deals in analogical relationships which reconcile perceived opposites. Primitive man can create *totems*. Even though he knows that he himself is not an animal, he may call himself a bear, another man a lion, a third a tiger. On the basis of this, structured analogies can be set up between nature and society. One man distinguishes himself from another in a social group in terms of strength, superiority or speed. Nature and culture come to mirror each other.

The isolation of the nature/culture opposition led to detailed examinations of food taxonomies in *The Raw and the Cooked* (1964) and partly in *From Honey to Ashes* (1966). Lévi-Strauss developed his argument on the basis of Jakobson's 'vowel/consonant triangles' to produce a 'culinary triangle' with its two sets of binary oppositions: culture/nature and raw/cooked. He distinguishes different ways of cooking food – roasting, boiling, and smoking – which he then categorizes as natural or cultural processes. Each society decides what is edible and what is not, and what sort of food shall be served on particular occasions. As with the Oedipus myth, he sets up homologies which reveal the relationship between kinds of food and between the special or ceremonial occasions on which such kinds of food are served. Man, then, is different from animals which merely eat their food raw.

Lévi-Strauss's influence on anthroplogy is enormous, even though some of his observations are regarded as inaccurate. His linguistics-based structuralist thinking is crucial for the part it played in fuelling the debate over 'realism'. No longer can we accept language as just referential. Although his study of myth has encouraged some literary critics to test his methodology on other textual material – and rewardingly, too, for example, A.J. **Greimas** and Fredric **Jameson** – other critics regard his generalizations either with scepticism or as little more than a theory in search of practice.

Main works

Elementary Structures of Kinship, trans. James Harle Bell, John Richard von Sturner and Rodney Needham, London: Eyre and Spottiswoode, 1969.

Tristes Tropiques, trans. John and Doreen Weightman, London, 1973.

Structural Anthropology, trans. Claire Jacobson, London, 1972.

'La structure et le forme: Réflexions sur un ouvrage de Vladimir Propp', Paris, 1960. *Cahiers de l'institut des Sciences Economiques Appliquées* 99: 3–37. The translation appears in *Structural Anthropology 2* 1976.

Lévi-Strauss, Claude and Didier Eribon, *Conversations with Claude Lévi-Strauss*, trans. P. Wissing, Chicago: University of Chicago Press, 1991.

The Savage Mind, London: Weidenfeld and Nicholson, 1966.

Totemism, trans. R. Needham, London: Merlin Press, 1964.

The Raw and the Cooked, trans. John and Doreen Weightman, New York: Harper and Row, 1970.

From Honey to Ashes, trans. John and Doreen Weightman, New York: Harper and Row, 1972.

The Origin of Table Manners, trans. John and Doreen Weightman, New York: Harper and Row, 1978.

The Naked Man, trans. John and Doreen Weightman, New York: Harper and Row, 1980.

Claire Jacobson and Brooke Erundfest Schoepf, *Structural Anthroplogy 2*, London, 1976.

Further reading

Boon, James A., *From Symbolism to Structuralism: Lévi-Strauss in a literary tradition*, Oxford, 1972.

Clark, Simon, *Foundations of Structuralism: A Critique of Lévi-Strauss and the Structuralist Movement*, Brighton: Harvester, 1981.

Gardner, Howard, *The Quest for Mind: Piaget, Lévi-Strauss and the Structuralist Movement*, New York: Alfred A. Knopf, 1972.

Leach, Edmund, *Lévi-Strauss*, London, 1970, revised 1974.

Paz, Octavio, *Claude Lévi-Strauss: An introduction*, Ithaca, NY; Cornell University Press, 1970.

Steiner, George, 'Orpheus with his myths: Claude Lévi-Strauss', in *Language and Silence*, London: Faber and Faber, 1967, pp. 267–79.

Lévinas, Emmanuel (1906–)

Lévinas was born into a Jewish community in Kovno, Lithuania. He left in 1923 for the University of Strasbourg. Once in France he joined the

Alliance Israélite Universelle, first set up in 1860 and devoted to integrating Jewish and Western European values. At Strasbourg he studied with Charles Blondel and Maurice Pradines, later attending a lecture course given by Husserl at the University of Freiburg, (1928–9). He was also present at the famous 1929 encounter between Heidegger and Cassirer at Davos. Henri Bergson's ideas of time and duration influenced Lévinas, and he became friends with Maurice Blanchot. In the 1930s he took French nationality. When war broke out, Lévinas was commandeered as a translator of Russian and German, but was soon made a prisoner of war. During his captivity he began to prepare the ideas which were to be published as *Existence and Existents* in 1946. After the war he became director of the Ecole Normale Israélite Orientale in Paris. At the Collège Philosophique founded by Jean Wahl he gave a series of papers in 1946–7 which became *Time and the Other*. His doctoral thesis of 1930, *The Theory of Intuition in Husserl's Phenomenology*, gained him an appointment at the University of Poitiers, followed in 1967 by Paris-Nanterre. In 1973 he was appointed Professor of Philosophy at the Sorbonne. Although Lévinas has published extensively, including volumes of Talmudic commentaries, his reception in the English-speaking world has been largely dominated by his two major works. *Totality and Infinity* in (1961) and *Otherwise Than Being or Beyond Essence* (1974).

Levinas's works might be considered to elaborate a single thought: ethics is first philosophy. The exposition of this thought constitutes a challenge to traditional thinking concerning the nature of ethical obligation and the connection between ethics and a just polity. The weight of the thought that ethics is first philosophy is borne by the combined radicality and novelty of the notion that ethical responsibility is *not a matter of thought at all*. Rather, it precedes and exceeds thought altogether. The claim is that the level at which an ethical summons is both given and received occurs beyond or before or outside of consciousness. Ethical significance [*sens*] does not become an object of thought for consciousness. Levinas's 'ethical turn' – a turn away from epistemology and ontology – is to situate ethical regard in a primordial and non-cognitive experience of a dimension of another person that transcends all thought. This transcending aspect, which eludes the grasp of consciousness, Levinas calls the 'Other' [*Autrui*] or the 'face' [*visage*]. The face signifies ethically as an originary revelation of the poverty, nudity, vulnerability and defencelessness of another human being. It is a call for help or a cry for aid, a summons to me to respond responsibly to the dependency and helplessness of the Other. Lévinas argues that the face speaks an ethical language which is heard, as it were, before all other forms of communication. For Lévinas, Abraham's

'Here I Am' for the Other reveals a state of originary passivity: I am affected by the face prior to all choice or reason.

In this way the Other resists being dominated by or reduced to whatever interests or assumptions condition my understanding. Indeed, the very structure of consciousness as such is for Lévinas always and inescapably a movement of appropriation. It is crucially important to him that ethical responsibility towards others not be grounded in any form of interestedness or understanding, for this would amount to taking possession of the Other as an element of my knowing self or ego where the Other is assumed to be essentially the same as me. Lévinas calls this a reduction of the Other to the Same [*le Même*]. It is to suppress the very otherness or absolute difference of the face. Far from genuine ethical regard, Lévinas calls this an egoism. To base ethical responsibility in any form of consciousness is thus precisely to have failed to respect the Other. The Other is exterior to any perception or conception of which I am capable, and stands above me in an infinite height. It is at this primordial pre-conscious level of encounter between me and the Other that, Lévinas claims, an ethical appeal is made.

Lévinas is thus preoccupied with showing how the face is a type of primordial language which carries a meaning or sense that is wholly otherwise than cognitive meaning. In *Otherwise Than Being* he calls the former domain of sense 'the Saying' [*le dire*] and the latter 'the Said' [*le dit*]. He considers that philosophy, with only a couple of exceptions (aspects of Plato and Descartes), has been concerned with the attempt to comprehend being. All forms of comprehension and perception belonging to the knowing self or subject Lévinas includes under the rubric of the Same. Philosophically working within the tradition of phenomenological thought, it is primarily through readings of his immediate predecessors, Edmund Husserl and Martin Heidegger, that Lévinas understands the logic of meaning-giving consciousness, the nature of phenomenological experience, and the constitution of what it means to be. He considers these two figures to have lent the most sophisticated and explicit voice to the governing prejudice of the Western philosophical tradition. That tradition has most often, he protests, been an egological ontology. Ontology is always a form of comprehension on some level, and takes itself not only to exhaust all possibilities of meaning, but also as fundamental or originary, with no other significance outside its purview. The attempt to comprehend the meaning of Being and beings has dominated the philosophical voyage; a bias towards what can be intelligible which has masked and englobed the Other. Western philosophy has deemed that the only province of sense is that belonging to the structures determining what can be intelligible. It has reduced the Other to the Same: to what can be accessible to consciousness. Lévinas's anxiety is that this way of thinking either results in or is coextensive with equally totalizing and repressive political structures.

Although the category of the Same allows Lévinas to exhibit forms of thought that exclude the Other as well as displaying this occlusion as a dominant tendency in Western philosophy, it is not an unproblematic category. To put the notion of the Same to work in this way involves a deliberate simplification of many complexities in previous philosophy, raising the objection that his blanket notion of the Same suffers from a lack of self-differentiation. For Lévinas to show how an ethically orientated conception of political justice has a purchase upon the sphere of reason and action requires this differentiation in order for us to recognize and distinguish between an ethical and an unethical act. However, for the notion of the Same to admit of levels, degrees, and distinctions within itself implies that the Other does not command an *absolute* respect in relation to *every* modality of the Same, as Lévinas claims.

Responding to Lévinas is a process which, in many fields, has only just begun. Although he is becoming an increasingly prominent figure in philosophy, the power of his thought is also exerting an insistent and growing ripple in other cultural disciplines, beginning with **Derrida**'s early monograph on Lévinas, 'Violence and metaphysics'. His impact on political thought has been the most far-reaching; see, for example, S. Critchley's *The Ethics of Deconstruction*, where Lévinas is read in conjunction with Derrida, Lacoue–Labarthe and Nancy, and the recent critical work of R. Bernasconi centring on the universalistic implications of Lévinas's thought within the problematic of cultural difference. Far from only interrupting categories of politico-ethical thought, however, many of Lévinas's studies cut into and disturb areas that are not specifically or necessarily concerned with ethics. The descriptions of obsession by the Other and fractures in the integrity of consciousness, for example, as well as his philosophy of language and intersubjective relationships, are acquiring attention in psychoanalytic, sociological and literary provinces.

Main works

Totality and Infinity, trans. A. Lingis, Pittsburgh, PA: Duquesne University Press, 1969.

Otherwise Than Being or Beyond Essence, trans. A. Lingis, The Hague: Martinus Nijhoff, 1974.

Collected Philosophical Papers, trans. A. Lingis, Dordrecht: Martinus Nijhoff, 1987.

Existence and Existents, trans. A. Lingis, Dordrecht/Boston/London: Kluwer Academic, 1988.

Difficult Freedon: Essays on Judaism, trans. S. Hand, London: The Athlone Press, 1990.

Emmanuel Lévinas: Basic philosophical writings, ed. R. Bernasconi, S. Critchley and A. Peperzak, Bloomington and Indianapolis: Indiana University Press, forthcoming.

Further reading

R. Bernasconi and S. Critchley (eds), *Re-Reading Lévinas*, Bloomington and Indianapolis: Indiana University Press, 1991.

R. Bernasconi and D. Wood, (eds), *The Provocation of Lévinas*, London: Routledge, 1988.

R.A. Cohen (ed.), *Face to Face with Lévinas*, Albany, NY: SUNY, 1986.

Critchley, Simon, *The Ethics of Deconstruction: Derrida & Lévinas*, Oxford/ Cambridge, MA: Blackwell, 1992.

Derrida, Jacques, 'Violence and Metaphysics' in *Writing and Difference*, trans. A. Bass, London and Henley: Routledge & Kegan Paul, 1978.

S. Hand (ed.), *The Lévinas Reader*, Oxford/Cambridge, MA: Basil Blackwell, 1989.

Glossary

'Other'[*Autrui*] and 'other' [*autre*]: These terms cannot be rendered unambiguously into English. In the original French Lévinas uses both locutions in the upper and lower case; nor is he consistent in his deployment of the terms.

Lukács, Georg (1885–1971)

Over the course of his long career Lukács worked in a wide variety of social and intellectual contexts. A lecturer in aesthetics at the University of Heidelberg before the First World War, he subsequently became a leading light in the Hungarian Communist Party and then one of the major theorists of twentieth-century Marxism, particularly in the fields of philosophy and literature. Variously active in Hungary, Austria,

Germany and Russia, Lukács ended his career in his native Hungary, his last academic appointment being as Professor of Aesthetics and Cultural Policy at the University of Budapest from 1945 onwards. He also had brief spells of ministerial office in the Hungarian Soviet government of 1919, and during the Hungarian uprising of 1956. After the latter event he was exiled from Hungary for a short time, and remained out of favour with the Communist authorities for most of the rest of his life.

Lukács first came to prominence in Hungarian and German intellectual circles as an essayist on aesthetics and literary matters in the pre-First World War period (the tone of his work, in line with prevailing intellectual trends, being pessimistic and world-weary), but by the end of the war he had become an enthusiastic convert to communism, and his writings from then onwards demonstrate an unshakable devotion to the Marxist cause. Lukács is one of the founders of what has come to be known as 'Western Marxism', whose concern with aesthetic and philosophical matters differentiates it from the more practically politically orientated Eastern (Soviet) variety. Nevertheless much of his career was spent in the Soviet bloc.

Hegel was a major influence on Lukács from his early career, and remained so, even though his Hegelian-inspired Marxism often came under attack from the Soviet authorities. His first major work of Marxist theory, *History and Class Consciousness*, with its vision of a proletariat on the verge of achieving the class consciousness required to liberate mankind from capitalism, was condemned for its Hegelian abstraction of reasoning at the 1924 Comintern Congress, and Lukács subsequently disowned the work (which underwent renewed popularity amongst student activists in the 1960s, much to the author's annoyance). *History and Class Consciousness* took a very undogmatic line on Marxism, insisting that it was above all a *method* rather than a body of doctrine to be defended at all costs. On that basis Lukács, to the dismay of the Soviet authorities, saw fit to attack Engels for deficiencies in his understanding of the Marxist method. Despite opposition Lukács continued to regard a grounding in Hegel as vital for any serious Marxist theorist, and *The Young Hegel* went on vigorously to defend its subject against charges of being an irrationalist romantic. For Lukács, Hegel was an early disciple of Adam Smith and the first thinker in Germany to explore, however tentatively, the links between economics and social being, thus notably prefiguring the work of Marx.

As a literary theorist Lukács is a pioneering figure in Marxist history in terms of establishing the relationship between narrative form (the novel being his prime concern) and socioeconomic developments. Probably the best-known, as well as most controversial, aspect of his literary work is his championship of realism. On the basis of a select group of models – most notably Scott, Balzac, Stendhal, Tolstoy, Gorki, and Mann – Lukács argued that realism was the only acceptable style for the novelist to adopt. In the work of such authors the leading characters were seen to be products of historical forces, essentially social beings responding to events unfolding around them (and in this sense 'typical' of their time and social context) rather than alienated individuals of the kind found in most naturalist or modernist fiction. Typicality plus a sense of historical process was what Lukács demanded of the novel form, not an attitude of political correctness on the author's part. Thus *The Historical Novel* could praise the work of Scott for what it revealed about great turning points in Western cultural history (the shift from feudalism to capitalism, for example) as seen through the eyes of typical characters, despite the obvious conservatism of the author's politics.

A subsequent series of studies on realism made similar claims about other 'great realists' such as Balzac and Tolstoy (with their reactionary politics again being discounted), whereas Flaubert and Zola were invariably attacked for the pessimistic picture they painted of modern social existence. Where the great realists made it plain that socio-historical developments affected and shaped social being, naturalists and modernists tended to present the 'human condition' as despairing and unalterable by individual endeavour. To Lukács this was to encourage an attitude of resignation to one's fate, and to serve the cause of capitalism indirectly. Modernism was viewed as a form of literary decadence, most notoriously in *The Meaning of Contemporary Realism*, where the styles of such twentieth-century modernist authors as Joyce, Beckett and Kafka were held to be deficient compared to Mann's 'critical realism'. For the modern bourgeois author, Lukács maintained, there was a stark choice to be made between the narrative methods of Kafka or Mann, and that choice had far-reaching ideological implications.

Lukács was also a notable critic of **Brecht** during the 1930s, and the two represent the different ends of the spectrum in Marxist aesthetics, realism and traditional methods versus modernism and formal experimentation. Yet for all his defence of realism, Lukács was ambivalent about socialist realism, the dominant Soviet aesthetic theory from the 1930s onwards, and frequently attacked it as a romanticized picture of reality more likely to retard than promote the growth of a socialist consciousness (towards the end of his life, however, he was to argue that Solzhenitsyn had revitalized the style). A guarded critic of Stalin's cultural policy during the dictator's lifetime, he was openly hostile to it after Stalin's death in 1953.

In his late writings on aesthetics Lukács pictured art as a special category located between the categories of the individual (the here and now) and the universal (the essential), which at its best, as in the work of the great literary realists, contrived to reveal the underlying reality of sociohistorical process. Great art (works which met the conditions of the category of speciality) had the capacity to change consciousness in a more or less cathartic manner.

Lukács has had an enormous impact on Marxist aesthetics, being a critical influence on the work of theorists such as Walter **Benjamin**, Theodor **Adorno** (and the Frankfurt School in general), Lucien **Goldmann** and Fredric **Jameson**. In the case of the latter two, *The Theory of the Novel* is probably the key text; for the others *History and Class Consciousness*. To a certain extent all Marxist literary theorists have to position themselves with regard to Lukács's work: realism has remained a highly contentious issue in Marxist aesthetics, and Lukács's vigorous defence of it has cast a long shadow. Although for much of his career his defence of realism made him seem somewhat old-fashioned (Brecht accused him of wanting authors to be little more than updated versions of great realists like Balzac and Tolstoy), the advent of postmodernism and its problematization of the modernist aesthetic has given Lukács's aesthetic theories a new topicality.

Main works

The Meaning of Contemporary Realism, trans. John and Necke Mander, London: Merlin Press, 1963a.

Die Eigenart des Asthetischen, Neuweid: Luchterhand, 1963b.

Essays on Thomas Mann, trans. Stanley Mitchell, London: Merlin Press, 1964.

Goethe and his Age, trans. Robert Anchor, London: Merlin Press, 1968.

The Historical Novel, trans. Hannah and Stanley Mitchell, London: Penguin, 1969.

Lenin: A study on the unity of his thought, trans. Nicholas Jacobs, London: 1970.

History and Class Consciousness: Studies in Marxist dialectics, trans. Rodney Livingstone, London: Merlin Press, 1971.

Studies in European Realism, trans. Edith Bone, London: Merlin Press, 1972.

Soul and Form, trans. Anna Bostock, London: Merlin Press, 1974.

The Young Hegel, trans. Rodney Livingstone, London: Merlin Press, 1975.

The Ontology of Social Being, I–II, trans. David Fernbach, London: Merlin Press, 1978.

Essays on Realism, trans. David Fernbach, London: Lawrence & Wishart, 1980a.

The Destruction of Reason, trans. Peter Palmer, London: Merlin Press, 1980b.

The Theory of the Novel, trans. Anna Bostock, London: Merlin Press, 1980c.

Further reading

Arato, Andrew and Paul Brienes, *The Young Lukács and the Origins of Western Marxism*, New York: Seabury Press, 1979.

Heller, Agnes (ed), *Lukács Revalued*, Oxford: Blackwell, 1983.

Kadarkay, Arpad, *Georg Lukács: Life, thought and politics*, Oxford and Cambridge, MA: Blackwell, 1991.

Lichtheim, George, *Lukács*, London: Fontana/Collins, 1970.

Löwy, Michael, *Georg Lukács – From Romanticism to Bolshevism*, trans. Patrick Camiller, London: New Left Books, 1979.

Sim, Stuart, *Georg Lukács*, Hemel Hempstead: Harvester Wheatsheaf, 1994.

Glossary

Critical realism: The twentieth-century version of great realism (see, for example, the work of Thomas Mann).

Great realism: The style espoused by certain approved nineteenth-century novelists, who gave a broad picture of society and demonstrated a keen awareness of historical process.

Lyotard, Jean-François (1924–)

Lyotard has worked in both the French and American academic worlds, notably as Professor of Philosophy at the University of Paris (Vincennes) and the University of California at Irvine, and was a founding member of the International College of Philosophy in Paris. In his early career he was heavily involved with the *Socialisme ou barbarie* group, whose critique of **Marx**ism from within Marxism, conducted in the group's journal of the same name, eventually led to a loss of faith in the theory itself among many of its members, Lyotard included.

Although he has published widely in several areas of philosophy, politics and the arts (painting being a major interest), Lyotard is nevertheless best known for his work as a theorist of postmodernism, and *The Postmodern Condition* has become one of the most frequently cited texts of the late twentieth century in the field of cultural studies. Although several commentators have argued that *The Postmodern Condition* is in fact one of Lyotard's least representative works, it is probably fair to say that it crystallizes in a very accessible form debates and ideas that run through Lyotard's works of the 1970s, when his thinking had undertaken a distinctively postmodern turn. Commentators are also prone to remark on the disparate nature of Lyotard's output, but there are recurrent themes and attitudes to be noted over the course of his career, such as a general distrust towards totalizing theory or entrenched authority, and a highly practical and pragmatic approach to political activity.

Lyotard's early work is in the Marxist tradition (with some forays into phenomenology), but in common with many of his colleagues in *Socialisme ou barbarie* – and, it should be said, the French intellectual community in general – he eventually turned against Marxism in the aftermath of the 1968 *événements* – in which he was actively involved as an organizer of protests at the University of Nanterre – to become a bitter critic of the theory and its advocates. This bitterness was expressed particularly in *Libidinal Economy* (a savage broadside which made him many enemies within the French Communist Party, and in the *Socialisme ou barbarie* group too) and then later in *The Postmodern Condition*. *Libidinal Economy* denounces theory, Marxism in particular, as a form of terror, and marks a clear break with Lyotard's militant past. *The Postmodern Condition* goes on to take a very critical line on the viability of universal theories, and argues that such 'grand narratives' (Marxism and Hegelianism being outstanding examples) have forfeited all credibility or claim to be taken seriously as sources of social or political guidance in the late twentieth century. One of Lyotard's definitions of postmodernism, in fact, is 'incredulity towards meta-narratives', and it is an incredulity that his work from *Libidinal Economy* onwards has been concerned actively to foster. The anti-theoretical imperative remains one of the critical components of Lyotard's brand of postmodernism.

Grand narratives are essentially authoritarian and curb human creativity, Lyotard contends, and he puts his faith instead in the 'little narrative' [*petit récit*] – that is, the narrative of the individual human being. Lyotard takes narrative to be an unproblematical foundation for discourse, arguing that it needs no justification, that it certifies itself in the mere act of telling (humans being naturally narrative-disposed creatures) and thus does not become embroiled in any epistemological complications of the 'what grounds the ground of discourse?' variety. His political philosophy is based on a belief in the little narrative's ability to offer a challenge to authoritarian systems (Lyotard leans somewhat towards the American model of 'issue politics' in this regard), and he considers it infinitely more flexible than grand narrative. Even marginalized individuals have the power to subvert repressive social systems, he believes, simply by acting in contrary and unpredictable ways. He has devised the concept of 'svelteness' to describe the kind of behaviour he thinks will be most fruitful in challenging entrenched systems at the individual level. Svelteness is a guerrilla-like attitude of flexible and creative response to pressures emanating from one's particular grand narrative – the ability to 'go to a ball in the evening and fight a war at dawn', as Lyotard rather romantically pictures it.

The Postmodern Condition sets out an agenda for postmodernism that takes account of the information technology revolution. It calls for a destabilization of institutions and multinational corporations, and an opening up to the general public of all the world's databanks. Lyotard appeals for a war on totality that will encourage difference at the expense of authority, and he is concerned to promote the cause of paradox and 'agonistics' in political discourse (there is in fact a strong political dimension to Lyotard's theorizing throughout his entire *oeuvre*). *The Postmodern Condition* draws freely on both catastrophe theory and chaos theory for its model of the world, and sees postmodern science (which produces not the known but the unknown, Lyotard argues) as pointing the way forward for social theorists and philosophers. One of the criticisms of this line of thought, however, has been that science does not so much produce the unknown as discover it as an area for further investigation – science is never content to leave the unknown in that state.

Lyotard's anti-authoritarianism and anti-foundationalism reveal themselves in the way he pursues the problem of the legitimation of authority in *The Postmodern Condition*. He argues that legitimation (of knowledge, for example) is a question not so much of truth or proof as of power, and that most institutions manipulate concepts like truth or proof to serve their own self-interested ends. As a case in point, multinational corporations fund science less to promote the cause of truth than to increase their power with respect to their competitors. It is against totalities such as these, with their fundamentally hostile attitude to the world of the little narrative, that Lyotard's arguments are directed. The postmodern condition is essentially a struggle between grand narrative and little narrative as to who controls knowledge (and the means to transmit that knowledge); hence the plea for open access to the databanks. Lyotard's ultimate objective is the destruction of narrative monopolies and the institution of a brave new world of little narratives freed from authoritarian control, and there is an unmistakably libertarian quality to his thought. There is also a bleaker, **Nietzsche**an side to Lyotardean postmodernism, however, in the sense that the struggle between grand and little narrative, modernism and postmodernism, is seen to be part of a recurring cycle: there have been postmodernisms in the past (Sterne is cited as an earlier postmodernist); there will be modernisms to come in the future.

Not surprisingly, perhaps, given his anti-foundationalist credentials, Lyotard has become increasingly concerned with the role and status of judgement in human affairs. Once foundations of discourse are problematized, then judgement becomes extremely difficult to legitimate – there being no self-evidently indubitable criteria to appeal to under such circumstances – and Lyotard has been one of the few postmodernists to address this problem in any detail, as he does in *The Differend* and *Just Gaming* in particular. True to his anti-totality bias, Lyotard argues (and approves of the fact) that we now live in a highly fragmented universe of discourse in which there are numerous incommensurable genres (truth and justice being just two examples). All we can do is to bear witness to what he calls 'the differend' (unresolvable conflict) that obtains between genres such as truth and justice, and not fall into the mistake of trying to apply the rules of one genre to another. *Within* a genre, judgements can be made (although Lyotard is at best a bit vague as to the process involved), but not *across* genres. Making judgements across genres is, in fact, a major characteristic of politics – which, as Lyotard notes, can be notoriously intolerant of *differends*; fundamentalist theocracy or extreme nationalism serve to make the point quite graphically. It is the duty of philosophers to identify differends and draw them to our attention rather than to waste effort attempting to resolve the unresolvable. This points to a radical politics – although, as Geoff Bennington has noted, not one with a specific programme to implement, hence not one likely to exercise much appeal on the left, where action, as well as change of consciousness, is a required element of the political realm.

Ultimately this is a philosopher who does not believe in absolute criteria of judgement, and whose approach to the act of judgement itself is highly pragmatic – it depends what will serve the interest of the little narrative at any one time in its conflict with grand narrative. His ideal of politics is 'paganism', defined as a situation in which one judges without criteria (presumably according to the needs of the particular little narrative applying at that time). Paganism has an obvious appeal, but it does not really address the question of what happens when entrenched power bases refuse to play by those rules (which in practice they always do). Lyotard has been felt by many on the left to display a certain naivety in his political philosophy on issues such as this.

Lyotard's later writing displays an increasing concern with the work of Kant, particularly the *Critique of Judgement* and the notion of the sublime. Once again, the search for differends is a prime motivation: the sublime, for Lyotard, constitutes a limit-point where judgement breaks down and we become aware of the differend between thought and feeling.

Lyotard's work, notably *The Postmodern Condition*, has had a considerable impact on cultural debate in the last decade or so, and he remains one of the most stimulating, and philosophically sophisticated, of postmodernist thinkers. *The Postmodern Condition* may take a broad-brush approach to cultural change, but Lyotard can also provide the fine detail elsewhere in his *oeuvre* (*The Differend*, for example, is a particularly closely argued piece of philosophical reasoning). The positive side of his work is its libertarian tone, which seems to offer up the possibility of the dissolution of grand-narrative power, however it manifests itself. In many ways, given what has happened in the old Soviet bloc over the last few years, *The Postmodern Condition* is a very prophetic work which has identified real weaknesses within the grand-narrative position, which can and does fall apart under certain conditions. On the negative side, however, Lyotard has a very romantic view of the little narrative and almost certainly overrates its ability, or opportunity, to challenge grand-narrative monopolies. He is often criticized for a certain naivety in his thinking in this respect, an assumption that institutional power is more vulnerable than it really is (multinationals have proved largely immune to the little narrative challenge, it could be objected). Nevertheless, there is no denying the considerable appeal that his libertarian views have exercised, and his work has been a catalyst for a whole range of debates across the field of cultural studies – debates which are still very much in process.

Main works

Discours, figure, Paris: Klinckseick, 1971.

Instruction païennes, Paris: Galilée, 1977a.

Rudiments païennes: genre dissertatif, Paris: Union générale d'éditions, 1977b.

Le Mur du pacifique, Paris: Galilée, 1979.

Tombeau de l'intellectuel et autres papiers, Paris: Galilée, 1984a.

The Postmodern Condition: A report on knowledge, trans. Geoff Bennington and Brian Massumi, Minneapolis: University of Minnesota Press, 1984b.

Just Gaming (with Jean-Loup Thébaud), trans. Wlad Godzich, Minneapolis: University of Minnesota Press, 1986.

The Differend: Phrases in dispute, trans. George Van Den Abbeele, Minneapolis: University of Minnesota Press, 1988a.

Peregrinations: Law, form, event, New York: Columbia University Press, 1988b.

Heidegger and 'the Jews', trans. Andreas Michel and Mark Roberts, Minneapolis: University of Minnesota Press, 1990.

The Inhuman: Reflections on time, trans. Geoff Bennington and Rachel Bowlby, Oxford: Blackwell, 1991.

Libidinal Economy, trans. Iain Hamilton Grant, London: Athlone Press, 1993.

Lessons on the Analytic and the Sublime, trans. Elizabeth Rottenberg, Stanford, CA: Stanford University Press, 1994.

Further reading

Bennington, Geoffrey, *Lyotard: Writing the event*, Manchester: Manchester University Press, 1988.

Callinicos, Alex, *Against Postmodernism: A Marxist perspective*, Cambridge: Polity, 1989.

Dews, Peter, *Logics of Disintegration*, London and New York: Verso, 1987.

Pefanis, Julian, *Heterology and the Postmodern: Bataille, Baudrillard, and Lyotard*, Durham, NC and London: Duke University Press, 1991.

Readings, Bill, *Introducing Lyotard: Art and Politics*, (London: Routledge, 1991).

Sim, Stuart, *Beyond Aesthetics: Confrontations with poststructuralism and postmodernism*, Hemel Hempstead: Harvester Wheatsheaf, 1992.

Glossary

Agonistics: Conflict over *différends*.

Grand narrative: Cultural paradigm (also referred to as 'metanarrative'); all-embracing explanatory theory taken to have universal application.

M

Maccabe, Colin (1951–)

Colin MacCabe became Professor at the University of Strathclyde after the non-renewal of his lectureship at Cambridge University in 1980; since 1985 he has been at the British Film Institute.

In an article published in the *Times Higher Education Supplement* (26 March 1976) Stephen Heath proposed, regarding film theory that 'content analysis' fails 'to engage with the ideological *operation* of the film' (original emphasis). By thinking together **Althusser**ian **Marx**ism, and **Lacan**ian psychoanalysis on the terrain of **Saussure**an semiology, the project aimed to produce a totalizing theory of signifying practice, responsive simultaneously to the demands for a specific account of textuality, its political implication, and its potential effects of the subjectivity of its reader. Coming from a solid background in contemporary linguistics, MacCabe – along with others grouped around the film journal *Screen* – hoped to use film somewhat as a stalking horse for the larger synthesis of what has been termed 'British post-structuralism'.

MacCabe's crucial interventions were made in film theory, particularly in seeking to analyze the realist tradition, implicitly defined as the preferred bourgeois mode in aesthetic representation, while holding up modernism as a potentially radical alternative. An essay of 1974 (written when MacCabe was 23), 'Realism and the cinema: notes on some Brechtian theses', acknowledges its debt to the German dramatist, but picks up the account of realism by **Barthes** in *S/Z* (1970), and extends it with reference to film and nineteenth-century fiction.

What is said in a language – how a language is *used* – can be distinguished from a higher order or *metalanguage* in which that first *object language* might be discussed (so, if a 'Teach Yourself French' book is written in Mandarin Chinese, French is the object language and Mandarin the metalanguage for it). MacCabe proposes that the different discourses of a realist text conform to a hierarchical categorization between object language and metalanguage. The classic realist film sets up what the characters know and say to each other as object language, a limited knowledge, in contrast to what we learn from the image as metalanguage: the whole truth (apparently) about the characters and their world. Corresponding to the empiricist view that knowledge can be obtained directly through experience, realism invites its reader to 'look through' the metalanguage, and so 'see' as if transparently and directly what is represented in the object language.

Althusser had argued that ideology operates to 'interpellate' the subject so that subjects appear to 'work by themselves', an account which in turn leans on Lacan's analysis of subjectivity as an effect of discourse. Drawing on these precedents, MacCabe asserts that realist discourse produces a position for the subject. Whether as Hollywood film or novel by George Eliot, 'the classic realist text ensures the position of the subject in a relation of dominant specularity' as though situated outside looking on (*Tracking the Signifier*). In so far as that discursive position is given, unquestioned, realism cannot represent the real as contradictory. In thus effacing contradiction, realism promotes an ideological practice determined in a relatively autonomous relationship to capitalist production.

But can Lacanian psychoanalysis, based in the concept of the unconscious, be held in place within historical materialism and its concern with history? A subsequent essay, 'Theory and film: principles of realism and pleasure' (1976) returns to the problem of realism, but with a more committedly Lacanian account of subjectivity as a process of desire rather than a point for vision and understanding. Again it is argued that realism is defined in 'the logic of that contradiction which produces a position for the viewer but denies that production' (*Tracking the Signifier*, p.69). But now that effect is far more problematic, and in an act of autocritique the second essay accuses its predecessor of being contaminated by Formalism. The first essay affirmed that the realist text *effaced* the process of the signifier, rendering it, as it were, of no account, so that the reader is passively hailed into position by a text given once and for all. In the revised view, however it is recognized that the relation between text and reader always takes place in an active dialectic in which neither term can stand as the fixed object for a structuralist analysis. In principle, then, a text could mean anything, and any confidence that textuality could be referred to the Hegelian – Marxist notion of inherent contradiction tends to dissolve.

James Joyce and the Revolution of the Word (1978) reworks the theoretical insights of the film essays in relation to Joyce's modernist texts. Arguably, the theoretical impasse reached in the second essay on realism is avoided by moving sideways, into the question of gender. A reading of Lacan suggests that sexual difference is analogous to linguistic difference, the order of the signifier described by Saussure as founded merely in oppositions and differences without positive terms.

Realism, seeking to master difference by holding it within a coherent narrative, is therefore implicitly phallocentric; Joyce's modernism, on the other hand, admitting difference at once textual and sexual, denies the reader's pleasure by opening his – or more significantly, her – desire.

During the 1970s in London the work of MacCabe and those associated with *Screen* was linked to the project of the 'Social Relations and Discourse' seminar organized by Paul Q. Hirst and others. The hoped-for theoretical synthesis between linguistics, historical materialism and Lacan's theory of the subject proved overoptimistic, for reasons evident in MacCabe's own work and admitted with robust honesty in an essay in *Tracking the Signifier*, 'Class of '68: elements of an intellectual autobiography 1967–81'. It was nevertheless admirably un-English in its rationalist ambition and in the seriousness with which it addressed issues of textuality, reading, ideology and gender. *Screen* was a communal project in which a number of writers – including (in alphabetical order) Stephen Heath, Colin MacCabe, Laura **Mulvey** and Jacqueline Rose – playing off each other, moved forward together into some territory whose strangeness made it as difficult as it was novel (then). Film theory has been transformed once and for all, with an influence moving out into literary theory itself and what is now recognized as the tradition of British cultural studies. MacCabe has gone on to promote work in cultural studies by editing a number of important collections in the field, and *James Joyce and the Revolution of the Word* (1978) can claim to be the first post-structuralist work of literary theory published in Britain.

Main works

James Joyce and the Revolution of the Word, London: Macmillan, 1978.

Godard: Images, sounds, politics, with Mick Eaton and Laura Mulvey, London: BFI/Macmillan, 1980.

(ed.), *The Talking Cure: Essays in psychoanalysis*, London: Macmillan, 1981.

Tracking the Signifier: Theoretical essays, Manchester: Manchester University Press, 1985.

(ed.), *High Culture/Low Culture: Analysing popular television and films* Manchester: Manchester University Press, 1986.

(ed.), *Futures for English*, Manchester: Manchester University Press, 1988.

Further reading

Andrew, Dudley, *Concepts in Film Theory*, New York: Oxford University Press, 1984.

Easthope, Antony, *British Post-Structuralism since 1968*, London: Routledge, 1988.

Heath, Stephen, *Questions of Cinema*, London: Macmillan, 1982.

Lapsley, Rob, and Michael Westlake, *Film Theory: An introduction*, Manchester: Manchester University Press, 1988.

Lodge, David, '*Middlemarch* and the idea of the classic realist text', in Arnold Kettle (ed.), *the Nineteenth Century Novel, Critical Essays and Documents* (rev. edn), London: Heinemann, 1981.

Mulvey, Laura, *Visual and Other Pleasures*, London: Macmillan, 1989.

McGann, Jerome J. (1937–)

Jerome J. McGann is Commonwealth Professor of English at the University of Virginia. His is the leading voice in the American New Historicist approach to Romantic poetry (exemplified in the work of McGann, Marjorie Levinson, David Simpson and Alan Liu), an approach which, alongside the related work of the English critic Marilyn Butler, became highly influential (and controversial) in Romantic studies in the last decade.

During the 1980s, New Historicists loudly proclaimed the importance of history to literary criticism. Whilst the likes of Stephen **Greenblatt** and Louis Montrose addressed Renaissance literature, McGann led the New Historicist charge into Romantic studies, the critical heartland of the then ascendant Yale School. His work is based on the simple contention that literature is best understood in terms of its social meaning. Repudiating what he sees as an ahistorical consensus in the non-**Marx**ist critical tradition, McGann argues that literary criticism 'must be grounded in a socio-historical analytic'. Historical analysis, far from simply supplementing formalist approaches, becomes the governing principle of literary study. Other critical methodologies (formal, structural, thematic, and so on) are arid, marginal undertakings unless they 'find their *raison d'être* in the socio-historical ground' (McGann, like **Jameson**, has a totalizing vision, one which leaves him open to the charge that he simply swaps one univocal brand of hermeneutics for another). McGann's prescriptive tone is attributable to his belief that literary criticism since the 1930s has been dominated by aggressively ahistorical methodologies which either address works of literature as self-contained verbal icons or bracket out sociohistorical matters from their field of inquiry. Such criticism (McGann includes New Criticism, structuralism, post-structuralism, reader-response theory and decon-struction) has ignored the fact that works of art are social products. American deconstruction is particularly culpable because of the 'extremity of [its] antihistorical position'. Instead of an emphasis on the contextless 'text', criticism should address the social meaning of the literary 'work'.

Though McGann has recently written about both modernist and postmodernist poetry, most of his work has addressed Romantic poetry. This area of study is particularly apposite to his wider argument, as critical ahistoricism is itself one of the products of what he calls 'the Romantic ideology'. In his short but highly influential book of that name, McGann discusses the Romantic poets' insistence that the products of the imagination transcend time and circumstance. A key part of the Romantic ideology is the idea that poetry 'has no relation to partisan, didactic, or doctrinal matters. Poetry transcends these things'. Thus the ahistoricism of twentieth-century literary criticism has Romantic antecedents.

McGann's project is to politicize the critical discourse of American Romantic studies. For him, Romanticism's sublimation of history has subsequently been rehearsed in the ahistoricism of Romantic critics. McGann deplores the tendency of the key Romantic scholars of the 1960s and 1970s (notably M.H. Abrams and the Yale critics **Hartman** and **Bloom**) to privilege imaginative vision over the socially specific in their readings of Romantic poetry. Their contextually minimalist accounts simply repeat the Romantics' own evasion of history. Like the Renaissance New Historicists, McGann insists that criticism, rather than being scientific or dispassionately analytical, is inevitably informed by ideological commitments, and what informs critical representations of Romanticism is often Romantic ideology. Romantic scholarship, unquestioningly grounded on its subject's own premises, is often as 'Romantic' as the poetry it studies – Hartman simply endorses and rehearses Wordsworth's apotheosis of the imagination. McGann, on the other hand, wants to place Romanticists (poets and scholars) in a critical context which understands them in terms 'other than their own self-definitions' (paradoxically, this gestures towards the idea, previously repudiated by McGann, of a 'neutral' and objective critical perspective). He implies that his self-conscious awareness of criticism's inevitable involvement in ideology grants him a conceptual privilege over his peers. In *Social Values and Poetic Acts*, McGann claims, perhaps optimistically, that 'hermeneutics – though necessarily an ideological activity – need no longer be subject to ideology'.

The Romantic ideology, as we have seen, is an attempt to transcend ideology and deal with timeless human themes. Romantic poetry is consequently 'marked by extreme forms of displacement . . . whereby the actual human issues with which the poetry is concerned are resituated and deflected in various ways'. McGann's interpretations of individual poems show how the traces of this displacement are manifested, demonstrating (and condemning) Romantic acts of socio-historical 'evasion'. Instead of celebrating (with Wordsworth, Abrams and Hartman) the Romantic imagination, McGann identifies the remnants of history in Romantic poetry. The Romantics developed 'artistic means with which to occlude and disguise their own involvement in a certain nexus of historical relations'. However, they never quite succeed in their project. McGann examines the Romantic struggle to sublimate, tracking down the half-erased traces of history. *The Romantic Ideology* contains a number of practical demonstrations of this provocative methodology. For example, Wordsworth's 'The Ruined Cottage' is seen as evading the historically specific origins of its heroine's pitiful tragedy in favour of endorsing a spiritual, politically quietist and supposedly universal truth of human sympathy.

McGann's preoccupation with absence and erasure echoes the critical vocabulary of deconstruction. His important essay 'Beginning again' (McGann, 1988) acknowledges that the lessons of deconstruction cannot be forgotten (especially those of **de Man**, 'the most impressive as well as the most troubling figure' in literary studies since the 1950s). Deconstructionist analysis is valuable in that it shows the tensions and contradictions evident in the teleological idealisms of both literature and criticism. Like de Man, McGann seeks to destabilize the self-conceptions of particular discourses. None the less, deconstruction remains preoccupied with formal issues, and is faulted for still preserving 'the distance between literature and its socio-historical ground'. In displaying the self-contradictions evident in Romantic poetry within a historical frame of reference, McGann is pressing deconstructionist procedures into the service of sociohistorical analysis (what Levinson has called 'deconstructive materialism').

Despite McGann's special pleading, it should be registered that political accounts of Romanticism are nothing new. However, it is the stress on textual absence (on what the work attempts to silence), rather than the exposition of 'explicitly' political aspects of Romantic poetry (what the work is actually saying), which differentiates his work from historical critics of Romanticism such as David Erdman and E.P. Thompson. McGann also borrows from theorists alien to traditional historical criticism, notably **Althusser** (Thompson's *bête noire*), **Macherey** and **Bakhtin** (**Foucault** is far less important to Romantic New

Historicism than he is to its Renaissance equivalent). 'Displacement' is a **Freud**ian concept, but McGann uses it in a politically charged manner which derives from Macherey. Macherey, following Althusser, argues that ideologies are built around that which they exclude. He goes on to develop this idea into a model of textual analysis. Macherey's examination of textual silence and his stress on 'dissimulation' as a way of speaking inform McGann's discussion of Romantic erasure, displacement and disguise. However, McGann repudiates Althusser and Macherey's privileging of art. Though he sees art as a vehicle for ideologies, Althusser contends that it can ultimately offer a 'retreat' from ideology. McGann argues that Althusser, in declaring 'I do not rate real art among the ideologies', is echoing Romantic idealism, the attempt to set poetry apart from ideology. Invoking **Eagleton**, McGann argues that literature is an ideological form rather than the means to escape ideology.

McGann has been highly influential in theorizing textual studies (ideas put into practice in his magisterial Oxford edition of Byron). He argues that the low esteem afforded the work of the textual scholar by the literary critic is paradigmatic of a pernicious extrinsic/intrinsic critical division in which the scholar (fearful of intruding into the critic's hermeneutical territory) simply delivers the text to the critic (who is generally ignorant of the work's textual variants, its bibliographical history and its reception history). McGann argues that far from being 'preliminaries' to aesthetic or ideological analysis, 'philological' methods (textual criticism, bibliography and palaeography) are central to criticism and interpretation. *The Beauty of Inflections* uses Bakhtinian thought to theorize modern textual studies and to derive practical procedural forms for its various methodologies.

McGann ends *The Romantic Ideology* with another Bakhtinian flourish, denying that supposedly 'historical' criticism which explains works *solely* 'in terms of the past historical contexts which penetrate them' is actually historical. Such 'fruitless' criticism, Marxist or non-Marxist, is (to use Bakhtin's term) 'monological'. 'Traditional' historical criticism attempts to posit clear historical referents, forgetting that 'historical contexts are multiple and conflicting: heteroglossial, as Bakhtin would say' (McGann, 1988) and forgetting also that criticism involves 'the dialectical relation of the analysed "texts" to present interests and concerns' (a notion clearly indebted to Bakhtinian dialogism).

McGann's attempt to wrest the high ground of Romantic studies from deconstruction (whilst borrowing many of its preoccupations) and his robust approach to Romanticism itself (and its critics) has made him the most controversial critic currently working in the area. He has also made a valuable contribution in bringing textual studies closer to the centre of contemporary theoretical debate.

Main works

The Romantic Ideology, Chicago: Chicago University Press, 1983a.

A Critique of Modern Textual Criticism, Chicago: Chicago University Press, 1983b.

The Beauty of Inflections: Literary investigations in historical method and theory, Oxford: Clarendon Press, 1985.

Social Values and Poetic Acts: The historical judgment of literary work, Cambridge, MA and London: Harvard University Press, 1988.

Towards a Literature of Knowledge, Oxford: Clarendon Press, 1989.

The Textual Condition, Princeton, NJ: Princeton University Press, 1991.

Further reading

Johnston, Kenneth R. (ed.), *Romantic Revolutions: Criticism and theory*, Bloomington and Indianapolis: Indiana University Press, 1990.

Levinson, Marjorie (ed.), *Rethinking Historicism*, Oxford: Blackwell, 1990.

Siskin, Clifford, *The Historicity of Romantic Discourse*, Oxford: Oxford University Press, 1988.

Macherey, Pierre (1939–)

Pierre Macherey is best known in the English-speaking world as a literary critic, but his background and his academic career are firmly located in philosophy and political economy. As Professor of Philosophy at the University of Paris, Macherey worked with his former teacher and fellow **Marx**ist philosopher Louis **Althusser** on the latter's major project of 'rereading' Marx, both of them for a long time being wrongly labelled 'structuralist Marxists'.

Although a number of commentators have tended to divide Macherey's work (as Althusser famously did with the work of Marx) into an 'earlier' and a 'later' – the latter representing a definite advance on the limitations and/or errors of the former – it is possible to see Macherey as continuously and progressively rethinking the terms of the relationship between literature, theory and ideology. Whether or not the 'early' Macherey contains errors and limitations to be transcended, it is certainly that phase which is responsible for his reputation as a theorist. *Pour une théorie de la production littéraire*, published in 1966 but not brought out in an English translation until 1978, has, for many, something of an epoch-making character, even if, for some, it marks a negative moment: as Robert Young says in *White Mythologies: Writing history and the West*, 'Marxist literary criticism has not produced a new theory in over twenty years. Not since Macherey's *A Theory of Literary Production* of 1966 has there been any fundamental theoretical inno-vation.' A book which proposes a different role and status for both author and reader, as well as a different model of the text and of its relation to society and history from either mainstream literary criticism or the dominant forms of Marxist theorizing: these give us some sense of how 'fundamental' Macherey's contribution was.

A different conception of the role of the author is the first important sense of 'production' in the title (and one which some critics do not get beyond). Its most obvious target is the widely held notion of the writer as creator of the text. In opposition to this traditional Romantic image of the quasi-God-like creator, Macherey offers that of the writer who, like a craftsman, works with a set of materials – including literary forms, literary language, generic conventions and, crucially, ideology – using the tools and techniques of his/her trade. None of these 'raw' materials is invented or created by the writer; on the contrary, they are pre-given, and have to be worked with and upon in order for the product – the literary text – to emerge:

> Now, art is not man's creation, it is a product (and the producer is not a subject centred in his creation, he is an element in a situation or a system) . . . Before disposing of these works . . . men have to *produce* them, not by magic, but by a real labour of production.

This quotation also highlights a further move away from 'the artist as individual genius' towards a recognition of the writer's involvement in 'systems' such as the publishing industry and literature as an institution. A final demoting of the author occurs in Macherey's rejection of the idea that authorial intention guarantees a single unified meaning for the work.

If the author is a producer, he/she is not the only one associated with the text, as Macherey envisages the reader (or, more precisely, a particular kind of reader) as active producer of its meanings (multiple and diverse, not singular and unified). Most importantly for Macherey, the reader as critic brings a theoretically informed prespective which allows him/her to produce a 'knowledge of the text', an explanation of why it is as it is, especially in relation to the workings of ideology. It is in this area that yet another type of 'production' occurs, as Macherey sees the text as a 'producer' of ideology. In order to explain that, however, we need to look first at Macherey's notion of the literary text.

The formal counterpart of the text as possessor of a unitary meaning is the image of it as whole, harmonious and unified, the text as 'verbal icon', which is as much part of twentieth-century Marxism (in, for example, the work of Lucien **Goldmann** or Georg **Lukács**) as it is part of the literary-critical mainstream. For Macherey, such unity and harmony are illusory; they may indeed be the desired aim of the author, but they are unrealizable as a result of the text's relation to ideology. Ideology, as the 'reality' in which we all live, is an inescapable component of literature. Its aims, however, are not those of literature. To put it simply: if literature exists to talk about things, ideology has a range of topics – social or historical facts, the 'real conditions of existence' – about which it must keep silent. Ideology imposes its silences on literature, which creates a source of tension within the text. At the same time, the text is giving a form to that (ideology) which outside the text tends to appear formless, spontaneous or 'natural'. In this way, the text reworks and 'produces' ideology; but this, once again, is a source of internal disruption: 'there is a conflict within the text between the text and its ideological content, conflict rather than contiguity'. These fissiparous tendencies in the text are compounded by the fact that it is 'composed from a real diversity of elements' which work against any simple textual unity.

All these conflicts, tensions, silences and contradictory projects result in a text which, in Macherey's words, is 'incomplete'. They are, at one and the same time, that which the reader as critic must account for, and the best point of entry to the text for the critic: these places of discernible strain being where the text has rendered ideology most visible. The 'incomplete' nature of the text does not, however, mean that the reader is supposed somehow to 'fill in the gaps', as a traditional critic might aim to do, to make up for the text's shortcomings – they are to be explained, not explained away.

The process of explanation is twofold. It is necessary both to analyze the text itself in detail, 'an accurate description which respects the specificity of this work', and to stand back from it: 'To know the work, we must move outside it.' The 'outside' is the history from which the text emerges, and about which its ideological content so frequently maintains a tense and uneasy silence. The relationship between text and ideology is very close to Althusser's well-known formulation which locates literature midway between ideology and theoretically informed knowledge (or 'science', as it is usually – and unhelpfully – translated). Although ideology is an important component, the literary text is never simply reducible to ideology; on the other hand, it can never achieve the kind of understanding which theory provides.

Macherey pursues the relationship between literature and ideology in later articles. While these may move away from a concern with aesthetics (which carries a particularly bourgeois stigma) towards a greater emphasis on social dimensions and an awareness of the way in which, following Althusser's famous article on Ideological State Apparatuses, literature is constituted through the apparatus of education and the linguistic practices it involves, this would seem to have more to do with the continued examination of a problem than the 'epistemological break' (in Althusser's words) or the self-transcendence some critics have discovered.

Macherey's standing has no doubt suffered from his association with Althusser, in terms of being overshadowed by his more famous contemporary as well as sharing the latter's subsequent fall from popularity. The fact that a number of Macherey's ideas about the role of reader and author may be found in later, but better-known, books and articles by **Barthes** also affects how he is seen. Some critics have been keen to deny any originality to his concept of literature as production, pointing out that it can be found in **Brecht** – and even more so in **Benjamin**'s writings on Brecht. Despite this, Macherey's impact has been considerable. For many, the combination of theoretical discussion, the elaboration of an analytical approach, and the demonstration of that approach in action was particularly exciting and enabling, showing theory as workable, rather than abstract and aloof. Macherey's approach also encouraged Marxist analysis to expand into areas not usually associated with it, and Peter Hulme's excellent *Colonial Encounters* is just one example of that widened horizon. One of the best testimonies to Macherey's influence was the way in which some of his ideas very rapidly became part of the 'common sense' of contemporary critical theory. This can sometimes make it harder to appreciate their radical force, but it should not be allowed to obscure it entirely.

Main works

Lire le Capital, Paris: Maspero, 1968 (with Louis Althusser and Etienne Balibar), trans. Ben Brewster as *Reading Capital*, London: New Left Books, 1968 – without Macherey!

Introduction to Renée Balibar, *Les français fictifs*, Paris: Hachette, 1974 (with Etienne Balibar).

'Problems of reflection', in F. Barker *et al.* (eds.), *Literature, Society and the Sociology of Literature*, Colchester: University of Essex, 1976.

A Theory of Literary Production, trans. Geoffrey Wall, London: Routledge & Kegan Paul, 1978a.

'On literature as an ideological form', *Oxford Literary Review* 3, 1 (1978b) (with Etienne Balibar).

Hegel ou Spinoza, Paris, 1979.

Comte: la philosophie et les sciences, Paris, 1989.

A quoi pense la littérature?: exercises de philosophie littéraire, Paris, 1990.

Further reading

Belsey, Catherine, *Critical Practice*, London: Methuen, 1980.

Eagleton, Terry, 'Macherey and Marxist literary theory', in *Against the Grain*, London: Verso, 1986.

Eagleton, Terry, *Marxism and Literary Criticism*, London: Methuen, 1976.

Forgacs, David, 'Marxist literary theories', in Ann Jefferson and David Robey (eds), *Modern Literary Theory*, London: Batsford, 1986, 2nd edn.

Hulme, Peter, *Colonial Encounters*, London: Methuen, 1986.

McLuhan, Herbert Marshall (1911–1980)

McLuhan was born in Edmonton, Alberta, Canada. He obtained a BA and an MA in English Literature from University of Manitoba, a BA and an MA in English Literature at the University of Cambridge (Trinity Hall) and a PhD from the University of Cambridge in 1943 with a dissertation on Thomas Nashe. During his years as a student, McLuhan converted to Roman Catholicism. He began his teaching career at the University of Wisconsin in 1936, moved to St Louis University in 1937, and then returned to Canada in 1944 to the Assumption University of Windsor, Ontario. In 1946 he took up a post at St Michael's College, University of Toronto, where he was to remain until his death. He became Professor of English Literature in 1952. As well as publishing articles on conventional literary topics, McLuhan, with his first book, *The Mechanical Bride* (1951), announced an interest in media and popular culture, which was sustained in the 1950s through an association with the journal *Explorations: Studies in Culture and Communication*. His *Understanding Media* (1964) contributed to the sudden acquisition of an astonishing fame, when he was discussed and fêted throughout America and beyond. He gave celebrity lectures and held packed public seminars, made frequent television appearances and, besides continuing to publish books, made a television film, and released a record. His celebrity declined sharply in the 1970s, though he continued to direct the University of Toronto's Centre for Culture and Technology, which he had founded in 1963. Some of McLuhan's researches of the 1970s became available posthumously, written up by his assistant, Bruce Powers, and his son, Eric McLuhan.

The choice of literary figures for discussion in McLuhan's early articles is telling: the querulous Catholic reactionary G.K. Chesterton; the mystic nationalist Yeats; the High Anglican T.S. Eliot; the Fascist sympathizer Ezra Pound; and above all the Catholic wordsmith James Joyce. Here is an opponent of the modern world, but not of modernism. McLuhan praised **Leavis** for his criticism of modern society and culture, warming to the backward-looking ruralist strain within that critique. For he came from the Western Provinces, where political Agrarianism flourished, and in the United States he wrote in defence of the agrarian South against the industrial North.

His remarkable first book, *The Mechanical Bride*, continued the criticism of modern society, though now through its popular culture. The book comprises a series of 59 short pieces on individual 'exhibits' drawn from newspaper front pages, popular periodicals, cartoon strips, advertisements and film posters. These are said to 'represent a world of social myths or forms' which constitute 'the folklore of industrial man'. Although it can in part be seen as an early manifestation of the American 'mass culture' debate of the 1950s, the book can also be considered an astonishing, reactionary prefiguration of **Barthes**'s *Mythologies* in its detailed attention to the social meanings of popular cultural texts and practices as expressions of modern myths. McLuhan's contributions during the 1950s to the innovative journal *Explorations* signalled many of the themes that were to run through his celebrated 1960s work: the problems of print culture, the 'media as art forms', the changing balance of the human sensorium.

The Gutenberg Galaxy damned the typographic revolution: print 'detribalizes' humanity and fosters individualism, while making for linearity, regularity, uniformity. It imposes the single private vantage point which he called the 'visual'. This drives out the 'audile-tactile' of traditional culture and its potential for polyphony. It was for their anticipation of the non-punctuality of the auditory field that McLuhan celebrated Cubist perspective, the polysemy of Joyce's prose, and the multiple melodies of jazz.

In *Understanding Media*, McLuhan widened his attention to media beyond print. As well as sustaining his preoccupation with alphabetization, literacy and printing, there are chapters on comics, the photograph, the newspaper press, advertisements, the telegraph, the typewriter, the telephone, the phonograph, movies, radio, television and information technology ('automation'). But for McLuhan 'media' are all the extensions of particular human senses or faculties, so he also devotes chapters to other technologies such as housing, clothing ('our external skin'), the motorcar and weapons. He explores the way each of these media or technologies reorganizes social life and the 'ratio' between the senses. McLuhan had thus begun to move away decisively from the attention to the meaning of media texts displayed in *The Mechanical Bride*, asserting instead that the real significance of media lay in their overall impacts on human perception and social interrelationships. Hence, he argued, the 'medium is the message' (a phrase he first used to title a 1960 article), claiming that 'all media are active metaphors in their power to translate experience into new forms', and that 'the "message" of any medium or technology is the change of scale or pace or pattern that it introduces into human affairs'. Most of the aphorisms and terms by which McLuhan became known are set forth in *Understanding Media*, the work on which his reputation rests: 'the "content" of any medium is always another medium' (so: 'The content of writing is speech, just as the written word is the content of print, and print is the content of the telegraph'); the distinction between a 'cool' medium – a low-definition medium that solicits a high intensity of involvement and participation (like television or the telephone) – and a 'hot' medium, which invites a relatively detached contemplation (like books or movies); 'the global village', which is the state of the world being brought into existence by the spread of instantaneous electronic communication. McLuhan was influenced by his compatriot, Harold Innis, whose work on the history of Canada attributed the particularity of that country's economic and social development to the historical specificity of its system of communications. In acknowledgement of his intellectual debt, he contributed an introduction to Innis's *Bias of Communication* (1964).

McLuhan's later work popularized his views, further explored the effects of the developing information technologies, or codified the 'laws of the media' as he saw them. Many of these books elaborated repetitiously on his fundamental positions, though a rekindling of interest in hermeneutics occurred in his final years.

McLuhan's Catholicism is never explicitly espoused in his mature writings, but it underwrites his most insistent theme: that the arrival of print was an event so catastrophic that it practically amounted to a second Fall. (The spread of printed Bibles played a significant part in the Reformation, and the association of print and Protestantism is a historiographical commonplace.) His idea of the potentially redemptive role of a coming worldwide network of electronic communications owes something to the concept of the 'noosphere' advanced by the palaeontologist and Jesuit theologian Teilhard de Chardin in his posthumous *The Phenomenon of Man* (1955). For Chardin, the 'noosphere' is the new layer or membrane on the earth's surface, above the hydrosphere, atmosphere and biosphere, the ⌐thinking layer⌐ inaugurated by the development of conscious thought in humanity, evolving to ever higher levels of development, making people more fully human and bringing humanity – and thus the earth's entire evolutionary process – closer to God. McLuhan affirms: 'Our new electric technology . . . extends our senses and nerves in a global embrace . . . The computer promises by technology a Pentecostal condition of universal understanding and unity.'

In many respects, McLuhan's cultural impact was enormous. He was profiled by Tom Wolfe for the *New York Herald Tribune*, made appearances in chat shows and broadcast interviews, was cast in a vignette in Woody Allen's *Annie Hall*. Because his theme was an endorsement of the burgeoning new electronic media against a mentally and spiritually imprisoning print culture, his media ubiquity became a part of making the case. He had constituencies in both corporate America, which received him as a futures guru, and within the counter-culture, whose generation of television and rock'n'roll took to his enthusiastic celebration of new media. Within more intellectually reflective milieux, his work was seldom well received. His bold epigrams, love of paradox and delight in sub-Joycean wordplay exasperated many. He was condemned as a technological determinist, and sometimes characterized as an apologist for technocratic neo-capitalism (Fekete). Jonathan Miller's *McLuhan* (1971), which took issue with many of McLuhan's theses and examples and first drew attention to the reactionary Agrarian values that underplay some of them, halted the momentum of any gathering cult in Britain. Nevertheless, something of McLuhan's agenda persisted in the preoccupations of Raymond **Williams**'s *Television, Technology and Cultural Form*. In Canada McLuhan is treated seriously as a major contributor to an important native tradition of communication studies.

McLuhan's reputation is currently in the ascendant. To the counter-culture epigones – the cyberpunks, computer hackers and techno-hippies of the Bay area – he is a sixties sage who features in the pages of *Mondo 2000* and is the idol of *Wired*, the magazine of information superhighways and multimedia. But more widely, various of McLuhan's concerns – the end of mechanization and the coming of post-industrialism, the growing significance of media and communications, the dissolution of the high culture/low culture opposition, the assault on linear rationality and unified consciousness, the championing of rhetoric, the information technology revolution, the contraction of time–space, even his invoking of the Holy Ghost – can be seen to foreshadow many of the themes in the contemporary characterization of postmodernity. Jean **Baudrillard** reviewed *Understanding Media* in 1967, and has continued to be attracted to an account of the media that regarded their manifest content as irrelevant, and proclaimed a version of the coming 'ecstasy of communication'.

Whether or not he should be considered a postmodernist *avant la lettre*, it can be said that McLuhan made an intervention in public debate in the sixties which, in boldly negating the behaviourist social-scientism of the 'effects' school and sloughing off the liberal-moralism of the 'mass culture' critics, helped to open the way for the displacement of 'the science of mass communications' by 'media studies'.

Main works

The Mechanical Bride: Folklore of industrial man, New York: Vanguard Press, 1951; London: Routledge & Kegan Paul, 1967.

(ed., with Edmund Carpenter) *Explorations in Communications: An anthology*, Boston, MA: Beacon Press, 1960.

The Gutenberg Galaxy: The making of typographic man, Toronto: University of Toronto Press, 1962; London: Routledge & Kegan Paul, 1962.

Understanding Media: The extensions of man, New York: McGraw-Hill, 1964; London: Routledge & Kegan Paul, 1964.

(with Quentin Fiore) *The Medium is the Massage: An inventory of effects*, New York: Bantam Books/Random House, 1967; Harmondsworth: Penguin, 1968.

(with Bruce R Powers) *The Global Village: Transformations in world life and media in the 21st century*, New York and Oxford: Oxford University Press, 1989.

Further reading

Fekete, John, *The Critical Twilight: Explorations in the ideology of Anglo-American literary theory from Eliot to McLuhan*, London and Boston, MA: Routledge & Kegan Paul, 1977.

Ferguson, Marjorie, 'Marshall McLuhan revisited: 1960s Zeitgeist victim or pioneer postmodernist?', *Media, Culture and Society*, 13 (1991): 71–90.

Kroker, Arthur, *Technology and the Canadian Mind: Innis, McLuhan, Grant* New York: St. Martin's Press, 1984.

Marchand, Pierre, *Marshall McLuhan the Medium and the Messenger*, New York: Tichenor & Fields, 1989.

Miller, Jonathan, *McLuhan*, London: Fontana, 1971.

Stearn, Gerald (ed.), *McLuhan: Hot & cool*, New York: Dial Press, 1967; Harmondsworth: Penguin, 1968.

Marcuse, Herbert (1898–1979)

Like many of his radical contemporaries, Marcuse came from a well-to-do bourgeois Jewish family which had benefited materially from industrial capitalism. In keeping with this background, his early education was typically isolated from political realities. At the Kaiserin Augusta Gymnasium he learned classical languages and history, but his extra-curricular reading involved forays into modern architectural theory and the works of such literary modernists as Gide, Stefan George, Thomas and Heinrich Mann. When, at the age of 17, he was conscripted into the Imperial German Reichswehr and subsequently assigned to the domestic reserves because of poor eyesight, Marcuse attended lectures at Berlin University, and one year later (1917) he registered his disillusionment with the war effort by joining the Social Democratic Party. When the military revolt precipitated the rise of Workers' and Soldiers' Councils, Marcuse was elected to the Reinicken-dorf *Soldatenrat*. He left the SDP in 1919 when the party's gradual embracing of government policies at the expense of a revolutionary socialist vision led directly to – in his opinion – not only the abandonment of the council movement, but the murder of Rosa Luxemburg and Karl Liebknecht. From 1919 to 1920 Marcuse studied at the Humboldt University in Berlin, where he met Walter **Benjamin** and Georg **Lukács**. Moving to Freiburg, he studied Hegel and attended classes by Husserl and later Heidegger, completing his doctoral dissertation on the German *Künstlerroman* in 1922, *magna cum laude*. After a nine year sabbatical, Marcuse returned to Freiburg to continue his study of philosophy with Edmund Husserl and Martin Heidegger.

The year 1932 saw the publication of his first book, *Hegel's Ontology and the Foundation of a Theory of Historicity*, which argued for a reading of the historical aspects of Hegel's thought over and above its philosophical systematization. This book prompted an invitation to join the Institute of Social Research in 1933. However, owing to the precarious position of the Jewish intellectual in Nazi Germany, Marcuse was forced, along with the other members of the Institute, to leave the country and adopt refugee status in the United States. He subsequently emigrated to the

United States to became a key figure – along with Max Horkheimer, Leo Löwenthal, Friedrich Pollock and Theodor **Adorno** – in what came to be known as the 'Frankfurt School of Critical Theory'.

Like that of most important intellectuals growing up in the revolutionary first third of the twentieth century, Marcuse's thinking demonstrates a dialectical relationship with socioeconomic changes. Nevertheless, more than any other member of the Frankfurt School Marcuse was compelled throughout his career to envisage a social whole which could aspire to 'utopian' objectives without being totalitarian: in this he was a self-confessed romantic. His lifelong commitment was to reconstructing a *Marxism* in crisis so that it would more adequately reflect the modern capitalist economy and the changing nature of alienated labour while retaining a classical **Marx**ist belief in the possibility of a truly emancipated socialist society, achieved through the growth and development of a decentralized political movement. His thought is generally seen to develop in three phases: the first concentrates on the problems of ontology and historicity in relation to dialectics; the second attempts to tease out the radical potential of Hegel's thought (see *Reason and Revolution*, 1941) and to read Marx in the light of his early writings, especially the *Economic and Philosophical Manuscripts*; and the third begins as a philosophical inquiry into **Freud** (*Eros and Civilization*, 1955) and culminates in an analysis of Soviet Marxism (*Soviet Marxism*, 1958) and modern technological culture (*One-Dimensional Man*, 1964).

In the 1930s and 1940s, Marcuse became involved in a study of authoritarian culture. At this time he also wrote a series of essays which would lay the ground for his later thinking. These essays, collected in *Negations* (1968) and *Studies in Critical Philosophy* (1972), range in topic from a study on authority to critiques of such concepts as essence and culture. It was primarily through these essays that the American institution was introduced to the brand of dialectical thinking characteristic of Marcuse's work and that of those associated with the Frankfurt School. Ironically, if these essays index a certain style and depth of thought which has since become the norm in the literary studies of the American and British left, then the foreword, written many decades after the essays themselves, reveals a pessimism which has come to mark the works of certain post-Marxist, postmodern writers. Nevertheless, because they were written before it was clear that superior technology would both facilitate the defeat of fascism and strengthen the social structure which allowed for its emergence in the first place, they demonstrate a hopefulness about the possibility of overcoming an 'irrational social organization'.

One-Dimensional Man (1964), perhaps Marcuse's best-known work and first published at a time of much student unrest, is sceptical of this early naivety. It argues that technology and bureaucracy no longer work for particular interests, as they once did, but operate as forms of institutional domination. Scientific rationality has become a formalism, *sui generis*, which underlies and determines a specific type of technological development. If the pacification of the struggle for existence is to take place, there must be a 'qualitative' change at the level of technology. But because the system of needs is controlled economically, politically and culturally, the possibility of a revolutionary consciousness is no longer made available: with the industrialized saturation of the social realm, the utopian moment when critical consciousness could liberate labour from fatigue and suffering, transforming it into an aesthetic activity – work and play, technique and art – is precluded. For Marcuse, the advance of this technological saturation removes the representation not only of critique, but of need and hope. In this, as Fredric **Jameson** notes, his understanding of technological culture insidiously replaces Freud's 'repressed unhappiness' which coincides with the growth and progress of civilization (*Civilization and its Discontents*) with a kind of complacent pleasure principle. This means that 'administered individuals' become implicated in their own oppression by virtue of the fact that they are psychologically formed in accordance with the needs of the system. The book ends with a note of pathos as he asks 'How can administered individuals, who have made their mutilation into their own freedom and gratification, reproducing it on an expanded scale, free themselves from themselves as from their masters?' (Marcuse, 1964).

Thus in the 1960s Marcuse became an advocate of what was known as 'marginal groups theory', a theory committed to the belief that revolutionary transformation would be facilitated by marginalized minority groups, those less integrated groups still conscious enough to refuse the values of advanced industrial capitalism. The basis of this great refusal would be a moral radicalism which might 'precondition man for freedom' by activating 'the elementary, organic foundation of morality'. In *An Essay on Liberation* (1969), he defines morality as a disposition rooted in 'the erotic desire to counter aggressiveness, to create and preserve "ever-greater unities" of life'. This organic foundation is therefore 'biological' and 'historical' in so far as 'the malleability of "human nature" reaches into the depth of man's instinctual structure':

> If biological needs are defined as those which must be satisfied and for which no adequate substitute can be provided, certain cultural needs can 'sink down' into the biology of man. We could then speak, for example, of the biological need of freedom, or of some aesthetic needs as having taken root in the organic structure of man, in his 'nature' or rather 'second nature'. (Marcuse, 1969)

The production of superfluous needs through capitalism and the advancing affluence of the proletariat effectively repress these 'human' needs. During the 1970s Marcuse maintained his belief in the critical potential of radical social movements for combating contemporary capitalism, supporting Third World national liberation organizations and certain European Communist parties; nevertheless, he also began to advocate the importance of democratic processes in bringing about political reform.

Marcuse virtually soared to academic prominence in the 1960s, when he took up a post in Philosophy and Politics at Brandeis University. As a leading exponent of critical theory, his work (in particular *One-Dimensional Man*) became central to the thinking and development of the New Left. However, his influence within the institution has receded since that time, in line with the fortunes of the political movements mobilized by the student unrest of the late 1960s. Nevertheless, the issues that preoccupied the Frankfurt School critical theorists continue to be a source of controversy, especially in departments of Cultural Studies.

Main works

Hegels Ontologie und die Grundlgung einer Theorie der Geschichlichkeit, Frankfurt-am-Main: V. Klosterman, 1932.

Reason and Revolution: Hegel and the rise of social theory, London: Routledge & Kegan Paul, 1941.

Eros and Civilization: A philosophical inquiry into Freud, Boston, MA: Penguin, 1955; 2nd edn (with 'Political Preface 1966').

Soviet Marxism: A critical analysis, New York: Columbia University Press, 1958.

One-Dimensional Man, Boston, MA: Beacon Press, 1964.

Negations: Essays in critical theory, Boston, MA: Beacon Press; London: Allen Lane/Penguin, 1968.

An Essay on Liberation, Boston, MA: Beacon Press; London: Allen Lane/ Penguin, 1969.

Five Lectures, Boston, MA: Beacon Press; London: Allen Lane/Penguin, 1970.

Studies in Critical Philosophy, trans. Joris de Bres, London: New Left Books, 1972a.

Counterrevolution and Revolt, Boston, MA: Penguin, 1972b.

Revolution or Reform: A confrontation, ed. A.T. Ferguson, Chicago/
Boston, MA: Penguin, 1976.

The Aesthetic Dimension, Boston, MA: Beacon Press, 1978.

Further reading

Geoghegan, V., *Reason and Eros: The social theory of Herbert Marcuse,*
London: Plato, 1981.

Katz, B., *Herbert Marcuse and the Art of Liberation,* London: NLB, 1982.

Kellner, David, *Herbert Marcuse and the Crisis of Marxism,* Basingstoke:
Macmillan, 1984.

Pippin, Robert, Robert Feenberg and Charles P. Webel (eds), *Marcuse:
Critical theory and the promise of Utopia,* Basingstoke: Macmillan, 1988.

Jay, Martin, *Marxism and Totality: The adventures of a concept from Lukács
to Habermas,* Cambridge and London: Polity, 1984.

Schoolman, Morton, *The Imaginary Witness: The critical theory of Herbert
Marcuse,* New York: Free Press, 1980.

Marx, Karl (1818–1883)

Karl Marx was born into a middle-class Jewish family in Trier,
Germany, in 1818. He studied jurisprudence, philosophy and history at
the universities of Bonn and Berlin. In 1842 he became editor of the
influential liberal newspaper *Rheinische Zeitung.* In 1843 he moved to
Paris, where he edited the socialist newspaper *Deutsch-französische
Jahrbücher.* It was during this period that he formed his lifelong
friendship with Frederick Engels and became a convinced communist.
Marx was expelled from France in 1845. He spent the next three years in
Brussels, until his expulsion in 1848. During this period he joined the
Communist League. Following the League's 1847 conference in
London, Marx and Engels were commissioned to write the Communist
Manifesto. In 1848 (the year of revolutions throughout Europe) Marx
moved back to Paris, then to Cologne to found the *Neue Rheinische
Zeitung.* In Cologne he was accused of incitement to armed rebellion.
Although he was acquitted, he was soon expelled. Marx moved to
London in May 1849. Here he remained, regularly travelling to Europe,
until his death in 1883. During this period he produced much of his

most significant work, and helped to found the International Working Men's Association (the First International) in 1864.

Despite his encyclopaedic knowledge of aesthetics and the arts, and the fact that as a young man he wrote poetry, a fragment of a verse drama and an unfinished comic novel, and that his work on politics, economics, philosophy, sociology and history is scattered with references to world literature, Karl Marx never produced a systematic theory of culture. Therefore, what is called Marxist cultural theory is in its explicit form a post-Marx development, constructed within Marxism on the basis of Marx's revolutionary analysis of society. It is, therefore, to Marx's general theory that we must turn, rather than his scattered comments on literature and the arts, if we are to establish the basis of a Marxist theory of culture.

A Marxist approach to culture is above all concerned to analyze the texts and practices of culture within their historical conditions of production (and in some later versions, the changing conditions of their consumption and reception). What makes Marx's methodology different from other 'historical' approaches to culture is his concept of history. The fullest statement of his approach to history is contained in *Preface and Introduction to A Contribution to the Critique of Political Economy*. Here Marx outlines the now famous 'base/superstructure' account of social and historical development. He argues that each significant period in history is constructed around a particular 'mode of production': that is, the way in which a society is organized (i.e. slave, feudal, capitalist, etc.) to produce the necessities of life: food, clothing, shelter, and so on.

Each mode of production produces different ways of obtaining the necessities of life, but it also produces different relations between 'workers' and 'non-workers', and different social institutions (including cultural ones). At the heart of this analysis is the claim that the way a society produces its means of existence (its particular mode of production) will ultimately 'condition' the political, social, and cultural shape of that society, and its possible future development. This claim is based on a revolutionary understanding of the relationship between base and superstructure.

The base consists of a combination of the 'forces of production' and the 'relations of production'. The forces of production refer to the raw materials, the tools, the technology, the workers and their skills, and so on. The relations of production refer to the class relations of those engaged in production. That is, each mode of production – besides being different, say, in terms of its basis in agriculture or industry – is also different in that it produces particular relations of production: the slave mode produces master/slave relations; the feudal mode produces

lord/peasant relations; the capitalist mode produces bourgeois/
proletariat relations. It is in this sense that one's class position is
determined by one's relation to the mode of production.

The superstructure consists of the institutions (political, legal,
educational, cultural, etc.), and 'definite forms of social consciousness'
generated by these (political, religious, ethical, philosophical, aesthetic,
cultural, etc.), which arise on the basis of the mode of production. The
relationship between base and superstructure is twofold. On the one
hand, the superstructure both expresses and legitimates the base. On
the other, the base is said to 'condition' the content and form of the
superstructure. This relationship can be understood in a range of
different ways. It can be seen as a mechanical relationship of cause and
effect: what happens in the superstructure is a passive reflection of
what is happening in the base ('economic determinism'). This often
results in a vulgar Marxist 'reflection theory' of culture, in which the
politics of a text or practice are read off from or reduced to the economic
conditions of its production. The relationship can also be seen as the
setting of limits, the providing of a specific framework in which some
developments are probable and others unlikely. However we interpret
the details of Marx's model, it is clear that he is making the general
claim that the way a society organizes the means of its economic
production will have a *conditioning* effect on the type of culture that
society produces.

What are the implications of Marx's conception of history for the
analysis of culture? First of all, to understand and explain a text or
practice it must first be situated in its historical moment of production;
analyzed in terms of the historical conditions which produced it. There
are dangers here: historical conditions are ultimately economic;
therefore cultural analysis can quickly collapse into economic analysis
(the cultural becomes a passive reflection of the economic). It is crucial,
as Marx warned, to keep in play a subtle dialectic between agency and
structure (we make history, but we are also made by history). A full
analysis of the nineteenth-century novel would have to weave together
and keep together in focus, for example, the economic changes which
produced its reading public, the new technologies of production and
distribution, and the literary traditions inherited from the past. The
same also holds true for a full analysis of nineteenth-century theatre. In
neither instance would literary or theatrical developments be reduced
to changes in the economic structure of society, but what would be
insisted on is that a full analysis of the novel or the theatre would not be
possible without reference to the changes in the reading public and
theatre attendance brought about by changes in the economic structure
of society, which in turn (however indirectly) produced, for example,
the performance and popularity of a play like *Black–Eyed Susan* and the
emergence and success of a novelist like Charles Dickens. Thus a

Marxist analysis would argue that ultimately, however indirectly, there is nevertheless a real and fundamental relationship between the development of the novel and the emergence of a new type of drama, and changes that took place in the capitalist mode of production. Although the economic base produces the superstructural terrain (this terrain and not that), the form of activity that takes place there is determined not just by the fact that the terrain was produced and is reproduced by the economic base (although this clearly sets limits and influences outcomes), but by the interaction of the institutions and the participants as they occupy the terrain. Therefore, although culture can never be, strictly speaking, the primary force in history, it can be an active agent in historical change or the servant of social stability. In *The German Ideology*, Marx and Engels claim that '[t]he ideas of the ruling class are in every epoch the ruling ideas, i.e. the class which is the ruling *material* force in society, is at the same time its ruling *intellectual* force'. By this they mean that the dominant class, on the basis of its ownership of and control over the means of material production, is virtually guaranteed to have control over the means of intellectual production. However, this does not mean that the ideas of the ruling class are simply imposed on subordinate classes. A ruling class is 'compelled . . . to represent its interest as the common interest of all the members of society . . . to give its ideas the form of universality, and represent them as the only rational, universal valid ones'. Given the uncertainty of this project, ideological struggle is almost inevitable. During periods of social transformation it becomes chronic. As Marx points out, it is in the 'ideological forms' of the superstructure that men and women 'become conscious of . . . conflict and fight it out'. For Marx, therefore, culture is one of the 'ideological forms' of the superstructure.

Defining culture as an 'ideological form' is premised on the view that society is structured around class conflict rather than social consensus. Cultural texts and practices inevitably take sides, consciously or unconsciously, in this conflict. This means that culture is itself a key site of class conflict. Therefore, the second feature of a Marxist approach to culture is the insistence that culture is political. That is to say, cultural texts and practices are always implicated in particular relations of power. They may, for example, implicitly or explicitly support the interests of the dominant groups who socially, politically, economically and culturally benefit from the economic organization of society. Thus cultural texts and practices are continually caught up in the politics of signification, the attempt to establish (or to articulate) and circulate specific social meanings, and to win readers and audiences to particular ways of seeing the world.

The Marxist approach to culture is often criticized for a tendency to reduce cultural texts and practices to questions of history, politics and economics. While it is certainly true that a Marxist cultural theory must always insist on the importance of the historical (including economic conditions) and the political for an adequate understanding, it is later Marxists, rather than Marx himself, who have been guilty of reducing this to a form of 'economic determinism'.

Although Marx did not produce a systematic theory of culture, it is almost impossible to overestimate his influence on cultural theory. Marx's general theory of society and of historical development has generated a huge and influential body of work which is now collectively known as Marxist cultural and literary theory.

Main works

The Eighteenth Brumaire of Louis Bonaparte, Moscow: Progress Publishers, 1954.

The Poverty of Philosophy, trans. S. Moore, Moscow: Progress Press, 1955.

Pre-Capitalist Economic Formations, trans. J. Cohen, London: Lawrence & Wishart, 1964.

The Communist Manifesto (with Frederick Engels), Harmondsworth: Penguin, 1967.

Selected Works in One Volume, Moscow: Progress Press, 1968.

Basic Writings on Politics and Philosophy, London: Fontana, 1969.

Theories of Surplus Value, trans. E. Burns, vols 1–3, London: Lawrence & Wishart, 1969, 1976.

Critique of Hegel's Philosophy of Right, trans. A. Jolin and J.O. O'Malley, London: Cambridge University Press, 1970.

Preface and Introduction to A Contribution to a Critique of Political Economy, trans. S.W. Ryazanskaya, London: Lawrence & Wishart, 1971a.

Early Texts, Oxford: Blackwell, 1971b.

Grundrisse, trans. M. Nicolaus, Harmondsworth: Penguin, 1973a.

On Literature and Art (with Frederick Engels), trans. L. Baxandall and S. Morawski, St Louis, MO: Telos Press, 1973b.

Political Writings, vols 1–3, Harmondsworth: Penguin, 1973c.

The German Ideology (with Frederick Engels), London: Lawrence & Wishart, 1974.

Early Writings, trans. R. Livingstone, Harmondsworth: Penguin, 1975.

Capital, trans. B. Fowkes, vols 1–3, Harmondsworth: Penguin, 1976.

Economic and Philosophic Manuscripts, trans. C. Dutt, C.P. Magill and W. Lough, Moscow: Progress Press, 1977a.

Selected Letters (with Frederick Engels), Peking: Foreign Languages Press, 1977b.

Critique of the Gotha Programme, Moscow: Progress Press, 1978.

Further reading

Eagleton, Terry, *Marxism and Literary Criticism*, London: Methuen, 1976.

Laing, Dave, *The Marxist Theory of Art*, Brighton: Harvester, 1978.

Lifshitz, Mikhail, *The Philosophy of Art of Karl Marx*, London: Pluto Press, 1973.

McLellan, David, *The Thought of Karl Marx*, London: Macmillan, 1971.

Prawer, S.S., *Karl Marx and World Literature*, Oxford: Oxford University Press, 1976.

Williams, Raymond, *Marxism and Literature*, Oxford: Oxford University Press, 1977.

Miller, J. Hillis (1928–)

The prominent American critic and theorist J. Hillis Miller, gained a PhD at Harvard University in 1951. He taught English at Johns Hopkins University for some twenty years, moving in 1972 to a Chair in English at Yale University. He remained at Yale until 1986, the year in which he also held the Presidency of the Modern Language Association. During this crucial period Miller was instrumental in introducing the work of the French post-structuralist philosopher Jacques **Derrida** into the Anglo-American academic community. In formulating his own brand of deconstructive literacy criticism he became known – along with colleagues Paul **de Man**, Geoffrey **Hartman**, Harold **Bloom** and Derrida himself – as one of the 'Yale Critics' or 'Yale Mafia'. Since 1987 Miller has been Distinguished Professor of English and Comparative Literature at the University of California at Irvine.

Miller's work focuses primarily on nineteenth- and twentieth-century English and American literature, with particular emphasis on the novel from Dickens to James. It falls, in broad terms, into two strikingly distinct – ultimately antithetical – phases. In the first phase (from 1958 to 1970) Miller is strongly influenced by the phenomenological criticism of the 'Geneva School', a group of critics dominated by Georges Poulet, whose colleague Miller had been for the first six years of his tenure at Johns Hopkins. For the Geneva School – or 'critics of consciousness', as they are sometimes called – the literary text is viewed (like the total *oeuvre* of which it is a part) as an imaginative projection of it author's unique mode of consciousness. By suspending his or her own individuated selfhood, the critic strives to enter into that consciousness, describing and re-presenting its distinctive structures in the act of critical writing. Miller was the earliest Anglo-American exponent of this approach in the initial part of his career, most notably in *The Disappearance of God: Five nineteenth-century writers* (1963). But as a critic trained in the traditions of New Criticism and 'close reading' which still held sway in America at this time (his dissertation was entitled *Symbolic Imagery in Six Novels of Charles Dickens*), Miller not only adopts but also modifies the methods of the Geneva School. This is illustrated by the fact that he is rather more willing than other 'critics of consciousness' to concern himself with the technical or objective elements of literary texts. Miller's early work thus supplements one critical tradition with another – European phenomenology with Anglo-American formalism.

Miller's second phase constitutes a dramatic shift from the phenomenological orientation of the first. Here he effectively reinvents his intellectual and critical identity. Poulet's influence gives way to that of the deconstructive philosophy of Derrida, and the focus of Miller's own critical practice moves accordingly from consciousness to language and textuality. Derrida's grand critique of the metaphysical assumptions of Western thought since Plato, and his concomitant insights into the radical instabilities of language, are taken up and deployed by Miller – within the narrower ambit of literary criticism and theory – as the basis for his own deconstructive procedures. With their concern for the 'words on the page', these procedures seem to share one of the characteristics of New Criticism. Yet both the presuppositions and effects of deconstruction as performed by Miller and others are drastically at odds with those of New Criticism. For New Criticism the literary text is a complex yet organic and determinate unity. But for Miller, texts – literary or otherwise – are structures that are 'self-subverting' or 'heterogeneous'. Deconstruction typically elucidates the contradictions which inhabit a text through a rigorous and vigilant analysis which is attentive, in particular, to those elements which seem anomalous, marginal or unaccountable in terms of the text as a 'whole'. Texts are thus shown to be 'undecidable', denying the reader any position from which to adjudicate between the warring meanings within them. It is important here to recognize that deconstruction does not contradict or go against the ostensible meaning of a text so much as illuminate how texts contradict *themselves*. As Miller states, deconstruction 'is not a dismantling of the structure of a text but a demonstration that it has already dismantled itself' ('Stevens' Rock and Criticism as Cure, II', *The Georgia Review* 30 [1976]).

After deconstruction reached its height in America in the early 1980s, an important issue to emerge in Miller's work concerns the relation between ethics and reading. This is first addressed in *The Ethics of Reading: Kant, de Man, Eliot, Trollope, James, and Benjamin* (1987) and further explored in *Versions of Pygmalion* (1990), where it is linked to problems of storytelling and personification from Kleist to Maurice Blanchot. For Miller, the ethical dimension of the act of reading is twofold. Reading is ethical first of all in so far as it entails a response to a text which is in some sense *inevitable* or *necessary* – an ' "I must". . . . I cannot do otherwise' (*Ethics*). Yet that which is demanded in reading is precisely *misreading*, since the meanings of texts can never be unequivocally fixed or arrested: 'the impossibility of reading', Miller declares, 'is a universal necessity' (*ibid.*). The kind of ethical reading he advocates arises out of an encounter with the 'language of literature itself' (*ibid.*). It openly excludes consideration of the relation between texts and their historical, social, political or psychological contexts. Yet at the same time Miller argues that the teacher's or critic's readings are located in the world as acts spurring other acts in their turn. Reading is thus ethical in a second sense, producing effects upon others for which critics must hold themselves responsible. It possesses, Miller insists, 'crucial implications for our moral, social, and political lives' (*ibid.*).

This assertion is indicative of Miller's concern, in much of his more recent work, to combat the stereotypical dismissal of deconstructive criticism as 'apolitical' or 'unworldly'. The development of such a concern is not surprising, since in the last ten years or so boundaries between literary and cultural studies have become increasingly blurred, leading to forms of debate which are in turn increasingly politicized. In order to avoid marginalization, deconstructive theory and practice must demonstrate their continuing relevance to the intellectual and institutional situation as it changes around them. This is indeed the explicit aim of Miller's latest book, *Illustration* (1992). While he recognizes the importance of cultural studies, Miller argues that its practitioners often move too rapidly through the 'evident features' of a cultural artefact in order to 'diagnose it as another case of the particular culture it manifests' (*Illustration*). As a corrective to such reductive tendencies, he proposes the incorporation within the work of cultural criticism of the kinds of techniques of reading developed by deconstruction. Because such techniques are designed to locate the contradictions within texts of all kinds, they can help to show how cultural forms disrupt and exceed the range of contextual meanings which they are usually said only to reflect. In making and supporting these claims,

Miller invokes an array of examples (from 'high' and 'popular' culture alike) which are neither purely literary nor purely textual but combine visual and verbal elements – titled paintings by Turner, an illustrated novel by Dickens, comic strips, magazine covers. *Illustration* is not only an elegant defence of the kind of critical reading Miller has practised since the early 1970s; it also breaks new ground.

Miller's significance lies principally in the part he has played in establishing and deploying deconstruction as a radical means of reading texts (albeit ones drawn mainly from the canon of Western literature) within the context of the North American university. His work has helped profoundly to challenge, if not wholly to displace, the assumptions, procedures and goals of traditional humanistic scholarship and criticism. Such influence, however is not without its ironies. Miller's deconstructive work has contributed to the emergence of other modes of analysis and critique – cultural studies, for example which now present, as *Illustration* suggests, a significant and growing threat to the kind of iconoclastic critical approaches which largely enabled them. Whether deconstruction can successfully negotiate that threat – perhaps in the ways proposed in *Illustration* – remains to be seen.

Main works

The Disappearance of God: Five nineteenth-century writers, Cambridge, MA: Harvard University Press, 1963.

Fiction and Repetition: Seven English novels, Oxford: Blackwell, 1982.

The Linguistic Moment: From Wordsworth to Stevens, Princeton, NJ: Princeton University Press, 1985.

The Ethics of Reading: Kant, de Man, Eliot, Trollope, James, and Benjamin, New York: Columbia University Press, 1987.

Theory Now and Then, Hemel Hempstead: Harvester Wheatsheaf, 1991.

Illustration, Cambridge, MA: Harvard University Press, 1992.

Further reading

Abrams, M.H., 'The deconstructive angel', *Critical Inquiry*, 3 (1977): 425–38.

Cain, William E., 'Deconstruction in America: the recent literary criticism of J. Hillis Miller', *College English*, 41 (1979): 367–82.

Harpham, Geoffrey Galt, 'Language, History and ethics', *Raritan: A Quarterly Review* 7, 2 (1987): 128–46.

Loesberg, Jonathan, 'From Victorian Consciousness to an Ethics of Reading: The Criticism of J. Hillis Miller', *Victorian Studies*, 37 (1993), pp. 98–122.

Pease, Donald, 'J. Hillis Miller: the other Victorian at Yale', in *The Yale Critics: Deconstruction in America*, ed. by Jonathan Arac, Wlad Godzich and Wallace Martin, Minneapolis: University of Minnesota Press, 1983, pp. 66–89.

Riddel, Joseph N., 'A Miller's tale', *Diacritics*, 5 (1975): 56–65.

Millett, Kate (1934–)

Kate Millett is a painter, scultor and writer. After studying at the University of Minnesota and St Hilda's College, Oxford, she spent three years in Japan, where she held her first one-woman exhibition. Her return to the USA to teach English saw her involvement with the Women's Movement and the beginnings of her radical feminism. Published in 1970, *Sexual Politics*, originally her PhD thesis, became one of the most influential texts of second-wave feminism. Its year of publication – which also saw the appearance of Germaine Greer's *The Female Eunuch*, Shulamith Firestone's *The Dialectic of Sex*, Eva Figes's *Patriarchal Attitudes*, and the anthology *Sisterhood is Powerful*, edited by Robin Morgan – can be seen as marking the emergence of second-wave feminism as a powerful theoretical and critical force. *Sexual Politics* itself established both the fundamental premises of radical feminism – that sexual relationships are essentially *political* – and the possibilities of a feminist cultural theory and criticism which would challenge existing academic boundaries.

Sexual Politics sets out to formulate 'a systematic overview of patriarchy as a political institution'. Defining 'politics' as 'power-structured relationships', Millett argues not only that sex must be seen as a 'status category with political implications' but that patriarchy is the *primary* form of human oppression, without whose elimination other forms of oppression – racial, political or economic – will continue to function. Patriarchy, she argues, operates as a social institution which pervades all other political, social or economic forms. It maintains power largely by ideological means, winning consent through the socialization of both sexes to sexual inequalities of temperament, role, and status.

Part One of *Sexual Politics* establishes this 'Theory of Sexual Politics'. Sexual difference is culturally, not biologically produced, established through language in which the male functions as norm, and reinforced psychosocially by patriarchy's chief institution, the family. Male domination is mediated by differences of class but, Millett argues, although class functions to set one woman against another – 'whore against matron' or career woman against housewife – women's class affiliations are superficial. Patriarchy is both independent of and anterior to economically determined class structures. Economic power is used to reinforce patriarchy, assigning women to work with little or no market value and denying them access to the power which comes with technological knowledge. Education furthers this segregation, confining women to the 'feminine' areas of the humanities, a restricted education that perpetuates power inequalities. Historically, we can trace the cultural expressions of patriarchy through from primitive myths to the development of religion and ethics, and into the contemporary myths of science. The result of such socialization is that women internalize the ideology of femininity, accepting their inferior status; but, in case of failure, patriarchy can also, like other 'total ideologies', call on force. Institutionalized force, from legal penalties for women's adultery to the lack of abortion rights, is paralleled by sexual violence – both in material form, as in rape, and as embodied in cultural forms, for example pornography and contemporary literature.

Part Two of *Sexual Politics* traces the 'first phase' of the sexual revolution (1830–1930) and its succeeding counter-revolution (1930–60), while Part Three examines the 'Literary Reflection' in the work of D.H. Lawrence, Henry Miller, Norman Mailer and Jean Genet. The first of these sections provides a blueprint for a sexual revolution as Millett conceives it. The end of patriarchy would see an end to sexual inhibitions, taboos and double standards, an integration of the 'separate sexual subcultures', and a re-examination and re-evaluation of characteristics labelled 'masculine' or 'feminine'. As a result, the patriarchal family would disappear, to be replaced by professionalized child care and voluntary sexual liaisons. While it fell well short of such goals, the 'first phase' did attack the most obvious abuses in the patriarchal structure. Its Women's Movement effected changes in legislative and other civil rights, suffrage, education and employment. Its polemicists, notably Mill and Engels, attacked sexual double standards, marriage and the family. Its literature provides expressions of 'revolutionary sensibility' such as Charlotte Brontë's *Villette*. Yet because it failed to challenge patriarchal ideology at a sufficiently fundamental level, this first phase of sexual revolution was vulnerable to counter-revolution.

The single most powerful counter-revolutionary force in the ideology of sexual politics, argues Millett, was **Freud**, for Freud's theories of sexual difference lent scientific respectability to patriarchal assumptions about 'natural' female inferiority. Confusing biology and culture, Freud ascribed 'what he took to be the three corollaries of feminine psychology, passivity, masochism, and narcissism', to 'penis envy'. Social conditioning is ignored, and what could be seen as an accurate *description* of the position of women in patriarchy becomes instead – and despite Freud's theory of an original bisexuality – the definition of an inherent femininity. As such, it serves as *justification* for male domination and cruelty – women enjoy suffering – and as therapeutic *prescription*: women must be helped to 'adjust' to their biologically determined role. 'Penis envy' provides sufficient explanation for women's dissatisfactions, whether social or sexual, and since the cause is biological, aspiration 'only forebodes frustration'. Psychoanalysis promises women instead 'fulfillment in passivity and masochism'. Freud's theories provided the counter-revolution with a framework and a vocabulary for its counterattack. This framework, argues Millett, was extended by Freud's followers and aided by functionalism which, ignoring history, justified sexual role differentiation as 'functional' for the patriarchal status quo.

The final section of *Sexual Politics* provides a critical reading of male writers whom Millett sees as both 'reflections' and cultural agents of the patriarchal counter-revolution. Millett's reading of Lawrence, Miller and Mailer refuses the position of respectful criticism. Instead, she reads their descriptions of sexual practice as carrying ideological and political implications, and insists that their writing be seen within its social and cultural context, in relation to ideological positions inscribed in other contemporary discourses. From Lawrence to Mailer she traces the growth of an open sexual hostility: Mailer's *machismo* is at once the most violent and the most precarious, threatened as it is by the emergence of a second phase in the sexual revolution. Finally Genet, alone of contemporary writers, is seen as recognizing women as an oppressed group and a revolutionary force, and as identifying with them. *Sexual Politics* ends optimistically: the social change required of a sexual revolution is a product of 'altered consciousness', and that consciousness is now evident in a growing radical coalition. Millett's work both urges and heralds the 'second wave of the sexual revolution'.

Sexual Politics had a powerful impact both inside and outside the Women's Movement. It was instrumental in the creation of radical feminist theory, providing a framework and a language within which the politics of gender could be addressed. Its attack on Freud set the terms for the ensuing feminist debate about the usefulness of psychoanalytic theory to feminism, and its emphasis on ideological forms of oppression was taken up by feminist cultural theorists from the 1970s onwards. Its analysis of the operation of patriarchal ideology in literature established feminist literary criticism, and paved the way for much later feminist literary and cultural criticism. Finally, its interdisciplinarity and its mixture of scholarship and personal anger established new possibilities for feminist theoretical writing. Millett's study, however, has not gone unchallenged. Later feminist theorists have criticized her concept of ideology as oversimplified and monolithic. Her attack on Freud is seen as similarly limited. In concentrating on the concept of penis envy, she ignores what is arguably Freud's most fundamental contribution to theories of ideology: the concept of the unconscious. Without a concept of the unconscious, patriarchal ideology can, for Millett, become a conscious conspiracy, and women's liberation merely a matter of re-education. For similar reasons, it has been argued, her literary analysis is oversimplistic. Her identification of the literary work with conscious authorial ideology makes it impossible for her to deal with textual ambiguities and contradictions, and very difficult for her to address female-authored texts. Finally, Millett's failure to acknowledge her own feminist precursors, and particularly her debt to Simone de **Beauvoir's** *The Second Sex*, has been heavily criticized by later feminist writers.

Millett's later writings have abandoned what she described as the 'abstract language' of *Sexual Politics*, concentrating instead on the personal and autobiographical, and on issues arising from personal experience. Her most recent book, *The Loony Bin Trip*, is an account of her experiences after being diagnosed as manic-depressive in 1973, and an attack on psychiatric incarceration as a 'system of social control'.

Main works

The Prostitution Papers, London: Granada, 1975a.

Flying, London: Granada, 1975b.

Sexual Politics, London: Virago, 1977.

Sita, London: Virago, 1979.

The Loony Bin Trip, London: Virago, 1991.

Film

Three Lives (1972).

Further reading

Kaplan, Cora, *Sea Changes: Essays on culture and feminism*, London: Verso, 1986.

Moi, Toril, *Sexual/Textual Politics*, London: Methuen, 1985.

Spender, Dale, *For the Record: The making and meaning of feminist knowledge*, London: The Women's Press, 1985.

Tong, Rosemarie, *Feminist Thought: A comprehensive introduction*, London: Unwin Hyman, 1989.

Morris, Meaghan (1950–)

As an 'avowed textualist, postmodernist, poststructuralist, and really a raging formalist' Morris's work is situated at the intersection of feminist theory, discourse analysis and cultural studies. Her collected essays have earned her the reputation of one of the most important cultural critics writing in Australia. Morris's interests are remarkably comprehensive and theoretically diverse. From work with an editorial collective producing *Working Papers: Studies in the discourses of sex, subjectivity and power* in the 1970s, she turned to film reviewing in the early 1980s and to cultural and critical theory later in the 1980s and 1990s. Currently a freelance writer in Sydney, Morris left academia twenty years ago, finding the frameworks of European philosophy less and less useful, and now focuses on aspects of Australian cultural history through the lenses of **Marx**ism, psychoanalysis, **Foucault** and **Deleuze**, publishing internationally on semiotics, cinema and cultural theory.

The context of Morris's thinking is postmodernism, whose theories help to explain changes in late-twentieth-century cultural practices. Postmodernism often effaces the frontiers between speech and writing, between literary and visual representations. Morris deploys postmodernism to attack the notion that the arts are in a separate and superior realm from life.

Meaghan Morris's main concern is with the role of intellectuals in effecting cultural change. Specifically, she is interested in the way in which women have actively participated in the modernization of social and cultural life since the Second World War, and questions 'modernism' as a historical phenomenon. Beginning with *Michael Foucault: Power, Truth, Strategy* which she co-edited with Paul Patton in 1979, through to her current interest in consumerism ('Things to do with shopping centres'), Morris utilizes Foucault's notions of knowledge/power and discursive fields, and applies these to the ways in which 'women' are constructed in discursive and non-discursive locations such as shopping centres and movies, and in feminist and postmodernist theory. *The Pirate's Fiancée* is an exemplary study of the grammar of culture and its conditions of production and reception. Taking her title from the 1969 film by Nelly Kaplan, Morris ranges through subjects as diverse as blockbuster movies (*Crocodile Dundee*), art photography (Lynn Silverman, Juan Davila and Richard Dunn) to the cultural critics Foucault, Mary Daly, Susan Sontag and Jean **Baudrillard**. Each essay is about discourse, or the social textual uses of language, and Morris successfully argues the case that feminist critics have made a major contribution to discourse analysis and changes throughout cultural studies, and specifically in relation to postmodernism. Morris argues that the future management of change to which feminist criticism needs to address itself will involve a scrutiny of practices *throughout* patriarchy – 'leisure centres, unemployment activity' as well as the sociology of consumerism. Fashion and shopping are particularly crucial topics for feminist criticism because, as Morris argues, these turn women into both *consumers* and *objects* of knowledge. She points out that women also *enjoy* fashion and shopping, and frequently consume in order to transform their everyday lives, and that they are quite capable of resisting cultural stereotypes. It was Foucault above all, in *The History of Sexuality*, who characterized power as a multiplicity of discursive fields with multiple resistances. Gender identity, Morris argues, can be only understood in terms of the complex and contradictory ways in which consumerism, pleasure and power and cultural languages are produced and institutionalized and then subverted and discredited in many 'fields', including shopping centres.

Morris's essays are explicitly concerned with representations of women and subjectivity in particular historical contexts. She concludes that postmodernism is double-coded. That is, material which postmodernism absorbs from popular culture might help its message to reach a wider audience outside the academy, while simultaneously, postmodernism's parodic use of historical forms (in art, architecture and writing) appeals to the trained academic.

What cultural studies has to confront, Morris argues, is the aestheticization of politics as well as the gap between the history of Australian culture and transnational critical discourses of feminism, Marxim and postmodernism.

Morris's self-interrogative challenge to grand theories and her analysis of the social conditions of critical practice have been taken up by cultural critics in Britain and America (for example, Angela McRobbie) in the current unprecedented international forum on feminism and post-structuralism. It could be argued that Morris's work contributes to the major reorientation within feminism which is affecting cultural politics in the 1990s as deeply as second-wave feminism did in the late 1960s. These projects are all engaged in some way with representations and attempting to revolutionize cultural institutions and practices.

Morris agrees with other feminist critics that literature and culture are contested by social power, and that only by pluralizing meanings can we open up fixed binary terms (man = culture), understand the politics of these terms, and move beyond them.

Main works

With P. Foss [eds], *Language, Sexuality and Subversion*, Sydney: Feral, 1978.

With P. Foss [eds], *Michael Foucault: Power, Truth, Strategy*, Sydney: Feral, 1979.

'Panorama: The Live, The Dead and The Living', in P. Foss (ed), *Island in the Stream: Myth of place in Australian culture*, Sydney: Pluto Press, 1988a.

The Pirate's Fiancée: Feminism, Reading, Postmodernism, London: Verso, 1988b.

'Banality in Cultural Studies', in P. Mellencamp (ed.), *The Logics of Television*, Bloomington: Indiana University Press, 1990.

Ecstasy and Economics: American essays for John Forbes, Sydney: Empress, 1992a.

'Great moments in social climbing: King Kong and the human fly', in B. Colomina (ed). *Sexuality and Space*, Princeton, NJ: Princeton School of Architecture, 1992a.

With J, Frow [ed]; *Australian Cultural Studies: A Reader*, Sydney: Allen & Unwin, 1993.

Further reading

During, Simon (ed.), *The Cultural Studies Reader*, London: Routledge, 1993.

Grossberg, Lawrence *et al.* (eds), *Cultural Studies*, London: Routledge, 1992.

Humm, Maggie, *A Reader's Guide to Contemporary Feminist Literary Criticism*, Hemel Hempstead: Harvester Wheatsheaf, 1994.

Sheridan, Susan, (ed.), *Grafts: Feminist cultural criticism*, London: Verso, 1988.

Mulvey, Laura (1941–)

Laura Mulvey is a feminist theorist and film-maker working in Britain whose work can be situated in the meeting of feminist politics, psychoanalytic cultural theory and avant-garde aesthetics which occurred in the 1970s. She is most widely known for her ground-breaking essay 'Visual pleasure and narrative cinema' (1975), though she has also co-directed (with Peter Wollen) a number of important feminist avant-garde films which take up the issues raised in her theoretical writings.

Laura Mulvey's essay 'Visual pleasure and narrative cinema', written in 1973 and first published in 1975, has become the single most anthologized essay in the field of feminist film criticism. Together with early work by Claire Johnston and Pam Cook, Mulvey's essay placed the question of sexual difference as central within film theory, both extending and challenging work on the cinematic apparatus and spectatorship by theorists such as Raymond Bellour, Jean-Louis Baudry and Christian Metz. It also shifted the direction of feminist film criticism away from the issue of 'positive' or 'negative' images of women and their relation to the existing or historical 'realities' of women's lives, and towards a feminist theory of narrative film as signifying system. Mulvey drew on psychoanalytic theory, semiotics and theories of ideology to analyze the way in which the codes and practices of dominant cinema – narrative, genre, *mise en scène*, and so on – work to construct these images, coding visual pleasure to fulfil the needs and unconscious desires of male fantasy.

According to Mulvey, the image of woman, central to patriarchal culture, stands not for the realities of women's lives but as a signifier for the male other, repository of male fantasies and obsessions. It is crucially important, therefore, for women to understand these mechanisms, and for Mulvey psychoanalysis becomes a political weapon in the drive to understand male cinematic pleasure, and thus clear the way for the production of feminist alternatives.

Mulvey describes two forms of visual pleasure identified by **Freud**. Voyeuristic scopophilia arises from pleasure in using another person as an object of sexual stimulation through sight, while the narcissistic gaze – suggested by Freud, but in Mulvey's formulation more fully identified with **Lacan's** account of the mirror stage – produces pleasure through identification with the image seen. As constructed in the cinema, this division corresponds to that between the eroticized (passive) image of the woman on the one hand, and the ideal figure of the (active) screen hero, object of ego identification, on the other. Mulvey goes on to describe how this active/passive heterosexual division also determines narrative structure, so that the image of woman as erotic spectacle interrupts the flow of narrative, while the central male figure advances the story and, as the ideal ego of male fantasy, controls both events and the erotic gaze.

The figure of woman, however, is also identified for the male spectator with threat – the threat of castration and, hence, unpleasure. Ultimately, the meaning of woman is sexual difference, and the anxiety thus produced is mitigated by film in two ways: by voyeurism or by fetishism. The first strategy asserts control and produces narratives (for example, in *film noir*) in which the woman is investigated and punished; the second turns the woman into fetish object, disavowing her threat so that she, the overvalued female star, becomes reassuring rather than dangerous. Finally, Mulvey turns to the narrative and visual codes through which film, uniquely, controls the dimensions of time and space, producing an illusion cut to the measure of (male) desire. Radical film-makers and feminist critics, in exposing and breaking these codes, must seek to destroy conventional pleasurable expectations and 'conceive a new language of desire'.

These identifications – of the realist aesthetics of mainstream narrative cinema with patriarchal oppression, and of feminism with the 'negative aesthetics' of avant-garde film – are developed further in the 1978 essay 'Feminism, film and the avant-garde'. Here Mulvey, while sympathetic to the early feminist documentary films which borrowed *cinéma vérité* techniques to enact, and stimulate, the process of consciousness-raising for an audience of women's groups, nevertheless rejects their use of realist techniques. These techniques, she argues, remain tied to a concept of film as a transparent medium, and to dominant processes of cinematic identification. What is needed (following **Kristeva**) is a subversion of the means of meaning-making itself; in order that a new language of cinema might be developed, the old must be subjected both to theoretical analysis and to the 'negative aesthetics' and radical politics of a politicized feminist avant-garde practice.

In a further move in 1981, in 'Afterthoughts on "Visual pleasure and narrative cinema" inspired by *Duel in the Sun*', Mulvey turned to the questions of the female spectator and the female central protagonist (usually found in melodrama), ignored in her earlier account of the 'masculinized' cinematic spectator. Her account again turns to Freud – this time to his account of female psychic development, with its conclusion that maturity for women is achieved through the repression of active desire and the assumption of passivity. Popular cinema re-enacts this loss, its 'masculine' genres offering the female spectator, through trans-sex identification, a temporary, uneasy 'fantasy of masculinization', whilst the melodrama replays the process of loss itself, with the female protagonist relinquishing her own 'fantasy of masculinization' in the course of the narrative.

The impact of 'Visual pleasure and narrative cinema' on both feminist theory and film criticism was enormous. For example, the division between classical (patriarchal) realist cinema and radical (feminist) avant-garde film which underlies both it and Mulvey's own film-making (with Peter Wollen) structured both E. Ann Kaplan's (1983) *Women and Film* and Annette Kuhn's (1982) *Women's Pictures*, and was a founding principle of the journal *Camera Obscura* (founded 1976); her work on spectatorship and sexual difference was further developed by Mary Ann Doane (the 'woman's film') and Linda Williams (the horror film); her focus on Hitchcock was extended by Tania Modleski. At the same time, however, its reliance on psychoanalysis, however polemical in intent – and Mulvey herself later (1985) described the essay as 'a polemic, a challenge to dominant cinematic codes' – created considerable problems for feminist theory. While the use of psychoanalysis freed feminist theory from a concern with an essentialist 'truth' about women's experiences against which film images might be measured, a theory based on women's silence and exclusion leaves little space for feminist action on either culture or society.

The problem has two aspects. The first concerns the relation of this theory of cinematic subject construction to the social structure. Mulvey's active/passive binary pattern leaves no space for an active female spectator, or for the intersection of gender with class, race or other social differences to produce differences *between* women spectators. The second concerns Mulvey's dominant cinema/counter-cinema paradigm. Later feminist theory has been less convinced either of the inevitable identity of realism and patriarchal/bourgeois ideology or of the subversive potential of what has been termed the 'avant-garde theory film'. Mulvey's own later work acknowledges the limitations both of the original dualistic frame of reference and of the 'negative aesthetics' of counter-cinema, seeing both as the product of a historical moment at which change 'seemed to be just around the corner'. Rather than developing her early work on cinema, however, Mulvey's later work has instead turned to the relationship between myth, narrative and the processes of historical change, seeking both to rework Freud's myth of the oedipal founding moment and to situate historically the arguments in her own early essay, an essay which has itself become a sort of 'founding moment' of feminist cultural theory.

Main works

'Visual pleasure and narrative cinema', *Screen*, 16, 3 (1975).

'Notes on Sirk and Melodrama', *Movie*, 25–26 (1976–7).

'Feminism, film and the avant-garde', *Framework*, 10 (1979).

'Afterthoughts on "Visual pleasure and narrative cinema" inspired by King Vidor's *Duel in the Sun*', *Framework*, 15–17 (1981).

'Changes: thoughts on myth, narrative and historical experience', *History Workshop*, 23 (1987).

Visual and Other Pleasures, London: Macmillan, 1989.

Films (co-directed with Peter Wollen)

Penthesilea (1974).
Riddles of the Sphinx (1977).
AMY! (1980).
The Bad Sister (1983).

Further reading

Doane, Mary Ann, Patricia Mellencamp and Linda Williams, *Re-vision: Essays in feminist film criticism*, Bloomington, IN: American Film Institute, 1984.

Kaplan, E. Ann, *Women and Film*, London: Methuen, 1983.

Kuhn, Annette, *Women's Pictures*, London: Routledge, 1982.

Mayne, Judith, *Cinema and Spectatorship*, London: Routledge, 1993.

Silverman, Kaja, *The Acoustic Mirror*, Bloomington: Indiana University Press, 1988.

N

Ngugi wa Thiongo (1938–)

Ngugi wa Thiongo was born in Kamiriithu, Limuru, Kiambu District, in Kenya. His parents were members of the peasantry who worked on land which was owned by an African landlord. Despite their poverty the family were able to send Ngugi to school, and in 1955, 'largely due to a credit in English', Ngugi won a coveted place at the Alliance High School.

In 1959 Ngugi entered Makerere University College, Uganda, where he achieved a upper-second-class Honours degree in English. He was then awarded a British Council scholarship, which enabled him to study for an MA at the University of Leeds. He did not complete his degree, partly owning to a growing dissatisfaction with the concept of what he considered to be elitist degrees. During his time at Leeds, Ngugi began to explore the work of writers such as **Fanon**, **Marx** and Engels and it was during this period that his first novel, *Weep Not, Child*, was first published. In 1967 Ngugi became the first African member of staff at University College, Nairobi Kenya. It is significant that he was instrumental in mobilizing the impetus for the study of African literatures at an African university; hitherto this had been virtually unheard of.

Ngugi has always been actively involved in the struggles of the Kenyan peoples against the oppressive structures of neo-colonialism and capitalism. In 1977 the licence for the performance of his play *Ngaahika Ndeenda (I Will Marry When I Want)* was revoked by the government after its debut performance; it can be surmised that this was partly due to its revolutionary stance. It seems that the subversive aspects of the text were twofold. First, the play was performed by members of a villagers cooperative in Kamiriithu, and the production challenged the received assumptions as to what constituted theatre and – more importantly – art in an African context. Secondly, the production openly addressed the economic and political issues which are endemic to Kenya's politics. Shortly after this, Ngugi was detained under the Public Security Act 'for possessing banned books'. In 1978 he was adopted as a prisoner of conscience by Amnesty International, and later that year he was released from prison. Following further problems with the Kenyan government, he went into exile in Britain in 1978.

Although Ngugi's first published novel was written in 1962, his most significant work was published in the late 1970s and early 1980s. It is possible to trace his primary ideas in the large body of work which he has produced. Ngugi's work has always taken an uncompromising stance on the issues of colonialism, capitalism and the destabilizing effect of the African elite on the nascent African nations. These concerns have been focused primarily through the the prism of revolutionary socialism. At the same time, his concerns about these issues have fed into a wider critical debate, namely around the problematic relationship between African literatures and the English language (see **Achebe**), the relationship between language and culture and the revitalization of indigenous African cultures, linked to the notion that the proletariat cultures in Africa are the driving force behind the construction of national cultures.

All these ideas are explored in the collection of essays which make up *Moving the Centre* (1993) and *Decolonising the Mind* (1981). His seminal essay 'The language of African literature', in the latter text, explores the central debate which emerged in the 1970s with regard to African literatures: *namely*, could the English language be a suitable medium for the expression of the political, cultural and social realities of the African nations? Or could English, as Achebe had argued, be fashioned by the African writer so that it could 'bear the weight of our experience'? Ngugi's counterargument to this claim was that the use of English by African writers was incontrovertible evidence of their cultural enslavement. He has critiqued the tradition of African literatures written in English, on a number of grounds, suggesting that there is a direct correlation between language and culture. Thus imperialism's most devastating weapon against colonized peoples has been the 'cultural bomb' of the English language, which has stifled and stunted the growth of indigenous African cultures by effecting a *spiritual* enslavement of the African peoples. Ngugi has also argued that the basis for a revolutionary or resistance tradition is to be found in the oral traditions of the proletariat. Hence, the use of English in modern African cultural forms is instrumental in preventing the cultural renaissance of African states: 'The choice of language and the use to which it is put is central to a people's definition of themselves in relation to their social environments.' The logical extension of this line of thought is that language constructs the political and economic realities of African people.

Ngugi feels that cultural, economic and political enslavement is an insidious form of capitalism, represented in Africa by the 'black skins, white masks' of the African bourgeoisie. He has argued, on legitimate grounds, that the political and economic functions of the colonizing nations, have been assumed by an indigenous petty-bourgeois class. Thus the ethnic, class, religious and regional factions which have riven the African continent can be explained in terms of the natural side-effects of a specific economic system. Consequently, he claims:

> We must wholly Africanize and socialize our political and economic life. We must break with capitalism whose imperialistic stage – that of colonialism and neocolonialism – has done so much harm to Africa and dwarfed our total creative spirit. Capitalism can only produce anti-human culture that is only an expression of sectional warring interests. (Ngugi, 1972)

Given these well-documented political and economic concerns of the African subcontinent Ngugi has quite pertinently asked: how does a writer function in such a society?

An exploration of his novels – particularly *A Grain of Wheat, Petals of Blood,* and *Devil on the Cross* – provides evidence of Ngugi's revolutionary and interventionist stance on the issues of capitalism and the attendant problem of the exploitation of the proletariat. It is significant that the form of *Devil on the Cross,* his first novel in Gikuyu, is imitative of the modes of traditional oral narrative. This novel therefore pulls together the multifarious threads of his political writings over two decades. Consequently, it seems that the answer to his question, as explicated by his novels, is that the African writer must work in harmony with the liberation struggles of the proletariat, as opposed to commenting on society as a teacher.

Ngugi's ideas – particularly with regard to the isues that surround the use of the English language and his commitment to a revolutionary socialism – have had enduring reverberations within the field of African literature. They have also been invaluable critiques of the cultural hegemony of the European metropole. His conversion to the use of Gikuyu in the late 1970s, together with his obvious commitment as a political activist and writer, have helped to shift the debates within post-colonialism from the construction of post-colonial literatures as 'universal' texts, which are judged by Western standards of literature and art, to a domain in which post-colonial literatures are understood in terms of the specific cultural, political, economic and historical circumstances in which they are produced.

Main works

Weep Not, Child, London: Heinemann, 1962.

A Grain of Wheat, London: Heinemann, 1966.

Homecoming, London: Heinemann, 1972.

I Will Marry When I Want, London: Heinemann, 1977.

Decolonising the Mind, London: Heinemann, 1981.

Devil on the Cross, London: Heinemann, 1982.

Further reading

Bjorkman, I., *Mother Sing for Me*, London: Zed Press, 1989.

Cook, David and Michael Okenimkpe, *Ngugi: an exploration of his writing*, London: Heinemann, 1983.

Killam, G.D., *An Introduction to the Writings of Ngugi*, London: Heinemann, 1986.

Robson, C.B., *Ngugi wa Thiongo*, London: Macmillan, 1979.

Sicherman, C., *Ngugi wa Thiongo: The making of a rebel*, London: Hans Zell, 1990.

Nietzsche, Friedrich (1844–1900)

Born in Saxony on 15 October 1844, Friedrich Nietzsche was educated in Naumburg from 1852 to 1858 before moving to the famous Protestant school Schulpforta, where he received a classical education and founded an artistic society, 'Germania'. In 1864, he entered the University of Bonn, where he became a protégé of the philologist Ritschl, with whom he moved to the University of Leipzig in the following year; here Nietzsche first came into contact with the philosophy of Schopenhauer. In 1868 Nietzsche met Richard Wagner for the first time, while in 1869, at the age of 24, he was nominated Professor of Classical Philology at the University of Basel, where he became friends with the historian Jacob Burckhardt. Nietzsche's academic career received its first significant setback in 1872, when he published *The Birth of Tragedy out of the Spirit of Music*, which was greeted with harsh reviews. Between 1872 and 1878, when he finally resigned from the university on grounds of ill-health, Nietzsche published his *Untimely Meditations* and the first book of *Human, All Too Human*, in which he moved away from the influences of Schopenhauer and, in particular, Wagner towards a 'historical philosophy'. In the next four years, this development continued as Nietzsche completed *Human. All Too Human, Daybreak* and *The Gay Science*. These works were followed, in the period from 1882 to 1889, both by a series of historical and philosophical reflections on morality – notably *On the Genealogy of Morality* and *Beyond Good and Evil*, in which Nietzsche developed the ideas of genealogy and will to power – and by his enigmatic masterpiece *Thus Spake Zarathustra*, in which the doctrine of eternal recurrence and the notion of the Übermensch was presented. In 1889, just as he was beginning to achieve recognition, Nietzsche suffered complete mental collapse (possibly brought on by syphilis) and continued to live in this state until his death in 1900. A collection of unpublished notes, *The Will to Power*, appeared first in 1901 and was expanded in the following decade, while in 1908 Nietzsche's 'autobiography' *Ecce Homo* was published.

Friedrich Nietzsche, who stands with **Marx** and **Freud** as one of the major interpreters of modernity, is concerned throughout his philosophical career with the question of culture and, more specifically, of great culture – a culture which is constitutive of noble human beings. The significance of this question for Nietzsche is tied to his recognition that nineteenth century Europe, and Germany in particular, are characterized by a state of cultural exhaustion and a decline into decadence. Whereas Marx's diagnosis of modernity as capitalism is tied to his philosophical concern with the ways in which humanity reproduces the material conditions of its own existence (economic production), Nietzsche's diagnosis of modernity as nihilism is tied to his philosophical concern with the ways in which humanity reproduces its ideal conditions of existence (cultural production) – that is, our will to power.

Nietzsche's reflections on modernity may be divided into three periods: first, his early phase, which is specifically tied to *The Birth of Tragedy*, the *Untimely Meditations* and other unpublished writings from 1872 to 1876; secondly, his 'positivist' period, which runs from *Human, All Too Human* in 1878 to *The Gay Science* in 1882; finally, his mature work, which encompasses *Thus Spake Zarathustra* and all the works published thereafter. In each of these phases Nietzsche addresses the question of cultural renewal: through an appeal to art in the first period, through an appeal to science in the second period, and finally through a post-metaphysical aestheticization of ethics.

In early reflections on this question, such as *The Birth of Tragedy* (1872), Nietzsche looked to Greek tragedy, understood as the synthesis of the Apollonian (restraint, harmony, form) and the Dionysian (transgression, dissonance, energy), as an exemplary cultural site for the articulation of nobility. He argues that Greek tragedy was displaced by Socratic philosophy but that the Socratic tradition has now exhausted itself, consequently, cultural renewal could be secured through an artistic Socrates. Here Nietzsche looked to the music of

Wagner and the philosophy of Schopenhauer. However, between 1872 and his break with Wagner in 1876, he became increasingly sceptical about the possibility of a purely artistic basis for cultural renewal.

In his 'positivist' period, which lasts until the publication of *The Gay Science* in 1882, Nietzsche addresses the question of culture by focusing on developing a 'natural history' of cultural phenomena. In this period, Nietzsche is particularly concerned with giving a naturalistic account of the development of both scientific and moral consciousness. In *Human, All Too Human* and *Daybreak*, he develops this mode of historical philosophy as an unmasking of morality as entrenched cultural prejudices, and locates cultural renewal in terms of the potential of scientific consciousness to produce an ethic of probity and, consequently, a culture of self-legislating beings. This trajectory finds its fulfilment in *The Gay Science*, in which work Nietzsche announces the death of God and charts its implications for knowledge, ethics and art.

It is in *Thus Spake Zarathustra*, commonly regarded as Nietzsche's masterpiece, and the works which follow it, that Nietzsche recognizes that his faith in science is simply a refined form of the ascetic ideal whereby life is devalued in the name of metaphysics. This metaphysical asceticism is constitutive of contemporary nihilism, the valuelessness of existence, on Nietzsche's account insofar as scientific consciousness displaces moral consciousness, only to find that in undermining all moral grounds of value for existence, science has also undermined any ground of value of truth. Scientific (causal) explanation rules out meaning, only to find that as a result the activity of science has become meaningless. To overcome nihilism, on Nietzsche's account, consequently requires the provision of a post-metaphysical ground of value for human existence which will transform our relation to both morality and knowledge. Nietzsche's attempt to provide such an overcoming of nihilism is the doctrine of eternal recurrence, in which the recognition of our becoming what we are as this-worldly activity is tied to the recognition of art as the only post-metaphysical ground of value. This produces an affective thought-experiment in which the affirmation of the eternal recurrence of one's existence acts as a test of the degree to which one's life is a work of art, and thus possesses intrinsic value. The *Übermensch* is the individual who exhibits the stylistic constraint demanded by the doctrine of eternal recurrence. Here the metaphysical understanding of ethical impartiality and cognitive objectivity as a God's-eye view is refigured in terms of the contestation of the plural perspectives of embodied and embedded agents.

The central problem with Nietzsche's mature response to the question of cultural renewal, a problem which is performatively enacted in *Thus Spake Zarathustra*, is that Nietzsche cannot legislate his post-metaphysical ground of value because he cannot ground the authority of either his diagnosis or his cure. Moreover, in refiguring ethics and knowledge as the contestation of plural perspectives, Nietzsche places the problem of judgement at the heart of contemporary thinking, yet provides no clear account of judgement in his work.

The depth of Nietzsche's cultural impact is almost unimaginable. His thought found a receptive audience among writers and poets such as W.B. Yeats, G.B. Shaw, Stefan Georg, Thomas Mann, Herman Hesse, D.H. Lawrence and Kenneth White. Before the period of the Nazi appropriation of his name, Nietzsche's thought was deployed by anarchist, feminist and socialist movements in German politics, and decisively influenced intellectuals such Georg Simmel and Karl Jaspers, while Max Weber commented that the honesty of the modern scholar could be judged by how much he acknowledged that Marx and Nietzsche are the foundations for modern thought. More recently, Nietzsche has been read as central to the existentialist thinking of **Sartre**, the aesthetic thinking of **Adorno**, the genealogical thinking of **Foucault**, the deconstructive approach of Heidegger and **Derrida**, the philosophy of desire presented by **Deleuze**, and the postmodernism of **Lyotard**.

Main works

Thus Spake Zarathustra [1883–5], trans. R.J. Hollingdale, Harmondsworth: Penguin, 1961.

Beyond Good and Evil [1886], trans. Walter Kaufmann, New York: Random House, 1966.

The Birth of Tragedy out of the Spirit of Music [1872]/ *The Case against Wagner* [1888], trans. Walter Kaufmann, New York: Random House, 1967.

Twilight of the Idols [1889]/ *The Antichrist* [1895], trans. R.J. Hollingdale, Harmondsworth: Penguin, 1968.

The Gay Science [1882], trans. Walter Kaufmann, New York: Random House, 1974.

Daybreak [1881], trans. R.J. Hollingdale, Cambridge: Cambridge University Press, 1982.

Untimely Meditations [1873–6], trans. R.J. Hollingdale, Cambridge: Cambridge University Press, 1983.

Human, All Too Human [1878–80], trans. R.J. Hollingdale, Cambridge: Cambridge University Press, 1986.

On the Genealogy of Morality [1887], ed. K. Ansell–Pearson, trans. C. Diethe, Cambridge: Cambridge University Press, 1994.

Further reading

Allison, David B., *The New Nietzsche*, New York: Dell Publishing, 1977.

Ansell–Pearson, Keith, *An Introduction to Nietzsche as Political Thinker: The perfect nihilist*, Cambridge: Cambridge University Press, 1994.

Deleuze, Gilles, *Nietzsche and Philosophy*, New York: Athlone Press, 1983.

Kaufmann, Walter, *Nietzsche: Philosopher, psychologist, antichrist*, Princeton, NJ: Princeton University Press, 1974.

Nehamas, Alexander, *Nietzsche: Life as literature*, Cambridge, MA: Harvard University Press, 1985.

Solomon, Robert and Kathleen Higgins (eds), *Reading Nietzsche*, Oxford: Oxford University Press, 1988.

Norris, Christopher Charles (1947–)

Christopher Norris, a London-born literary critic and history of ideas specialist, is Professor in the Department of Philosophy at the University of Wales College of Cardiff. In 1975 Norris was awarded a PhD for his work on William **Empson** and the philosophy of literary criticism, and in 1978, having taught at University College, London and the University of Duisburg, West Germany, he accepted a post in the English Department of the University of Wales Institute of Science and Technology, Cardiff, where, in 1985, he became a Reader. In 1987 he moved to the English Department at the College of Cardiff, and received a Personal Chair that same year. Norris has held visiting professorships in the Department of Rhetoric at the University of California, Berkeley, and in the Graduate Center at City University in New York, and has been an Associate Fellow at the University of Warwick Centre for Research in Philosophy and Literature since 1990. He is currently on the editorial advisory board of *The Southern Review, Contemporary Literary Criticism, The Belgrade Circle, Philosophy and Literature* and *Prose Studies,* and was the reviews editor for *Textual*

Practice until 1993. He is also general editor for the 'Critics of the Twentieth Century' series, published by Croom Helm.

Norris's work to date is as wide-ranging as it is critical. It is unique in that it represents an almost single-handed attempt to recover what he views as the critical potential of deconstruction by foregrounding its relationship to analytical philosophy. This project has both led him to defend the autonomy of philosophy as a discipline committed to reasoned argument, a discipline grounded in an epistemological truth not reduced simply to 'what's God in the way of belief', and, ironically, made him contribute to the deconstruction of traditional disciplinary boundaries by his mere participation, as a literary critic, in the debate between neo-pragmatists and analytical philosophers. Arguing specifically against a radical pragmatism which 'has the effect of levelling out truth-claims to a point where they all appear as options thrown up by different kinds of cultural self-interest' (Norris, 1985), Norris charges certain American and continental philosophers (Richard **Rorty**, Jean-François **Lyotard** and Jean **Baudrillard** in particular) with deliberately dismantling a philosophical machinery – theory, dialectics, mediating concepts – which would 'challenge that "naturalized" relation between history, reason and present-day consensus values' (*ibid.*). He holds up Jürgen **Habermas** as one who has engaged the postmodern 'legitimation crisis' (Lyotard) – the fact that Enlightenment values seem to have no positive influence in the late modernist context – but has refused to relinquish rational critique to the blind demands of consensus. By far the bulk of Norris's work has been directed towards – in both the literary and philosophical contexts – preventing the uncritical conflation of the content of thought with its formal expression, and it is this commitment that becomes apparent in his reading of deconstruction.

Deconstruction: Theory and practice (1982), an early attempt to popularize the basic assumptions behind a critique of Western metaphysics and to indicate its implications for literary theory, is arguably Norris's best-known book worldwide. Two later books – *Jacques Derrida* (1987) and *Paul de Man: Deconstruction and the critique of aesthetic ideology* (1988) – deal in more depth with the two leading thinkers in the field: In *Derrida* he draws on the philosophical underpinnings of **Derrida's** work, explicating in the process what makes deconstruction, as a non-method and non-strategy, critically both intertextual (and hence 'literary') and not anti-philosophical. The double negative is important here, for it designates Derrida's desire for a 'non-site, or a non-philosophical site, from which to question philosophy', and it is precisely this orientation – this anti-position position – that, for Norris, makes deconstruction a potent ideological critique. Norris's work remains unique among Derrida's commentators in the way it consistently distinguishes between those essays that pursue a rigorous and unrelentingly reasoned critique of philosophy, and those that enact the excessive literariness of all texts.

In *Paul de Man*, the philosophy/literature dichotomy that Derrida's work calls into question is again foregrounded in what Norris reads as the critical potential of **de Man**'s deconstruction of the category of the aesthetic, in particular as it is articulated in Romantic ideology. Here, literary criticism is seen as colluding with philosophy in claiming to read a reconciliation between phenomenal or sensory perception, cognition and rhetoric, the conditions necessary for communicative felicity, and ultimately knowledge. Norris places de Man firmly in the tradition of 'radical *Ideologiekritik*', along with **Marx**, **Adorno** and **Althusser**. This book was written primarily before the 1987 revelation of de Man's wartime journalism, the early articles written in *Le Soir* during the Nazi occupation of Belgium which were demonstrably anti-Semitic. But in a 'postscript' to the 1988 publication of this book, Norris acknowledges the possible autobiographical impulse behind de Man's thinking, reiterating Derrida in making a distinction between the case of Heidegger (his deliberate and forthright participation in developing an ideology which would 'spiritualize' National Socialism and confirm the inevitable destiny of everything Germanic) and de Man's youthful indiscretions. Rather than viewing de Man's career as an attempt to cover up an unfortunate insinuation into fascist ideology, Norris sees him as 'a conceptual rhetorician, one for whom all truth-claims must be called into question through a close examination of language in its suasive and tropological modes, but for whom nevertheless such questioning conduces to better, more enlightened thought' (1988).

Much of Norris's late work has been directed towards redressing what he sees as an unfortunate appropriation of deconstruction in much 'postmodern' speculation, one that dispenses with the rigorous and unrelenting arguments of its original practitioners. The effects of this wholesale abandonment of all forms of enlightened critique capable of referencing political realities – a critique still implicit in deconstruction at its best – were borne out during the Gulf War: Jean Baudrillard's initial claim that the Gulf War would not happen because war was now simply a word cast up in the management of public opinion, an imaginary construct bearing no reliable, unmediated relation to reality, and his later claim that the outbreak of war could not be read as an event without its declaration, effectively reduced the catastrophe to a mere simulation. In *Uncritical Theory: Postmodernism intellectuals and the Gulf War* (1992), Norris argues that the sheer outrage of this thesis is made possible by

> a half-baked mixture of ideas picked up from the latest fashionable sources, or a series of slogans to the general effect that 'truth' and 'reality' are obsolete

ideas, that knowledge is always and everywhere a function of the epistemic will-to-power, and that history is nothing but fictive construct out of the various 'discourses' that jostle for supremacy from one period to the next (1992).

The undoubted hero of this book is Noam **Chomsky**, who – despite the general reluctance or outright refusal of intellectuals to take a stand on what Norris views as another instance of American imperialism at its most blatant – 'maintains the continued relevance of a critical-rationalist outlook that rejects the *tout court* equation of reason and truth with current consensus beliefs' (1992). Norris attributes this essentially ethical disposition directly to a theory of language which does not dissolve human reason in unlimited semiosis.

The impact of Norris's work, in particular his defence of deconstruction, can be measured by the prolific nature of his writing. He has been proclaimed 'the most philosophically astute of all British literary theorists, and increasingly one of the most politically important, subjecting the jaded scepticisms of our time to a scintillating critique' (**Eagleton**). What Eagleton's statement highlights is Norris's consistent attempt to foreground the political implications of all theory, even that which aspires to the status of non-theory.

Main works

William Empson and the Philosophy of Literary Criticism, London: Athlone Press, 1978.

Deconstruction: Theory and practice, London: Methuen, 1982, second edn (expanded and revised) London: Routledge, 1991.

The Deconstructive Turn: Essays in the rhetoric of philosophy, London: Methuen, 1985a.

The Contest of Faculties: Philosophy and theory after deconstruction, London: Methuen, 1985b.

Jacques Derrida, London: Fontana and Cambridge, MA.: Harvard University Press, 1987.

Paul de Man: Deconstruction and the criticism of aesthetic ideology, New York and London: Routledge, 1988a.

Deconstruction and the Interests of Theory, London: Pinter and Norman, Oklahoma University Press, 1988b.

What's Wrong with Postmodernism: Critical theory and the ends of philosophy, Hemel Hempstead: Harvester Wheatsheaf and Baltimore, MD: Johns Hopkins University Press, 1990a.

Spinoza and the Origins of Modern Critical Theory, Oxford: Blackwell, 1990b.

Uncritical Theory: postmodernism, intellectuals and the Gulf War, London: Lawrence & Wishart and Amherst, MA: University of Massenchusetts Press, 1992.

The Truth about Postmodernism, Oxford: Blackwell, 1993.

Truth and the Ethics of Criticism, Manchester: Manchester University Press, 1994.

Further reading

Rorty, Richard, 'Two meanings of "logocentrism": a reply to Norris', in Dasenbrock, Reed Way (ed.), Re-*Drawing the Lines: analytic philosophy, deconstruction and literary theory*, Minneapolis: University of Minnesota Press, 1989, pp. 189–203, 204–16.

Postmodern Jurisprudence: the law of text in the texts of law, Douzinas, Costa, Ronnie Warrington, Shaun McVeigh, chapter 2, 'Law (un)Like literature – who's afraid of pragmatism?', London: Routledge, 1991, pp. 136–50.

Kermode, Frank, 'Theory and Truth', *London Review of Books*, 13, 22, (1991) 9–10.

Nuttall, A.D. 'Return of the real', *London Review of Books*, 14 (23 April 1993) 5–6.

Paine, Michael, Introduction to *Spinoza and the Origins of Modern Critical Theory* (Norris, 1990), pp. 1–10.

P

Propp, Vladimir Yakovlevich (1895–1970)

Propp, having graduated in Russian and German Philology at Petrograd University in 1918, became a language teacher in schools. He returned to the University to work first in languages and then, from 1938, as a folklorist, having been appointed professor. He was never a member of OPOYAZ (Russian acronym for the society for the study of Poetic Language), but he was close to the Formalists in his thinking. Like the Formalists, he was attacked in the 1930s and 1940s.

Dissatisfied with the then orthodox approach to the study of folktales, especially methods of classification which tended to stress themes, motifs, or names – e.g. The Tale of the Tsar who had three daughters – Propp, following **Shklovsky**, turned his attention to the basic structures of the folktale, and in *The Morphology of the Folktale* (1928) he published his findings, based on a study of 100 Russian tales from the Afanasiev collection. He compared the following events, taken from different tales:

1. A tsar gives an eagle to a hero. The eagle carries the hero away to another kingdom.

2. An old man gives Suchenko a horse. The horse carries Suchenko away to another kingdom.

3. A sorcerer gives Ivan a little boat. The boat takes Ivan to another kingdom.

4. A princess gives Ivan a ring. Young men, appearing out of the ring, carry Ivan away to another kingdom.

These statements possess variables and constants. The characters and their attributes change, the action and the function do not. That is: A gives X to Y. X carries Y away.

A (tsar; old man; sorcerer; princess)

X (eagle; horse; little boat; ring)

Y (hero; Suchenko; Ivan; Ivan)

Action + function = constants: 'giving in order to carry away'.

According to Propp, the Tale is predicated on sets of rules, whereby the function is the basic component of the tale; the number of functions is limited to 31; the sequence is always constant. The absence or presence of functions (no tale gives evidence of all 31) serves as the basis of a classification of plots, of which there are four: development through a struggle or victory; development through the accomplishment of a difficult task; development through both; development through neither. Each function is given a letter of the alphabet, beginning with A *Villainy* through H *The hero struggles with the villain* I *Victory over the villain* M *Difficult task* N *Solution of the difficult task* and ending with W *Wedding or Accession to the Throne*. Tales might be made up of two series of functions called moves. For example, the first might end with the hero's rescue, return home and marriage. A further villainy ushers in a second move. The tale, however, remains a single tale. Finally, Propp distinguished seven fields of operation in the plot: villain; donor; helper; princess (a sought-for person) and her father; dispatcher; hero; false hero. A character might be a donor in one tale or a helper in another.

An annotation of one of Propp's own examples of an analysis of a tale will clarify the approach. This is a simple, single-move tale, H–I classification. The kidnapping of three daughters constitutes the villainy A1, the beginning of the 'zavyazka' ('Complication'). A preparatory section, represented by Greek letters, incorporates the following: 'Once upon a time there lived a tsar who had three daughters' (α). 'The daughters went for a walk in the palace garden' ($\beta3$ – departure of younger persons). 'Here they tarried, even though they had been commanded by their father not to do so' ($\delta1$: violation of command). 'The dragon kidnapped them' (A1). 'They called for help' (B1). 'Three heroes, hearing their cries, set out' (C$\uparrow$). 'Three battles were fought with the dragon' (H1–I1). 'The heroes rescued the daughters' (K4). 'They returned home' ($\downarrow$). 'The heroes were rewarded' (Wo).

The analysis would be expressed thus:

$$\alpha \ \beta3 \ \delta1 \ A1 \ B1 \ C\uparrow \ H1{-}I1 \ K4 \ \downarrow \ Wo$$

Although Propp has become known as the father of narratology, he did not in fact set himself the task of trying to establish the laws governing all narrative. That is clear from the title of his pioneering study. The *Morphology of the Folktale*. The title in Russian and English is partly to blame. The Russian editors removed the adjective 'magic'. The Afanasiev collection were all tales in which a magical agent played a part. *Morphology of the Wondertale* would be a more accurate translation. Later he preferred 'Composition' to 'Morphology'. In other words, he is dealing with a particular genre. Propp replied to **Lévi-Strauss's** criticisms (1960) in the introduction to a 1966 Italian version of the *Morphology*. In an old-worldly, gentlemanly manner he rejected Lévi-Strauss's view that one begins with a method and then decides where to apply it. Propp acted in an empirical fashion, scrupulously observing the wondertales and reaching the conclusion that functions are their basic components. He dismissed Lévi-Strauss's charge of ahistorical formalism, arguing that his *Morphology* found a logical extension in 'Historical roots of the wondertale' (1946), which revealed a more detailed, more explicit conjoining of empirical observation and historical explanation. As early as 1928 he had begun to explore this in 'Fairy tale transformations'? Finally, he argued that Lévi-Strauss's work on myth prevented him from fully appreciating not only his (Propp's) choice of subject for study – wondertales rather than myths – but also his goal.

Initially Propp had scant influence in his own country, because he was being tarred with the brush of Formalism. His work was, however, recognized there in the late 1960s. From the moment of his 'discovery' by the West in the 1960s Propp profoundly influenced continental and Anglo-American structural anthropologists and structuralist thinkers alike. His isolation of action and function as constant elements in the structure of the tales has, interestingly enough, been the starting point for the exploration of how narrative in general works. In France, Lévi-Strauss, despite his disagreements with Propp, acknowledged the importance of his *Morphology:* as did **Greimas**, who wished to establish universal structures lying beneath the surface of the plot, and dechronologized Propp's functions, regrouping them in terms of homologies and oppositions. Bremond left aside existing texts, and tried to assess text potentiality. Despite the criticism that Propp's theoretical work in *Morphology* is capable of only limited application, there have been some impressive results, notably in the area of arguably less sophisticated texts: the formulaic plots of Hollywood Dream Factory films, Hitchcock films, myths, detective and mystery stories.

Main works

The Morphology of the Folktale, trans. Laurence Scott; Austin and London: University of Texas Press American Folklore Society Bibliographical and Special Series Volume 9, 1958.

'Fairy tale transformations' in *Readings in Russian Poetics*, Ladislav Matejka and Krystyna Pomorska (eds), Cambridge MA: Massachusetts Institute of Technology Press, 1971.

'Ritual laughter in folklore. A propos of the Tale of the Princess who would not laugh', in Vladimir Propp; *Theory and History of Folklore*, trans. Ariadra Y. Martin and Richard P. Martin, Manchester: Manchester University Press, 1984.

'Istoricheskie korni volshebnoi skazki', Leningrad, 1946. Extracts translated as 'Historical roots of the wondertale', in *Theory and History of Folklore*

'Russkii geroicheskii epos', Leningrad, 1955. Extracts translated as 'Russian heroic poetry', in *Theory and History of Folklore*. This work also contains Propp's reply to Lévi-Strauss.

Further reading

Lévi-Strauss, Claude, 'Structure and form: reflections on a work by Vladimir Propp', in *Structural Anthropology 2* (1973), Harmondsworth: Penguin, 1976.

Liberman, Anatoly (ed.) Introduction to *Vladimir Propp Theory and History of Folklore*, Manchester: Manchester University Press, 1984, pp. ix–lxxxi.

Meletinsky, E., 'The structural-typological study of the folktale', in P. Maranda (ed.), *Soviet Structural Folkloristics*, vol. 1, The Hague: Mouton, 1974.

Shukman, Ann, 'The legacy of Propp', in *Essays in Poetics*, 1/2, Keele: University of Keele, 1976.

Wollen, Peter, '*North by North West*: a morphological analysis', *Film Form*, 1, London, 1976, pp. 19–34.

R

Rich, Adrienne (1929–)

Adrienne Rich was born in Baltimore in 1929. She graduated from
Radcliffe College in 1951, the same year in which her first collection of
poetry, *A Change in the World*, was published. Subsequent publications
have established Rich as one of America's most distinguished modern
poets. However, her poetry is only part of her contribution to
contemporary culture, for she has also published a number of
provocative and well-known prose works in which she has, in various
ways, not only developed new categories which have become central in
cultural analysis, but also provided a difference of view with respect to
methodology and focus. Her early poetry and prose writings can be
seen as part of a movement of women's voices in the 1960s and 1970s
(such as those of Betty Friedan, Germaine Greer, Juliet Mitchell, Tillie
Olsen and Shulamith Firestone) which has had a profound and
sustained impact on the development of feminism both within and
outside the academy.

Adrienne Rich is more frequently discussed with respect to her work as
a poet, but she has also made a substantial contribution to feminist
thought, knowledge and practice. It is necessary here to focus on her
prose essays and polemics. This in many respects is not wholly
appropriate, because one of Rich's concerns as a writer is to explore the
connections and intersections between all aspects of what it is to be a
woman living, working, writing within a particular culture. Her whole
body of work is therefore testimony to the development and working
through of many ideas on this, and her work draws on history,
mythology, anthropology, medicine, psychology and literature, as well
as her own experience and memory. In this respect Rich is an example
of a particular methodological approach which has been adopted,
adapted and analyzed within what we might want to label as cultural/
women's studies within the academy. Rich acknowledges in her new
foreword to the latest edition of *Of Woman Born* how her early writings
were informed in particular by the 'instruments then most familiar to
me: my own experience, literature by white and middle-class Anglo–

Saxon women'. She notes also how these writings became a lens she looked through in order to frame her analysis.

The centrality of ideas about perception and perspective are a vital concern for Rich, and she is constantly looking at the tensions and contradictions in any of the specific areas in which she is engaged. From her collection *Of Lies, Secrets and Silences* one can gain an instant insight to her areas of investigation: these range from the more literary to specific essays on working conditions, teaching and learning as a woman in the university system, motherhood and lesbianism. It is in the essays 'When we dead awaken: writing as re-vision' and 'Toward a woman-centred university' that some of her main ideas can be found. In the first essay Rich is at pains to point out the need for a new approach to research into literature and literary traditions. This essay, written in 1971, can be seen as one of the first articulations of the now perceived school of feminist criticism that has grown up since. The key to Rich's essay is the importance of re-vision and the way in which this provides both a basis for critical practice and a methodological position. Through the adoption of this approach Rich maintains that 'a whole new psychic geography' is there to be explored. This approach has been of central importance in feminist scholarship particularly in the analysis of literary texts of the past.

In 'Towards a woman-centred university', Rich is issuing a warning to women as feminists who are working in the academy. The essay works as a valuable insight into the role that universities play as cultural institutions within patriarchal society. This essay, written in 1973–4, is concerned to build upon the work of feminists of the past, such as the eighteenth-century feminist Mary Wollstonecraft, who had believed that when women had equal educational opportunities with men, the latter would no longer have an assumed superiority and power. Rich's argument works to suggest that in the twentieth century this has not actually been the case, for even though women and men appear to have equal access to educational opportunity, what is actually happening within the institutions is that women have to learn and fulfil masculine criteria, and follow a masculine curriculum and expectations. Rich not only extends the arguments of Mary Wollstonecraft but also uses ideas from Virginia Woolf's polemic *Three Guineas* (published in 1938) in which Woolf notes the exclusion of female-centred ideas and values in public forums, and how educational institutions are largely responsible for this continuation. Like Woolf, Rich wants to see on the curriculum the histories of women, their experiences and their ideas. For Rich, the presence of women within the academy was not enough to indicate change. She states that change will be made possible only when 'the centre of gravity shifted'; only then 'will women really be free to learn, to teach, to share strength, to explore, to criticize, and to convert knowledge to power'.

In *Of Woman Born: Motherhood as experience and institution*, Rich was one of the first feminists to provide a historical analysis of motherhood. In this she works to unravel the myths of 'the Mother' and the regulatory practices within various cultures to control and constrain this role for society's own ends. One of the central concerns in this book was to become the foundation for a later work, *Compulsory Heterosexuality and the Lesbian Experience*, for Rich was concerned to ask why, 'if heterosexuality was so natural', was it necessary to have such regulatory practices to keep women in their place? In the later work, published in 1981, she is thus concerned to take on what Dale **Spender** calls 'the taboo against questioning heterosexuality', a taboo that has been deliberately constructed, according to Rich, to keep patriarchal discourse and power at the centre. In this work Rich is at pains to provide a new category and language in which to discuss lesbianism. Her terms 'lesbian existence' and 'lesbian continuum' are an attempt to distance herself from the ways in which patriarchal discourse works with these terms in respect of 'sex'. Rich wants to move further to construct a woman-centred terminology.

In forging these categories Rich is concerned to extend the discussions of relationships between women, and the ways in which they share and support beyond the 'genital sexual experience'. In this way she wants to create a way of thinking which moves away from the compulsion of seeing men and heterosexuality at the centre of all women's relationships and activities.

An extension of arguments about similarities and differences between women also appears in Rich's essay, 'Disloyal to civilization: feminism, racism, gynephobia', published in 1980. Here she investigates the complexities, the contradictions and the painful debates that have occurred between feminists over the issue of race. She points out that even though women cannot be held responsible in the first instance for racism and imperialism, there is a danger for all of us in colluding in and perpetuating dominant ideas about race and gender. In order to avoid this, she asserts that even issues which are painful have to be discussed openly between women, and not hidden in silence or organized to perpetuate hierarchical ways of thinking about oppression.

Adrienne Rich's contribution both to literary criticism and feminist/ cultural studies works to connect the personal and the public world and to assert the importance of the personal as a category for criticism. Central to Rich's work has been the need to foreground the importance of gender, class, race, nationality and sexual orientation in the development of new ideas and knowledge. Her ideas about the need for 're-vision' have been taken up by other feminists working in cultural theory, literary criticism and women's history. 'Toward a woman-centred university' still has resonance and influence for women working within the academy today, and has provided a framework for debates on teaching, learning, gender and power. In Norway the influence has been made much more concrete by the efforts of Bent Ås, who – as Dale Spender records – attempts to establish a feminist university as opposed to trying to work within the structures and institutions already in existence.

The indebtedness of feminists working in a range of disciplines to the work of Adrienne Rich is profound, but may not always appear fully to acknowledge her early work in the areas which have now become the familiar territory of cultural studies as well as feminist criticism: investigation into gender, sexual orientation, race, class and power.

Main works

Of Woman Born: Motherhood as experience and institution, London: Virago, 1977.

Women and Honour: Notes on lying, London: Onlywomen Press, 1979.

On Lies, Secrets and Silences: Selected Prose 1966–1978, New York: Norton, 1979, London: Virago, 1980.

Blood, Bread and Poetry, London: Virago, 1987.

Poetry and Prose, New York: Norton Critical Editions, 1993.

Further reading

Gilbert, Sandra and Susan Gubar (eds), *Shakespeare's Sisters: Feminist essays on women poets*, Bloomington: Indiana University Press, 1985.

Gunew, Sneja (ed.), *Feminist Knowledge: Critique and construct*, London: Routledge, 1990.

Gunew, Sneja (ed.), *A Reader in Feminist Knowledge*, London: Routledge, 1991.

Miller, Jane, *Seductions: Studies in reading and culture*, London: Virago, 1990.

Spender, Dale, *For the Record: The making and meaning of feminist knowledge*, London: The Women's Press, 1985.

York, Liz, *Impertinent Voices: Subversive strategies in contemporary women's poetry*, London: Routledge, 1991.

Glossary

Re-vision:

The act of looking back, of seeing with fresh eyes, of entering an old text from a new critical direction – is for women more than a chapter in cultural history: it is an act of survival. Until we can understand the assumptions in which we are drenched we cannot know ourselves. And this drive to self-knowledge, for women, is more than a search for identity, it is part of our refusal of the self-destructiveness of male-dominated society.

Richards, I.A. (1893–1979)

Ivor Armstrong Richards was one of the most influential figures in twentieth-century Anglo-American literary criticism. His theoretical position was largely established in a series of books written during the 1920s, as a member of the recently founded English School at Cambridge University (though his own training was primarily in philosophy). After teaching in China during the 1930s, he became lecturer in literary criticism, then Professor of English, at Harvard University, where he remained Professor Emeritus until his death in 1979, outlasting the period of his greatest influence but remaining an important reference point for critical theory in the United States until the 1960s.

Richards draws eclectically upon a range of earlier writers, including Coleridge, Arnold, Mill and G.E. Moore, as well as upon contemporary work in semantics, psychology and neurophysiology, in his project of setting literary criticism on a 'scientific' footing for the first time. His theory can be summarized, with some simplification and some merging of ideas from different works, as follows.

A symbol, such as a word, is connected to the object it symbolizes by virtue of being used to communicate a reference to that object. (The term 'reference' is distinctively employed by Richards to denote not an utterance but a mental act, perhaps best explained as the registering or 'finding' of an object. A 'belief' is a compound of simple references, united by relations which give the belief its logical form.) There is no direct or necessary relation between symbol and object. The meaning of a symbol is given by its use, and to ascribe inherent meaning to symbols is to invite error. A word can have a multitude of meanings depending on the contexts in which it is used; distinguishing among these is a crucial task for the literary critic or other interpreter.

A symbol is a special kind of 'sign', used for communication. A sign is a part of a psychological complex formed by constantly conjoined memories: the sign serves to evoke the entire complex, as hearing the dinner-gong evokes the complex idea of dinner. The interpretation of an utterance or other symbolic act needs to take account of this complex context or 'sign-situation', not merely of the referent. The phrases 'morning star' and 'evening star', to borrow Frege's example, refer to the same referent, but we have no difficulty in recognizing that their meaning is different because each is a part of a different psychological complex.

Metaphor is a 'transaction between contexts', linking two otherwise separated psychological complexes by virtue of a shared feature, and so producing a new complex; it is therefore no mere decorative adjunct, but a fundamental creative and integrative principle of all language. Richards notes that the 'tenor' and 'vehicle' of a metaphor – terms he himself introduced into literary criticism – have a varying relation: sometimes, as in Symbolist poetry, the vehicle is more important than the tenor; often the expressive force of the metaphor lies in the (emotionally significant) difference between the contexts as much as in their (intellectually significant) resemblance, as when Hamlet speaks of such fellows as himself 'crawling', vermin-like, between earth and heaven.

Language is used not only to communicate 'references' but for many other purposes, including the expression or promotion of 'attitudes' (which are other components of the psychological complex associated with the symbol, and are to be understood as affective or intentional states of mind). The use which terminates in references is the scientific use of language; that which aims to bring about or to support attitudes, either by means of the references or by the immediate effect of the 'arrangements of words', is the emotive use of language, characteristic of 'poetry' in the widest sense.

The purpose of literature, and of the arts in general, is therefore radically severed from that of science. It lies not in the transmission of factual knowledge but in the communication of states of mind which are of high psychological value. Richards rejects the idea, propounded by Kant and Schopenhauer, that these states are of a special kind, 'disinterested' because dissociated from our general emotional life; on the contrary, they are ordinary experiences subjected to a particular kind of organisation by the artist. Richards advances a sophisticated utilitarian theory of value: the satisfaction of psychical 'impulses' is a good (though some impulses lead to more valuable experiences than others); impulses, however, are liable to impede one another's satisfaction, and the fortunate are those who have or develop psychical 'clearing-houses' in which the claims of different impulses are adjusted to one another. Aesthetic organization accomplishes just such a balancing and reconciliation of impulses, promoting an ideal psychosomatic equilibrium which makes for heightened 'vigilance', for 'freedom and fullness of life'. The Kantian disinterestedness is reinterpreted as liberation from the tyranny of the particular, singular impulse. The poet (as Eliot also famously affirmed) is distinguished by his ability to connect and synthesize disparate experiences, to achieve 'an intricately wrought composure'. The benefit for readers lies not in the transient intensity of ecstatic moments, as Pater had maintained, but in 'permanent modifications to the structure of the mind' which, according to Richards, may be produced in a person by the experience of art, and may subsequently be communicated to others.

The most concrete and detailed application of Richards's ideas to literary texts is in his enormously influential volume *Practical Criticism* (1929). Richards presented the comments of Cambridge undergraduates (aged 19 or 20 in most cases) on a number of unseen poems, and drew on his theory in analyzing, evaluating, and (usually) disparaging their responses and judgements. Confusion of poetic utterance with 'scientific' statement, inattention to the integrative use of metaphor, misinterpretation of words through neglect of context, are duly excoriated. Yet the strength and the weakness of the book both lie in the extent to which its strictures escape the confines of Richards's theory and fix upon two relatively simple discoveries: firstly, that readers often – indeed, normally, on a first encounter – read texts partially, and with obstructive presuppositions derived from the experience of other texts or from other cultural sources; secondly, that emotional experience and maturity, or lack of them, influence the reading of a poem. The book consequently presents a powerful case not so much for Richards's specific aesthetic as for a sustained practice of close reading and collaborative analysis, and for a recognition that the significance of a literary text for different readers, or the same reader at different times, will vary.

The dominance, over half a century, of 'practical criticism' as a teaching strategy and a basis for literary analysis is the most unambiguous testimony to Richards's influence. It is harder to authenticate his influence on other writers, since common sources such as Arnold or Eliot may also be in play, but there are few English-language critics of the middle third of the century whose work does not in some way emulate or resemble Richards's. His Cambridge pupil William **Empson** developed Richards's insight into the polyvalency of metaphor in his *Seven Types of Ambiguity* (1930). F.R. and Q.D. **Leavis** eschewed Richards's psychological and semantic theories, and his preference for systematic argument, while amplifying, and moralizing, his claim that the educative power of literature lies in communicating rich possibilities of valuable experience. The American 'New Critics' preferred to play down the affective element in Richards's theory (**Wimsatt and**

Beardsley implicitly accusing him of confusion between 'the poem and its results'), but followed him in their view of the poem as achieving a unique integration of experience, through a structure which is not essentially that of its logical meaning or its versification but, rather, a linguistic complex characterized by organizing metaphor.

Richards's influence has now entirely faded – partly as a result of the cycle of fashion but partly, and ironically, because of his over confident appeal to 'scientific' psychological and linguistic models which enjoyed the prestige of modernity in the 1920s but now appear superseded. His semantic theory has elements which anticipate the later Wittgenstein (most obviously the identification of meaning with use in context), but it is Wittgenstein who is still read, or at least cited, by literary theorists. Richards's style – pedagogic, painstaking, confidential, liable to capitalized abstractions and heavy-handed jokes – looked professional in the 1920s but looks amateurish or at least dated now. His claims for the transformative power of literature seem overstated, in part because they are tied to an insufficiently grounded concept of emotional 'belief' supposedly engendered by art (in counterposition to the intellectual belief commanded by science) and likened by Richards to 'the state which follows the conclusive answering of a question'. In his later writings, culminating in the significantly titled *Beyond*, a meditation on Homer, Plato, Dante and the Book of *Job*, little is added to the main features of his theory, but the pedagogic manner becomes increasingly allusive, obscure and exhortatory, sometimes switching focus disconcertingly between the most ambitious perspectives on the human condition and the most narrowly academic concerns. One senses at times an approach to a religious or mystical intuition of value that the humanist Richards, unlike Coleridge or Eliot, never felt able to claim. His reserve in this respect is consistent with the intellectual honesty, tireless spirit of inquiry, and refusal to simplify which characterize his whole career.

Main works

(Richards's output of literary, linguistic, aesthetic and educational theory, literary criticism, poetry, translations and miscellaneous writings is immense. His theoretical works include, in addition to those cited below, *The Philosophy of Rhetoric*, *How to Read a Page*, and *Interpretation in Teaching*. *Speculative Instruments* and *Complementarities* are collections of essays. Richards also published a number of writings advocating the use of 'Basic English' [a simplified version with a vocabulary of fewer than 1000 words] as an international language.)

The Meaning of Meaning (with C.K. Ogden), London: Routledge & Kegan Paul, 1923.

Principles of Literary Criticism, London: Routledge & Kegan Paul, 1924.

Science and Poetry, London: Routledge & Kegan Paul, 1926; reissued as *Poetries and Sciences* with a commentary by the author, 1970.

Practical Criticism, London: Routledge & Kegan Paul, 1929.

Coleridge on Imagination, London: Kegan Paul, Trench, Trubner & Co., 1934.

Beyond, New York: Harcourt Brace Jovanovich, 1974.

Further reading

Constable, John (ed.), *Selected Letters of I.A. Richards*, Oxford: Oxford University Press, 1990.

Ransom, John Crowe, *The New Criticism*, Norfolk, CT: New Directions, 1941.

Russo, J.P., 'Introduction' to I.A., Richards, *Complementarities: Uncollected essays*, Manchester: Carcanet New Press, 1977.

Schiller, Jerome P., *I.A. Richards' Theory of Literature*, New Haven, CT.: Yale University Press, 1969.

Wimsatt, W.K. and M.C. Beardsley, 'The affective fallacy', in W.K., Wimsatt, *The Verbal Icon: Studies in the meaning of poetry*, Lexington, KY: University Press of Kentucky, 1954.

Wimsatt, W.K. and Cleanth Brooks, 'I.A. Richards: a poetics of tension', in *Literary Criticism: A short history*, New York: Knopf, 1957.

Ricoeur, Paul (1913–)

Pupil of the Catholic existentialist writer Gabriel Marcel and disciple of the phenomenological and hermeneutic traditions, Ricoeur became a university professor of philosophy in 1948. From 1956 to 1970 he taught at Paris-Nanterre, becoming Dean of the Faculty of Letters and President of the International Institute of Philosophy. He then moved to the University of Chicago, where he is still an emeritus professor of divinity. He has straddled a remarkable range of philosophical and intellectual discourses – theology, psychoanalysis, philosophy, phenomenology, literary theory, history – making unique contributions to them for both European and Anglo-Saxon intellectual circles.

Until the early 1960s, Ricoeur's work reflected on the existentialist writers and on the philosophy of action within a Christian frame of reference. Then, starting in the mid 1960s, he began to supplement his theological/mythic/poetic discussions of human action and evil with hermeneutical investigations intended to account for and interpret human meaning. He expounded a modern hermeneutics 'of suspicion', through which theory – as, for example, in the psychoanalysis of **Freud** – may counter the evasion of meaning. He undertook studies of meaning as analyzed in the sciences of language. In due course, this led Ricoeur to rework the topic of human action: in a magisterial study of time and narrative, and in further reflections on human identity. Overall, his work has developed unique concepts of metaphor and narrativity in the pursuit of his lifelong concerns with freedom, responsibility and progressive humanism.

Starting in the phenomenological and hermeneutic traditions of philosophy, Ricoeur has redefined for literary theory the metaphysical character and human status of various dimensions of the literary text. The problematic of his *Time and Narrative* typifies the route taken. The book starts in the classic 'aporias' of time, set out in the work of Aristotle and Augustine. These are the theoretically unbridgeable gaps between past, present and future: each separate moments of a continuum, which are somehow held *concurrently* in consciousness. The account of narrativity in stories develops as a response to the *philosophical* problem of the consciousness of time: 'between a story and the temporal character of human experience, there is a correlation . . .: *time becomes human to the extent that it is articulated in the narrative mode . . . narrative attains its full significance when it becomes a condition of temporal existence'*. Ricoeur finds the nature of narrative, then, not in the text but in the form of human consciousness.

The same route can be found in Ricoeur's study of *The Rule of Metaphor*. To be sure, the book sets out its stall among the sciences of language. Ricoeur argues that metaphor exceeds the 'crystalline purity' imposed on meaning by structuralist semiotics *à la* **Saussure**. Likewise, he opposes the new rhetoric of **Greimas** and others in the 1960s, which confines metaphors as mere deviations of meaning to be comprehended within an overarching semantic structure. The book deploys Anglo-Saxon semantics in a development of **Jakcobson's** account of the interplay between code and message. The way it stimulates that interplay makes metaphor the apogee of the creative powers of language in human consciousness. As the original, French title suggests, Ricoeur's deeper, philosophical agenda is to show how metaphor 'lives' in the phenomenology of consciousness.

In Ricoeur's theory, metaphor functions both at the level of the sentence and at that of the individual word. Likewise, semantics is conjoined to semiotics. Metaphor possesses a unique fecundity for consciousness, precisely because it embraces a perpetual tension between the unique act of naming (the natural territory of semantics, and of the individual word) and the imaginative act of predicating (the territory of semiotics and of the sentence). Operating as both reference and predication, metaphor enables the human imagination perpetually to *extend* meaning. For Ricoeur (as for **Bachelard**, whose influence he acknowledges), imagery is, then, more than figures of rhetoric or device within language, which substitute one expression for another that can be associated with it psychologically: the image is 'not a dying perception, but a language being born'. By continuously encompassing the identity *and* the difference within the world of our experience, metaphor enables us to make a trade-off between the two. It is thus the creative source of both meaning and discovery.

In a similar way, Ricoeur's view of narrative turns the reading of a story text into something deeper than an act of mere analysis. This is so because the narrative mode which makes time 'human' is shared: for reader, as for writer, human life is 'an activity and a passion in search of a narrative'. The act of emplotment in human consciousness continually reshapes the open field of the future. Initially we 'pre-figure' – that is, envisage it as possibilities of action. Emplotment then 'configures' that open field into a comprehensible, temporally structured totality where the sequence of past events has unfolded. To read a narrative, then, is is to apply the phenomenal schema with which consciousness makes coherent time out of haphazard events and deeds: 'To understand the story is to understand how and why the successive episodes led to this conclusion, which, far from being predictable, must in the end be accepted as consistent with the assembled episodes.'

What is more, humans require 'narrative identity' for their own selfhood: that is to say, they require to be *permanent* in time without being merely *the same* over time. This further extends the significance of the act of reading: 'In the course of the application of literature to life, what we carry over and transpose into the exegesis of ourselves is [the] dialectic of the self and the same.' In sum, Ricoeur's hermeneutics of the literary experience shows readers' acts of emplotment developing their deeper knowledge of the objective world, of each other and of self.

It may be too early to determine Ricoeur's impact on literary theory, and he has not himself engaged in specifically literary studies. On the other hand, his hermeneutical analyses have generated literary insights: such as his view of how the characters in modern novels perpetually balance 'narrative identity' and its loss in the contemporary world. Furthermore, Ricoeur's account of the power of narrative *per se* provided a counter-strategy, *avant la lettre*, to the attacks on 'Grand Narrative' launched by **Lyotard** and other postmodernists. In the 1980s literary theorists began, in the light of Ricoeur's thought, to reassess the relation of meaning to symbol, the nature of narrative and the act of reading.

Main works

Gabriel Marcel et Karl Jaspers: Philosophie du mystère et philosophie du paradoxe, Paris: Sevil, 1948.

Freedom and Nature: The voluntary and the involuntary, Evanston: Northern University Press, 1966.

Fallible Man, trans. Charly A. Kelbley, Chicago: Henry Regnery, 1965.

The Symbolism of Evil, trans. E. Buchanan, New York and London: Harper and Row, 1967.

Freud and Philosophy: An essay on interpretation, trans. D. Savage, New Haven, CT and London: Yale University Press, 1970.

The Rule of Metaphor: Multi-disciplinary studies of the creation of meaning in language, trans. R. Czerny, London: Routledge and Kegan Paul, 1977.

Hermeneutics and the Human Sciences: Essays on Language, action and interpretation, ed. and trans. J.B. Thompson, Cambridge: Cambridge University Press, 1981.

Time and Narrative, trans. K. McLaughlin and D. Pellaur, three volumes, Chicago: Chicago University Press, 1984–7.

Lectures on Ideology and Utopia, ed. and trans. George S. Taylor, New York: Columbia University Press, 1986.

Oneself as Another, trans. Kathleen Blamey, Chicago: University of Chicago Press, 1992.

Further reading

Adams, Hazard, *Philosophy of the Literary Symbol*, Tallahassee, FL: University of Florida State Press, 1984.

Clark, S.H., *Paul Ricoeur*, London and New York: Routledge, 1990.

Kemp, T. Peter and David Rasmussen, *The Narrative Path: The later works of Paul Ricoeur*, Cambridge, MA and London: MIT, 1989.

Thompson, John, *Critical Hermeneutics: A study of the thought of Paul Ricoeur and Jürgen Habermas*, Cambridge: Cambridge University Press, 1981.

Valdes, M. (ed.) *A Ricoeur Reader: Reflection and imagination*, Hemel Hempstead: Harvester Wheatsheaf, 1991.

Wood, David (ed.), *On Paul Ricoeur: Narrative and interpretation*, London and New York: Routledge, 1991.

Rorty, Richard (1931–)

Rorty has worked in the American university system at Princeton University and the University of Virginia, where he is currently University Professor of Humanities. He is a philosopher by training – the studies that first brought him to public notice were in the 'history of philosophy' mode – but his later work also ventures into other areas such as literary criticism and social theory.

Rorty's work is in the tradition of American philosophical pragmatism dating back to philosophers like John Dewey and C.S. Peirce, whom he acknowledges as abiding influences on the development of his thought and refers to frequently in his writings, but he has also shown himself to be highly receptive to recent continental philosophy, in particular to the work of **Derrida** and the post-structuralist movement. Both *Philosophy and the Mirror of Nature* and *Consequences of Pragmatism* take a broad overview of philosophy from the point of view of pragmatism. For Rorty, pragmatism involves dispensing with large-scale philosophical problems such as the nature of truth and goodness (or even the attempt to define such terms) on the grounds that these are now non-problems from discourses that have outlived their cultural usefulness. Pragmatism is a position of scepticism with regard to such discourses and their problems (essentially manufactured ones, in Rorty's view) and has no desire to enter into the argument either for or against – all that pragmatists wish to do, Rorty claims, is 'to change the subject'. Rorty's mission, as he sees it, is to *dissolve* rather than to solve the traditional problems of philosophical history. His stance is unmistakably post-philosophical and anti-foundationalist in intent.

Philosophy and the Mirror of Nature sets out to undermine the reader's confidence in theories of mind and knowledge, as well as in philosophy as it has been practised since the time of Kant. Rorty notes that although he is prepared to discuss the various solutions offered to the problems of mind and knowledge in the philosophical literature, his objective in doing so is merely to reveal that these problems do not really exist. Although it is written in the language of analytical philosophy, the study is not willing to make any special claims for that

343

method – analytical philosophy being merely one style among many as far as Rorty is concerned, with no particular purchase on truth or knowledge. Rorty's approach to his subject is determinedly historicist, and he is critical of most traditional forms of philosophy as attempts to escape from history and give the discipline a spuriously timeless air. Most philosophical problems can be reduced to historical origins in Rorty's opinion, and he sees Western philosophy as dominated by the idea of the mind as a mirror containing representations of reality (some accurate, some not). The ultimate goal of the study is to argue that truth is, in William James's formulation, 'what it is better for us to believe', rather than the more traditional philosophical notion of 'the accurate representation of reality'.

Rorty makes a key distinction between 'systematic' and 'edifying' philosophy. Edifying philosophy – that found in the pages of Wittgenstein, Heidegger and Dewey, for example – aims to help its readers break free from outmoded discourses (such as analytical philosophy as usually practised) rather than to provide them with some eventually dubious system for determining 'truth', and for Rorty it is the only form of philosophy that is worth our while pursuing.

Consequences of Pragmatism continues in a similar vein, stating uncompromisingly that 'truth is not the sort of thing that one should expect to have a philosophically interesting theory about'. Although such theories certainly exist, they tell us little about the world: the world they *do* tell us about being a 'world well lost'. Rorty goes on to argue that coherence and correspondence theories of truth (that truth is a matter of the coherence of our beliefs with one another, or the correspondence between our beliefs and reality) are in fact 'noncompeting trivialities' from which we should be making every effort to break free. Drawing on Dewey, Rorty claims that theories ought to be judged in terms of their usefulness (in bringing us greater happiness, for example) rather than on their truthfulness. The kind of philosophical style that we should be fostering is philosophy as commentary, not philosophy, as a critique of our claims to know, the latter always turning out to be an arid area of inquiry that contributes little of benefit (if anything at all) to our understanding of the world in which we live.

Contingency, Irony, Solidarity proceeds to push Rorty's antiphilosophical bias to its logical conclusion and moves out of philosophy altogether, in this instance into the domains of literature and social theory. Rorty sees literature as providing us with an ironic perspective on the human condition that is extremely valuable at the personal level – where it helps to promote a sense of human solidarity – and approvingly cites the novels of Orwell and Nabokov as models in this respect. Philosophy is held to be deficient in achieving such a desirable goal. An ironic perspective is one that is always aware of the contingency of the individual's central beliefs and desires, as well as of the manifest impossibility of there ever being any grand unified theory that will succeed in explaining totally the nature of things, or reconciling the conflicting demands of the public and the private. The condition we should aspire to is that of 'liberal ironism', and the culture that would best express such an ideal would be a post-metaphysical one where fiction, rather than philosophy, would be the main agent of moral change and progress. In a liberal ironist world philosophers should align themselves with poets instead of with physicists (Rorty is scathing on the use of science as a means of grounding philosophical inquiry), and cease to manufacture false problems (about truth or knowledge, etc.) or dwell on non-existent difficulties that exasperate or alienate non-philosophers. Poets are praised in almost Shelleyan fashion as being in 'the vanguard of the species'.

Ultimately Rorty does not see philosophy as an arbiter of disputes or a final court of appeal, or even as a field of professional inquiry (the traditional assumption made in 'history of philosophy' exercises), but as a form of conversation – something on the lines of academic common-room discussion, perhaps, in which various viewpoints are aired but no ultimate victory for any one viewpoint is objectively possible, or even really desirable. Indeed, the whole point about edifying philosophy, Rorty argues, is simply to keep the conversation going rather than discover something called 'objective truth'. His liberal politics, which he proudly proclaims repeatedly over the course of his *oeuvre*, are very evident in such a vision of the subject, which some on the left consider to be politically somewhat naive, or at the very least overly idealistic about human nature and its ability to remain disinterested about questions of power.

Rorty has become a name to drop in cultural studies because of his enthusiastic espousal of continental philosophy and the generally anti-foundationalist tenor of his work, which is much in tune with late twentieth-century post-philosophical thinking. His pragmatism has an obvious appeal for an age generally sceptical of grandiose theory and system-building (he describes himself as against the study of anything initialized, such as Truth, Absolute Knowledge, or The Will To Power) and has been widely evoked. Rorty's work also has the virtue of being considerably more accessible than that of most of the continental theorists he champions – 'the only post-modernist anyone can understand, or the poor-person's Derrida', as Jonathan Ree has put it in commending Rorty's stylistic clarity (although the irony here is that Rorty himself tends to praise theorists with a 'noisy', difficult style that keeps the reader in a state of tension). His recent forays into areas such as literary criticism and social theory, and his claim that they probably have more to teach us than philosophy does, point up the post-philosophical implications of his position, and throughout his career he often sounds as if philosophy is a stage in modern thought to be transcended as soon as practicable: as he puts it in *Consequences of Pragmatism*, 'Pragmatists are saying that the best hope for philosophy is not to practise Philosophy.'

Main works

Philosophy and the Mirror of Nature, Oxford: Blackwell, 1980.

Consequences of Pragmatism, Brighton: Harvester, 1982.

Philosophy in History (with J.B. Schneewind and Quentin Skinner, eds), Cambridge: Cambridge University Press, 1984.

Contingency, Irony, Solidarity, Cambridge and New York: Cambridge University Press, 1991a.

Objectivity, Relativism and Truth: Philosophical papers, Vol. 1, Cambridge and New York: Cambridge University Press, 1991b.

Essays on Heidegger and Others: Philosophical papers, Vol. 2, Cambridge and New York: Cambridge University Press, 1991c.

Further reading

Hollinger, Robert (ed.), *Hermeneutics and Praxis*, Notre Dame, 1985.

Lang, Berel, *The Anatomy of Philosophical Style*, Oxford, 1990.

McGowan, John, *Postmodernism and its Critics*, Ithaca, NY and London: Cornell University Press, 1991.

Neilsen, Kai, *After the Demise of the Tradition: Rorty, critical theory and the fate of philosophy*, Boulder, CO, 1991.

Ree, Jonathan, 'Timely meditations', *Radical Philosophy* 55 (1990).

S

Said, Edward W. (1935–)

Edward Said was born in Jerusalem, in what was mandatory Palestine, into an Anglican family. His family left Palestine permanently at the end of 1947 and settled in Egypt, where he attended British colonial schools. He completed his secondary education in the United States in the early 1950s, and went on to study English and History at Princeton University. He did his doctoral dissertation at Harvard University, later published as his first book, *Joseph Conrad and the Fiction of Autobiography* (1966). He has spent most of his career teaching at Columbia University, New York, where he is currently University Professor of English and Comparative Literature. In addition to his academic career, Said has been prominent in the American media as a spokesperson for the cause of Palestinian self-determination. While he insists that he has never been a member of a political party, he was appointed to the Palestine National Council (the Palestinian parliament in exile) in 1977. Said has commented extensively in interviews and elsewhere on the effect of the various displacements and expatriations which he has experienced in his life: 'The sense of being between cultures has been very, very strong for me. I would say that's the single strongest strand running through my life: the fact that I'm always in and out of things, and never really *of* anything for very long' (Salusinszky, 1987).

Said's first sustained engagement with modern literary and cultural theory (especially the new French thought) occurs in *Beginnings: Intention and method* (1975). His analysis of 'beginnings' in canonical literary and cultural texts proceeds not so much through a philosophically rigorous interrogation of the terms 'intention' and 'method' as through an extensively illustrated meditation on the act of beginning a work of writing. The book's most assured focus in its early chapters is the nineteenth-century European novel, but the final chapter, entitled '*Abecedarium Culturae*', moves into a critical but nevertheless considered treatment of the work of **Barthes**, **Foucault**, **Deleuze** and **Derrida**, iconoclastic figures in the American literary establishment at the time.

The account of Foucault is particularly full, and in its receptivity to the idea of the relationship between knowledge and power it suggests an engagement which is central to some of Said's later work, particularly *Orientalism*. The remit of *Beginnings* makes it appear as if it is addressed to an earlier generation of American scholars and critics who had taught or influenced Said (such as Auerbach, Blackmur and Trilling), and his cautious attitude to structuralism seems to be a result of his loyalty to this liberal, humanist critical tradition. Yet in the conclusion to *Beginnings*, Said seeks to align modern French literary and cultural theory with an earlier manifestation of humanism, Vico's *New Science*. What the methodologies of Vico and the structuralists have in common, according to Said, is a post-Enlightenment loss of faith in origins, hence a secular view of the role of the writer in modern society: 'The state of mind that is concerned with origins . . . is theological. By contrast, . . . beginnings are eminently secular, or gentile, continuing activities.' The notion of the validity of secular criticism is further developed in the introduction to the collection *The World, The Text, and The Critic* (1983), which contains essays on literature and criticism written between 1969 and 1981.

Said's most influential work so far has undoubtedly been *Orientalism*, a book he has reflected upon persistently since its publication in 1978 (with most concentration in his essay '*Orientalism* Reconsidered'). The texts examined in *Orientalism* include novels, political writings and travel narratives concerning the Orient (i.e. the Middle East), primarily by English and French writers from the late eighteenth century until the aftermath of World War II. Said's argument is that the representation of the Orient in Western discourse has always been predicated upon an unequal relationship of economic, political and imaginative power. Of several not entirely compatible definitions of the term 'Orientalism' offered in the book, the following captures the overriding spirit of Said's usage: 'Orientalism can be discussed and analyzed as the corporate institution for dealing with the Orient – dealing with it by making statements about it, authorizing views of it, describing it, by teaching it, settling it, ruling over it: in short, Orientalism is a Western style for dominating, restructuring and having authority over the Orient.' In addition he posits the mutually binding force of this relationship (shades of Hegel and **Freud** are apparent in its articulation): the Orient is one of Europe's 'deepest and most recurring images of the Other'; it has helped 'to define Europe (or the West) as its contrasting image, idea, personality, experience'.

While he is acknowledged as a foundational text in the new field of post-colonial theory, critique rather than acclaim has been the more usual response to *Orientalism* in recent years. Dennis Porter has criticized Said's characterization of Orientalism as a systematic and unitary attitude to the East when in fact exceptions to his thesis – or at least, examples of contradictions within specific Western discourses – are plentiful. As James Clifford has pointed out, this blindness to historical complexity signals a painful irony: *Orientalism* can sometimes appear to verge towards Occidentalism in the way it replicates the totalizing force of a method of representation whose ills it had sought to diagnose. The major methodological problem appears to be that Said swerves between a thoroughgoing adherence to the post-structuralist idea that there are only representations in discourse and the contradictory claim that Orientalism is a form of distortion. In his brilliant Marxist critique, Ahmad sees the roots of such contradictions as lying in the book's attempt to effect several virtually impossible reconciliations. First, Said is both faithful to the great works of Western literature in his choice of examples, yet – unlike one of his mentors, Auerbach – his concern is to offer the reader the means through which to be critical rather than reverential towards this canon. Second, he seeks to reconcile his humanism with a Nietzschean anti-humanist suspicion of truth, associated with Foucault's discourse theory. Each of these ambiguities, as Ahmad points out, makes for considerable uneasiness in the course of the book.

Orientalism came to be viewed by Said as the first of a trilogy of studies on the relationship between Islam, the Arabs, and the Orient on the one hand, and the West on the other. The second and third books of the trio, *The Question of Palestine* (1979), an account of the contemporary political struggle for self-determination by the Palestinians, and *Covering Islam* (1981), on the representation of Islam and the Arabs in the contemporary American media, form part of a distinct strand of his *oeuvre* concerned with the ongoing debate over a future Palestinian state, and the portrayal of the Arab world in the Western press. Other works in this vein are the poignantly composed *After the Last Sky* (1986), in which Said's textual commentary is interwoven with photographs of contemporary Palestinian lives by Jean Mohr, and *Blaming the Victims* (1988).

Culture and Imperialism [*CI*] (1993) addresses several of the charges levelled at *Orientalism*, in particular the view that Said's reluctance to treat non-Western texts and perspectives in the earlier book seriously damaged his case. But *CI*, especially in its opening two chapters, largely operates as a kind of reprise of earlier themes. Texts examined on previous occasions, such as Conrad's *Heart of Darkness* and *Nostromo*, are revisited, and though there is new material on the relationship between the novel and imperialism – illustrated with readings of Austen's *Mansfield Park*, Kipling's *Kim*, and Camus's *L'Etranger*, among others – the dominant focus is still the Western canon. The third chapter, entitled 'Resistance and Opposition', addresses the perspective of the colonized intellectual, with readings of Yeats's poetry, and Third World historians such as C.L.R. James and Ranajit Guha, a prominent member of *Subaltern Studies* co-operative. The final chapter, written during Operation Desert Storm, reflects on the way contemporary issues (the *fatwa* against Salman Rushdie and the Gulf War itself) confirm the urgency of Said's desire to analyze East–West relations critically. Overall, while there is much of interest in *CL*, it seems to lack an adequate overall structure, as if the contents, written for the most part in discrete units over a long period, resist being shaped into a coherent argument that measures up to the ambitious title.

Said must be considered a major figure in modern literary and cultural theory, but the interest of his legacy may come to lie less in the coherence of his most well-known theory, Orientalism, than in the extraordinary range and diversity of his output. The breadth and ambition of his work, and his unreconstructed celebration of canonical literature (particularly fiction), invite comparison with European and American criticism of an earlier era. But Said's courage and resilience in confronting awkward and embarrassing questions concerning the politics of theory and criticism, as well as his interventions in debates concerning the future of the Middle East, mark him out as a distinctively engaged literary and cultural critic.

Main works

Joseph Conrad and the Fiction of Autobiography, New Haven: Harvard University Press, 1966.

Beginnings: Intention and method, Baltimore: Johns Hopkins University Press, 1975.

'Interview/Edward W. Said', *Diacritics*, 6, 3 (1976): 30–47.

Orientalism, London: Routledge & Kegan Paul, 1978.

The Question of Palestine, New York: New York Times Books, 1979.

(ed.), *Literature and History: Selected papers from the English Institute*, Baltimore: Johns Hopkins University Press, 1980.

Covering Islam: How the media and the experts determine how we see the rest of the world, London: Routledge & Kegan Paul, 1981.

The World, the Text, and the Critic, Cambridge, Mass.: Harvard University Press, 1983.

'Orientalism reconsidered', in Francis Barker *et al.* (eds), *Europe and Its Others*, Proceedings of the Essex Conference on the Sociology of Literature 1984, 2 vols, University of Essex, 1985, vol. 1, pp. 14–27.

After the Last Sky: Palestinian lives, London: Faber, 1986.

(ed., with Christopher Hitchens), *Blaming the Victims: Spurious scholarship and the Palestinian question*, London: Verso, 1988.

Musical Elaborations, London: Chatto & Windus, 1991.

Culture and Imperialism, London: Chatto & Windus, 1993.

Further reading

Ahmad, Aijaz, *In Theory: Classes, nations, literatures*, London: Verso, 1992, pp. 159–219.

Bove, Paul A., *Intellectuals in Power: A genealogy of critical humanism*, New York: Columbia University Press, 1986.

Clifford, James, *The Predicament of Culture: Twentieth-century ethnography, literature and art*, Cambridge, Mass.: Harvard University Press, 1988, pp. 255–76.

Porter, Dennis, '*Orientalism* and its problems', in *The Politics of Theory*, Proceedings of the Essex Conference on the Sociology of Literature 1982 (University of Essex, 1983), pp. 179–93.

Salusinszky, Imre, Interview with Edward Said, in *Criticism in Society*, London: Methuen, 1987, pp. 123–48.

Sprinker, Michael, ed., *Edward Said: A Critical Reader* Oxford: Blackwell, 1992.

Sartre, Jean-Paul (1905–71)

Sartre is one of the twentieth-century's leading intellectual figures; his fame rests mainly on his philosophical endeavours as the major theorist of Existentialism, although he was also a successful novelist, playwright, essayist, journalist and broadcaster. In the mid 1930s Sartre was a fellow at the Institut Français in Berlin, then from 1937 to 1944 he taught at the Lycée Pasteur in Paris. When Existentalism became a cult after the Second World War, Sartre was propelled to international fame, and he was far and away the dominant intellectual figure of his generation in France, editor of the influential journal *Les Temps Modernes* and the centre of a group that included such other well-known personalities as de **Beauvoir**, Camus, and the philosopher Merleau–Ponty. The break in relations between Sartre and Camus in the early 1950s over Camus's *The Rebel*, which was unfavourably reviewed in *Les Temps Modernes* by Sartre's associate François Jeanson, was front-page news in France, and testimony to Existentialism's hold on the public imagination at the time. Sartre flirted with **Marx**ism for much of his later career, the *Critique of Dialectical Reason* being his major work in this idiom, although he remained a very unorthodox Marxist. In 1964 he was awarded, but refused to accept, the Nobel Prize for Literature.

Existentialism has been one of the most powerful cultural movements of modern times, one of the few philosophical theories to gain popular currency (even if, in Sartre's opinion, it was almost universally misunderstood and trivialized in the process). *Being and Nothingness* is its main source, although many of the ideas presented there can be found in a more accessible form in Sartre's prewar novel *Nausea*, a powerful study of individual alienation and breakdown within a stifling bourgeois society unwilling to acknowledge how precarious human existence really is. Sartre was heavily influenced by the philosophy of Heidegger, and existentialism as a whole owes much to the phenomenological movement. Like Heidegger, Sartre believes that human existence is absurd and contingent (Heidegger spoke of our 'thrownness-into-being', Sartre of our being 'abandoned' into existence), which leaves a vacuum at the centre of the individual's life. How to create a meaning for one's existence is a fundamental problem of such a philosophy, and Sartre contends that we try to hide the fact of life's contingency from ourselves – the phenomenon he calls 'bad faith'. In a famous example of bad faith in action he cites the condition of a waiter in a cafe, where his practised ability to lose himself in his role amounts to an avoidance of the unpalatable facts of existence on his part (bad faith [*mauvaise foi*] is sometimes glossed as self-deception). Sartre also argues that most of us are in a state of bad faith most of the time.

Being has two forms in Sartre: being-in-itself (the being of inert objects) and being-for-itself (that associated with human being and consciousness). Human beings are in fact *both* beings-in-themselves *and* beings-for-themselves who experience the world through consciousness, which is aware of its separation from the rest of the world by a gap, or nothingness. Being is constantly confronted by the possibility of non-being (nothingness), a condition which causes acute anxiety as we come to realize the sheer contingency of our individual existence. Authentic existence is lived in the shadow of this realization of the eternal threat posed by nothingness, which 'lies coiled in the heart of being – like a worm'. We carry non-being around within us at all times; hence our anxiety at the precariousness of our state, which is, in effect, the human condition.

Freedom plays a crucial role in Sartre's philosophical scheme, and he is one of the great defenders of free will in modern philosophy, believing that at any moment in our lives we are free to make choices, even if those choices are sometimes extremely limited in scope.

Freedom is a condition of considerable personal insecurity, since the passage of time continually condemns us to face new and often difficult situations, forcing new and often difficult choices to be made in their turn. Choice cannot be avoided – *not* to choose is also a form of choice. Existential anguish is the product of the realization of the constant necessity of choice, as well as the groundlessness of any such choice in an absurd and contingent universe. Nor can we claim that we are not free if we are thrust into situations not of our own choosing: even under torture we are free, Sartre insists, since the choice always exists to give in to or to resist the torturer's demands.

Overall, Sartre contends that man is what he makes of himself through his choices, and that vision of existence can have very positive connotations. In the final analysis we are not bound by tradition, fate, or forces outside our control: the individual is free to choose to oppose all such entities. As Sartre saw it, Existentialism was an optimistic philosophy which showed individuals the extent of their freedom.

Freedom of choice entails accepting responsibility for our choices and the impact they have. Our choices have significance for the rest of the world, since they alter the situations of choice – and thus the chances and opportunities – of others. The one choice we are enjoined *not* to make is suicide, since that amounts to surrendering to nothingness and the absurd.

Commitment is one of the major ways of coping with the contingency and anxiety that lie at the heart of the human condition, and it involves committing oneself to some larger cause (the Resistance movement during the Second World War, for example), and making that cause one's own. It then becomes a case of acting as if one were acting for the rest of humanity: one's actions become directed at others; one assumes responsibility for the world.

Sartre's main contribution to the field of literary theory is *What is Literature?*, a work which stakes out a role for the writer in the troubled postwar world. What Sartre demands of the writer is a clear commitment to addressing the problems of modern existence, and he is critical of any literature that can be described as escapist (that being another example of bad faith in action). The writer has a duty to involve himself/herself in sociopolitical issues of public significance. The best way to do this, Sartre felt, was by presenting 'extreme situations' in which the fictional characters had to choose whether to commit themselves to others or not. Sartre saw writing as a weapon in the political struggle taking place, and argued that the writer had no option but to take sides. Certainly his own fiction of the period faces up to the pressing political issues of postwar life, and unashamedly takes sides.

Sartre's literary output in general deals with recognizably philosophical themes, such as free will and commitment in *Crime Passionel*, and self and other in *No Exit*, for example. In general both his novels and plays come into the 'literature of ideas' category, and are also fairly traditional in form for a period when modernism was in vogue, but Sartre's inherently dramatic world-view, with its preference for the extreme situation as a way of making metaphysical points, means that his literary endeavours do have a life of their own outside the philosophy that generated them.

Although its heyday is past, Existentialism's impact on twentieth-century thought runs deep, although it is probably fair to say that of late it has had more effect on the creative arts than on philosophy or cultural studies. In the case of the former, the existentialist world-view, with its vision of alienated individuals caught in an absurd and contingent universe, has exercised a considerable emotional appeal. Nevertheless, there is probably more of Sartre's influence within the post-structuralist and postmodernist movements in France than its major figures would probably care to admit: at the very least, Sartre can be credited with being the prime mover behind the 'phenomenological turn' in recent French philosophy.

Main works

Existentialism and Humanism, trans. Philip Mairet, London: Methuen, 1948.

Crime Passionnel, trans. Kitty Black, London: Hamish Hamilton, 1949.

What is Literature?, trans. Bernard Frechtman, London: Methuen, 1950.

Being and Nothingness, trans. Hazel E. Barnes, London: Methuen, 1957.

In Camera, trans. Stuart Gilbert, Harmondsworth: Penguin, 1958.

'Roads to Freedom' trilogy:

The Age of Reason, trans. Eric Sutton, Harmondsworth: Penguin, 1961.

The Reprieve, trans. Eric Sutton, Harmondsworth: Penguin, 1963a.

Iron in the Soul, trans. Gerard Hopkins, Harmondsworth: Penguin, 1963b.

The Flies, trans. Stuart Gilbert, Harmondsworth: Penguin, 1962a.

Sketch for a Theory of the Emotions, trans. Philip Mairet, London: Methuen, 1962b.

Saint Genet: Actor and Martyr, trans. Bernard Frechtman, New York: G. Braziller, 1963c.

Words, trans. Irene Clephane, London: Hamish Hamilton, 1964.

Nausea, trans. Robert Baldick, Harmondsworth: Penguin, 1965.

Critique of Dialectical Reason, trans. Alan Sheridan-Smith, London: Verso, 1991.

Further reading

Aron, Raymond, *Marxism and the Existentialists*, New York, 1969.

Bree, Germaine, *Camus and Sartre: Crisis and commitment*, New York, 1972.

Danto, Arthur, *Sartre*, Glasgow, 1975.

Jameson, Frederic, *Sartre: Origins of a style*, New York and Guildford, 1984.

Murdoch, Iris, *Sartre: Romantic rationalist*, London, 1953.

Warnock, Mary, *The Philosophy of Sartre*, London, 1965.

Glossary

Extreme situation: Situation of crisis which demands definite response (that is, choice) from participants.

Saussure, Ferdinand de (1857–1913)

Saussure's academic career was spent at the Ecole Pratique des Hautes Etudes, Paris, and the University of Geneva, where he was Professor of Linguistics and gave the series of lectures (1907–11) that was subsequently put together in book form as the now-famous *Course in General Linguistics* by several of his ex-students after his death. He is one of the founders of modern linguistics, and the *Course in General Linguistics* did much to organize the subject on scientific lines (hitherto it had had a largely historical bias). The only work of Saussure's published during his lifetime was a study of the vowel system of early Indo-European language (*Mémoire sur le système primitif des voyelles dans les langues indo-européennes*), which was heavily influenced by the neo-grammarian school of historical linguists, whom he had encountered during his studies at the University of Leipzig.

Saussure's influence extends well beyond the discipline of linguistics. The model of language he constructed in the *Course in General*

Linguistics has proved enormously influential in the field of cultural studies, providing the basis for structuralist and semiological methodology. His primary concern in the *Course in General Linguistics* is to establish a methodology for linguistics such that it can become a subject of scientific inquiry. He sees his task as being threefold: (1) to trace the history of all observable languages; (2) to deduce general laws for the forces permanently at work in all languages; (3) to delimit and define linguistics' field of inquiry. Saussure's critical insight is his realization that language is above all a system, a self-contained, self-regulating system with its own internal 'grammar' (the game of chess being used as an analogy). Language as a system [*langue*] is differentiated from language as a set of particular utterances [*parole*], and it is with *langue* that Saussure's interest primarily lies in the *Course in General Linguistics*. *Langue/parole* is just the first of a series of binary divisions around which Saussure's linguistic theory is structured, and which constitute one of its most characteristic – and most imitated – features.

At the centre of Saussurean linguistics is the concept of the sign, an entity consisting of a signifier and a signified. When signifier and signified (word and concept) are united in an act of understanding in the mind, they constitute the sign. Language is to be regarded as a system of signs bound together by internally consistent grammatical rules and regulations, and it forms a model for how all other sign systems work, thus providing the basis for semiology. The sign is seen to be conventional, or arbitrary. This means that any word at all can be deployed to describe a given object in a given language, as long as there is general consent among that language's speakers to use it in that particular way. As evidence of this arbitrariness, and lack of any necessary connection between word and object, Saussure cites the fact that different words are used across the family of languages to describe the same object (tree, *arbre*, *baum*, etc.). If language were a mere naming process where appropriate word was matched to appropriate object, then such diversity could not happen.

The identification of arbitrariness appears to raise the spectre of instability and indeterminacy of meaning (and post-structuralists have been only too happy make just that connection), but Saussure himself had no such radical purpose in mind, and was content to settle for what he called a 'relative' arbitrariness where the sign was concerned. This relative arbitrariness allows the sign to change over time (but not at any individual's whim; there has to be consensus among language-users), and Saussure discriminates between language in its synchronic and diachronic forms. In its synchronic form language is a static totality complete with its constant elements (its internal grammar); in its diachronic form, on the other hand, language is in an evolutionary phase where change – as in the meanings of words – can occur (but again, only with general consensus). Once more, chess provides a useful analogy: the game plus its rules is the synchronic whole; the game during play is in a diachronic phase.

In a further binary division Saussure identifies two main types of relations applying to words: syntagmatic and associative (or, as it has since come to be known, paradigmatic). A syntagm is a sequence of two or more words structured according to the laws of grammar ('The cat sat on the mat', for example), such that the words relate to each other in a linear, rule-bound fashion. Associative relations between words are much looser than syntagmatic, being acquired from outside formal discourse as such, as in the process known as association of ideas, where sound-quality or individual memory might come into play and link words together in someone's mind for reasons other than grammatical ones (punning, and indeed, all wordplay, depends on the associative principle).

The system-orientated nature of Saussure's thought is particularly evident when it comes to his views on value and identity. Value, for Saussure, is system-bound and formally defined. Terms have value only within the system in question, and that value is a matter of their relationship to other terms. This is to say that there is no such thing as intrinsic value, which is one of the more radical notions to emerge from the *Course in General Linguistics*. Identity is equally a matter of relationship: the 8.25 Geneva – Paris train, as Saussure points out by way of analogy, derives its identity from its place within the system of the train timetable, even though its rolling stock and personnel may change from day to day, or it fails to leave on time at 8.25.

Saussure also subscribed to a theory that Latin poetry contained concealed anagrams of proper names placed there by the poets, although he failed to produce conclusive evidence for this belief, and never published anything on the subject despite filling many notebooks with probable examples of such anagrams. Post-structuralists, however, have been very much drawn towards this aspect of Saussure's thought, seeing it as further proof of the arbitrariness of the sign and the fundamental instability (and infinite plurality) of meaning, and several associated with the radical French journal *Tel Quel* have been inspired to conduct similar exercises.

Saussure's importance for the development of cultural studies can hardly be overestimated. Structuralism has been one of the paradigms of twentieth-century intellectual inquiry, and the linguistic model it appropriated from Saussure has proved an extremely powerful analytical method, with applications in almost all areas of human endeavour – there are in fact few areas which have *not* been the subject of structuralist analysis at one time or another. Structuralist methodology adopts a recognizably Saussurean approach to analysis, whatever the phenomenon that happens to be under investigation. First of all, the boundaries of the system in question are established, then the system's internal grammar is identified and examined in both diachronic and synchronic perspective. A large amount of apparently disparate data (the *parole* in question) can be reduced to ordered patterns [*langue*] in this manner – as in **Barthes**'s work on fashion and advertising, or **Lévi-Strauss**'s on myth. The method is particularly fruitful for the way it sets up the conditions for comparative analysis (say within or across artistic genres), and structuralism has been notably successful in this sphere. Post-structuralism similarly owes a large debt to Saussurean linguistics in taking as one of its starting points the arbitrariness of the sign.

It is also true to say that Saussure has often been very selectively interpreted, and his work has been credited with philosophical implications that were undoubtedly quite foreign to the nature of his inquiry, which, it should always be remembered, was first and foremost a linguistic one. Some recent commentators (Leonard Jackson, for example, in *The Poverty of Structuralism*) have been highly critical of the French tendency to turn Saussure into a proto-idealist philosopher, and it is also most unlikely that the somewhat anarchic procedures of post-structuralism would have found favour with such a systematic thinker who was, after all, *concerned* at the prospect of unrestrained arbitrariness, and sought to find ways of limiting it. Nevertheless, Saussure's linguistic model remains a richly suggestive source for cultural studies.

Within the discipline of linguistics itself Saussure's influence can be discerned at work in the development of structural linguistics (**Jakobson** and the Prague School, for example) as well as in **Chomsky**'s trans-formational-generative grammar.

Main works

Recueil des publications scientifiques de F. de Saussure, Geneva, 1922; contains *Mémoires*.

Course in General Linguistics, ed. by Charles Bally, Albert Sechehaye and Albert Reidlinger, trans. Wade Baskin, London, 1960.

Further reading

Aarsleff, Hans, *From Locke to Saussure*, London, 1982.

Culler, Jonathan, *Saussure*, London: Fontana/Collins, 1976.

Culler, Jonathan, *Structuralist Poetics*, London and Henley: Routledge and Kegan Paul, 1975.

Holdcroft, David, *Saussure: Signs, system, and arbitrariness*, Cambridge, 1991.

Koerner, E.F.K., *Ferdinand de Saussure: The origin and development of his linguistic thought in Western studies of language*, Braunschweig, 1973.

Starobinski, Jean, *Words upon Words: The anagrams of Ferdinand de Saussure*, New Haven, CT, 1979.

Glossary

Semiology: The study of sign systems (from the Greek word for sign, *semeion*).

Signified: The mental image or concept lying behind a word.

Signifier: A word, whether spoken or written.

Shklovsky, Viktor Borisovich (1893–1984)

Russian–Jewish writer and critic Viktor Shklovsky was born in St Petersburg. Having studied literary history at the University, he became a founding member of OPOYAZ, a Russian acronym for the Society for the Study of Poetic Language. Pro-avant-garde at the time of the February Revolution of 1917 and anti-Bolshevik in October, he served as a commissar in the war for the Provisional Government. He became Professor at the Institute of the Arts, and also lectured at the Institute of Literature. In 1918 he joined the Underground Union for the Rebirth of Russia, which wanted to restore the Constituent Assembly. Although he was obliged to flee to Ukraine, he was allowed to return to Petrograd in 1919. His former anti-Bolshevik attitudes led to exile in Berlin, whence he returned in 1923. He rejoined the Serapion Brothers ('sympathetic fellow-travellers') and became a member of LEF (Left Front of Art). The Party was not prepared to grant hegemony in the literary field to any one group: LEF collapsed. Shklovsky continued to pursue his formalist theoretical writings, though when Formalism was criticized for being out of touch with political reality, he moved into cinema, working for Goskino as the writer of intertitles (*The Prostitute*, 1927), as scriptwriter (*By the Law*, 1926; *Bed and Sofa* [a.k.a *Third Meshchanskaya*] 1927; *The House on Tribunaya*, 1927) and as critic, adapting formalist studies to film. His work on Western literary

359

influences, the continuing critique of Formalism and his support for writers like Mandelstam resulted in his being attacked in 1936–7. Shklovsky came to prominence once more in the post-Stalin era, contributing valuable, though as yet untranslated, essays on Russian writers and prose.

In 'The resurrection of the word' (1914) Shklovsky began his attack on mainline literature. He supported Futurist poetry because of its fresh approach, its introduction of unpoetic and, thereby, revitalized vocabulary. If the Futurists, with their often outrageous vocabulary, wanted to 'épater le bourgeois', Shklovsky's intention was to 'épater le critique' with his unconventional views. His article 'Art as technique' (1916) can be regarded almost as the Manifesto of the early Russian Formalists, members of the the the Moscow Linguistic Circle (1915) and the Petrograd OPOYAZ (1916) who radically challenged the accepted basis of literary study dismissing extra-textual dimensions (psychology, sociology, biography, inspiration) in order to concentrate on form rather than content. They flourished in the 1920s and were suppressed in the 1930s. In his article Shklovsky took issue with Potebnya's view – a view shared by the Russian Symbolists – that poetry was 'thinking in images', arguing that it is the devices [*priemy*] themselves that distinguish poetry from prose. Devices such as assonance, alliteration, metre, parallelism, repetition, and retardation constitute literature's 'literariness'. An image, then, is just one device among many. The key to understanding how literature works is perception. Ordinary language – or practical language, as the Formalists preferred to term it – does not call attention to itself; it has become automatic, habitual: 'The purpose of art is to impart the sensation of things as they are perceived. The technique of art is to make objects "unfamiliar", to make forms difficult, to increase the difficulty and length of perception.' Here Shklovsky introduces the device of defamiliarization [*ostranenie*], whereby that which has become habituated becomes revitalized; is seen afresh, no longer just recognized. It therefore draws attention both to itself and to the dynamic transformational process.

Shklovsky first embarked on the theory of prose in 'The connection between devices of plot-formation and general stylistic devices (1919), arguing that compositional and stylistic devices are closely correlated. In his monograph on Sterne's *Tristram Shandy* he provocatively sets out to demonstrate that this novel is the most typical novel in world literature. The term 'typical' might be best appreciated through the substitution of the word 'conventional', which means 'of or connected with convention', and convention is another word for device. One would expect a novel with the title *The Life and Opinions of Tristram Shandy* to take the reader through the major events of the hero's life, yet this hero is not born until Book 4; the Preface appears in the middle of the novel; some chapters are omitted; there are long digressions and interruptions. The story-line, its raw material [*fabula*], is thus defamiliarized by 'laying bare' the device of retardation. The process of retardation is the plot [*syuzhet*] of the novel. The novel speaks of its own coming into being. Shklovsky is to argue in 'The mystery novel' that detective stories work on the same retardation principle. Shklovsky agreed with later Formalists in seeing literary evolution in terms of a dynamic. In process is a combination of the downgrading of overfamiliar devices and the upgrading of older devices.

Many critics see Shklovsky's *Zoo* (1923), *Third Factory* (1926) and article in *Literaturnaya Gazeta* 'A monument to scientific error' (1930) as signs of his political surrender, though Sheldon disputes this, suggesting that *The Third Factory* in particular, though on the surface a sort of memoir, is in fact a spirited defence of formalist principles. Russian Formalism was criticized for failing to pay attention to history or to provide a systematic linguistic theory of its own. Shklovsky was certainly against a vulgar sociological approach, as his article 'In defence of the sociological method' (1927) makes clear. Furthermore, questions of ideology were considered – not the ideological colouring, merely the place that ideology occupied within the structure of the text. None the less it has to be admitted that Formalism and **Marx**ism are incompatible.

Shklovsky can be rightly regarded as the precursor of **Propp**. His influence on **Brecht** cannot be denied, Brecht's *Verfremdungseffekt* being the political equivalent of Shklovsky's *ostranenie*. And Shklovsky's ideas on literary evolution – refined by another Formalist, Tynyanov – forced intellectuals, at least, to question the view of history as a progressive evolution. Many of Shklovsky's concepts have been usefully and effectively exploited by literary scholars in the West.

Main works

'The resurrection of the word' in *Russian Formalism: A collection of articles and texts in translation*, ed. Stephen Bann and John E. Bowlt, Edinburgh: Scottish Academic Press, 1973, pp. 41–7.

'Art as technique' in Lee T. Lemon and Marion J. Reis, trans., *Russian Formalist Criticism: Four essays*, Lincoln, NA: University of Nebraska Press, 1965, pp. 5–24. Also in Robert Con Davis and Ronald Schleifer, *Contemporary Literary Criticism*, London: Longman, 1989, pp. 55–66.

'The connection between devices of plot-formation and general stylistic devices', in Bann and Bowlt, pp. 48–72.

'Sterne's *Tristram Shandy*: stylistic commentary' in Lemon and Reis, pp. 25–57.

Zoo, or Letters not about Love, trans. Richard Sheldon, Ithaca, NY: Cornell University Press, 1971.

V. Shklovsky Sentimental Journey: Memoirs, 1917–1922, trans. Richard Sheldon, Ithaca, NY: Cornell University Press, 1970, reprinted 1984.

The Theory of Prose, trans. Benjamin Sher, Elmwood Park, IU: Dalkey Arch, 1991.

Third Factory, trans. Richard Sheldon, Ann Arbor, MI: Ardis, 1977.

'Poetry and prose in the cinema', trans. Richard Taylor, in *Russian Poetics in Translation*, Keele: University of Keele, vol. 9, 1982, pp. 87–9.

'In defence of the sociological method', trans. Ann Shukman in *Russian Poetics in Translation*, Keele: University of Keele, vol. 4, 1977, pp. 92–9.

Mayakovsky and his Circle, trans. Lily Feiler, London: Pluto Press, 1972.

Further reading

Erlich, Victor, *Russian Formalism: History and doctrine*, New Haven: Yale University Press, 1965.

Jackson, Robert Louis and Rudy, Stephen (eds), *Russian Formalism: A retrospective glance. Festschrift in honor of Victor Erlich*, New Haven: Yale University Press, 1985.

Sheldon, Richard, 'The formalist poetics of Viktor Shklovsky', *Russian Literature Triquarterly*, 2, Ann Arbor, MI: Ardis, 1972.

Sheldon, Richard, *Viktor Shklovsky: An international bibliography of works by and about him*, Ann Arbor, MI: Ardis, 1976.

Sherwood, Richard J., 'Viktor Shklovsky and the development of early Formalist theory on prose literature', in Stephen Bann and John E. Bowlt (eds), *Russian Formalism: A collection of articles and texts in translation*, Edinburgh: Scottish Academic Press, 1973.

Striedter, Jurij, *Literary Structure, Evolution and Values: Russian Formalism and Czech Structuralism reconsidered*, Cambridge, Mass.: Harvard University Press, 1989.

Showalter, Elaine (1941–)

Elaine Showalter was born in Cambridge, Massachusetts in 1941, and studied at the University of California. From 1967 to 1984 she taught English and Women's Studies at Rutgers University, where she became Professor of English. She is currently Chair of the Department of English at Princeton University. Since the publication of her groundbreaking *A Literature of Their Own: British women novelists from Brontë to Lessing* in 1977 and her essays on feminist literary theory, 'Towards a feminist poetics' (1979) and 'Feminist criticism in the wilderness' (1981) she has been acknowledged as one of the leading feminist critics in North America. Since the mid 1980s she has been especially prolific, producing editions of literary texts, critical writings or monographs almost annually. Her concerns in several of her more recent works have diversified beyond the literary into feminist cultural history and analysis.

Elaine Showalter is generally considered a pioneer of Anglo-American feminist literary criticism. Whereas early seminal works of second-wave feminism had, as part of an overall political enterprise, almost unselfconsciously showed literature, along with other cultural forms, to reflect and contribute to patriarchal structures, and had looked at both men's and women's writings (famously displaying to ridicule and condemnation the misogyny of canonical male writers such as D.H. Lawrence and Henry Miller) feminists such as Showalter, Ellen Moers and Patricia Meyer Spacks were committed to a new strand of feminist analysis which focused exclusively on women's writing. This marked the emergence of feminist methodologies and concerns as a serious challenge to established and orthodox approaches within existing academic disciplines. *A Literature of Their Own* is a detailed, scholarly work which became a classic critical text in the study of women's writing on English and Women's Studies courses, as well as having a wider readership outside the academic world. In it, Showalter, as her title implies, sets out to delineate a British female literary tradition from the 1840s to the present. She fills in the gaps between well-known women writers such as Jane Austen, the Brontës, George Eliot and Virginia **Woolf**, restoring to literary history the works of their once widely read, but by the 1970s largely forgotten, contemporaries. She defines the female literary tradition as a 'subculture', stressing the need not only to consider what unifies women's literary concerns across time, but also to examine these in relation to wider changes in 'women's self-awareness' and their social and cultural roles at different historical moments. Showalter contributed crucially to the movement to make obscured women writers visible once more. This similarly motivated the founding of publishers such as Virago in Britain, and recovery of lost women's writings became, and remains, an important aspect of feminist literary scholarship. Many of the forgotten women writers she draws attention to – such as Margaret Oliphant, Rhoda Broughton, Harriet Martineau, Mrs Humphrey Ward – have continued to receive sustained critical attention. Work such as Showalter's enabled feminists to reveal and question the political underpinnings of the conventional literary canon.

Showalter presents women's literary tradition, like other subcultures, as passing through developmental stages. She names these the *Feminine* (the phase of writing from 1840, when the male pseudonym for women writers appeared and when women's fiction was, she argues, shaped by male models, to 1880 and the death of George Eliot); the *Feminist* (from 1880 to 1920, the period of suffrage protest and first-wave feminism, concluding with the winning of the vote for women); and the *Female* (1920 to the present, a period of self-discovery, especially marked by a shift towards increased self-awareness from about 1960.) Throughout *A Literature of Their Own*, her emphasis is on the relationship between women's experience and their fictional concerns, and she charts a general, if not uniform, movement beyond restriction and inhibition in the fictional depiction of socially contextualized, authentically female experience across the nineteenth and twentieth centuries in Britain. It is this unproblematized assumption of realist criteria for assessing women writers' degrees of successful achievement of 'femaleness' which has attracted most criticism of her work.

Showalter's theoretical position is not made explicit in *A Literature of Their Own*. In 1979, however, in 'Towards a feminist poetics', she distinguishes 'feminist critique', the work of women critics who probe and expose the ideological assumptions of male authors, from criticism which deals with women's writing. She invents the term 'gynocritics' to identify this second, woman-centred, practice, which aims to draw a historical map of forms and concerns of women writers, to analyze 'the psychodynamics of female creativity' in general and to study closely particular women authors and works. Her 1981 essay 'Feminist criticism in the wilderness' extends this argument. In it she takes stock of the aims and theoretical bases of feminist criticism in the United States, Britain and France to date, and reiterates her own distinction between 'feminist critique' (now renamed 'feminist reading'), an interpretative activity, and 'gynocritics'. In this rather confusing essay, Showalter rejects use of male critical theory, while proposing a cultural model of women's writing based on the work of the cultural anthropologists Shirley and Edwin Ardener and Clifford Geertz. But at the same time she suggests that she does not wish 'to enthrone Ardener and Geertz as the new white fathers in place of Freud, Lacan and Bloom'. She attempts to disentangle herself from this knot of contradiction by concluding with a reaffirmation of her belief that what is most important is 'close and extensive knowledge of women's texts'.

In the best-known and most influential of her more recent writings, *The Female Malady: Women, madness and English culture* (1987) and *Sexual Anarchy: Gender and culture at the* fin de siècle, Showalter's methods are those of a cultural historian working in a largely empirical tradition. *The Female Malady* investigates the historical association between women and madness. Her aim in this book is twofold: to examine the powerful linking of women and irrationality – whereby the irrational is seen as feminine and the feminine comes to be symbolized by madness, through analysis of cultural texts – and to construct a feminist history of psychiatry. She incorporates readings of medical writings, the diaries and narratives of women diagnosed as insane, novels, paintings and photographs into her detailed, forceful and often distressing account. In *Sexual Anarchy*, Showalter takes on the theory of 'endism'. Through a juxtaposition of the cultural and social preoccupations of the 1890s and the closing decades of the twentieth century, she points to parallel features, leading her to speculate on the meanings of the ends of centuries. Are they borderlines in time? Or do they suggest cycles of social and cultural crises clustered around an apocalyptic 'sense of an ending'? In this book, Showalter presents and examines, with characteristic wit, detail and range of reference, 'myths, metaphors, and images of sexual crises and apocalypse that [mark] both the late nineteenth century and our own *fin de siècle*'.

Showalter remains an important and acclaimed feminist critic and cultural historian. Her work is recognized as embodying the greatest strengths but also many of the problems of Anglo-American feminist thought. Her early work has been criticized, most notably by Toril Moi, for its unconscious political and aesthetic assumptions. Moi highlights Showalter's apparent belief that successful feminist literary texts are those which reflect the writer's authentic female experience (preferably positively) and transmit a powerful sense of experience to the reader. As Moi demonstrates, this valuing of 'realist images of women' is, in fact, a demand that all feminist writers should use realist fictional forms. And this, correspondingly, depends on a particular (liberal humanist) notion of society as comprising unitary individuals. Those writers whose works Showalter perceives as flawed are precisely those, such as Virginia Woolf or Doris Lessing, who 'radically undermine the notion of the unitary self, the central concept of Western male humanism' and who, through a ' "deconstructive" form of writing', reject 'the metaphysical essentialism underlying patriarchal ideology'. Moi sets up Showalter's assumptions and methods as antithetical to those of French post-structural feminists. Showalter's suspicion of theory, which she has tended to characterize as male, has similarly been criticized by Moi and others. Although these criticisms refer mainly to her early writing, similar problems can be identified in her later work. The relation between texts and historical and social event is not problematized, so that a rather simple reflective model is assumed; and her notions of the self, and even the gendered self, remain uncomplicated. *The Female Malady* reads as descriptive of the historical association of women and madness rather than offering any structural analysis of the relationship between actual psychic distress, social oppression and textual representation.

Main works

A Literature of Their Own: British women novelists from Brontë to Lessing, Princeton, NJ: Princeton University Press, 1977.

'Towards a feminist poetics', in Mary Jacobus (ed.), *Women Writing and Writing About Women*, London: Croom Helm, 1979.

'Feminist criticism in the wilderness', 1981, reprinted in Elizabeth Abel (ed.), *Writing and Sexual Difference*, Chicago: University of Chicago Press, 1982.

The New Feminist Criticism: Essays on Women, literature and theory, New York: Pantheon, 1985; London: Virago, 1986.

The Female Malady: Women, madness and English culture, London: Virago, 1987.

Sister's Choice: Tradition and change in American women's writing, Oxford: Clarendon Press, 1989a.

(ed.), *Speaking of Gender*, New York: Routledge, 1989b.

Sexual Anarchy: Gender and culture at the fin de siècle, London: Bloomsbury, 1991.

Further reading

Moi, Toril, *Sexual/Textual Politics: Feminist literary theory*, London and New York: Methuen, 1985.

Sinfield, Alan (1941–)

Alan Sinfield is Professor of English in the School of Cultural and Community Studies at the University of Sussex, where he convenes the MA programme 'Sexual Dissidence and Cultural Change', the title of which comes reasonably close to summarizing the development of his interests during a period in Britain and America which had seen the rise of the political and cultural backlash of the Thatcher/Reagan years, when the left saw the gains of the 1960s and 1970s at least partially clawed back, though not without a fight; when men and women, in some respects, had less control over their lives and bodies than before and when, by the mid 1980s, after the defeat of the miners, organized labour seemed at its weakest since the war.

While Sinfield had written and edited books on dramatic monologue and Shakespeare's tragedies during the 1970s, it was as if the political swing to the right was an impetus for him to consider explicitly political questions to do with the representation of gender and social change and, by the mid 1980s, to formulate and articulate a particular method of analysis; cultural materialism, which, broadly, is a version of the British **Marx**ist tradition of ideological critique which has absorbed the insights of post-structuralist and post-**Freud**ian continental theory. The beginnings of this kind of analysis, and some of its most important principles, are to be found in work published in the early 1980s.

In 'Against appropriation' (1981), Sinfield suggests that literary texts will serve us better if we allow them to 'challenge rather than confirm ourselves'; the real relevance of texts from the past, for instance, resides precisely in their distance from our time, their 'otherness', a quality critics in the humanist tradition seek to suppress. The reason for this, Sinfield argues in *Literature in Protestant England 1560–1660* (1983), is that this tradition holds that literature expresses enduring human values, and it is by these very same values that we should evaluate it. This also means that the rigours and contradictions of Reformation religious doctrine, its very strangeness, becomes obscured.

Modern criticism of this period tends to highlight the more moderate Christian values of thinkers like Erasmus because it is much easier to reconcile these views with the criticism's own. Critics tend to slant interpretations towards what is acceptable to the modern reader. One of Sinfield's examples is *Macbeth*. Critics tend to say that the witches in the play are really psychological projections informed by Macbeth's ambition. Against this kind of thinking, which sees the plays as repositories of universal human truths, Sinfield points out that in a period when witchcraft was a matter of common belief, when witches could still be put to death, the witches are, first and formost, witches. To deny this is to suppress the drama's cultural difference and to play down its distance from us. Sinfield suggests that critics will put a genial humanistic gloss on superstitious beliefs, rather than admit that Shakepeare may not be for all time, and that *Macbeth*, in certain major respects, has a less than universal meaning. This, for Sinfield, is a form of appropriation, and though such appropriations may be impossible to avoid, we should try to resist and reduce them in our own reading.

This is not to say that Sinfield accepts, for instance, Tillyard's *The Elizabethan World Picture* (1943), where literary texts reflect a world-view shared by all. Texts do not passively reflect their context, neither do they transcend it; they do not simply 'reflect' a world-view in the realm of ideas, but actively play a part in the making of meaning, and are themselves sites of ideological struggle. What Sinfield is suggesting is that we reverse the principle of relevance; earlier writing illuminates not because it appeals to enduring needs but because it offers an alternative perspective, a chance to question unexamined assumptions.

In *Literature in Protestant England 1560–1660* Sinfield is looking for a theory that will speak to the authoritative role of official doctrine and the opportunities for dissidence and change, and to the relationships between them. He finds the beginnings of it in the work of Raymond **Williams**, Stuart **Hall** and others, which argues that the dominant culture of a complex society is never homogeneous, but layered, reflecting different interests within the dominant class as well as containing traces from the past, and emergent and subordinate elements. This theoretical position later became a more fully worked-out set of principles when Sinfield co-authored them with Jonathan **Dollimore** and called the result 'cultural materialism'; this piece constituted the Foreword to the influential collection *Political Shakespeare* (1985). Dollimore and Sinfield take the term from the work of Raymond Williams, who defined 'cultural materialism' as 'the analysis of all forms of signification, including quite centrally writing, within the actual means and conditions of their production'. They adopted Williams's term because it insisted that culture was material (the product of a given society at a particular moment in time) and because it implied a radical politics – that is, taking up an oppositional role in relation to the dominant culture: 'cultural materialism does not pretend to political neutrality. It knows that there is no cultural practice that is without political significance' (Sinfield and Dollimore, 1985).

One piece of cultural practice was Sinfield's *Literature, Politics and Culture in Postwar Britain* (1989), a history of the postwar period that set out to show what had been gained and lost in that time, and particularly in the ten years of New Right government the publication of the book marks. It weighs up the possibilities for a dissident cultural politics more fully explored in Sinfield's work in the 1990s, initially in *Faultlines: Cultural materialism and the politics of dissident reading* (1992). Sinfield chooses the term 'dissident' over 'transgressive' or 'subversive' because these other terms imply that something has already happened, something has been subverted, transgressed and contained. 'Dissidence' implies a refusal of some aspect of the dominant without prejudging the outcome. The book examines the way texts produce plausible stories and construct subjectivities, and the faultlines through which dissident readings can be made. This takes the form of ideological critique, but the book is also a meditation on the relationship between dominance and subversion in texts and culture as they are presented in the work of American New Historicists and British cultural materialists.

The work of Michel **Foucault** is often read as giving powerful accounts of the workings of ideology as an unbreakable continuum. If the ruling ideas in society are those of the ruling class, as Marx suggested, and we come to consciousness with a language that is continuous with the power structures that sustain the social order, how, Sinfield asks, can we conceive of, let alone organize, resistance? For him, political awareness comes not from a notion of an irreducible self but from involvement in a subculture; it is through sharing modes of thinking with others that we build a plausible oppositional selfhood. To argue for the real possibility of a dissident reading of both politics and literature, Sinfield takes on the New Historicist argument that dissidence is always contained, and that subversion is just an effect of the dominant. Quite simply, there are extra-discursive forces at work; in *Macbeth*, Duncan has all the legitimacy, but Macbeth is the better fighter. For a materialist, when either dominance or resistance turns out to be the more successful, it is *not* in the nature of things, but depends on the balance of forces. If dissidence provokes brutal repression, then this is surely evidence that it could not be just a ruse of power to consolidate itself.

As Dollimore has pointed out, a dominant discourse that speaks of subversion is also giving it a voice. Sinfield takes his example from Foucault's work, against the usual reading of him. Nineteenth-century discourses on homosexuality made possible new forms of control, but also enabled a 'reverse discourse' whereby homosexuality began to speak for itself, often using the very terms by which it was subordinated. A contemporary example would be the adoption of the pejorative terms 'dyke' and 'queer' by lesbians and gay men.

Sinfield relates the notion of the definitive role of the extra-discursive in determining the outcome of an event to literary criticism. It means that formal textual analysis alone cannot decide whether a text's subversion is contained, because the historical conditions in which it is being deployed are crucial; meaning cannot be adequately deduced from the words on the page. For Sinfield, a text is always a site of cultural contest, but never a self-sufficient site. The theory which is the Other of both essentialist humanism and literary formalism is an unfashionable one; Marxism, a materialist theory and practice abandoned by intellectuals (as Dollimore has written) 'scared stiff of appearing less than totally sophisticated and up-to-date' (1990).

Sinfield's most recent writings have been on queer politics, marginality and dissidence. His book on Oscar Wilde traces the history of 'queerness' and effeminacy and its fraught relation to the literary: while his notion of dissident writing has taken on a further dimension from this context: the book examines forms of identity politics, while asserting, as in the rest of Sinfield's work, that identity is a social construct. For Sinfield, Wilde's 'queerness' was not discovered in court; he examines how the very demonizing of Wilde as homosexual opens up the possibilities for an alternative homosexual identity.

Sinfield's work has both informed and been a part of the explosion of materialist studies of Renaissance texts. 'Political Shakespeare' in this context indicates both an explicitly political reading of the text, examining its ideological underpinnings, and an examination of the 'politics of Shakespeare' which would involve looking at the institutional meanings encrusted upon the dramas; the way Shakespeare has been produced in the schoolroom and the theatre. Sinfield's own work has taken both forms, and as co-editor of a series of books under the general title 'cultural politics' he has been instrumental in the dissemination of these approaches both inside the academy and in the literary press – not least in an acrimonious and long-running debate in *The London Review of Books* (March 1990 – September 1991) where, for those attacking cultural materialism, the phrase 'political Shakespeare' is an oxymoron.

Main works

'Against appropriation', *Essays in Criticism*, 31, 3 (1981): 181–95.

Literature in Protestant England 1560–1660, Beckenham: Croom Helm, 1983a.

(ed.) *Society and Literature 1945–1970*, London: Methuen, 1983b (contains two essays by Sinfield).

(ed. with Jonathan Dollimore) *Political Shakespeare*, Manchester: Manchester University Press, 1985 (contains two essays by Sinfield).

Alfred Tennyson, Oxford: Blackwell, 1986.

Literature, Politics and Culture in Postwar Britain, Oxford: Blackwell, 1989.

'Culture and textuality: debating cultural materialism', *Textual Practice*, 4, 1 (1990).

Faultlines: Cultural materialism and the politics of dissident reading, Oxford: Oxford University Press, 1992.

'Should there be lesbian and gay intellectuals?', in Joseph Bristow and Angela R. Wilson (eds), *Activating Theory*, London: Lawrence & Wishart, 1993.

The Wilde Century: Effeminacy, Oscar Wilde and the queer moment, London: Cassell, 1994a.

Cultural Politics – Queer Reading, London: Routledge, 1994b.

Further reading

Felperin, H., *The Uses of the Canon*, Oxford: Oxford University Press, 1990.

Greenblatt, Stephen, *Shakepearean Negotiations*, Oxford: Oxford University Press, 1988.

Howard, J. and O'Connor, M. (eds), *Shakespeare Reproduced: The text in history and ideology*, London: Methuen, 1987.

Wilson, R. and Dutton, R. (eds), *The New Historicism and Renaissance Drama*, Harlow: Longman, 1992.

Smith, Barbara Herrnstein (1932–)

Barbara Herrnstein Smith is an American literary critic/theorist, Professor of English and Communications at the University of Pennsylvania; she was educated at City University in New York and Brandeis University, where she received her BA in 1954, her MA in 1955, and her PhD in 1965. She rose to prominence in 1968, when her book *Poetic Closure*, an ambitious attempt to discover how a wide range of poetry – Elizabethean lyric, free and syllabic verse, concrete poetry – works as poetry, won the Phi Beta Kappa Christian Gauss Award and the Explicator Award.

Smith is a left-liberal literary theorist whose critical orientation is usually considered part of literary semiotics – specifically, the kind of semiotic study that attempts to isolate the distinctive features of literary discourse. Her work engages the the arguments of speech act theory, replacing an understanding of a static symbolic text with the action of the literary text in reading construction. Her second book, *On the Margins of Discourse: The relationship of literature to language* – a collection of essays which deal with the question of the relation between literature, language, and other art forms – established her reputation as an analytical thinker of some insight and depth. This volume, which is a response to Nelson Goodman's *Languages of Art*, is theoretically grounded in not only the traditional opposition between 'art' and 'nature', but the early Russian Formalists' discrimination between poetic and ordinary language, and the structuralist culture/nature dichotomy. In defining 'marginal discourse', Smith makes a distinction between 'natural' and 'fictive' discourse: fictive discourse is a second-order discourse which is a fabrication or reproduction, a product of design, a representation or deliberate 'making appear' of counterfeit forms of natural phenomena which 'reflects our impatience with nature'; natural discourse, on the other hand, remains independent of desire, true to the real existence of things in nature:

> By 'natural discourse' I mean here all utterances – trivial or sublime, ill-wrought or eloquent, true or false, scientific or passionate – that can be taken as someone's saying something, somewhere, sometime, that is, as the verbal acts of real persons on particular occasions in response to particular sets of circumstances. In stressing all these particularities, I wish to emphasize that a natural utterance is a historical *event*; like any other event, it occupies a specific and unique point in time and space. (Smith, 1978)

Poetry is a fictive discourse, which distinguishes itself from other mimetic art forms and other verbal compositions in two ways. In the first instance, it represents *discourse,* not worlds, scenes, ideas, or even feelings; in the second, a poem is not a natural utterance, occupying a specific and historical point in time and space, but the *representation* of one. Here the crucial difference, for Smith, resides in the nature of the speech act itself, for she is not claiming that a poem is fictive because the 'character' or 'persona' utilized in it is distinct from the poet, or that the events, emotions, or audience alluded to are fictional; the point is that the *'the speaking, addressing, expressing, and alluding are themselves fictive verbal acts'*. Thus poetry is defined neither by its use of 'poetic language' or those tropes and figures, nor by its distortion of syntax or use of idiomatic expression or diction, nor even by its use of imagery and allusion. Rather, it is defined by its *fictiveness*. Consequently, any attempt by literary historians or biographers to restrict the context of a poem to historical particulars, or to suggest that the meanings of a poem are to be confined exclusively to a historically determinate context, is to be rigorously resisted. For the 'meaning' of any poem, like its value, is the product of linguistic contexts and culturally defined conventions which evolve in time. This notion of the meaning and significance of a literary work recalls the reader-response orientation of such theorists as Hans Robert **Jauss** and Wolfgang **Iser**, for whom the reception of any literary work takes place within a context of expectations the horizon of which has been established by previous works; the work's significance, its value and merits, change and evolve over time through its accumulative reception from generation to generation.

In *Contingencies of Value* (1988), Smith extends her examination of the relation between literature and language into the discourses of taste and value. Central to her argument is the question of the way in which a piece of literature gains both meaning and value. Although this focus is not new, it extends some of her long-abiding philosophical concerns into the area of the production and reception of literary and non-literary texts. Here her observations begin to coincide with some contemporary pragmatists such as Richard **Rorty**, whose own attack on philosophical foundationalism, published in 1989, is entitled *Contingency, Irony, and Solidarity*. The following passage, taken from *Contingencies of Value*, might have been penned by Rorty himself.

> All value is radically contingent, being neither a fixed attribute, an inherent quality, or an objective value of things, but rather an effect of multiple continuously changing and continuingly interacting variables or, to put this another way, the product of the dynamics of a system, specifically, an *economic* system. (Smith, 1988)

While this quotation may seem to be a prelude to a **Marx**ist evaluation of literary production, in point of practice Smith is conceptually closer to Darwin than to Marx: the reference to an economic system here gives a more general context to an account of canon-formation, redefining in the process the concept of evaluation, taking it beyond any simple or discrete gestures of 'approval' (or disapproval) into a wide range of selective activities. These activities, which involve a complex of individual preferences and choices, have broad social/cultural conse-quences. Thus, the production and endurance of cultural products – literary works, intellectual production, social practices – is better understood as a kind of *natural selection*. Smith's retelling of the making of a 'classic', for example, in an essay entitled 'Endurance, otherwise a response to Martin Mueller', focuses on a kind of pragmatic process of selection rather than on the 'genius' of a given author or on any enduring, eternal, inherent 'greatness' that any classic possesses. These works are defined by the fact that they are repeatedly offered up as valuable: they get insinuated into other texts through, among other things, citation, translation and commentary. In other words, they become woven into a cultural fabric by the very fact that they remain prevalent in the texts and teaching practices of successive communities of thinkers.

The influence of Barbara Herrnstein Smith's work falls within the scope of those twentieth-century literary critics who have engaged issues raised in the area of modern philosophical aesthetics, and have thus been concerned with retaining an understanding of distinctiveness and value regarding literature, meanwhile replacing the notion of a literary text as a static object with an emphasis on reading as a process of constructing, rather than discovering, meaning. In this she stands beside such thinkers as Wolfgang Iser and Monroe **Beardsley**.

Main works

Poetic Closure: A study of how poems end, Chicago: University of Chicago Press, 1968.

On the Margins of Discourse: The relationship of literature to language, Chicago: University of Chicago Press, 1978.

Contingencies of Value: Alternative perspectives for critical theory, Cambridge, MA: Harvard University Press, 1988.

The Unquiet Judge: Relativism and legal/political agency, Toronto: University of Toronto Press, Faculty of Law, 1990.

'Endurance, otherwise a response to Martin Mueller', *Salmagundi*, 88–9 (Fall 1990–Winter 1991): 455–68.

Further reading

Connor, Steven, *Theory and Cultural Value*, Oxford and Cambridge, Mass.: Blackwell, 1992.

Harpham, Geoffrey, *The Ascetic Imperative in Culture and Criticism*, Chicago and London: University of Illinois Press, 1987.

Natoli, Joseph, *Tracing Literary Theory*, Urbana and Chicago: University of Illinois Press, 1987.

Norris, Christopher, *Spinoza and the Origin of Modern Critical Theory*, Oxford and Cambridge, Mass.: Blackwell, 1991.

Rorty, Richard, *Essays on Heidegger and Others*, Cambridge and New York: Cambridge University Press, 1991.

Soyinka, Wole (1934–)

Wole Soyinka, Africa's first Nobel Laureate for Literature, received the prize particularly for his work as a dramatist, but he is also an important poet and (occasional) novelist. In addition, he has held a number of academic positions, and is currently Professor of Comparative Literature at the University of Ife, Nigeria.

Although Soyinka is obviously best known as a producer of literature, he has also been a consistent commentator on questions regarding the relation between culture and society, the nature of literature and the role of the artist, resembling in this his famous contemporaries, the novelists Chinua **Achebe** and **Ngugi wa Thiongo**. Understandably, though many of his essays concern African culture and the theatre as his principal area of cultural production, they are far from being restricted to them; similarly, although one might wish to characterize Soyinka's essays as, broadly, polemical interventions, there is more to them than that. Nevertheless, from his earliest articles, Soyinka's writing on culture has been strongly polemical, and frequently better-known for the controversy surrounding it than for the substance of the arguments. The main engagements have been with **Marx**ist critics (variously categorized as 'Leftocrats' or 'radical chic-ists') and, at the other end of the theoretical spectrum, the nativist school of cultural criticism as personified in the 'Troika' of Chinweizu, Jemie and Madubuike, best known for their book *The Decolonisation of African Literature*. Although the disagreements are often aggressively personalized, they also raise cultural and theoretical issues which are important for Africa, but which in addition – if such justification were needed – have a wider resonance.

Rejection of Chinweizu-style nativism could be seen as the latest version of one of Soyinka's early battles, with the Négritude movement, in essays such as 'From a common backcloth' and 'And after the narcissist?'. Soyinka's dislike of what he considered the self-regarding and self-promoting nature of Négritude is encapsulated in his well-known remark 'A tiger does not *proclaim* his tigritude, he pounces.' (This perceived exclusive concern with talking about things rather than doing them is something he later attacks Marxist critics for.) The particular failing of Négritude lies elsewhere, however: in its acceptance of negative Western descriptions of black people – even if it hopes ultimately to overturn them. A too-easy or uncritical acceptance of Western categories and ideologies, coupled with a reluctance to give African culture the praise it deserves, is something which Soyinka has opposed throughout his career, more recently in the work of left-wing African critics. It is worth nothing, however, the element of possible *rapprochement* with Négritude implied in the desire to give proper weight to African culture. This is increased by the position taken in *Myth, Literature and the African World*, where, especially in the essay 'The fourth stage', Soyinka develops his vision of tragic drama and its relation to African culture through traditional categories, particularly ones based in myth and ritual. What is important for him is to demonstrate that 'the self-apprehension of the African world' in terms of concepts and categories can be embodied in properly African cultural forms, forms which can be considered to have artistic merit.

Daringly – shockingly for many – Soyinka argues that a conceptual system based on traditional Yoruba deities such as Ogun (god of iron, war, creation, transitions) and Obatala ('the embodiment of the suffering spirit of man'), is not only relevant to contemporary Africa but also its most appropriate means of expression. Refusing to accept that the use of mythic or ritual concepts implies cultural stasis or retrogression, Soyinka contends that Ogun, as god of lightning, for example, very easily becomes god of its modern technological equivalent, electricity. Less simply gods for Soyinka than complex nodes of principles and processes, Ogun and Obatala embody, respectively, action, primal energy (both disruptive and generative), rebellion and celebration and, on the other hand, passivity, rationality, contemplation and resolution of conflicts. They thus form a complementary pair (like Dionysus and Apollo), as well as a cycle involving destruction and rebuilding which operates both at the level of the literary text and at that of the individual and collective in society. Their characteristics of rebellion and suffering on the one hand translate into the martyred hero of tragic drama and, on the other, emphasize the degree of self-sacrifice involved in any revolutionary political struggle.

The relation between culture and political process is something of which Soyinka is very aware. Again, one of the shortcomings of Négritude for him was the fact that its practitioners seemed to disregard the way in which cultural texts can function as political weapons – either as conscious interventions or, more disturbingly for the writer, as open to appropriation by political forces. In view of this acute awareness, the fact that critics have deemed a number of

Soyinka's works apolitical comes as something of a surprise, but it is also a pointer to the frequently complex or contradictory nature of the positions Soyinka adopts, as well as that of the relation between his critical essays and his literary output.

A more frequent charge levelled at Soyinka is that his work is ahistorical, essentialist or idealist. Certainly, along with the Caribbean poet and critic Derek Walcott, Soyinka is probably the most important contemporary writer consistently to give myth priority over history. Walcott sees this as an act of courage on the part of the writer, and it is doubtful whether Soyinka would disagree. In addition, Soyinka sees no problem in construing society and politics in an ahistorical or essentialist manner, arguing, for instance, that 'all socio-political systems believe in "the final resolution of things" ', or 'What will always be intolerable is any attempt to suggest that the explication of social history and attitudes may not be expressed symbolically.' ('Who's afraid of Elesin Oba?', in *Art, Dialogue and Outrage*). At the same time, he is just as likely to mount a vigorous defence of his concepts against charges of essentialism or political quietism. In the case of the Ogun and Obatala cycle, for example, he asks critics who accuse him of adopting a static and essentialist view how they can be so sure that every revolution in the cycle will leave society or the individual in precisely the place they started out from. Nevertheless, it may still seem that a term like revolution in Soyinka's writings is to be understood more as a cyclical movement than a large-scale political upheaval. (This being the case, it is perhaps no coincidence that a 1975 lecture entitled 'Drama and the Revolutionary Ideal' came to be renamed 'Drama and the Idioms of Liberation'.)

Here again, however, there is an apparent contradiction between this attenuation of the political and Soyinka's lifetime of political activism – most notably when, during the Nigerian Civil War, he objected to the treatment of the (enemy) Ibo people, and was imprisoned for several years as a result. The latter would certainly fit his idea of the proper role of the writer (creative or critical) as someone prepared to act in accordance with their pronouncements, while also confirming that 'practical' politics matter more than the textual variety. In his scathing attack on left-wing critics, 'The critic and society', he says: 'It is time to pronounce the rigorous question "What are you really contributing to society while awaiting the revolution?" ' (*Art, Dialogue and Outrage*). The question, and the essay as a whole, typify Soyinka – for better or worse. On the one hand, his strictures on the complacency of his left-wing compatriots may well be justified, as is his call for greater (self-)awareness of the cultural, social and institutional location of the critic. At the same time, asking someone what real contribution they are making to the social order whose very overthrow they are (presumably) eagerly awaiting sounds distinctly strange, while the description of Marxism as a system which believes itself 'complete, controlled and controlling: an immanent reflection of every facet of human history, conduct and striving' scarcely does credit to the sophistication or credibility of his argument.

It may well be, then, that the greatest impact or importance of Soyinka's articles and essays lies in their status as polemic, rather than sustained cultural meditation. As the former, their success is assured; as the latter, it is somewhat more precarious – although a former adversary like Biodun Jeyifo is now prepared to see 'The fourth stage' as 'the finest document of modern African idealist philosophy', other critics (and not just his obvious Marxist or nativist opponents) feel that it and others like it have been accorded too much importance, both within Soyinka's *oeuvre* and beyond, and that reassessment is due. Ogun would no doubt approve.

Main works

(as novelist) *The Interpreters*, London: André Deutsch, 1965.

Season of Anomy, London: Rex Collings, 1973.

(as dramatist) *Collected Plays*, vols I & II, Oxford: Oxford University Press, 1973, 1974.

Death and the King's Horseman, London: Methuen, 1975.

(as critic) *Myth, Literature and the African World*, Cambridge: Cambridge University Press, 1976.

Art, Dialogue and Outrage: Essays on literature and culture, London: Methuen, 1993.

Further reading

Chinweizu, Jemie, Ilechukwn Onwuchekwa Madubuike, *The Decolonisation of African Literature*, Washington, DC: Howard University Press, 1983.

Gibbs, James (ed.), *Critical Perspectives on Wole Soyinka*, Washington, DC: Three Continents Press, 1980.

Irele, Abiola, *The African Experience in Literature and Ideology*, London: Heinemann, 1981.

Jeyifo, Biodun, 'Wole Soyinka and the tropes of disalienation', Introduction to Soyinka, *Art, Dialogue and Outrage*, London: Methuen, 1993.

Katrak, Ketu, *Wole Soyinka and Modern Tragedy*, Westport, CN: Greenwood Press, 1986.

Spender, Dale (1943–)

Australian feminist Dale Spender was educated at the Universities of Sydney, New South Wales and New England. She is the founding editor of Women's Studies International Forum, and co-founder of Pandora Press, London.

Dale Spender first came to prominence with the publication of *Man Made Language* in 1980. Her contention in this book follows the deterministic theories of Sapir and Whorf in asserting that language structures the way in which we view our world: 'Language is *not* neutral. It is not merely a vehicle which carries ideas. It is itself a shaper of ideas, it is the programme for mental activity' [Spender, 1980]. Spender argues that language is in fact patriarchal, created in order to express a male-dominated perspective. Women are forced to live within this male-dominated world-view, their linguistic marginalization leading inevitably to their cultural and social subordination to men.

The first part of *Man Made Language* critically examines the state of current linguistic research into sexism in language. Spender sees this research going in two different directions – what she terms 'sexist' research reinforces the linguistic status quo, while feminist research in the same area has consciously aimed to challenge the conventional construction of female discourse as 'inferior' to male discourse. The findings of sexist research are dismissed unequivocally by Spender, who claims that the researchers' methodology is flawed by their invariable bias in favour of the male. Feminist research, on the other hand, in its interrogation of the logical order upon which the entire dominant discourse is based, poses a genuine challenge to patriarchal assumptions. The formulation of an alternative, woman-centred frame of reference which is based upon its own system of values and assumptions enables the silence of women denied access to a viable discourse to be exposed.

The rest of Spender's book is concerned with elaborating on the strategies by which such a silence has been constructed. In so doing, her argument moves away from purely linguistic concerns towards a discussion of the particular problems faced by women writers. Modern feminism may have gained them increased social acceptance, but even the most self-conscious feminist attempting to write is faced with the problem of her subordinate postition in discourse. Every woman writer thus becomes inevitably involved in the struggle to formulate a new discursive system capable of articulating their own, female, reality.

Man Made Language, therefore, is not just a straightforward sociological examination of the differences between male and female speech. Although Spender does analyze conversation according to sociolinguistic models in the course of her argument, she is primarily concerned with a wider consideration of how meaning, knowledge, and ultimately reality itself, are constructed through language. The gender which has linguistic superiority also controls the generation of meaning, with the consequence that women live within a view of reality which keeps them perpetually marginalized. In an essay written in 1983, Spender clearly articulates the ideological conviction which has motivated all her work from *Man Made Language* onwards:

> If meaning is arbitrary in the sense I am suggesting that it is, then I will put my energies into constructing meanings that help to explain things that were inexplicable under patriarchal rules, and that help to show me, and women, in a positive rather than negative light . . . which has been the case while males have been in charge of constructing meaning. (In Bowles and Duelli Klein, 1983)

It is this attempt to formulate and maintain a woman-centred discursive system based on a recovered tradition of women's writing and intellectual endeavour that links her wide and fairly diverse body of publications. If *Man Made Language* can be viewed as setting out the agenda for the development of a woman-centred perceptual framework, *Mothers of the Novel* (1986), which overturns the popular conception of the status and productivity of women writers in the eighteenth century, is a good example of Spender's subsequent development of that agenda. In her Introduction she claims initially to have planned the book according to the conventional assumption that women's writing began with the advent of Jane Austen at the beginning of the nineteenth century. However, Spender says, her subsequent research revealed that Austen was far from being the first woman novelist, or even the first successful woman novelist. Instead, she was consciously writing out of a long tradition of women's fiction stretching back for well over a century.

Some of the writers discussed in *Mothers of the Novel* are at least vaguely familiar to the literary reader – Aphra Behn and Ann Radcliffe, for example – but Spender reveals that there were many more women writers whose work received widespread acclaim in the eighteenth century, and who did not deserve the obscurity to which they were subsequently assigned. Spender's project in this book is twofold – not only does she recover these women through synopses of their lives and work, she also goes on to expose the processes by which they were relegated to such obscurity in the first place. She argues that a double standard arose by which men's writing and women's writing were assessed differently, women's being categorized as stylistically second

-rate and concerned with such 'inferior' subjects as romance and domestic concerns. Once it was generally accepted that only men wrote 'good' literature, claims Spender, it became easy for influential critics such as Ian Watt to dismiss the female contribution to the development of the novel altogether.

Mothers of the Novel, therefore, does not intend just to rediscover the life and work of forgotten women writers, but also to construct a critique of the institutions of scholarship and education for upholding and perpetuating the erroneous assumption that, as men created the novel form, their consequent domination of it is quite natural. In writing this book, Spender opens the door to a woman-centred literary history, giving her readers access to information that reveals the misogynistic bias concealed in long-established and hitherto virtually unquestioned conventions.

According to Spender's argument, however, women continue to write and think, despite the fact that they do so within a discourse which persistently obliterates their efforts in order to rewrite history in its own patriarchal image. If this is so, her project to recover a tradition of female history and intellectual endeavour is absolutely vital. In books such as *Women of Ideas* (1982), Spender argues against the conventional history of feminism as a primarily twentieth-century phenomenon, revealing a forgotten history of women questioning their social and intellectual subordination to men dating from the seventeenth century. Her unwillingness to allow her own work, and that of her feminist contemporaries, to become subject to similar censorship motivates *For the Record* (1985), which outlines the views of the most influential thinkers within the modern feminist movement. Arguing that 'unless we keep reminding each other of our heritage we endanger it, we risk losing it as we contribute to our own amnesia' (Spender, 1985), Spender energetically defends a female intellectual space which she sees as being under constant threat from the dominant discourse it intends to challenge.

Spender's work is not particularly original, in that her argument for the reclamation of feminist knowledge is one that motivates the work of other women writers, such as Adrienne **Rich** and Joanna Russ (whose book *How to Suppress Women's Writing*, published in 1983, closely echoes Spender's debate in *Mothers of the Novel*). Furthermore, Spender's methodology in *Man Made Language* has been questioned by feminist linguists such as Deborah Cameron, who regards her treatment of linguistic determinism as somewhat inconsistent. However, Spender's work is widely read, and has motivated much discussion concerning women's place in education, literature and language. It is extremely accessible, and this is due not only to the popularity of her subject matter but also to her readable style. Her writing is characterized by its frequent appeal to her own personal experience, and her willingness to 'write herself' into her work in this way contributes to its accessibility.

Main works

Man Made Language, London: Routledge & Kegan Paul, 1980.

Women of Ideas and What Men Have Done to Them, London: Pandora Press, 1982.

'Theorising about theorising', in Gloria Bowles and Renati Duelli Klein (eds), *Theories of Women's Studies*, London: Routledge & Kegan Paul, 1983.

For the Record: The making and meaning of feminist knowledge, London: The Women's Press, 1985.

'What is feminism? A personal answer', in Juliet Mitchell and Anne Oakley (eds), *What is Feminism?*, Oxford: Blackwell, 1986a.

Mothers of the Novel: 100 good women novelists before Jane Austen, London: Pandora Press, 1986b.

Writing a New World: Two centuries of Australian women writers, London: Pandora Press, 1988.

The Writing or the Sex? or Why You Don't Have to Read Women's Writing to Know It's No Good, Oxford: Pergamon Press, 1989.

Further reading

Black, Maria and Coward, Rosalind, 'Linguistic, social and sexual relations: a review of Dale Spender's *Man Made Language*, in Deborah Cameron, (ed.), *The Feminist Critique of Language: A reader*, London: Routledge, 1990.

Cameron, Deborah, *Feminism and Linguistic Theory*, London: Macmillan, 1985.

Spivak, Gayatri Chakravorty (1941–)

Gayatri Spivak was born in Calcutta in West Bengal and has described her origins as 'solidly metropolitan middle class' (Spivak, 1990). She did her undergraduate degree at the University of Calcutta, and has identified herself with the 'first generation of intellectuals after [Indian] independence' (*ibid.*). She went to the United States in the early 1960s to do graduate work at Cornell University, where she was taught by Paul de Man. She has since taught at the universities of Iowa, Texas–Austin, Pittsburgh, and Emory. She has also lectured and taught widely outside the United States: in Australia, Saudi Arabia, India (in 1987 she held a visiting professorship at the Centre for Historical Studies at Jawaharlal Nehru University, New Delhi) and elsewhere. She is currently Professor of English and Comparative Literature at Columbia University, New York.

Rather than book-length projects united by a single sustained thesis, Spivak's published work customarily takes the form of an essay or, more recently, an interview (two of her books are collections of essays and one is a collection of interviews, though by no means all her work is collected within the covers of these three works). Her first book, *In Other Worlds: Essays in cultural politics* (1987), is divided into three sections. The first consists of post-structuralist readings of canonical literary texts from *To the Lighthouse* to the *Vita Nuova* and *The Prelude*; the second, of more explicitly theoretical pieces on feminism, **Marx**ism and deconstruction. In the final section, there are two translations (by Spivak herself) of short stories by the Bengali fiction writer Mahasweta Devi, along with two essays – one on the version of post-colonial historiography inaugurated by Marxist Indian historians known as *Subaltern Studies*, the other a symptomatic reading of one of Devi's stories entitled 'A Literary Representation of the Subaltern: A Woman's Text from the Third World'. *The Post-Colonial Critic* [*P-CC*] (1990), her second book, is a collection of twelve edited interviews published and/ or broadcast in Australia, Canada, India, the United States and Britain between 1984 and 1988. The dialogic mode of the interview is one to which Spivak feels herself particularly suited: 'It's always interesting to see one's own slips, or, where one falls back. These are things that you don't really get in other situations' (*P-CC*). Her most recent book, (*Outside in the Teaching Machine* [*OTM*] (1993), addresses the 'explosion of marginality studies in college and university teaching in the United States' since the late 1980s. While she revisits many of her favourite haunts – such as **Derrida**, Marx, **Foucault**, French feminism, and the work of Mahasweta Devi – there is a marked shift towards considerations of post-colonial texts (such as Kureishi's *Sammy and Rosie Get Laid* and Rushdie's *Satanic Verses*). The theme which appears to unite the essays in *OTM* is a critique of the contemporary practice of cultural studies. The title refers to the paradoxical position she inhabits: on the one hand she interrogates the politics of culture from the margin or the 'outside' (without seeking to be determined as simply 'marginal'); on the other, she is professionally located within specific institutions and pedagogical practices – 'in the teaching machine'.

Spivak has not objected to being described as a 'feminist, Marxist, deconstructivist', and she has no difficulty in reconciling these strands of her theoretical make-up with one another (nor with her more recent interest in post-colonial theory). Her intellectual formation as a graduate student in the United States in the early 1960s and as a young Assistant Professor from 1965 no doubt contributed to her theoretial orientation. In each of her three collections, questions within Marxism, feminism and post-colonial theory are examined through the lens of deconstruction. It is a source of irony and satisfaction to her that she is frequently perceived to be an anomaly by each of these 'schools': 'My position is generally a reactive one. I am viewed by the Marxists as too codic, by feminists as too male-identified, by indigenous theorists as too committed to Western theory. I am uneasily pleased about this' (*P-CC*).

Deconstruction is the thread which runs through all her work, and underpins all her theoretical engagements. Her first major publication (1976) was a translation of Jacques Derrida's *De la Grammatologie*, prefaced by a long introductory essay in which she sketched the philosophical traditions upon which Derrida draws in this work, examining his debts to **Nietzsche**, **Freud**, Heidegger and Husserl, and analyzing his relationship to French structuralism. Both translation and translator's preface constituted an important event in terms of the dissemination of Derrida's thought within the English-speaking world. Despite proving her competence in the discipline of philosophy in this project, Spivak resolutely describes herself now as a literary critic. Her own graduate training under de Man (among others) undoubtedly drew her towards Derrida's work and taught her 'the importance of reading absolutely literally' (*P-CC*). This, perhaps, explains her comment: 'When I first read *Of Grammatology*, I felt I had understood what it was saying, and that it was a better way of describing what I was already trying to do' (*ibid.*). However, her attitude to deconstruction as a theoretical enterprise is not uncritical and is sharply distinguished from those, especially North American academics, who are happy to describe themselves as practitioners of deconstruction. She has said of herself: 'although I make specific use of deconstruction, I'm not a deconstructivist' (*ibid.*). By this she suggests that she is sceptical of the very idea that deconstruction can be practised, let alone that it constitutes a political programme of any kind.

Spivak's intervention in feminist debates can be best exemplified through two essays: 'French feminism in an international frame' (first published in *Yale French Studies* 62 [1981]) and 'Displacement and the discourse of woman' (1983). In 'French feminism in an international frame' Spivak presents a critique of **Kristeva**'s book *About Chinese*

Women (1977). Kristeva is taken to task for her apparent obliviousness to the limitations of her own cultural perspective in using the predicament of Chinese women to further an articulation of Western feminist theory. Spivak also finds fault with Kristeva and **Cixous** for their 'presupposition of the *necessarily* revolutionary potential of the avant-garde, literary or philosophical', thus distancing herself from a tendency in French feminist theory to equate modernist, avant-gardist practices with political radicalism. But she also grants that Kristeva's double programme for women, '*against* sexism and *for* feminism', is politically suggestive and useful (such an acknowledgement of the politically strategic uses of essentialism can also be found in her endorsement of the *Subaltern Studies* project). In 'Displacement and the discourse of woman', she begins with the proposition that 'It would be possible to assemble here a collection of "great passages" from literature and philosophy to show how, unobtrusively but crucially, a certain metaphor of woman has produced (rather than merely illustrated) a discourse that we are obliged "historically" to call the discourse of man.' As Easthope and McGowan put it: 'It is Spivak's argument that within the irreducibly material dimensions of sexual difference male deconstructivists [she has in mind Derrida in particular] desire the displaced position of woman as their own, and that in taking that position for themselves they displace the figure of woman twice over' (1992). Elsewhere (e.g. in 'Feminism and critical theory' [1986] in *In Other Worlds* [*IOW*]. Spivak has commented on both the virtues and the dangers of deconstruction for feminism. On the one hand, it is 'the deconstructive view that keeps me resisting an essentialist freezing of the concepts of gender, race, and class . . . This aspect of deconstruction will not allow the establishment of a hegemonic "global theory" of feminism.' On the other, it is not simply that deconstruction has opened a way for feminists but, more problematically, 'the figure and discourse of women opened the way for Derrida as well'. While the critical deconstruction of phallocentrism, in Derrida's early work, is useful for a socially engaged critic sympathetic to feminism and Marxism, '[it is] when he writes under the sign of woman that his work becomes solipsistic and marginal'.

Spivak has described the work of the *Subaltern Studies* group, led by Ranajit Guha, as 'the most active example of deconstructive historiography that I have seen' (*P-CC*). The word 'subaltern', a British military term for 'an officer below the rank of captain' (*OED*), is used by Guha and the others in **Gramsci**'s sense of 'proletarian'. In 'Can the subaltern speak?' (first given as a paper in 1983) Spivak locates the project in terms of a wider questioning of historiography and historical method in the work of Foucault and others, while at the same time positing the (im)possibility of representing the colonial subaltern subject. Laura Chrisman has summarized Spivak's argument thus: 'she focuses on the figure of the subaltern South Asian woman, whose contradictory constructions and control by traditional patriarchal authority and by English colonialism, instanced in the history of *sati* (widow-burning), provide an illustration of the aporias of colonial discourse theory, and a challenge to both empiricist and idealist notions of "the subaltern" subject's historical representability' (1993). In 'Subaltern Studies: deconstructing historiography' (1985) Spivak argues that even as the project describes itself as an attempt to rethink Indian colonial historiography from the perspective of the 'discontinuous chain of peasant insurgencies during the colonial occupation', it is still caught within the vestiges of a positivist historiography. Nevertheless, she supports what she identifies in *Subaltern Studies* as 'a *strategic* use of positivist essentialism in a scrupulously visible political interest' (*IOW*).

Spivak's contribution to modern theoretical debate lies in her attempt to negotiate a constant critique of Marxism, post-colonial theory and feminism through the use of deconstruction. While her interests are resolutely focused on issues of race, class and gender, she is also adept at avoiding the pitfalls of marginality. As she put it in 'Explanation and culture: marginalia' (1979): 'The only way I can hope to suggest how the center itself is marginal is by not remaining outside in the margin and pointing my accusing finger at the center' (*IOW*). She has also provided access, through her translations from Bengali, to questions of race, class and gender in Third World literary texts.

Main works

(translation of, and introduction to) Jacques Derrida, *Of Grammatology*, Baltimore: Johns Hopkins University Press, 1976.

'Displacement and the discourse of woman', in Mark Krupnick, (ed.), *Displacement: Derrida and after*, Bloomington, IN: Indiana University Press, 1983, pp. 169–95.

In Other Worlds: Essays in cultural politics, London: Methuen, 1987.

'Can the subaltern speak?', in Cary Nelson and Larry Grossberg (eds), *Marxism and the Interpretation of Culture*, Chicago: University of Illinois Press, 1988a, pp. 271–313.

(ed., with Ranajit Guha) *Selected Subaltern Studies*, Oxford: Oxford University Press, 1988b.

The Post-Colonial Critic: Interviews, strategies, dialogues, ed. Sarah Harasyam, London: Routledge, 1990.

Outside in the Teaching Machine, London: Routledge, 1993.

Further reading

Eagleton, Mary (ed.), *Feminist Literary Criticism*, London: Longman, 1991.

Easthope, Anthony and Kate McGowan, *A Critical and Cultural Theory Reader*, Duckingham: Open University Press, 1992.

Williams, Patrick and Laura Chrisman (eds), *Colonial Discourse and Post-Colonial Theory: A reader*, Harvester Wheatsheaf: Hemel Hempstead, 1993.

Young, Robert, *White Mythologies: Writing history and the West*, London: Routledge, 1990.

T

Todorov, Tzvetan (1939–)

Tzvetan Todorov, poetician, narratologist and genre theorist, was born in Bulgaria in 1939, but has lived in France (where he is Directeur de Recherche, CRNS, Paris) since 1963. During the 1960s Todorov, **Barthes** and Gérard **Genette** became the leading figures in French structuralist literary theory. Todorov is particularly associated with the revival of interest in poetics, and founded (with Genette and Hélène **Cixous**) the influential journal *Poétique* in 1970.

In 1957, Northrop **Frye**'s *Anatomy of Criticism* attempted to outline the general principles of literature, heralding the return to poetics which informs the structuralism of Todorov, Genette and Barthes. Todorov – like the Russian Formalists who influenced him so deeply, and the structuralist *manqué* Frye – sees criticism as a science, declaring in 1973: 'structural analysis of literature is nothing other than an attempt to transform literary studies into a scientific discipline'. Consequently, structuralism needs poetics, 'a coherent body of concepts and methods aiming at the knowledge of underlying laws'. Todorov begins his most influential work, *The Fantastic: A structural approach to a literary genre,* (1975), with an extended discussion of Frye, whose ideas provide a 'point of departure' for structuralist poetics. However, Todorov dismisses Frye's identification of archetypes as the link between an individual text and the literary 'universe'; it is genres which 'are precisely those relay points by which the work assumes a relation with the universe of literature'. Consequently, the study of genre assumes a central place in Todorovian poetics. Todorov also rebukes Frye for ignoring linguistics. He shares Barthes's desire to see 'the structural analysis of narrative be given linguistics itself as founding model', arguing in *The Poetics of Prose* that 'All knowledge of literature will follow a path parallel to that of the knowledge of language.' Both Barthes and Todorov identify **Saussurean** linguistics (which also claim to be universal and scientific) as particularly relevant to structuralist poetics. Todorov acknowledges that the Russian Formalists had already identified the relevance of linguistics to poetics and, drawing upon his

Eastern European heritage, his work is influenced by the Formalists Viktor **Shklovsky** and Roman **Jakobson** (notably his 'Linguistics and poetics'), and by the related writings of the folklorist Vladimir **Propp**. Todorov is an important propagandist for the Formalists, and his 1965 anthology *Théorie de la littérature: Textes du Formalistes russes* was instrumental in renewing interest in their work.

Saussurean linguistics draws a distinction between *langue* (linguistic systems, with their norms and rules) and *parole* (the individual use of the system), and focuses on the system rather than its particular manifestations. Similarly, structuralist poetics tends to address the general structures of literature as they are manifested in the individual text rather than the 'meaning' of those texts. To borrow Saussure's terms, Todorov identifies the *langue* of narrative which is realized in the *parole* of the individual text. The critical emphasis is placed on the way in which narratives are intertextually conditioned through the operation of genres rather than on the 'autonomous', 'organic' text. Genette declared: 'literature had been regarded as a message without a code for so long that it became necessary momentarily to regard it as a code without a message', and one of the defining characteristics of structuralist criticism is this move away from asking what texts mean in favour of an examination of how meaning is produced. Todorov extends the structuralist shift in focus from content to form into an argument that content is itself often a meditation upon form. Borrowing from Shklovsky, he stresses the preoccupation of literary texts with their own fictionality, and the concomitant self-exposure of that fictional status: 'the meaning of a work lies in its telling itself, its speaking of its own existence'.

Despite his emphasis on general form and structure, Todorov does not neglect the individual text in favour of dislocated generalization. It becomes the poetician's source document, 'the means by which one can describe the properties of literature in general'. Todorov's most famous examination of an individual text is his *Grammaire du Décaméron*. Both here and in *The Fantastic*, Todorov identifies three key 'aspects' of the literary work: the 'verbal' (the sentence units which constitute the text), the 'syntactical' (the relationship between its structural 'parts') and the 'semantic' (its themes or content). His main emphasis is on the syntactical aspect. He posits the existence of a 'universal grammar' which informs all languages, and attempts to trace the 'imprint' of this grammar in the *Decameron*. Boccaccio's tales are paradigmatic for structural analysis, as each story is part of a wider 'abstract structure'. Todorov labels his examination of narrative structures in general 'the science of narrative' or 'narratology'.

Narratology provides the general theoretical basis for genre theory, which examines the different narrative 'species' or 'subgroups'. In *The Fantastic*, his most sustained examination of genres, Todorov argues, in true Saussurean manner, that a genre is defined by its difference from other related genres, 'defined in relation to the genres adjacent to it'. The fantastic is bounded by the uncanny and the marvellous. The uncanny text ultimately explains away its horrors in rational terms, while the marvellous presents us with a world where the supernatural is the norm. The fantastic, however, is characterized by the 'uncertainty' felt by the reader when, during the process of reading a narrative (or even after completing it), he or she is unable to decide if its events are uncanny or marvellous, 'real' or 'imaginary'. This hesitation between the real and the unreal typifies the 'literary' (which the *Introduction to Poetics* calls the 'least linguistically transparent' form of language). It means that the fantastic, far from being a minor genre, is 'the quintessence of literature'. *The Fantastic* follows Jakobson in drawing a distinction between 'literary' language and 'ordinary' language. While literary texts are 'the product of a pre-existing combinatorial system', they can also 'transform' that system. Thus genres are comprised of narratives which are interdependent, conditioning each other. Though individual linguistic acts do not alter the linguistic systems in which they are manifested, the literary *parole* can, in certain circumstances, transform the literary *langue*. This, however, is not to deny the validity of genre analysis; a knowledge of generic norms and structures is essential, as 'For there to be a transgression the norm must be apparent'.

Post-structuralist and **Marx**ist theorists have identified what they see as the fault lines in Todorovian structuralism. **De Man** makes the charge that Todorovian structuralism imports linguistics into poetics in a naive and uncritical manner. **Macherey** attacks structuralism in general for its ahistoricism, **Lacan** for its pretensions to a scientific 'metalanguage'. **Derrida**'s work, insisting as it does that all language is characterized by the play of *différance*, repudiates the Formalist/ structuralist boundary between literary and non-literary discourse. In the light of the post-structuralist insistence that criticism should acknowledge its own status as a rhetorical construct, Todorov's scientific vocabulary leaves him open to the charge that his work marks the death throes of an unproblematically rationalist model of literary analysis.

Todorov is wrestling with some of these problems in the final chapter of *The Fantastic*. The radical 'uncertainty' engendered by the fantastic confronts us with the difficulty of positing the 'real' world in a literary text. If ordinary language attempts to transcribe the real, literary language inscribes the impossibility of doing so ('combats the metaphysics of everyday language'). Thus literary language disrupts attempts to use language for the transparent representation of truth and reality: 'literature is a kind of murderous weapon by which language commits suicide'. From here it is only a small step to deconstruction. What marks Derrida's work off from Todorov's is his insistence that *all* language is 'literary' in Todorov's sense – that it defers the presence of the signified.

During the 1960s and 1970s, Todorov was a central figure in the rise of French literary structuralism and in the revival of poetics. His championing of **Bakhtin** and the Russian Formalists has been instrumental in the rediscovery of these important but previously neglected theorists. *The Fantastic* remains a classic of genre theory, and has been of great importance in the renewal of critical attention on forms of literature which have often been maligned as flippant escapism. In the last decade, New Historicists have developed the ideas of *The Conquest of America*, Todorov's meditation on colonialism and alterity (c.f. **Greenblatt**).

Main works

The Fantastic: A structural approach to a literary genre, trans. Richard Howard, Ithaca, NY: Cornell University Press, 1975.

The Poetics of Prose, trans. Richard Howard, Ithaca, NY: Cornell University Press, 1977.

An Introduction to Poetics, trans. Richard Howard, Minneapolis: University of Minnesota Press, 1981.

Theories of the Symbol, trans. Catherine Porter, Ithaca, NY: Cornell University Press, 1982.

Symbolism and Interpretation, trans. Catherine Porter, London: Routledge & Kegan Paul, 1983.

The Conquest of America: The question of the Other, trans. Richard Howard, New York: Harper, 1984.

Genres in Discourse, trans. Catherine Porter, Cambridge, Cambridge University Press, 1990.

Further reading

Brooks-Rose, Christine, *A Rhetoric of the Unreal: Studies in narratives and structure, especially of the fantastic*, Cambridge: Cambridge University Press, 1981.

Culler, Jonathan, *Structuralist Poetics: Structuralism, linguistics and the study of literature*, London: Routledge & Kegan Paul, 1975.

Hawkes, Terence, *Structuralism and Semiotics*, London: Methuen, 1977.

V

*Voloshinov, Valentin Niokolaevič (c.1895–)**

Voloshinov, a musicologist, was a member of what has become known as the **Bakhtin** Circle – a group of writers and intellectuals active in the Russian districts of Neval and Vitebsk between 1918 and 1924 (the early years of the Soviet Union).

The texts entitled *Freudianism: A Marxist critique and Marxism and the Philosophy of Language* are ascribed to V.N. Voloshinov, but it is important to note that the critic and philosopher M.M. Bakhtin claimed, late in his life, to be the author of these texts. This entry, while acknowledging the dispute, assumes that the texts are the work of Voloshinov. Although Voloshinov's first book suggests an interest in **Freud**ian psychoanalysis, the subtitle – *A Marxist critique* – gives a stronger indication of his theoretical orientation, and his commitment to the intellectual practice of critique. In many ways the critique that Voloshinov advances against psychoanalysis in *Freudianism* is best approached by way of his second and most influential book, *Marxism and the Philosophy of Language,* in which he articulates a sociohistorical theory of the sign, thus enabling the development of trends in recent literary and cultural theory which are critical of the legacies of both **Saussure**an structural linguistics and Romantic aesthetic ideology.

Voloshinov outlines two trends of thought in the philosophy of language: individualistic subjectivism and abstract objectivism. Individualistic subjectivism holds that language is activity, an unceasing process of creation realized in individual speech acts, and that the laws of language creativity are the laws of individual psychology (Voloshinov, 1973). This trend of thought can be traced to the idealist philosophy of Wilhelm von Humboldt. From the point of view of the field that Voloshinov's ideas critique, it is important to remember that Humboldt's idealism was shaped by late-eighteenth-century German Romanticism,

---

* NB: Voloshinov disappeared during Stalin's purges of Soviet Russia in the 1930s; precise date (and cause) of death are unknown.

which was important in the development of a predominantly subjectivist nineteenth- and twentieth-century aesthetic ideology. Abstract objectivism is the antithesis of individualistic subjectivism; it ignores the main object venerated by individualistic subjectivism, the individual utterance, and concentrates instead on the objective language system that makes utterance possible. This trend of thought can be traced to the linguistic theory of Ferdinand de Saussure. Saussure's theory of the sign as a systemically determined but ultimately arbitrary unit of meaning is itself historically grounded in a tradition of abstract, rationalist thought about language dating back at least to the eighteenth century; again, it is this tradition that Voloshinov's theory sets out to critique.

It is Voloshinov's theory of the ideological sign that acts as the basis for this critique. The world of physical objects is separate from the world of the sign, but the moment a physical object becomes a referent, a version of it functions as a sign and has entered the socio-historical domain of ideology. For Voloshinov it is language, or the *word*, which is 'the ideological phenomenon *par excellence*' (Voloshinov, 1973); this because of its '*social ubiquity*', or the fact that the word is implicated in each and every act or contact between people (*ibid.*). It is this social basis to the ideological sign, exemplified in the word, that enables Voloshinov to develop a united critique of the two major trends in the philosophy of language, for both individualistic subjectivism and abstract objectivism overlook the social nature of the sign. The privileged terrain of individualistic subjectivism – so-called private thought and introspection which is distinct from and perverted by 'expression' in Romantic theory – is in practice mediated by 'inner speech', or signs which have their origin in the ideological domain of the social world. And abstract objectivism fails to acknowledge the sign as a shared social phenomenon – a phenomenon that is defined by an utterance which passes between (at least two) subjects. However, Voloshinov's theory avoids being a simple account of intersubjectively recognized meaning based around the norm inherent in the principle of a code, and it is his commitment to a **Marx**ist model of social analysis which ensures this. For according to Voloshinov, signs are 'understood' (*ibid.*); and understanding implies the faculty of manipulating and apprehending the socially sensitive adaptability of the sign. While speakers inhabit a common sign community, the fact that the community is divided along class lines means that speakers will accent the signs at their disposal in different ways: 'each living ideological sign has two faces, like Janus' (*ibid.*). Thus ideology is the process of social struggle that is carried on through and embodied in forms of utterance and writing.

In respect of the theory of ideology, *Marxism and the Philosophy of Language* might be said to be grounded in the much fuller exposition of the concept which is undertaken in Voloshinov's first book, *Freudianism* to which we should now turn. *Freudianism* presents psychoanlysis as an ideology in a classically Marxist sense; that is to say, as a symptomatic expression of a historically bankrupt bourgeois class, a body of ideas which occludes the economic and social determinants of being, clings to individualism, and so distorts knowledge of material reality (Voloshinov, 1976). Voloshinov argues that Freudian psychoanalysis is potentially important from a Marxist point of view precisely because, as a post-Darwinian theory, it posits conflict as the essential condition underpinning the operation of the individual psyche (*ibid.*). From the perspective of a Marxist critique, however, it is essential that this conflict be recognized as social in origin. Voloshinov argues that the Freudian model of the psyche is reductively subjectivist, and hides the true conditions of existence of the material on which it grounds its analysis of the psyche's conflict – that is, the language of the analysand. Moreover, the language of the analysand has to be seen as inner speech which is prompted by an interlocutor – the analyst – and so the psychoanlytic encounter is charged by a social context and all that this implies, given the multi-accentual nature of the sign. As such, the signs comprising the utterances of both analyst and analysand must be viewed as ideological behaviour, and interpreted through the same framework of ideological analysis as Freudianism itself has been (*ibid.*). It will be clear, then, that many of the concerns which are elaborated at greater length in *Marxism and the Philosophy of Language* are present in this earlier work.

Voloshinov elaborates an important theory of discourse: a theory of utterance or inscription which holds that meaning is dependent on social context. However, some of his examples of the operations of discourse – for instance, in the essay 'Discourse in life and discourse in poetry' – might strike the reader as underdeveloped, given the weight of exemplarity they are asked to carry. And one could argue that Voloshinov's emphasis on the sign as the main focus for discourse analysis keeps his project too close to the structuralist framework that it is seeking to surpass; it is notable that later theorists of discourse who have rejected structuralism, such as **Ricoeur**, have tracked their quarry through more complex units of analysis – the sentence and the categories of speech act theory in Ricoeur's case. Finally, Voloshinov's critique of the ideological asociality displayed by Freudian psychoanalysis strongly resonates with the assumptions of early-twentieth-century Marxism. These assumptions have been challenged by **Lacan**ian psychoanalysis, which arguably 'socialized' Freudianism by emphasizing language as a symbolic system constitutive of social relations – and this socially regenerated psychoanalysis underpins the socialist feminism of literary and cultural critics such as Juliet Mitchell and Cora Kaplan.

In terms of the history of literary critical ideas, Voloshinov is, as Wiliam Garrett Walton has argued, most important for his place in the early-twentieth-century debate between Russian Formalism and Marxist aesthetics. For Voloshinov's theory of the socially dialogic sign, accounting for both internal and external speech as well as inscription, effectively opened the way for a 'marriage' between the textually intrinsic criticism of the Russian Formalists and the extrinsic sociology of early Marxist literary theory. Because of the unertainty over the authorship of *Marxism and the Philosophy of Language* and *Freudianism*, it is difficult to assess Voloshinov's wider cultural impact: if we follow a critic like Michael Holquist (1990) in arguing that Voloshinov is really M.M. Bakhtin, then his cultural impact has been extensive – but this is tantamount to abolishing Voloshinov and the specifically Marxist nature of his contribution to theory. Even so, texts such as *Marxism and the Philosophy of Language* have been important to a Marxist strain in British cultural studies which has attempted to resist the dominance of structural linguistics; the pivotal chapter on language in Raymond **Williams**'s *Marxism and Literature* is organized around Voloshinov's critique of Saussure, and James Donald's analysis of the history of language, literacy and schooling in Britain draws upon Voloshinov's theory of the sign.

Main works

'Discourse in life and discourse in poetry' (1926), trans. John Richmond in *Bakhtin School Papers*, ed. Ann Shukman, Oxford: Russian Poetics in Translation, 1988.

Freudianism: A Marxist critique (1927), trans. I.R. Titunik, New York and London: Seminar Press, 1976.

Marxism and the Philosophy of Language (1929), trans. Ladislav Matejka and I.R. Titunik, New York and London: Seminar Press, 1973.

Further reading

Donald, James, 'Language, literacy and schooling', in *The State and Popular Culture 1*, Open University, Popular Culture Block 7, Milton Keynes: Open University Press, 1982.

Gardiner, Michael, *The Dialogics of Critique: M.M. Bakhtin and the theory of ideology*, London: Routledge, 1992.

Holquist, Michael, *Dialogism: Bakhtin and his world*, London: Routledge, 1990.

Walton, William Garrett Jr, 'V.N. Voloshinov: a marriage of Formalism and Marxism', in *Semiotics and Dialectics: Ideology and the text*, ed. Peter V. Zima, Amsterdam: John Benjamins B.V, 1981.

Williams, Raymond, *Marxism and Literature* (1977), Oxford: Oxford University Press, 1985.

W

White, Hayden V. (1928–)

Historian of ideas and theorist of culture and narrativity Hayden White is Professor of the History of Consciousness at the University of California at Santa Cruz.

Hayden White has critically explored the consequences of the linguistic turn in the human and social sciences for the discipline of history and the practice of historiographical writing. In *Metahistory*, White argues that historical consciousness is structured by linguistic tropes, or the foundational devices through which linguistic units are selected and combined to generate figures of speech or thought. White points to four basic tropes: metaphor, metonymy, synecdoche and irony. For the historian, the consequences that follow from this linguistic determinism are profound: the historian can no longer claim to have an innocent approach to the materials that constitute the historical field, for her/his approach is always 'prefigured' by the tropical workings of language. Moreover, White takes a radically sceptical view of the historical field, claiming that there is no inherent truth to be found in the documentary materials that constitute it. He advances an anti-referential theory of language, severs the relationship between documentary writing and the referent, and undermines the correspondence theory of truth on which orthodox historical epistemology depends. This has major implications for the historiography that a historian writes: it can no longer be seen as a mirror held up to the past; instead, it is a verbal artefact generated by tropes which themselves select and combine to determine additional layers of linguistically constructed explanation.

White claims that there are three additional layers of construction: explanation by formal argument, explanation by ideological implication, and explanation by emplotment. The first and second of these layers relate, respectively, to representations of different versions of historical causation, and representations of different ideological versions of political society. The third, explanation by emplotment, is derived from literary conventions. According to White, an historiographical work is emplotted as a romance, a comedy, a tragedy or a satire. This is crucial as, to White, the essence of historical knowledge is a tropically generated narrative form in which the historian selects, from a limited number of possible combinations, her/his image of the historical process, political society, and the plot form in which these attain significance. *Metahistory* demonstrates this contention by means of detailed and sophisticated readings of nineteenth-century European historical texts by Michelet, Ranke, Tocqueville, Burckhardt, **Marx** and **Nietzsche**. Because Marx has had such an impact on literary and cultural studies, and because the issue of reading Marx has been intensively debated in cultural theory, it will be useful to demonstrate White's structuralism in nation by sketching a simplified version of his reading of Marx's historical writings.

According to White (*Metahistory ch.8*), Marx's philosophy of history is a narrative which is simultaneously metonymic and synecdochic (at the level of rhetoric), and tragi-comic (at the level of plot). The dominant trope organizing Marx's thought is that of metonymy (a figure of speech in which parts reductively stand for wholes through relations of contiguity), and metonymy organizes Marx's conception of historical causation, which, for White, is mechanistic (or cause-and-effect). This, White points out, generates the dimension of Marx's system classically defined as the 'base', or the means of production. However, this rhetorical system is not responsible for representing human consciousness in relation to the means of production. The trope used by Marx to represent human consciousness and its potential for moral growth is synecdoche – a figure of speech similar to metonymy, but stressing integration between part and whole rather than reduction. White argues that synecdoche introduces a different rhetoric of historical 'process' into Marx's writings which is organicist and, in terms of emplotment, potentially comic in its narrative resolution. He argues, however, that Marx has to emplot the prelude to this comic resolution in tragic form – a tragedy comprising an image of enslaved humanity, its consciousness alienated from a mechanistic means of production. White's reading of Marx argues that Marx's historical materialism does not have an epistemological (let alone a scientific) foundation. Instead, it is generated by forms of rhetoric which can be legitimate only as forms of moral and aesthetic *choice*. History is not a form of knowledge; it is a moral and aesthetic practice – but no less important to rapidly changing human societies for all that.

Marx takes his place in a broader story about change and loss which White tells in *Metahistory*, regarding the way in which post-Enlightenment Western societies came to downgrade the moral and aesthetic functions of historical writing. According to White, only Hegel commanded a theoretical viewpoint which simultaneously looked back to the Enlightenment historians (Voltaire, Gibbon) and forward to the nineteenth-century 'realist' historians (Michelet, Ranke, Tocqueville, Burckhardt). The Enlightenment historians asserted the primacy of the moral and aesthetic function of history, while the realists took social change seriously and tried to represent it in 'realistic' ('cognitively responsible') forms. White argues that Hegel was important because he was a *metahistorical* thinker (self-consciously making historiography confront philosophy, demonstrating historical consciousness's dependence upon rhetoric, and its consequences for ethics). Hegel's cognitively responsible approach to the representation of social change was extended only by the rhetorical and narrative complexity manifest in writings of the 'master' realist historians; while later, only Marx and the ironic, self-conscious Nietzsche came anywhere near to extending Hegel's ambitious metahistorical project. White argues that apart from the 'heroic' writers he deals with in *Metahistory*, historians in nineteenth-century Europe came to be domesticated by the universities of politically conservative nation-states as practitioners of a narrowly conceived, ideologically motivated discipline. Wedded to a correspondence theory of truth, historiography became selective in its representation of the 'reality' of the past, and disparaging of philosophy and theory (1973).

In his later writings, particularly the collection *The Content of the Form*, White considers in more detail the political effects and consequences of this narrowing of the discipline around a restrictive ideological discourse. The essays in *The Content of the Form* display a shift to a theory of ideology which resembles **Althusser's**, showing the extent to which White has developed a concern for the way in which the rhetoric of historiography plays a specific role in the general process of constructing the social subject in discourse. White is concerned about the politically limiting effects that the conventional liberal-academic discourse of history will have upon struggles experienced by persecuted, repressed or emergent communities of subjects whose interests are not advanced by a discipline whose conventions serve the status quo. In the most important essay in the collection, 'The politics of interpretation: discipline and de-sublimation', he considers this issue in relation to the interlocking problems of interpretation and representation thrown up by the Holocaust, modern Zionism and the Palestinian problem. According to White, none of these events or causes, and the communities most deeply affected by them, are adequately served by the standard conventions of historiographical writing. To compensate, he suggests that genuinely radical modern historiographers who seek to promote change need to rediscover the Romantic concept of the sublime, which was written out of the 'official' discourses of aesthetics and politics as they became ideologically respectable in the early nineteenth century. What is required is a historiography in which the sublimity or meaninglessness of an event like the Holocaust – a panorama of sin, suffering and terror – is set before subjects, to goad them into a determination to make life different for themselves and their children.

Although White wrote 'The politics of interpretation' in an explicit attempt to show his adversaries that his relativism can take a cognitively and ethically responsible position on an event such as the Holocaust, it has not done enough to convince some critics, such as Christopher **Norris**, that epistemologically sceptical positions such as White's do anything other than play into the hands of right-wing revisionist historians (see *Deconstruction and the Interests of Theory*, 1989). Norris's critique is advanced from a position which still holds that historical facts are ascertainable, and from a similar position Arnaldo Momigliano has argued that White fundamentally misunderstands the nature of the historian's relationship to archival research – which is based on a desire to discover new evidence, and not simply the need to find new ways of telling old stories. In addition, Momigliano argues that White's history of the elision of rhetoric from historical writing, in being centred on the nineteenth century, is far too limited in its focus.

Hayden White's exploration of the linguistic basis of historiography has enabled the work of Dominic La Capra (1983) and Sande Cohen (1987), though their post-structuralist approaches are in many ways critical of White's position. Wulf Kansteiner has recently argued (1993) that a major problem with White is that he has shifted his ground in his later work without using that shift to reassess fundamentally the viability of his earlier structuralism. In a sense, White's project has been so theoretically eclectic that such a thoroughgoing autocritique would reveal too many disabling contradictions: his structuralism owes at least as much to Northrop **Frye** and Kenneth Burke as it does to **Saussure** and **Jakobson**. Furthermore, while White has drifted closer to the post-structuralism of Althusser, he has been highly critical of post-structuralism and deconstruction in general (see his essay 'The absurdist moment in contemporary literary theory', in *Tropics of Discourse*). This eclecticism and tendency to distance himself from what he is apparently close to has probably lessened his cultural impact, as has the fact that he has been either ignored or denigrated by historians. But as Kansteiner has argued, some of White's most recent work (1989) has brought him closer to theorists of literary history; and White's astute and challenging readings of the philosophical texts of Kant and Hegel, in *Metahistory* and elsewhere, should mean that his work will find a new audience of literary theorists who are seeking to read their practices in the light of histories of philosophy and philosophies of history.

Main works

Metahistory: The historical imagination in nineteenth-century Europe, Baltimore, MD and London: Johns Hopkins University Press, 1973.

Tropics of Discourse: Essays in cultural criticism, Baltimore, MD and London: Johns Hopkins University Press, 1978.

The Content of the Form: Narrative discourse and historical representation, Baltimore, MD and London: Johns Hopkins University Press, 1987.

' "Figuring the nature of times deceased": literary theory and historical writing', in Ralph Cohen (ed.), *The Future of Literary Theory*, New York: Columbia University Press, 1989.

Further reading

Cohen, Sande, *Historical Culture: On the re-coding of an academic discipline*, Berkeley: University of California Press, 1987.

Kansteiner, Wulf, 'Hayden White's critique of the writing of history', *History and Theory*, 32, 3 (1993): 272–95.

Kellner, Hans, 'Narrativity in history: poststructuralism and since', *History and Theory*, 26, 4 (1987): 1–29.

Kellner, Hans, *Language and Historical Representation: Getting the story crooked*, Madison: University of Wisconsin Press, 1989.

La Capra, Dominic, *Rethinking Intellectual History: Texts, contexts, language*, Ithaca, NY: Cornell University Press, 1983.

Momigliano, Arnaldo, 'The rhetoric of history and the history of rhetoric: on Hayden White's tropes', *Comparative Criticism*, 3, Cambridge: Cambridge University Press, 1981, pp. 259–68.

Williams, Raymond (1921–88)

Raymond Williams came from a rural working-class background in South Wales. His English degree and Communist Party political activites at Cambridge were interrupted by active service in World War II (1941–5). After completing his degree, between 1946 and 1961 he was Staff Tutor, Oxford University Tutorial Classes Committee (adult education), after which he was elected to Jesus College, Cambridge, as Fellow. In 1974 Raymond Williams was appointed Professor of Drama,

Cambridge. He retired from university teaching in 1983, though he continued to write and lecture right up until his unexpected death in 1988.

Williams wrote prodigiously and across a number of discrete acamdemic fields. The resulting work analyzes 'culture' in the broadest sense, which, for Williams, was a particular way of life expressive of certain meanings and values, not only in art and learning, but also in institutions and everyday behaviour (Williams, 1965). Throughout his career as a cultural theorist and critic Williams sought to analyze the space constituted by the interaction of social relations, cultural institutions and forms of subjectivity (Eagleton, 1984). One might add here that this space, for Williams, was always a product of material history. While he wrote prodigiously, it is in two central texts – *The Long Revolution* (1961) and *Marxism and Literature* (1977) – that his distinctive contributions to cultural theory are articulated.

Although *Culture and Society* (1958) is a seminal history of the *idea* of 'culture' in writing in English between 1780 and 1950, it is in *The Long Revolution* that Williams first theorizes his sense of the historically developing relationship between social relations, cultural institutions and forms of subjectivity from an avowedly democratic, socialist and materialist perspective. He traces three interacting forms of developmental energy in modern history. First there is a growing desire for self-government whereby communities can become decision-makers, without conceding to any particular group, nationality or class (Williams, 1965). Second, there is the continued development of capitalist structures and social relations of production – and while these can advance democracy, they are more likely to exert controlling pressures which frustrate democratic desires. Third, there is a revolutionary expansion in communicative technologies and possibilities, from basic literacy to electronic media. The revolution in communications is the most ambiguous in its effects in that it can be used to extend both the democratic desire and the tendency of capitalism to frustrate participation. Williams admits that the difficulty in fully comprehending and interpreting the relations between these developmental energies is immense; yet the aim of his project is to trace the gradual emergence of progressive trends in the histories of these developments (it is and has been a *long* revolution), and to urge the extension of these trends into the realization of a democratic 'common' (socialist) culture in the future.

Williams's analysis is conducted by means of his distinctive methodological contributions to cultural theory: 'selective traditions' and 'structures of feeling'. He appropriates the concept of cultural tradition from earlier cultural critics such as Matthew Arnold, T.S. Eliot and F.R. **Leavis**, but modifies it by drawing attention to the necessity of its constructedness, selectivity and formation within material social relations. For Williams, while a culture is much more than its documents, access to cultural meanings of the past can be obtained only through its documents, and here he looks to art forms: especially the mimetic forms of drama – his academic specialism – and the novel. Cultural institutions and forms of social power – class interests – play a powerful role in *selecting* which documents will be preserved *as they are produced*. The process does not stop there, for in receiving and preserving documents from a particular epoch, educational institutions at other points in history will interpret the documents and the 'tradition' they represent in the light of the meanings, values and interests which express their cultural identity. The formation of 'selective traditions' is thus forever active, because in any given period there will be three different generations producing and interpreting cultural meanings.

Cultural meaning is to be interpreted as a 'structure of feeling', which is a manifestation of a form of lived experience. For Williams, the value of certain documents from the past resides in the fact that they are inscribed in equal measure by, first, meanings which are 'a very wide possession', a 'structure' which will be common to more than one generation, and, second, a 'feeling', or a specific form of emergent subjectivity which is distinctive to a generation but communicable to others (Williams, 1965). Discrimination is central to the analysis of a 'structure of feeling', and as Williams argues in *Marxism and Literature*, not all art relates to a contemporary structure of feeling (Williams, 1985). Here Williams means that while most forms of cultural production reproduce a dominant set of conventions and cultural meanings, a few take shape 'at the very edge of semantic availability' (*ibid.*) In other words, they demand to be selected for attention because, first, they put new meanings into circulation; and second, these new meanings disrupt previously held but moribund ideological certainties. Williams's persistent emphasis on the novels of the 1840s by the Brontës and Dickens can be seen as a protracted attempt to analyze an emergent 'structure of feeling' which critiqued mid-nineteenth-century social ideologies by means of a new and intense articulation of lived experience (see *The Long Revolution*, Chapter 2, and 'Form of English fiction in 1848' in *Writing in Society* (1984)). For Williams, a 'structure of feeling' is artistically creative, but its appearance is not restricted to one privileged form, such as literature; in the case of Dickens and the Brontës it was literary and print based, but it may be dramatic and televisual in the later twentieth century, as he demonstrated in his work as a television critic for *The Listener* in the late 1960s and early 1970s (Pinkney, 1989). The privileged and autonomous position of the 'literary' as a cultural category (shared by Leavis and the New Critics) is radically critiqued by Williams's materialism in *Marxism and Literature*.

Williams's theory of 'selective traditions' and 'structures of feeling' undergoes considerable elaboration by the time of *Marxism and Literature*, drawing upon such analytical categories as the 'formation' (groupings of producers and interpreters of meaning, and a refinement of the early emphasis on generations) and 'dominant, residual and emergent' patterns of cultural production. These new categories underpin a more detailed and sophisticated theory of 'cultural materialism'. This theory argues against the traditional deterministic distinction drawn by **Marx**ist thought between the productive economic base and the superstructure of ideas (Williams, 1985). Under cultural materialist analysis cultural objects such as literary artefacts, for instance, are no longer expressions of 'ideas' determined by a material base; rather, they are systems of printed signs and notations, the 'meaning' of which is produced by the material interplay between social relations, cultural institutions, forms of subjectivity and available conventions. Such a form of cultural materialist analysis is exemplified in Williams's earlier investigation (in *The Country and the City*, ch. 3) of the network of relations which produced the country-house poems of Jonson and Carew. *Marxism and Literature* marks the point at which Williams's project went beyond its roots in Anglo-American literary critical and British socialist thought, and selectively aligned itself with a wider European tradition of Marxist cultural analysis, embracing **Gramsci**'s theory of hegemony and **Goldmann** on the 'collective subject'. By Williams's own account, the chapter on language (I 2), which embraces V.N. **Voloshinov**'s Marxist theory of the dialogical sign, social consciousness and ideology, was 'pivotal' (Williams, 1979). By adopting these positions in *Marxism and Literature* and *Problems in Materialism and Culture* (1980), Williams saw himself as defending a particular version of the European Marxist tradition against emergent structuralist-Marxist positions in literary and cultural studies, particularly those which had been developed out of the structural linguistics of **Saussure**, Jacques **Lacan**'s account of subjectivity, and the Marxism of Louis **Althusser** (*ibid.*). It is to these emergent positions that we should turn in order to examine, briefly, the most trenchant critique to which Williams has been subjected.

Marxism and Literature was, in part, written in response to and against the first wave of Althusserian Marxism to establish itself in English literary and cultural theory. However, Terry **Eagleton**'s *Criticism and Ideology* (1976) had already decisively distanced itself from Williams. Eagleton's opening chapter critiques Williams because of his continuing commitment to the concept of 'lived experience'. For Eagleton, Williams's work dangerously conflated productive modes, social relations, ethical, political and aesthetic ideologies, merging them into a vacuous humanist abstraction of 'culture' which was as empty and politically disabling as the concept of 'lived experience' on which it ultimately depended (Eagleton, 1976). Eagleton's Althusserian baseline of discursively constructed subjectivity eats at the heart of William's analytical dependence upon 'structures of feeling' which refer to concrete, living forms of subjectivity which both pre-exist language and evade, in part, ideological determination. While Eagleton has moved on from this position, and has in many ways realigned himself with Williams (see his *The Function of Criticism*) his arguments can still be seen as representative of a way of critiquing, first, Williams's assumptions about subjectivity, and second, his method of analyzing subjectivity in relation to social, political and linguistic structures – though as Peter Middleton has argued, Williams's dealings with the problem of the subject through his concept of 'structure of feeling' may not be as naive as Eagleton once thought (Middleton, 1989). Certain feminist critiques of Williams have, it anything, been more telling, especially, as with Jane Miller's, when they articulate the same desire for social inclusiveness as Williams's own project, and find Williams's project to be either silent or naive on a major impediment to social inclusiveness, gendered structures of language and thought. However, perhaps the most impressive form of critique to which Williams was subjected were the interviews comprising *Politics and Letters* (1979), for in response to the interviewers' question he provides a remarkably frank form of auto-critique.

When Williams died in 1988, a large number of publications and broadcasts appeared testifying to his huge impact on two generations of the British New Left. Williams's impact on the formation of the discipline now known as cultural studies has been seen as decisive (Hall, 1980). Indeed, it was Williams who, in Britain, first helped to make television a medium for serious cultural analysis, and his concept of 'total flow', which analyzes, in place of discrete programmes, the total movement and intertextual relations of TV images, has passed into the analytical vocabulary of television studies. In other ways, though, Williams's impact looks profound but has actually been supplemented – some may say weakened – by the very movements he resisted. For instance, the school of Renaissance drama critics who have fashioned themselves as cultural materialists (led by Alan **Sinfield** and Jonathan **Dollimore**) have championed Williams's work, yet embraced, in some work, forms of the post-structuralism which Williams referred to critically as a new conformism. And there have been few who have specifically worked with Williams's most personal contribution to cultural theory: 'structures of feeling'. For Williams this was an essential – though in many ways conceptually unsatisfactory – analytical tool in cultural studies; most have simply found it conceptually unsatisfactory. An important exception here is a new generation of literary and cultural critics, including Tony Pinkney (editor of Williams's posthumously published *The Politics of Modernism* [1989]), Carol Watts, Peter Middleton and Ken Hirschkop, who have, in recent work, returned to the specific categories structuring Williams's intellectual work in an attempt to rethink them in the light of the problem of postmodernity.

Main works

Culture and Society, Harmondsworth: Pelican, 1961.

The Long Revolution, Harmondsworth: Pelican, 1965.

The Country and the City, St Albans: Paladin, 1975.

Marxism and Literature, Oxford: Oxford University Press, 1977.

Politics and Letters, London: New Left Books, 1979.

Problems in Materialism and Culture, London: Verso, 1980.

Writing in Society, London: Verso, 1984.

Further reading

Eagleton, Terry, *Criticism and Ideology*, London: New Left Books, 1976.

Eagleton, Terry, *The Function of Criticism*, London: Verso, 1984.

Hall, Stuart, 'Cultural studies and the centre: some problematics and problems', in S. Hall *et al.* (eds), *Culture, Media, Language*, London: Hutchinson, 1980.

Middleton, Peter, 'Why structure feeling?', *News from Nowhere*, 6 (1989): 50–57.

Miller, Jane, 'The one great silent area', in *Seductions: Essays in reading and culture*, London: Virago, 1990.

Pinkney, Tony, 'Raymond Williams on television', *News from Nowhere*, 6 (1989): 73–7.

Wimsatt, William K. (1907–75) and Beardsley, Monroe C. (1915–85)

William K. Wimsatt was educated in Washington, DC, and taught at numerous universities in the United States, including Yale. An expert on the prose of Samuel Johnson, Wimsatt is best known for his subtle readings of poetry and his theorizing, in two very influential essays written with Monroe C. Beardsley in the 1940s, concerning the relationship of the text to author and reader. These polemical essays became two of the most important theoretical statements of what was by this time called the New Criticism (flourishing in America from the 1930s to the 1960s) which aimed at objectivity in critical analysis.

Monroe C. Beardsley was born in 1915 and taught for many years at Temple University. Beardsley wrote extensively on aesthetics, and brought the New Criticism's principles to bear on both literature and art. His *Aesthetics* (1958) has the status of a reference book, and is generally considered to be the most influential work on the philosophy of art published in America since World War II.

Wimsatt and Beardsley's 'The intentional fallacy' (1946) and 'The affective fallacy' (1948) can be seen as a two-pronged attack; in the first essay it is on Romantic or expressive criticism which saw literature in terms of the imaginative act that produced it; and in the second on late-nineteenth-century Aestheticist criticism, which was fascinated by the effect of literature upon the reader, without a concomitant interest in how that effect was achieved. Over the next thirty years, the two critics refined but still vigorously defended the critical position outlined in their early collaborative work.

In looking at the author/text/reader relation, Wimsatt and Beardsley argued that criticism, as a form of evaluation and judgement, should focus its attention on the text itself, because an orientation on either producer or receiver, author or reader, deflected attention from what a poem (the New Critic's paradigmatic literary object) really was: a piece of complex, public language that could be understood by those willing to study it carefully.

Wimsatt and Beardsley's work was part of a general attempt by the New Critics to examine literature as literature and not as a form of psychology, biography or sociology, and to produce a criticism that was none of these things either. Much later, Beardsley reflected that his and Wimsatt's early work:

> was a kind of banner or rallying cry for those literary theorists who could no longer put up with the mishmash of philology, biography, moral admonition and sheer burbling that made up what was thought of as literary criticism in academic circles. (Beardsley, 1982)

In the first of the attacks on this 'burbling'. 'The intentional fallacy', Wimsatt and Beardsley argued 'that the design or intention of the author is neither available or desirable as a standard for judging the success of a literary work of art' (Lodge, 1972). It begins, they suggest, by trying to derive the standards of criticism from the psychological causes of the poem, and ends in biography and relativism. Knowing or establishing the author's aims does not explain the work. If the poem is successful, then the poem itself will show what the poet was trying to do.

Generally, the intentionalist sees the text as a relatively unproblematic expression of the author's intention. This seems unobjectionable, but it raises many complex questions: outside the text itself, what counts as evidence of intention? Can intention speak with more than one voice? What about unconscious intention? Wimsatt and Beardsley would answer that these are very interesting questions, but they are the province of history and biography. Evidence of T.S. Eliot's mental breakdown may be found in 'The Waste Land', and may have inspired it, but this information gives us nothing by which to judge the poem *as a poem*.

Wimsatt and Beardsley do not deny that writers intend meanings when they write: Beardsley's *Aesthetics* defines art as an intentional act; Wimsatt comments that 'an artwork is something which emerges from the private, intentionalist realm of its maker's mind' (1976). That the designing intellect is the cause of a poem does not mean that the author's intention is the standard by which to judge works. Criticism, according to Wimsatt and Beardsley, should examine the text – not against some notion of intention, nor as access to some prior state of mind, but according to the standards of literary criticism. We should ask, for instance, if it is ultimately a coherent and satisfying work of art. For this task, the only history we need is the history of the words themselves.

For Wimsatt and Beardsley in the second of their polemical essays, the Affective Fallacy is a

> confusion between the poem and its *results* (what it *is* and what it *does*) . . . it begins by trying to derive the standard of criticism from the psychological effects of the poem, and ends in impressionism and relativism. (Lodge, 1972)

Moreover, 'the affective report is either too psychological or it is too vague' (*ibid.*). They do not, of course, suggest that poetry has no emotional effect, just that there must be a reason for the emotion, which depends upon the descriptive and contextual aspects of the words themselves; we should investigate the causes of the effect.

Behind both these essays, and the New Criticism generally, is a particular way of looking at poetry – what amounts to the reconstruction of the poem as a particular kind of object – and, as Beardsley pointed out, the first thing you need for an objective criticism is an object to be criticized. For Wimsatt, 'the poem itself is an abstraction produced by the author/text/reader relation, 'but if it is to be a critical object, it must be hypostatized' (1954) – that is, it must be given a certain substance which allows us to find what poetic discourse is. For Wimsatt and Beardsley, the poem becomes 'a feat of style by which a complex of meaning is handled all at once' (Lodge, 1972).

This 'complex of meaning' was explained in a number of similar ways by a variety of New Critics, each using a key term as a way of defining the 'poetic' – **Empson**'s 'ambiguity'; Tate's 'tension'; Brooks's 'irony'. These terms are evaluative for the New Critics; they define not poetry, but *good* poetry. Obviously, certain kinds of poetry responded well to this type of analysis, and the New Critics tended to privilege the immensely difficult and complex writings of the Metaphysical and Modernist poets. However (in, for example, Cleanth Brooks's *The Well-Wrought Urn* (1947), poetry from different parts of the literary canon came to be examined in this fashion.

The publication of Wimsatt and Beardsley's collaborations comes at the apex of the New Criticism's cultural hegemony in the American universities, giving theoretical justification to many book-length studies and the production of classroom textbooks, such as Brooks and Warren's influential *Understanding Poetry* (1938), a set text for a generation of American students. Wimsatt and Beardsley's work was important because in the kinds of criticism they attack, 'the poem itself, as an object of specifically critical judgement tends to disappear' (Lodge 1972). As they assert the autonomy and integrity of the literary text, they are asserting the autonomy and integrity of literary criticism as a discipline, and are themselves part of the professionalization of literary studies that marked the postwar period.

'The intentional fallacy' (reproduced eighteen times in various collections) provoked a debate which challenged but never fully answered it – from E.D. **Hirsch** in the 1960s to Knapp and Michaels in the 1980s (see Iseminger). It seems to have become the accepted wisdom in literary studies that the meaning or intention of the text cannot be delimited or established by any prior or subsequent statements by the author. Both **Derrida**'s and **Barthes**'s concepts of 'writing' rely on the fact that texts can mean in ways that the author cannot control, as Wimsatt and Beardsley pointed out in a footnote to their original essay.

It was the social and intellectual upheavals of the late 1960s that dissolved the New Critical object, and along with it the dominance of New Critical thinking. While privileging complexity in poetry, the New Critics saw it held in check by various elements that produced the poem as – in their final and most important critical move – an organic, unified, whole. The more radical post-1960s kinds of analyses, produced under the influence of continental critical theory, replaced such concepts as 'ambiguity' and 'unity' with more disturbing ones: 'contradiction', 'aporia', 'fragmentation'. By the end of the 1960s, the integrity of the text had been challenged in important ways; it was dissolved first by post-structuralism to become 'intertextuality', where texts are seen as woven from numerous other texts and discourses; and secondly by a reader-response criticism that directly challenged 'The affective fallacy' by asserting that what the text does *is* what it means. Ideological, black and feminist criticism, which was frankly engaged and committed, challenged the decorum of political neutrality in criticism, and exposed the ideological and aesthetic assumptions at work in the New Criticism. Wimsatt and Beardsley's legacy may well be the close reading for which the New Critics were noted, and a combative relish for argument and debate over the philosophical principles at work in literary criticism.

Main works

'The intentionalist fallacy' and 'The affective fallacy', in *20th Century Literary Criticism: A reader*, ed. David Lodge, London: Longmans, 1972.

William K. Wimsatt

Hateful Contraries, Lexington: University of Kentucky Press, 1965.

The Verbal Icon, London: Methuen, 1970. Contains the two collaborative essays above.

Day of the Leopards: Essays in defence of poems, New Haven, CT: Yale University Press, 1976.

Monroe C. Beardsley

The Possibility of Criticism, Detroit: Wayne State University Press, 1970.

Aesthetics: Problems in the philosophy of criticism, Indianapolis, IN: Hackett, 1981.

The Aesthetic Point of View, ed. M.J. Wreen and D.M. Callen, Ithaca, NY: Cornell University Press, 1982.

Further reading

Barthes, Roland, 'The death of the author', in *Music/Image/Text*, ed. and trans. Stephen Heath, London: Fontana, 1977.

Derrida, Jacques, 'Signature event context', in *Margins of Philosophy*, trans. Alan Bass, Brighton: Harvester, 1982.

Fish, Stanley, *Is There a Text in this Class?*, Cambridge, MA and London: Harvard University Press, 1980.

Iseminger, Gary (ed.), *Intention and Interpretation*, Philadelphia, PA: Temple University Press, 1992.

Newton-De Molina, David (ed.), *On Literary Intention*, Edinburgh: Edinburgh University Press, 1976.

Wittig, Monique (1935–)

Monique Wittig was born in the Haut-Rhin region of France in 1935. She is a Professor in the Department of French and Italian at the University of Arizona. A notable writer of innovative novels, short stories and plays, Wittig is also a significant contributor to the field of lesbian critical theory. Her 'materialist lesbian' critical position has been developed in part through her engagement with **Marxist** critique and with the recent wave of the French Women's Liberation Movement. Wittig has been involved with the latter since its emergence, having published her first experimental radical lesbian novel, *Les Guérillères* in 1969, after the student and worker protests in France; the 1968 'revolution' was a catalyst to the increased visibility of French radical women's groups under the umbrella term, attributed by the press, of the MLF ('Mouvement de Libération des Femmes') in 1970. During this year, Wittig's affiliation to French radical feminism was demonstrated when she participated in the widely publicized and iconoclastic ceremony of attempting to place on the tomb of the unknown soldier in Paris a wreath dedicated to 'the unknown wife of the soldier'. Later, in 1970, Wittig also became spokesperson for the newly formed radical group 'Féministes révolutionnaires', which staged activities calculated to disrupt the patriarchal order in France.

Throughout her work, Wittig has presented a radical critique of what she conceives of as the 'political regime' of heterosexuality. This position was initially elaborated in the essays which she contributed to the 'new materialist' feminist journal *Questions Féministes*, which was launched in 1977 under the editorship of Simone de **Beauvoir**, and has been sustained through her subsequent contributions to the American journal *Feminist Issues*. Several of these essays are now collected in *The Straight Mind and Other Essays*. The term 'materialist feminism' was coined by Christine Delphy – one of the original contributors, with Wittig, to *Questions Féministes* – to describe a theoretical approach which both appropriated and criticized the paradigms of classic **Marxist** analysis. Such feminists regarded regarded Marxist theory as being blind to the fundamental exploitation of women through reproduction, as well as production, in capitalist patriarchal societies. Materialist feminists set out to to address the way in which the economic, social

411

and political forces of heterosexual societies operate primarily through the oppression of women, thus constituted as a 'class'.

Wittig's own materialism has been combined with elements of post-structuralist theory to produce a focus upon the power of language, itself understood to be an 'order of materiality', as society's primary constitutive force. In a world ordered by the discourses of hetero-sexuality, which articulate what Wittig has conceptualized as the logic of 'the straight mind', the human subject is positioned within a structure of binary oppositions. From Aristotle and Plato onwards, Wittig observes, human thought has been organized around such dualisms as 'One/Many', 'Male/Female', 'Light/Dark' and 'Good/Bad'. These dualisms are structured hierarchically such that the second term is always the negative of the first. Wittig argues that it is through this binary structure that sexual difference itself is produced: in hetero-sexual society, the masculine and the feminine are projected as being 'natural' or 'given' in order to legitimate the economic and cultural oppression of women.

In maintaining this position, Wittig differs from both those liberal feminists who demand 'equality in difference' and those radical feminists who have claimed the specificity of women as an occasion for both celebration and political unity. In her essay 'The category of sex', Wittig extends her anti-essentialist argument further, proposing that 'the category of sex' is a linguistic construct which has been naturalized to give it the appearance of biological substance and which, indeed, constitutes a 'political category' which is fundamental to the social contract that binds heterosexual society. Through heterosexual dis-courses, Wittig maintains, 'woman' is always sexualized. 'Sex', she concludes, 'is a category which women cannot be outside of.' Unlike most other feminist theorists, Wittig does not distinguish between 'sex' and 'gender': both are political categories, produced in language. Moreover, she contends that there is only one gender, the feminine: women alone bear the particularizing and hence fracturing inscription of gender, while men are 'total subjects' ('The mark of gender'). In this way, Wittig extends de Beauvoir's proposition that 'one is not born, but becomes a woman'. Not only is the idea of a generalized 'Woman' a myth; 'woman' is a construct of heterosexual ideology, produced always as the negative of 'man' in order to maintain the oppression of the subjects thus conceptualized. Within this system, 'woman' is always in the relation of slave to the master, 'man'. The concept of 'woman' is irredeemable: the redistribution of power in the world can be brought about only by 'its whole reorganization with new concepts, from the point of view of . . . the oppressed' ('One is not born a woman').

It is from this radical perspective that Wittig has advanced her controversial formulation that 'lesbians are not women'. The lesbian, she claims, is an 'escapee' or 'fugitive' from the class of women constructed by the system of heterosexuality. Hence the lesbian, who refuses the economic and political power of men, maintains a privileged position and point of view from outside the world constructed by heterosexual discourse. The lesbian, therefore, is singularly placed to expose the artifice of that regime which constructs its subjects as 'men' and 'women'. 'Lesbianism', Wittig contends, 'provides for the moment the only social form in which we can live freely. Lesbian is the only concept I know of which is beyond the categories of sex . . .' ('One is not born a woman'). Other critics have taken issue with Wittig's conceptualization of lesbianism, arguing that in societies where heterosexuality is the dominant mode, the formation of lesbian subjectivity is always imbricated with it. It has been pointed out that Wittig's work appears to be premised upon a double ontology: whereas through her anti-essentialist critique she emphasizes that the categories of 'man' and 'woman' are socially produced, she posits the lesbian as existing within a different order of being which antecedes and transcends heterosexual formations in a 'free' space where full subjectivity may be attained. Other critics have expressed reservations about Wittig's totalizing view of heterosexual society and the ahistorical nature of her vision of a homogeneous lesbian society or culture.

The arguably essentialist element of her work notwithstanding, Wittig's deconstruction of heterosexual discourse to disclose a vision of disengendered societies in which power is distributed equally has made a valuable contribution to radical lesbian feminist critique. According to Wittig, the balance of power in society is to be changed not only through the transformation of economic relations but also through the transformation of language. Unlike other French theorists such as Hélène **Cixous** and Luce **Irigaray**, however, she does not propound a concept of 'feminine writing'. Indeed, she strongly criticizes this notion, arguing that it invokes the naturalized concept of 'woman' and is rooted in a celebration of the difference of the female body, in particular that of the maternal body. Wittig also rejects what she interprets as the normative heterosexual paradigms or 'myths' of psychoanalysis, paradigms which inform the theories of many of her poststructuralist contemporaries, as she proposes that psychoanalysis (primarily **Lacan**ian) is currently one of the dominant oppressive discourses of heterosexual society.

Wittig stresses that under the current regime of heterosexuality, each speech act contributes to the material oppression of women. Yet she also draws attention to the plasticity of language which, she suggests, renders it amenable to radical transformation. Through the creation of new 'key concepts' the currently dominant formations of gender can be altered. Again, the lesbian writer, with her 'oblique' point of view, is ideally positioned to bring about such transformation.

For her, literature, like the Trojan Horse, is a 'war machine' which can pulverize existing literary forms which enforce the binary division of gender in order to create new linguistic structures productive of alternative economies of subjectivity and pleasure. Wittig's theory is put into practice in her fiction, where narrative and textual violence are combined to deconstruct existing phallocentric structures in order to present a utopian vision of societies in which 'whole' subjectivity is restored to women, and the lesbian point of view is universalized. In particular, her fiction enacts the deconstruction of the gender division maintained by pronouns in the French language. In *Les Guérillères*, for example, a generalized 'elles' erases the hierarchized opposition between masculine and feminine; and in *The Lesbian Body* the pronominal 'j/e' is used to indicate a full rather than split subjectivity. Existing genres and tropes are reappropriated to create a new lesbian mythology.

Since the 1970s, the envisioning of lesbian subjectivity and society offered by Wittig's work has been a central reference point for many European and American lesbian critics. The controversial insights offered by her deconstruction of concepts relating to gender and sexuality continue to stimulate debate among both post-structuralist feminists and the theorists of 'queer politics'.

Main works

The Opoponax, trans. H. Weaver, New York: Daughters, 1976.

Les Guérillères, trans. D. Le Vay, Boston, MA: Beacon Press, 1986a.

The Lesbian Body, trans. D. Le Vay, New York: Beacon Press, 1986b.

Lesbian Peoples: Material for a dictionary, co-authored with Sande Zeig, New York: Avon, 1979a.

'Paradigm', in George Stambolian and Elaine Marks (eds), *Homosexualities and French Literature*, Ithaca, NY: Cornell University Press, 1979b.

Across the Acheron, London: The Women's Press, 1989.

The Straight Mind and Other Essays, Hemel Hempstead: Harvester Wheatsheaf, 1992.

Further reading

Butler, Judith, 'Monique Wittig: bodily disintegration and fictive sex', in *Gender Trouble*, New York: Routledge, 1990.

Fuss, Diana, 'Monique Wittig's anti-essentialist materialism', in *Essentially Speaking*, New York: Routledge, 1989.

Marks, Elaine and Isabelle de Courtivron (eds), *New French Feminisms*, Brighton: Harvester, 1981.

Shaktini, Namascar, 'Displacing the phallic subject: Wittig's lesbian writing', *Signs*, 8, 1 (1982): 29–44.

Wenzel, Helen Vivienne, 'The text as body/politics: an appreciation of Monique Wittig's writings in context', *Feminist Studies*, 7, 2 (1987): 264–87.

Wolfe, Susan J. and Julia Penelope (eds), *Sexual Practice, Textual Theory*, Cambridge, MA: Blackwell, 1993.

Woolf, Virginia (1882–1941)

Virginia Woolf was a prominent British writer, reviewer and cultural critic of the early twentieth century. Never formally educated, Woolf was almost entirely self-taught. She read avidly, and accrued a great deal of knowledge of the arts and of politics throughout the course of her life. Throughout the 1920s and 1930s she was an active member of the literary and art circle known as the 'Bloomsbury Group', which included among its members Lytton Strachey, Roger Fry, her sister Vanessa Bell, and Leonard Woolf, whom she married in 1912. Highly critical of the society in which she lived, Woolf was also actively involved in the Women's Cooperative Guild and was, throughout her life, a confirmed pacifist.

Though her academic achievements as a cultural theorist have sometimes been overshadowed by critical fascination with her bouts of depression, attempts at suicide and 'scandalous' romance with the writer Vita Sackville-West, Virginia Woolf was none the less a prolific writer. She wrote regularly for *The Guardian*, *The Times Literary Supplement* and *The New Statesman*, published countless reviews of contemporary writing, wrote polemical tracts denouncing militarism, the Empire and capitalism, and theorized the nature both of writing and of gender. She was also, of course, an important figure in the early-twentieth-century development of the novel, and one of the earliest writers to experiment with a form of textual style which broke explicitly with realism. Between 1915 and 1941 she published nine novels, two short stories, one play text, two biographies, and eleven books of essays and literary criticism.

In 1917, together with Leonard Woolf, she founded the Hogarth

Press, which published most of her subsequent writings as well as the earliest translations of the work of Sigmund **Freud**.

———————————

A Room of One's Own (probably the most widely known of Woolf's works) deals explicitly with the questions of gender and of writing for which Woolf herself has subsequently become renowned. It is a complex text informed by a number of theoretical threads which are also developed elsewhere in her writing.

As a theory of literary production, it is at times materialist. Works of art, it argues, are not the products of individual genius but, rather, of historical and material conditions. In particular, it stresses the material inequalities of gender and class which serve to deny women access to the means and the mode of literary production. This is both an economic and an ideological argument. Not only do women generally lack the material conditions of production, in terms of money and a room of their own, but they also lack an adequate education and a tradition of writing in which to situate themselves.

If this situation is to be resolved, Woolf argues, the whole position of women in society must be changed. That in itself is a difficult task, since questions of gender are inextricably linked in her thinking to issues of 'the British Empire, our colonies . . . the growth of the middle class and so on . . .' ('Professions for women').

While she is undoubtedly concerned with the material conditions of British society at the turn of the century, however, the focus of Virginia Woolf's writing is much more sharply tuned to the question of ideology. Structures of power, it would seem, replicate themselves ideologically through the production of people as subjects of ideology. If resolutions of material inequalities are to be achieved, then the whole way in which a culture thinks about itself, and about relations between the subjects it produces, must be questioned.

Influenced by psychoanalysis, the model of the subject which Woolf presumes is an unstable and fragmented one. Unconscious drives and desires exert an unsettling pressure upon our conscious thoughts and actions thereby continually threatening to disrupt the rationalist governance of subjective being upon which systems of power depend. On the whole, Woolf argues, women are closer to this disruptive unconscious force than men. In *A Room of One's Own* she states that women often experience what she calls 'a sudden splitting off of the consciousness'. In her argument, women constantly move from being a part of 'civilization' to being outside of it, 'alien and critical', and this is both a material and a psychic state. In order to maintain a state of mind which is civilized in this sense, Woolf argues that 'one is unconsciously holding something back, and gradually the repression becomes an effort'.

That the repression of unconscious forces is both an effort, *and* a necessity to reproducing a stable social order, is explored elsewhere in

Woolf's writing. The novel *Mrs. Dalloway*, for example, is a damning critique of the forces of society which demand repression in order to perpetuate the status quo. But it is also, subversively, a testimony to the precarious nature of that repression and, in the end, a prediction of its impossibility. Now in her fifty-second year, Clarissa Dalloway struggles, for the sake of 'civilization itself', to draw together the fragmented parts of herself. Try as she might, however, the repressed unconscious of her lesbian desire for Sally Seton, and her socialist ideals of abolishing private property and the state, leak out from the retaining grasp of the socially conscious position of the subject which Mrs. Richard Dalloway is supposed to represent.

This notion of the multiple and fragmented subject is pursued more thoroughly in relation to the question of gender in *Orlando*. Ostensibly a tale about a transhistorical man who becomes a woman, *Orlando* represents an unsettling of the binary classifications of gender which cultures construct as natural, obvious and true. Gender identity for Orlando is not inevitable but, rather, a position which can be taken up and discarded. In other words, it is not an essentially defining characteristic of human identity, but a position within the symbolic order. And with 'two thousand and fifty-two' selves all 'ticking in the mind at once', taking up positions of gender again requires acts of repression which cannot always be guaranteed.

If conventional meanings of gender (for example) are structured and sustained not by nature but by the symbolic order, then the fragmentation of that order is necessary if conventional meanings are to be challenged. The unconscious must be brought into play. It must be allowed to exert its pressure upon the regimes of the symbolic order which serve to repress it. It is in this sense that Virginia Woolf most successfully unites the two main concerns in her work: women and writing. Since women are, she argues, closer to the forces of the unconscious than men, they must write from the place of that unconscious. The 'woman's sentence' which she posits in *A Room of One's Own* is the sentence which 'we might call the psychological sentence of the feminine gender' ('Revolving lights') – a sentence, that is, which 'breaks with the expected sequence' (*Room*).

While a great deal of Woolf's writing is explicitly conceptual and political, it is difficult to separate the questions of theory and of politics from the question of aesthetics within her work. Ahead of her time, perhaps, Woolf practised a playfully unsettling form of deconstructive writing within which language itself is fractured, and concepts of truth and reality are not easily tolerated. In this sense, she not only practised what she preached in conceptual terms, but also deftly located the debate about ideas very firmly within the debate about language which is only now, some sixty-four years later, coming fully to fruition.

The cultural importance of Woolf's work lies in its challenge to the humanist and essentialist notions of the subject as stable human individual. In its positing of the notion of the structuring of the subject in and through language, Woolf's *work* not only disrupts what counts for common sense within our culture, but offers us glimpses of possible resistances to the order our culture creates. The fact that resistance to that structuring is located in writing also indicates something of her contribution to the development of debates about language and gender in the present day. With the work of theorists like Julia **Kristeva** and Hélène **Cixous** in the 1970s and 1980s, the notion of feminine writing as subversive cultural force is now fully at the heart of feminist literary criticism.

Main works

The Voyage Out, London: Duckworth, 1915.

Mrs. Dalloway, London: Hogarth, 1925.

To the Lighthouse, London: Hogarth, 1927.

Orlando, London: Hogarth, 1928.

A Room of One's Own, London: Hogarth, 1929.

The Waves, London: Hogarth, 1931.

Three Guineas, London: Hogarth, 1938.

Between the Acts, London: Hogarth, 1941.

Further reading

Bowlby, Rachel, *Virginia Woolf: Feminist destinations*, Oxford: Blackwell, 1988.

Ferrer, Daniel, *Virginia Woolf and the Madness of Language*, trans. Geoffrey Bennington and Rachel Bowlby, London: Routledge, 1990.

Marcus, Jane, *New Feminist Essays on Virginia Woolf*, London: Macmillan, 1981.

Minnow-Pinkney, Makiko, *Woolf and the Problem of the Subject*, Brighton: Harvester, 1987.

Moi, Toril, 'Who's afraid of Virginia Woolf?' in *Sexual/Textual Politics*, London: Methuen, 1985.

Moore, Madeline, *A Short Season Between Two Silences: The mystical and political in the novels of Virginia Woolf*, London: Allen & Unwin, 1984.

Z

Zhdanov, Andrey Aleksandrovich (1896–1948)

Constituting part of the European debate around the merits or otherwise of modernist and Formalist innovations in cultural production in the first half of the twentieth century, Zhdanov's was a virulent line arguing for the social function of literature. As he put it, 'only in our country [the Soviet Union] is such enhanced importance given to literature and to writers'. This was allied to an overwhelming distrust of the radical experimentation of both Western and Soviet modernisms, whose practitioners were described by Zhdanov as 'thieves, police sleuths, prostitutes, hooligans'. In place of what he called the 'riot of mysticism, religious mania and pornography' characteristic of bourgeois culture, Zhdanov championed Soviet socialist realism, in all cultural forms. This was the official approach to cultural production resulting from the Stalinist Soviet state's political intervention in literary, artistic and other cultural spheres following the Revolution and World War II. Subjective or bourgeois forms, including modernist experimentation, were virulently criticized, and a new orthodoxy of 'tendentious' literature, committed to the Revolution and to Party dogma, was constructed and enforced. It is important to remember that Zhdanov could make influential interventions in the cultural sphere because he was himself a powerful politician in the Stalinist era, once viewed as Stalin's probable successor. (He made the cover of *Time* magazine in 1946.) His methods could be brutal and intimidatory. He fomented Party activity through purges and acts of censorship against Soviet writers and artists which contributed to the curtailment of the radical cultural experimentation that followed the Revolution. This was combined with an increasingly chauvinistic perspective, directed against perceived Western influence on Soviet cultural practices. Towards the end of his life Zhdanov was himself purged from office, and almost certainly murdered. His main published texts in translation are surprisingly few, consisting of collections of and extracts from his speeches. *On Literature, Music and Philosophy* contains both the 1934 address to the First Soviet Writers' Congress and the 1947 'Report on the journals *Zvezda* and *Leningrad'*. His work is much anthologized in short extracts.

The main tenets of socialist realism are: *partiinost'* ('party-ness', the extent to which it follows Party dogma), *narodnost'* ('people-ness', relevance and accessibility to the people), *ideinost'* (ideological content), and *klassovost'* (class content). It has often argued that the first of these embraces the other three, since what is correct in ideological and class terms, and relevant and accessible to the people, must by virtue of these facts also be closest to Party dogma. Retrospectively constructed precursors of socialist realism include Lenin's short 1905 article 'Party organization and Party literature', which was taken to argue that all literature must serve the purposes of the Party, and Maxim Gorky's early novel *Mother* (1907), which features another favoured textual device of socialist realism, the representation of the Positive Hero. Not necessarily always fairly, socialist realism has come to be seen in the West as the extreme of revolutionary Party dogma: in fiction, the staple plot is 'boy meets tractor' (see Luker's collection); in visual art, the staple genre is portrait of Leader in heroic pose (see those of Stalin by Aleksandr Gerasimov). For an illustrative orthodox comparative reading of socialist realism in relation to modernism see Karl Radek's 'James Joyce or socialist realism?', which was delivered at the 1934 Congress (in Scott). In his modernist epic *Ulysses*, argues Radek sardonically, Joyce writes ' "great art", which depicts the small deeds of small people'. Modernist fiction is subjective, indulgent, innately conservative, its focus on alienation cancelled out by its absence of a materialist critique. Socialist realism, on the other hand, is revolutionary, inspiring, accessible, 'a great literature of love for all the oppressed, of hatred for the exploiting class'. Yet in Zhdanov's 1934 speech, calling for a 'tendentious' (i.e. politically committed) literary practice, there are tensions, unresolved contradictions. In clarifying the phrase 'writers [are] the engineers of human souls' (attributed to Stalin but possibly of Zhdanov's own invention), Zhdanov argues that 'our literature . . . cannot be hostile to romanticism, but it must be a romanticism of a new type, revolutionary romanticism'. Apparently *not* jettisoning tradition or rejecting innovation Zhdanov here urges writers to employ 'all genres, styles, forms and methods of literary creation' to produce a revolutionary 'culture of language', as he puts it.

Zhdanov is primarily remembered today as Stalin's henchman in cultural affairs (though see below). There are, though, two distinct periods of Zhdanov's influence, clustered round the 1934 speech and the not dissimilar 1947 report. The 1934 address signalled the start of a brutal end to the extensive post-revolutionary radical culture, and its replacement by a set of tightly-regulated conventions. The state began to control and centralise cultural activity in order ostensibly to protect the revolution. The 1934 Congress was a ground-breaking event, opening in a carnival atmosphere, with portraits of Shakespeare, Cervantes, and Tolstoy adorning the walls. The energy and range of the debates by writers and critics is easily missed in the retrospective shadow cast by socialist realism: within a year of the Congress books were being removed from library shelves. Zhdanov was responsible for propaganda on the Central Committee; indeed, it could be argued that his primary role lay in propagandising socialist realism, while others theorised it (this would perhaps explain both the comparative lack of translated published texts, and the clear theoretical problems in those texts: see above). At the 1934 Congress, Radek discusses Soviet and international fiction, Nikolai Bukharin argues for the positive pluralism of Soviet poetry (a provocative line, apocryphally referred to as Bukharin's suicide note), and A.I. Stetsky celebrates the increasing range of experiential voices in proletarian culture. Stetsky identifies 'a new phenomenon in our literature': 'the fact that our people had produced heroes who not only accomplish feats of heroism but are able to recount the story both of themselves and of their feats'. It remained for Zhdanov to translate these various critical approaches into state policy. Following a relative thaw in cultural expression during World War Two, Zhdanov's second attack came under the guise of criticism of two Leningrad journals, while focusing on two writers, the social satirist Mikhail Zoshchenko and the subjective poet Anna Akhmatova. Satire and subjectivity are not Zhdanovist virtues. This second wave did much both to reinstate the Stalinist dogma in the cultural sphere, and to cut the Soviet Union off once more from wider cultural influence and experimentation. This later period of Zhdanov's clamp-down on cultural practice, from 1946 to 1948, is known as the *Zhdanovshchina* ('the Zhdanov time'). More recently there has been some critical effort aimed at rehabilitating Zhdanov, by new readings of both his historical actions and his public utterances. Hahn, for instance, has sought to reconstruct the later Zhdanov *not* as the source of militant orthodoxy but as a comparative moderate in Stalin's regime. Lahusen questions the accuracy of the entire negative narrative of socialist realism, as the literature of a totalitarian regime. Groys suggests that socialist realism itself was continuous rather than discontinuous with the efforts of Soviet modernism, at least in so far as both were non-mimetic and transformative stylistic strategies.

Main works

H.G. Scott (ed.), *Problems of Soviet Literature: Reports and speeches at the First Soviet Writers' Congress*, translator unknown, London: Martin

Lawrence, 1935. Includes unabridged translation of Zhdanov's speech to the 1934 Congress. This book is also printed as Maxim Gorky *et al.*, *Soviet Writers' Congress 1934: The debate on Socialist Realism and Modernism in the Soviet Union*, London: Lawrence & Wishart, 1977.

On Literature, Music and Philosophy, trans. E. Fox, S. Jackson and H.C. Feldt, London: Lawrence & Wishart, 1950.

Further reading

Bisztray, George, *Marxist Models of Literary Realism*, New York: Columbia University Press, 1978.

Groys, Boris, *The Total Art of Stalinism: Avant-garde, aesthetic dictatorship and beyond*, Princeton, NJ: Princeton University Press, 1982.

Hahn, Werner G., *Postwar Soviet Politics: The fall of Zhdanov and the defeat of moderation 1946–1953*, Ithaca, NY: Cornell University Press, 1982.

Kemp-Welch, A., *Stalin and the Literary Intelligentsia, 1928–1939*, London: Macmillan, 1991.

Mathewson, Rufus W., *The Positive Hero in Russian Literature*, Stanford, CA: Stanford University Press, 1975.

Robin, Regine, *Socialist Realism: An impossible aesthetic*, Stanford. CA: Stanford University Press, 1992.

Glossary

socialist realism: The official approach to cultural production resulting from the Stalinist Soviet state's political intervention in literary, artistic and other cultural spheres following the Revolution and World War II. Subjective or bourgeois forms, including modernist experimentation, were virulently criticized, and a new orthodoxy of 'tendentious' literature, committed to the Revolution and to Party dogma, was created, led by A.A. Zhdanov.

Zhdanovshchina: ('the Zhdanov time'). The later period of Zhdanov's clampdown on cultural practice, 1946 to 1948. Followed by a relative thaw in the Soviet state's cultural intervention, after both Zhdanov's and Stalin's deaths.

Index